"An admirably lu[...] [...]mics' drove us to disaster . . . Thi[...] [...]erives most of its narrative energy [...] [...]t and exposition."
—[...] Pressley, *Bloomberg*

"An essential, grittily intellectual, yet compelling guide to the financial debacle of 2009." —Geordie Greig, *Evening Standard* (London)

"John Cassidy [is] a fine journalist with a long-standing interest in economic and financial matters . . . He tells his story extremely well . . . Many of his chapters—on the development of general equilibrium theory (how everything in the economy systematically depends on everything else), for example, or marginalism (why prices are determined by what we're prepared to pay for the very last item of something we buy, rather than what the whole amount is worth to us)—would make useful supplementary reading in an undergraduate economics course." —Benjamin M. Friedman, *The New York Review of Books*

"A well constructed, thoughtful and cogent account of how capitalism evolved to its current form." —Edmund Conway, *The Daily Telegraph* (London)

"[*How Markets Fail*] is more than just an account of the failures of regulators and the self-deception of bankers and homebuyers, although these are well covered. For Cassidy, the deeper roots of the crisis lie in the enduring appeal of an idea: that society is always best served when individuals are left to pursue their self-interest in free markets . . . An ambitious book, and one that mostly succeeds." —*The Economist*

"An elegant, readable treatise on economics . . . Cassidy delivers on the promise of his title, but he also offers a clear-eyed look at economic thinking over the last three centuries, from Adam Smith to Ben Bernanke, and shows how the major theories have played out in practice, often not well . . . Cassidy writes with terrific clarity and a finely tuned sense of moral outrage, yielding a superb book."

—*Kirkus Reviews* (starred review)

"Both a narrative and a call to arms, [*How Markets Fail*] provides an intellectual and historical context for the string of denial and bad decisions that led to the disastrous 'illusion of harmony,' the lure of real estate and the Great Crunch of 2008. Using psychology and behavioral economics, Cassidy presents an excellent argument that the market is not in fact self-correcting, and that only a return to reality-based economics—and a reform-minded move to shove Wall Street in that direction—can pull us out of the mess in which we've found ourselves."

—*Publishers Weekly*

JOHN CASSIDY

HOW MARKETS FAIL

John Cassidy has been a staff writer at *The New Yorker* since 1995. He lives in New York City.

ALSO BY JOHN CASSIDY

*Dot.con: How America Lost Its Mind and Money
in the Internet Era*

HOW MARKETS FAIL

THE RISE AND FALL OF FREE MARKET ECONOMICS

JOHN CASSIDY

PICADOR

FARRAR, STRAUS AND GIROUX • NEW YORK

To Lucinda, Beatrice, and Cornelia

Picador
120 Broadway, New York 10271

Copyright © 2009, 2010 by John Cassidy
Preface copyright © 2021 by John Cassidy
All rights reserved
Printed in the United States of America
Originally published in 2009 by Farrar, Straus and Giroux as *How Markets Fail: The Logic of Economic Calamities*
First Picador paperback edition, 2010
This Picador paperback edition, 2021

Grateful acknowledgment is made for permission to reprint material from *Irrational Exuberance*, Second Edition, by Robert J. Shiller, copyright © 2005 by Princeton University Press. Reprinted by permission of Princeton University Press.

The Library of Congress has cataloged the Farrar, Straus and Giroux hardcover edition as follows:
Cassidy, John, 1963–
   How markets fail : the logic of economic calamities / John Cassidy.
      p. cm.
   Includes bibliographical references and index.
   ISBN: 978-0-374-17320-3 (hardcover)
   1. Financial crises.   2. Stock exchanges.   3. Monetary policy.   4. Banks and banking.   I. Title.

   HB3722.C37 2009
   381—dc22

2009029529

Picador Paperback ISBN: 978-1-250-78128-4

Designed by Abby Kagan

Our books may be purchased in bulk for promotional, educational, or business use. Please contact your local bookseller or the Macmillan Corporate and Premium Sales Department at 1-800-221-7945, extension 5442, or by email at MacmillanSpecialMarkets@macmillan.com.

Picador® is a U.S. registered trademark and is used by Macmillan Publishing Group, LLC, under license from Pan Books Limited.

For book club information, please visit facebook.com/picadorbookclub or email marketing@picadorusa.com.

picadorusa.com • instagram.com/picador
twitter.com/picadorusa • facebook.com/picadorusa

10 9 8 7 6 5 4 3 2 1

CONTENTS

Preface to the 2021 Edition   vii
Introduction: The Great Financial Crisis   3

PART ONE: UTOPIAN ECONOMICS

1. Raghuram Rajan's Prescient Warning   17
2. Adam Smith's Invisible Hand   25
3. Friedrich Hayek's Telecommunications System   37
4. Markets and Welfare: Walras and Pareto   49
5. Arrow and Debreu's Famous Proof   61
6. The Market Evangelist: Milton Friedman   72
7. Eugene Fama and the Efficient Markets Hypothesis   85
8. Robert Lucas and the Triumph of Utopian Economics   97

PART TWO: REALITY-BASED ECONOMICS

9. Climate Change, Spillovers, and Professor Pigou   111
10. Francis Bator's Taxonomy of Market Failures   125
11. The Prisoner's Dilemma and Rational Irrationality   139
12. George Akerlof's Market for Lemons   151
13. Keynes's Beauty Contest Theory of Investing   166

14. Herd Behavior and the Dot-Com Bubble 177
15. Psychology and Economics: Kahneman and Tversky 192
16. Hyman Minsky and Ponzi Finance 205

PART THREE: THE GREAT CRUNCH
17. Alan Greenspan Shrugs 221
18. The Lure of Real Estate 235
19. The Subprime Chain 251
20. In the Alphabet Soup 268
21. A Matter of Incentives 285
22. London Bridge Is Falling Down 299
23. Socialism in Our Time 317

Conclusion 335
Afterword: The Great Disconnect 347
Notes 363
Acknowledgments 391
Index 393

PREFACE TO THE 2021 EDITION

W hen I sat down, in the winter of 2008–2009, to write a book about economics and the Great Financial Crisis, I quickly realized that I was really writing three books in one: an account of the crisis; a history of economics; and a call to arms for economists, policymakers, and concerned citizens to embrace what I termed "reality-based economics." In the fall of 2009, when *How Markets Fail* was first published, it was gratifyingly well received. Since then I have been thrilled to get, at regular intervals, notes from readers in many different countries saying how useful they have found the book in explaining contemporary economic issues, and/or as an introduction to economics as a subject. Hopefully, this new edition will prove equally helpful to a new generation of readers.

The subject matter is certainly just as pressing as it was back in 2008–2009. Indeed, there are many parallels between then and now. Once again, we are living through the aftermath of an enormous shock to the economy—the coronavirus pandemic—that resulted in a deep recession. Once again, policymakers have pumped trillions of dollars into the economy and the financial markets. And once again, the uneven rebound from the depths of recession has highlighted some deep-seated problems and inequities. In the original paperback edition of this book, which appeared at the end of 2010, I pointed out a grotesque irony: many of the Wall Street banks whose irresponsible risk-taking had helped bring about the Great Financial Crisis emerged from its aftermath bigger and more profitable than ever. In 2020, something similar happened. Months after the Federal Reserve's emergency policy interventions triggered a rapid rebound in the financial markets, Goldman Sachs and Morgan Stanley announced record, or near-record, profits at the same time that the poverty rate was rising. The biggest winners of the pandemic were technology behemoths—such as Amazon, Facebook, Google, and Microsoft—whose businesses (and stock prices) benefited greatly from the shift to remote activity. On the other side of the ledger, the big losers were low-income workers, particularly those employed in heavily impacted industries, such as retailing and hospitality. Even before the virus struck, these people tended to be badly paid and less equipped to handle periods of economic hardship. The pandemic delivered to them a double blow. As well as being vulnerable to losing their jobs, they were more likely to contract the virus and die from it.

This book doesn't deal with COVID-19 specifically, but it does address many of the broader economic issues and conflicts that the pandemic raised. These include private interests versus the public interest; Wall Street versus Main Street; monopoly versus competition; free enterprise versus government intervention; and the challenge of managing finance-driven economies in the face of severe shocks. Ultimately, this is a book about how free market capitalist economies work, the types of behavior they incentivize, the things they are good at, and the sorts of failures they are vulnerable to. These are all age-old issues in economics, and in addressing them I adopt a broad historical approach. To begin with, I explore the free market tradition of Adam Smith, Léon Walras, and Milton Friedman, which I refer to as utopian economics because it rests on the illusion that markets, left to their own devices, almost always produce desirable outcomes. Then, I move on to a rival intellectual tradition that emphasizes how flawed incentives, herd behavior, and other features absent from the utopian model lead to market failures. This approach is associated with economists like John Maynard Keynes, Hyman Minsky, and Joseph Stiglitz. I call it reality-based economics.

During the two decades leading up to the collapse of Lehman Brothers, in September 2008, utopian economics was in the ascendancy. In many Western nations, policymakers and the economists who advised them acted as if the big questions in economics had been largely settled. They believed that as long as countries opened up their economies to free trade, deregulated their industries, balanced their budgets, and kept inflation under control, the market would take care of things: prosperity would rise, financial stability would be assured, and human well-being would gradually increase. The shattering experience of 2008 and 2009, when for a time the global financial system appeared to be on the brink of collapse, punctured this complacent optimism. It also prompted a critical reexamination of economic thinking that is still ongoing.

Even before the coronavirus pandemic, the issues of income and wealth inequality and the capture of the political system by economic elites had moved to the center of the political debate. In the years immediately following the Great Financial Crisis, many European countries adopted austerity policies, slashing spending on social programs and other public projects. The eurozone sank into a lengthy sovereign debt crisis, and a lot of places, including the United Kingdom, which wasn't even in the currency zone, experienced a lost decade of economic growth. In the United States, the economic recovery was somewhat more vigorous, but it was very lopsided. High income groups captured most of the income growth, whereas median household income—the income of the household right in the middle of the income distribution—didn't surpass its 2007 level until 2016. Inevitably, these economic developments had political ramifications. The Occupy Wall Street movement of 2011 was followed, in 2016 and 2020, by the insurgent presidential campaigns of Senator Bernie Sanders, a self-described democratic socialist who garnered a great deal of support, especially from young voters. Even though the Occupy movement eventually lost steam, and Sanders twice failed to win the Democratic nomination, the left arguably won the ideological contest.

According to a widely discussed opinion survey that Gallup carried out in 2018, just 45 percent of Americans aged eighteen to twenty-nine thought positively of capitalism, whereas 51 percent thought well of socialism. In a country where no socialist candidate for president has ever received even 10 percent of the vote—the highest figure was

Eugene Debs's 6 percent in 1912—the Gallup finding was pretty remarkable. Moreover, growing skepticism about free market capitalism and globalization wasn't confined to the young and left-leaning. In recent years, right-wing populist politicians in many different countries have enjoyed success by selling economic nationalism, protectionism, and anti-immigration policies to disaffected members of the working class, old and young. In 2016, Donald Trump put together a warlock's brew of protectionist economics, antielitism, and racial incitement that took him all the way to the White House. (When he got there, he and his Republican allies promptly gave a big tax cut to his fellow plutocrats and major corporations, but that is another story.)

Most mainstream economists still frown upon protectionism and the broader agenda of Trumpian economics. But they haven't been spared from the tumult around them. Back in 2010, I wrote: "Utopian economics is on the defensive, just like it was in the 1930s." Many of the people leading the criticism were economics students. In 2014, students from nineteen countries issued a manifesto calling for a more pluralistic approach, arguing that the traditional one, "limits our ability to contend with the multidimensional challenges of the 21st century— from financial stability to food security and climate change." At least some teachers of economics have responded to the demands for reform. In 2012, Wendy Carlin, of University College London, and Sam Bowles, of the Santa Fe Institute, launched the CORE Project, an open-access online teaching platform that emphasizes current economic problems, such as climate change, financial crises, and the economic impact of the coronavirus. "The textbook model is definitely broken," Carlin wrote in 2018.

For anyone looking for a fresh but rigorous approach to learning economics, the CORE website is a good place to start. Unlike many older textbooks, it emphasizes data, practical examples, and history. This is no accident. Arguably, the biggest shift in academic economics over the past twenty years has been a turn from abstract theorizing to empirical research, using new data sets and statistical techniques. The most talked about economics book of the past decade was Thomas Piketty's *Capital in the Twenty-First Century*, which illuminated, in great detail, the long-term trends in inequality of income and wealth across a variety of countries. "Too much energy has been and still is being wasted on pure theoretical speculation without a clear specification of the economic facts one is trying to explain or the social and political problems one is trying to resolve," Piketty wrote.

With the old orthodoxy on the defensive, and new data sources and statistical methods providing fresh insight into many important policy questions, the discipline that Thomas Carlyle dubbed the "dismal science" is far from stationary. "Economics is in a state of creative ferment that is often invisible to outsiders," the economists Suresh Naidu, Dani Rodrik, and Gabriel Zucman wrote in a 2019 essay, "Economics after Neoliberalism," which appeared in the *Boston Review*. Rodrik is the author of the 1997 book *Has Globalization Gone Too Far?*, which provided a prescient warning about how opening domestic markets to cheap foreign competitors could lead to job losses and "social disintegration." Naidu and Zucman are part of a younger generation of economists that is looking to refashion the subject, or, at least, the public perception of it. Adopting the name Economics for Inclusive Prosperity, the three scholars have set up a group of economists to provide policy recommendations in a number of different areas, including trade, finance, and labor markets. Their goal, they wrote, is to "provide an overall vision for economic policy that stands as an alternative to the market fundamentalism that is often—and wrongly—identified with economics."

When I read the essay in the *Boston Review*, it struck home. One of the original goals of *How Markets Fail* was to reframe public perceptions of economics as a subject, and to emphasize that economists have always studied the downsides of markets as well as their strengths. In Part I, I examine the rise and fall of market fundamentalism, from Adam Smith to the Chicago School. In Part II, I describe the evolution of reality-based economics, beginning with Arthur Cecil Pigou, an English economist who was a contemporary of John Maynard Keynes at Cambridge in the early decades of the twentieth century. A hundred years on, Pigou is perhaps best known for his opposition to the Keynesian revolution in macroeconomics, but he also made an enormous positive contribution to economics that is often overlooked. In his 1920 book *The Economics of Welfare*, Pigou explained how unfettered free markets can sometimes produce disastrous outcomes because they fail to take into account the effects of economic spillovers (or "externalities"). Spillovers can be positive or negative. The most glaring example of a negative spillover is climate change, which arises partly because the prices of fossil fuels don't reflect the damage they do to the environment.

From climate change, I move on to describe many market failures, and the factors that lead to them. Asset price bubbles of the sort that preceded the Great Financial Crisis are largely the product of trend following, which Keynes wrote about in his 1936 magnum opus, *The General Theory of Employment, Interest and Money*. Banking blowups on the 2008 model often result from disaster myopia—a concept that draws on work done in the 1970s by Daniel Kahneman, the only psychologist ever to be awarded a Nobel for economics, and his research partner Amos Tversky. Many of the drawbacks with private health insurance systems are the result of information problems that restrict access and raise prices—a problem that the American economist Kenneth Arrow, another Nobel recipient, pointed out back in 1963. Monopoly power has been a pet subject of economists going all the way back to John Stuart Mill, who discussed it in his 1848 textbook *Principles of Political Economy*, and Karl Marx, who wrote about the "centralization of capitals" in *Das Kapital*. The theory of "imperfect competition" dates back to the 1930s, when Joan Robinson, at Cambridge, and Edward Chamberlin, at Harvard, developed it independently.

To any serious student of economics, all of these market failures should be familiar. According to Naidu, Rodrik, and Zucman, most upper-level university courses now spend "more time on market failures and how to fix them than on the magic of competitive markets." But while this is an encouraging development, it would be folly to assume that utopian economics has been consigned to the history books. In her 2018 article about CORE, Carlin pointed out the simple textbook model of perfect competition "continues as the backbone of much undergraduate teaching." It's also still very influential in policy-making circles, in some parts of the media, and in the court system. Between 2017 and 2020, Donald Trump appointed hundreds of conservative judges to the federal bench. Almost all of them were heavily influenced by the free market "Law and Economics" school, which emerged from the University of Chicago, and other universities, during the 1970s.

Whether they emanate from conservative jurists or free market think tanks, generalized arguments about market efficiency are often dubious. It is certainly legitimate to question whether carbon taxes, antitrust rulings, limits on financial leverage, minimum wage laws, and other efforts to counter market failures are effective in practice. But it is disingenuous to ignore market failures entirely, or to try to explain them away—two tactics that remain popular in some conservative circles. If the period since this book was first published has taught us anything, it is that chronic market failures don't go away of their own accord. And in many cases, they are stubbornly resistant to supposed policy fixes.

Back in 2009 and 2010, the immediate issue facing policymakers and reality-based economists was how to tame a risk-addled financial system. Seeking to increase its resiliency and prevent another blowup, governments around the world forced big banks to hold more capital, which they could call on in times of stress. The Dodd-Frank Wall Street Reform and Consumer Protection Act of 2010 placed further restrictions on big financial firms, including tightening some of the rules for trading risky securities, such as credit default swaps. Reflecting public anger about the taxpayer bailouts of stricken Wall Street firms that the Bush and Obama administrations had introduced, the Dodd-Frank legislation also limited the Fed's ability to provide emergency financing to nondepository institutions, such as insurance companies, certain Wall Street firms, and nonfinance companies.

Necessary as many of these postcrisis reforms were, they didn't eliminate the problems of excessive risk-taking, financial fragility, and the idea of "too big to fail"—the concern that allowing one big bank to fail could bring them all down. In March 2020, as in the Great Financial Crisis, some parts of the global credit system virtually seized up. In another echo of 2008, the Fed and other central banks moved to inject trillions of dollars into the credit markets. As part of this rescue program, the Fed purchased a whole range of borrowing instruments, including Treasury bonds, high-grade corporate bonds, junk bonds, municipal bonds, and bonds backed by auto loans and credit card receivables. It also started lending directly to corporations, a move that required the U.S. Congress to reverse part of the Dodd-Frank Act. That didn't take long. In the $2.2 trillion Coronavirus Aid, Relief, and Economic Security Act—also known as the CARES Act—which passed in the final week of March, Congress allotted $454 billion to the Fed, thus enabling it to launch rescue programs on an even bigger and broader scale than it had done in 2008.

In the words of one observer, the Fed went from being a lender of last resort for banks to being a lender of last resort for the broader economy. To be clear, nothing in this book should be taken to suggest that this policy response was inappropriate. The pandemic was an unprecedented natural disaster with dire global repercussions. Switching on the Fed's money hose may well have headed off an immediate financial collapse, and it also gave governments time to introduce vital fiscal measures, including wage subsidies and expanded unemployment benefits, which helped to head off another Great Depression. But the policy response of 2020 came at a great cost to taxpayers, and to the utopian ideal of a self-regulating, self-sustaining economy.

The experiences of 2008 and 2020 demonstrated how, in a modern financial system, individual banks, insurance companies, and institutional investors aren't the true bearers of risks that can't be diversified away: taxpayers are. In essence, taxpayers provide an implicit guarantee to big financial institutions that if they get into serious trouble they will be rescued, directly or indirectly. As I explain at length in Part III of this book, which is devoted to the Great Financial Crisis, this is one of the perennial problems that policymakers face. Since many different parts of the financial system are closely interlinked and many of the individual players are highly leveraged—meaning they have borrowed heavily— there is always the potential for a self-reinforcing downward spiral that collapses the entire edifice. Although it sounds tempting to let such a collapse proceed and force risk-takers to absorb their losses, policymakers very rarely choose this option, partly because it would see pension funds and individual investors suffer grievous harm alongside the big banks, hedge funds, and billionaires. So, financial crises usually lead to bailouts of various kinds, often accompanied by plaintive cries of "never again." Then the risk-taking starts over, with the cycle getting bigger and more perilous every time.

Climate change is in a category of its own as a policy challenge, but it's also another market failure that is getting more serious by the year. In my aforementioned chapter on Pigou and the theory of spillovers, I recall how, in October 2006, Sir Nicholas Stern, a well-known British economist, issued an official report that described climate change as "the greatest market failure the world has ever seen." In a talk at MIT in 2019, Stern noted that the concentration of carbon dioxide in the atmosphere is now more than four hundred parts per million, a level last reached about three million years ago, when oceans levels were much higher than they are today. If similar conditions returned, it "would be Oxford-by-the-Sea," Stern noted. "Bangladesh would be completely underwater." Already, the signals are unmistakable. As I was getting started on this new preface in the fall of 2020, huge wildfires were consuming great swaths of California, Washington, and Oregon. Experts were warning that changing weather patterns could displace 1.2 billion people by 2050.

To be sure, there are efforts afoot to take climate change seriously, including the Paris Agreement, which was signed in 2016; the "net zero" movement, which sets a target of zero carbon emissions by 2050; and the Green New Deal. But there have also been significant setbacks, including the Trump administration's vow to withdraw from the Paris Agreement (since reversed by the Biden administration) and the abject failure of the U.S. Congress to act decisively by introducing carbon taxes, or other remedial measures—a failure that dates back to well before the Trump presidency. "It has seemingly become impossible to amend the Clean Air Act or to pass other legislation to address climate change in a serious and economically efficient manner," the economists Richard Schmalensee and Robert Stavins noted in the *Journal of Economic Perspectives* in 2019.

Rising monopoly power is yet another market failure that the U.S. government has taken little action to address. After decades of corporate mergers, industries ranging from airlines to hospitals to the manufacture of domestic appliances have become far less competitive than they used to be. There is now plentiful evidence that, as the number of competitors in these industries has shrunk, prices and profit margins have risen, which is just what you would expect to see when a handful of businesses gain monopoly power. In 1985, corporate profits accounted for 7.5 percent of U.S. GDP; by 2016, the share had risen to 11 percent.

It is now widely accepted that the monopoly problem is particularly serious in the tech sector, where companies like Amazon, Apple, Google, and Facebook exercise a great deal of market power. In explaining why tech industries are particularly susceptible to monopolization, I point to the work of W. Brian Arthur, an economist at the Santa Fe Institute, on how network effects can cause the markets for things like web browsers and social networks to "tip" in the direction of a single product, which then acquires a dominant position. Once a market has tipped, the incumbent can exploit its position in many different ways. The European Union has fined Alphabet, Google's parent company, more than eight billion euros for various anticompetitive practices, including favoring its own products in its online search results and forcing users of its AdSense product to sign exclusive agreements. In October 2020, the U.S. Department of Justice filed suit against Alphabet, claiming it illegally exploited its dominant position to stifle competition in search and search advertising. Amazon and Apple stand accused of gouging third-party companies that use their platforms to sell products and apps. In one particularly egregious misuse of monopoly power, Facebook supplied personal user data from tens of millions of users to Cambridge Analytica, the controversial data research firm that was involved in the 2016 Brexit referendum and the 2016 Trump campaign.

From the standpoint of reality-based economics, none of this is particularly surprising. In chapter 10, I recount how abusive behavior on the part of giant companies was a potent political issue during the Gilded Age of the late nineteenth century. Huge "trusts," such as Standard Oil and U.S. Steel, dominated their industries and crushed potential competitors. Eventually, Congress passed the Sherman Antitrust Act of 1890, which outlawed efforts to establish a monopoly, and the Clayton Antitrust Act of 1914, which proscribed a number of predatory tactics, including price-fixing, exclusive dealing contracts, and anticompetitive mergers. Since both of these pieces of legislation are still on the books, one may ask how today's tech giants, and monopolistic companies in other sectors, achieved their positions of dominance. Part of the answer goes back to my point about the U.S. court system and the role of utopian economics.

By prioritizing a very narrow view of "economic efficiency," judges influenced by the Law and Economics approach have greatly restricted the ability of the Justice Department and the Federal Trade Commission to block megamergers and other forms of anticompetitive behavior. But conservative judges aren't the only ones to blame. Even in instances when the courts might have been persuaded to act, administrations from both major parties have proved reluctant to challenge the tech giants, which have a great deal of clout in Washington. "Google, Amazon, and Facebook are conglomerates who monopolized ad markets, and have done so through a range of tactics and mergers that were until very recently illegal," Matt Stoller, a former fellow at the Open Markets Institute, wrote in his 2019 book *Goliath: The 100-Year War Between*

Monopoly Power and Democracy. "And in so doing, they have become governing powers."

The growth of monopoly power stifles competition and innovation. It also contributes to other serious problems, such as political corruption and glaring inequality. In the first eight months of 2020, a period in which tens of millions of Americans were furloughed or laid off, the net worth of Amazon's founder, Jeff Bezos, rose by more than $85 billion as the firm's stock price soared. "COVID-19 has been tragic for the many but good for a privileged few," noted Chema Vera, the executive director of Oxfam International, which issued a coruscating report about the economic impact of the pandemic.

Much like the Great Financial Crisis did, the coronavirus pandemic has raised anew many of the central issues of economics, including the age-old divide between utopian economics and reality-based economics. As I hope I have made clear in the pages that follow, this division runs through the entire history of economics, and it is likely to survive into the future. And yet, there is one thing both sides should be able to agree on: the proper goal of economics is to enhance the welfare of everybody, not just the rich and privileged. How to achieve this end is always going to be the subject of vigorous debates, some of which will be distorted by special-interest pleading and the promulgation of bogus theories. It is my hope that this new edition of *How Markets Fail*, in some modest way, helps to advance these debates in the direction of promoting the common good.

HOW MARKETS FAIL

INTRODUCTION:
THE GREAT FINANCIAL CRISIS

"I am shocked, shocked, to find that gambling is going on in here!"
—*Claude Rains as Captain Renault in* Casablanca

he old man looked drawn and gray. During the almost two decades he had spent overseeing America's financial system, as chairman of the Federal Reserve, congressmen, cabinet ministers, even presidents had treated him with a deference that bordered on the obsequious. But on this morning—October 23, 2008—Alan Greenspan, who retired from the Fed in January 2006, was back on Capitol Hill under very different circumstances. Since the summer of 2007, when the market for subprime mortgage securities had collapsed, leaving many financial institutions saddled with tens of billions of dollars' worth of assets that couldn't be sold at any price, the Democratic congressman Henry Waxman, chairman of the House Committee on Oversight and Government Reform, had held a series of televised hearings, summoning before him Wall Street CEOs, mortgage industry executives, heads of rating agencies, and regulators. Now it was Greenspan's turn at the witness table.

Waxman and many other Americans were looking for somebody to blame. For more than a month following the sudden unraveling of Lehman Brothers, a Wall Street investment bank with substantial holdings of mortgage securities, an unprecedented panic had been roiling the financial markets. Faced with the imminent collapse of American International Group, the largest insurance company in the United States, Ben Bernanke, Greenspan's mild-mannered successor at the Fed, had approved an emergency loan of $85 billion to the company. Federal regulators had seized Washington Mutual, a major mortgage lender, selling off most of its assets to JPMorgan Chase. Wells Fargo, the nation's sixth-biggest bank, had rescued Wachovia, the fourth-biggest. Rumors had circulated about the soundness of other financial institutions, including Citigroup, Morgan Stanley, and even the mighty Goldman Sachs.

Watching this unfold, Americans had clung to their wallets. Sales of autos, furniture, clothes, even books had fallen, sending the economy into a tailspin. In an effort to restore stability to the financial system, Bernanke and the Treasury secretary, Hank Paulson, had obtained from Congress the authority to spend up to $700 billion in taxpayers' money on a bank bailout. Their original plan had been to buy distressed mortgage securities from banks, but in mid-October, with the financial panic intensifying, they had changed course and opted to invest up to $250 billion directly in bank equity. This decision had calmed the markets somewhat, but the pace of events had been so frantic that few had stopped to consider what it meant: the Bush administration, after eight years of preaching the virtues of free markets, tax cuts, and small government, had turned the U.S. Treasury into part owner and the effective guarantor of every big bank in the country. Struggling to contain the crisis, it had stumbled into the most sweeping extension of state intervention in the economy since the 1930s. (Other governments, including those of Britain, Ireland, and France, had taken similar measures.)

"Dr. Greenspan," Waxman said. "You were the longest-serving chairman of the Federal Reserve in history, and during this period of time you were, perhaps, the leading proponent of deregulation of our financial markets . . . You have been a staunch advocate for letting markets regulate themselves. Let me give you a few of your past statements." Waxman read from his notes: "'There's nothing involved in federal regulation which makes it superior to market regulation.' 'There appears to be no need for government regulation of off-exchange derivative transactions.' 'We do not believe a public policy case exists to justify this government intervention.'" Greenspan, dressed, as always, in a dark suit and tie, listened quietly. His face was deeply lined. His chin sagged. He looked all of his eighty-two years. When Waxman had finished reading out Greenspan's words, he turned to him and said: "My question for you is simple: Were you wrong?"

"Partially," Greenspan replied. He went on: "I made a mistake in presuming that the self-interests of organizations, specifically banks and others, were such that they were best capable of protecting their own shareholders and their equity in the firms . . . The problem here is something which looked to be a very solid edifice, and, indeed, a critical pillar to market competition and free markets, did break down. And I think that, as I said, shocked me. I still do not fully understand why it happened and, obviously, to the extent that I figure out what happened and why, I will change my views."

Waxman, whose populist leanings belie the fact that he represents some of the wealthiest precincts in the country—Beverly Hills, Bel Air, Malibu—asked Greenspan whether he felt any personal responsibility for what had happened. Greenspan didn't reply directly. Waxman returned to his notes and started reading again. "'I do have an ideology. My judgment is that free, competitive markets are by far the unrivaled way to organize economies. We have tried regulations. None meaningfully worked.'" Waxman looked at Greenspan. "That was your quote," he said. "You had the authority to prevent irresponsible lending practices that led to the subprime mortgage crisis. You were advised to do so by many others. Now our whole economy is paying the price. Do you feel that your ideology pushed you to make decisions that you wish you had not made?"

Greenspan stared through his thick spectacles. Behind his mournful gaze lurked a savvy, self-made New Yorker. He grew up during the Great Depression in Washington Heights, a working-class neighborhood in upper Manhattan. After graduating from high school, he played saxophone in a Times Square swing band, and then turned to the study of economics, which was coming to be dominated by the ideas of John Maynard Keynes. After initially embracing Keynes's suggestion that the government should actively manage the economy, Greenspan turned strongly against it. In the 1950s, he became a friend and acolyte of Ayn Rand, the libertarian philosopher and novelist, who referred to him as "the undertaker." (In his youth, too, he was lugubrious.) He became a successful economic consultant, advising many big corporations, including Alcoa, J.P. Morgan, and U.S. Steel. In 1968, he advised Richard Nixon during his successful run for the presidency, and under Gerald Ford he acted as chairman of the White House Council of Economic Advisers. In 1987, he returned to Washington, this time permanently, to head the Fed and personify the triumph of free market economics.

Now Greenspan was on the defensive. An ideology is just a conceptual framework for dealing with reality, he said to Waxman. "To exist, you need an ideology. The question is whether it is accurate or not. What I am saying to you is, yes, I found a flaw. I don't know how significant or permanent it is, but I have been very distressed by that fact." Waxman interrupted him. "You found a flaw?" he demanded. Greenspan nodded. "I found a flaw in the model that I perceived as the critical functioning structure that defines how the world works, so to speak," he said.

Waxman had elicited enough already to provide headlines for the following day's newspapers—the *Financial Times*: "'I made a mistake,' admits Greenspan"—but he wasn't finished. "In other words, you found that your view of the world, your ideology, was not right," he said. "It was not working?"

"Precisely," Greenspan replied. "That's precisely the reason I was shocked. Because I had been going for forty years, or more, with very considerable evidence that it was working exceptionally well."

This book traces the rise and fall of free market ideology, which, as Greenspan said, is more than a set of opinions: it is a well-developed and all-encompassing way of thinking about the world. I have tried to combine a history of ideas, a narrative of the financial crisis, and a call to arms. It is my contention that you cannot comprehend recent events without taking into account the intellectual and historical context in which they unfolded. For those who want one, the first chapter and last third of the book contain a reasonably comprehensive account of the credit crunch of 2007–2009. But unlike other books on the subject, this one doesn't focus on the firms and characters involved: my aim is to explore the underlying economics of the crisis and to explain how the rational pursuit of self-interest, which is the basis of free market economics, created and prolonged it.

Greenspan isn't the only one to whom the collapse of the subprime mortgage market and ensuing global slump came as a rude shock. In the summer of 2007, the vast majority of analysts, including the Fed chairman, Bernanke, thought worries of a recession were greatly overblown. In many parts of the country, home prices had started falling, and the number of families defaulting on their mortgages was rising sharply. But among economists there was still a deep and pervasive faith in the vitality of American capitalism, and the ideals it represented.

For decades now, economists have been insisting that the best way to ensure prosperity is to scale back government involvement in the economy and let the private sector take over. In the late 1970s, when Margaret Thatcher and Ronald Reagan launched the conservative counterrevolution, the intellectuals who initially pushed this line of reasoning—Friedrich Hayek, Milton Friedman, Arthur Laffer, Sir Keith Joseph—were widely seen as right-wing cranks. By the 1990s, Bill Clinton, Tony Blair, and many other progressive politicians had adopted the language of the right. They didn't have much choice. With the collapse of communism and the ascendancy of conservative parties on both sides of the Atlantic, a positive attitude to markets became a badge of political respectability. Governments around the world dismantled welfare programs, privatized state-run firms, and deregulated industries that previously had been subjected to government supervision.

In the United States, deregulation started out modestly, with the Carter administration's abolition of restrictions on airline routes. The policy was then expanded to many other parts of the economy, including telecommunications, media, and financial services. In 1999, Clinton signed into law the Gramm-Leach-Bliley Act (aka the Financial Services Modernization Act), which allowed commercial banks and investment banks to combine and form vast financial supermarkets. Lawrence Summers, a leading Harvard economist who was then serving as Treasury secretary, helped shepherd the bill through Congress. (Today, Summers is Barack Obama's top economic adviser.)

Some proponents of financial deregulation—lobbyists for big financial firms, analysts at Washington research institutes funded by corporations, congressmen representing financial districts—were simply doing the bidding of their paymasters. Others, such as Greenspan and Summers, were sincere in their belief that Wall Street could, to a large extent, regulate itself. Financial markets, after all, are full of well-paid and highly educated people competing with one another to make money. Unlike in some other parts of the economy, no single firm can corner the market or determine the market price. In such circumstances, according to economic orthodoxy, the invisible hand of the market transmutes individual acts of selfishness into socially desirable collective outcomes.

If this argument didn't contain an important element of truth, the conservative movement wouldn't have enjoyed the success it did. Properly functioning markets reward hard work, innovation, and the provision of well-made, affordable products; they punish firms and workers who supply overpriced or shoddy goods. This carrot-and-stick mechanism ensures that resources are allocated to productive uses, making market economies more efficient and dynamic than other systems, such as communism and feudalism, which lack an effective incentive structure. Nothing in this book should be taken as an argument for returning to the land or reconstituting the Soviets' Gosplan. But to claim that free markets always generate good outcomes is to fall victim to one of three illusions I identify: the illusion of harmony.

In Part I, I trace the story of what I call utopian economics, taking it from Adam Smith to Alan Greenspan. Rather than confining myself to expounding the arguments of Friedrich Hayek, Milton Friedman, and their fellow members of the "Chicago School," I have also included an account of the formal theory of the free market, which economists refer to as general equilibrium theory. Friedman's brand of utopian economics is much better known, but it is the mathematical exposition, associated with names like Léon Walras, Vilfredo Pareto, and Kenneth Arrow, that explains the respect, nay, awe with which many professional economists view the free market. Even today, many books about economics give the impression that general equilibrium theory provides "scientific" support for the idea of the economy as a stable and self-correcting mechanism. In fact, the theory does nothing of the kind. I refer to the idea that a free market economy is sturdy and well grounded as the illusion of stability.

The period of conservative dominance culminated in the Greenspan Bubble Era, which lasted from about 1997 to 2007. During that decade, there were three separate speculative bubbles—in technology stocks, real estate, and physical commodities, such as oil. In each case, investors rushed in to make quick profits, and prices rose vertiginously before crashing. A decade ago, bubbles were widely regarded as aberrations. Some free market economists expressed skepticism about the very possibility of them occurring. Today, such arguments are rarely heard; even Greenspan, after much prevarication, has accepted the existence of the housing bubble.

Once a bubble begins, free markets can no longer be relied on to allocate resources sensibly or efficiently. By holding out the prospect of quick and effortless profits, they provide incentives for individuals and firms to act in ways that seem individually rational but immensely damaging—to themselves and others. The problem of distorted incentives is, perhaps, most acute in financial markets, but it crops up throughout the economy. Markets encourage power companies to despoil the environment and cause global warming; health insurers to exclude sick people from coverage; computer makers to force customers to buy software programs they don't need; and CEOs to stuff their own pockets at the expense of their stockholders. These are all examples of "market failure," a concept that recurs throughout the book and gives it its title. Market failure isn't an intellectual curiosity. In many areas of the economy, such as health care, high technology, and finance, it is endemic.

The previous sentence might come as news to the editorial writers of *The Wall Street Journal*, but it isn't saying anything controversial. For the past thirty or forty years, many of the brightest minds in economics have been busy examining how markets function when the unrealistic assumptions of the free market model don't apply. For some reason, the economics of market failure has received a lot less attention than the economics of market success. Perhaps the word "failure" has such negative connotations that it offends the American psyche. For whatever reason, "market failure economics" never took off as a catchphrase. Some textbooks refer to the "economics of information," or the "economics of incomplete markets." Recently, the term "behavioral economics" has come into vogue. For myself, I prefer the phrase "reality-based economics," which is the title of Part II.

Reality-based economics is less unified than utopian economics: because the modern economy is labyrinthine and complicated, it encompasses many different theories, each applying to a particular market failure. These theories aren't as general as the invisible hand, but they are more useful. Once you start to think about the world in terms of some of the concepts I outline, such as the beauty contest, disaster myopia, and the market for lemons, you may well wonder how you ever got along without them.

The emergence of reality-based economics can be traced to two sources. Within orthodox economics, beginning in the late 1960s, a new generation of researchers began working on a number of topics that didn't fit easily within the free market model, such as information problems, monopoly power, and herd behavior. At about the same time, two experimental psychologists, Amos Tversky and Daniel Kahneman, were subjecting rational economic man—*Homo economicus*—to a withering critique. As only an economist would be surprised to discover, humans aren't supercomputers: we have trouble doing sums, let alone solving the mathematical optimization problems that lie at the heart of many economic theories. When faced with complicated choices, we often rely on rules of thumb, or instinct. And we are greatly influenced by the actions of others. When the findings of Tversky, Kahneman, and other psychologists crossed over into economics, the two strands of thought came together under the rubric of "behavioral economics," which seeks to combine the rigor of economics with the realism of psychology.

In Part II, I devote a chapter to Kahneman and Tversky, but this book shouldn't be mistaken for another text on behavioral economics. Reality-based economics is a much broader field, a good part of which makes no departure from the axioms of rationality, and it is also considerably older. I trace its development back to Arthur C. Pigou, an English colleague and antagonist of John Maynard Keynes who argued that many economic phenomena involve interdependencies—what you do affects my welfare, and what I do affects yours—a fact that the market often fails to take into account. After using global warming to illustrate how such "spillovers" arise, I move on to other pervasive types of market failure, involving monopoly power, strategic interactions (game theory), hidden information, uncertainty, and speculative bubbles.

A common theme of this section is that the market, through the price system, often sends the wrong signals to people. It isn't that people are irrational: within their mental limitations, and the limitations imposed by their environment, they pursue their own interests as best they can. In Part III, The Great Crunch, I pursue this argument further and apply it to the financial crisis, using some of the conceptual tools laid out in Parts I and II. The mortgage brokers who steered hard-up working-class families toward risky subprime mortgages were reacting to monetary incentives. So were the loan officers who approved these loans, the investment bankers who cobbled them together into mortgage securities, the rating agency analysts who stamped these securities as safe investments, and the mutual fund managers who bought them.

The subprime boom represented a failure of capitalism in the presence of bounded cognition, uncertainty, hidden information, trend-following, and plentiful credit. Since all of these things are endemic to the modern economy, it was a failure of business as usual. In seeking to deny this, some conservatives have sought to put the blame entirely on the Fed, the Treasury Department, or on Fannie Mae and Freddie Mac, two giant mortgage companies that were actually quasi-governmental organizations. (The U.S. Treasury implicitly guaranteed their debt.) But at least one prominent conservative, Richard Posner, one of the founders of the "Law and Economics" school, has recognized the truth. "The crisis is primarily, perhaps almost entirely, the consequence of decisions taken by private firms in an environment of minimal regulation," he said in a 2008 speech. "We have seen a largely deregulated financial sector breaking and seemingly carrying much of the economy with it."

How could such a thing happen? Bad economic policy decisions played an important role. In keeping interest rates too low for too long, Greenspan and Bernanke distorted the price signals that the market sends and created the conditions for an unprecedented housing bubble. Greed is another oft-mentioned factor; stupidity, a third. (How could those boneheads on Wall Street not have known that lending money to folks with no income, no jobs, and no assets—the infamous "NINJA" mortgage loans—was a bad idea?) In the wake of the revelations about Bernie Madoff and his multibillion-dollar Ponzi scheme, criminality is yet another thing to consider.

At the risk of outraging some readers, I downplay character issues. Greed is ever present: it is what economists call a "primitive" of the capitalist model. Stupidity is equally ubiquitous, but I don't think it played a big role here, and neither, with some obvious exceptions, did outright larceny. My perhaps controversial suggestion is that Chuck Prince, Stan O'Neal, John Thain, and the rest of the Wall Street executives whose financial blundering and multimillion-dollar pay packages have featured on the front pages during the past two years weren't sociopaths, idiots, or felons. For the most part, they were bright, industrious, not particularly imaginative Americans who worked their way up, cultivated the right people, performed a bit better than their colleagues, and found themselves occupying a corner office during one of the great credit booms of all time. Some of these men, perhaps many of them, harbored doubts about what was happening, but the competitive environment they operated in provided them with no incentive to pull back. To the contrary, it urged them on. Between 2004 and 2007, at the height of the boom, banks and other financial companies were reaping record profits; their stock prices were hitting new highs; and their leaders were being lionized in the media.

Consider what would have happened if Prince, who served as chief executive of Citigroup from 2003 to 2007, had announced in 2005, say, that Citi was withdrawing from the subprime market because it was getting too risky. What would have been the reaction of Prince's rivals? Would they have acknowledged the wisdom of his move and copied it? Not likely. Rather, they would have ordered their underlings to rush in and take the business Citi was leaving behind. Citi's short-term earnings would have suffered relative to those of its peers; its stock price would have come under pressure; and Prince, who was already facing criticism because of problems in other areas of Citi's business, would have been written off as a fuddy-duddy. In an interview with the *Financial Times* in July 2007, he acknowledged the constraints he was operating under. "When the music stops, in terms of liquidity, things will be complicated," Prince said. "But as long as the music is playing, you've got to get up and dance. We're still dancing." Four months later, Citi revealed billions of dollars in losses on bad corporate debts and distressed home mortgages. Prince resigned, his reputation in tatters.

In game theory, the dilemma that Prince faced is called the prisoner's dilemma, and it illustrates how perfectly rational behavior on the part of competing individuals can result in bad collective outcomes. When the results of our actions depend on the behavior of others, the theory of the invisible hand doesn't provide much guidance about the likely outcome. Until the formulation of game theory in the 1940s and 1950s, economists simply didn't have the tools needed to figure out what happens in these instances. But we now know a lot more about how purposeful but self-defeating behavior, or what I refer to as rational irrationality, can develop and persist.

In Part III, The Great Crunch, I show how rational irrationality was central to the housing bubble, the growth of the subprime mortgage market, and the subsequent unraveling of the financial system. Much as we might like to imagine that the last few years were an aberration, they weren't. Credit-driven boom-and-bust cycles have plagued capitalist economies for centuries. During the past forty years, there have been 124 systemic banking crises around the world. During the 1980s, many Latin American countries experienced one. In the late 1980s and 1990s, it was the turn of a number of developed countries, including Japan, Norway, Sweden, and the United States. The collapse of the savings-and-loan industry led Congress to establish the Resolution Trust Corporation, which took over hundreds of failed thrifts. Later in the 1990s, many fast-growing Asian countries, including Thailand, Indonesia, and South Korea, endured serious financial blowups. In 2007–2008, it was our turn again, and this time the crisis involved the big banks at the center of the financial system.

For years, Greenspan and other economists argued that the development of complicated, little-understood financial products, such as subprime mortgage–backed securities (MBSs), collateralized debt obligations (CDOs), and credit default swaps (CDSs), made the system safer and more efficient. The basic idea was that by putting a market price on risk and distributing it to investors willing and able to bear it, these complex securities greatly reduced the chances of a systemic crisis. But the risk-spreading proved to be illusory, and the prices that these products traded at turned out to be based on the premise that movements in financial markets followed regular patterns, that their overall distribution, if not their daily gyrations, could be foreseen—a fallacy I call the illusion of predictability, the third illusion at the heart of utopian economics. When the crisis began, the markets reacted in ways that practically none of the participants had anticipated.

In telling this story, and bringing it up to the summer of 2009, I have tried to relate recent events to long-standing intellectual debates over the performance of market systems. The last ten years can be viewed as a unique natural experiment designed to answer the questions: What happens to a twenty-first-century, financially driven economy when you deregulate it and supply it with large amounts of cheap money? Does the invisible hand ensure that everything works out for the best? This isn't an economics textbook, but it does invite the reader to move beyond the daily headlines and think quite deeply about the way modern capitalism operates, and about the theories that have informed economic policies. We tend to think of policy as all about politics and special interests, which certainly play a role. However, behind the debates in Congress, on cable television, and on the Op-Ed pages, there are also some complex and abstract ideas, which rarely get acknowledged. "Practical men, who believe themselves to be quite exempt from any intellectual influences, are usually the slaves of some defunct economist," John Maynard Keynes famously remarked on the final page of *The General Theory of Employment, Interest and Money*. "Madmen in authority, who hear voices in the air, are distilling their frenzy from some academic scribbler of a few years back."

Keynes had a weakness for rhetorical flourishes, but economic ideas do have important practical consequences: that is what makes them worthy of study. If the following helps some readers comprehend some things that had previously seemed mystifying, the effort I have put into it will have been well rewarded. If it also helps consign utopian economics to the history books, that will be a bonus.

PART ONE

UTOPIAN ECONOMICS

1. RAGHURAM RAJAN'S PRESCIENT WARNING

common reaction to extreme events is to say they couldn't have been predicted. Japan's aerial assault on Pearl Harbor; the terrorist strikes against New York and Washington on September 11, 2001; Hurricane Katrina's devastating path through New Orleans—in each of these cases, the authorities claimed to have had no inkling of what was coming. Strictly speaking, this must have been true: had the people in charge known more, they would have taken preemptive action. But lack of firm knowledge rarely equates with complete ignorance. In 1941, numerous American experts on imperial Japan considered an attack on the U.S. Pacific Fleet an urgent threat; prior to 9/11, al-Qaeda had made no secret of its intention to strike the United States again—the CIA and the FBI had some of the actual plotters under observation; as far back as 1986, experts working for the Army Corps of Engineers expressed concerns about the design of the levees protecting New Orleans.

What prevented the authorities from averting these disasters wasn't so much a lack of timely warnings as a dearth of imagination. The individuals in charge weren't particularly venal or shortsighted; even their negligence was within the usual bounds. They simply couldn't conceive of Japan bombing Hawaii; of jihadists flying civilian jets into Manhattan skyscrapers; of a flood surge in the Gulf of Mexico breaching more than fifty levees simultaneously. These catastrophic eventualities weren't regarded as low-probability outcomes, which is the mathematical definition of extreme events: they weren't within the range of possibilities that were considered at all.

The subprime mortgage crisis was another singular and unexpected event, but not one that came without warning. As early as 2002, some commentators, myself included, were saying that in many parts of the country real estate values were losing touch with incomes. In the fall of that year, I visited the prototypical middle-class town of Levittown, on Long Island, where, in the aftermath of World War II, the developer Levitt and Sons offered for sale eight-hundred-square-foot ranch houses, complete with refrigerator, range, washing machine, oil burners, and Venetian blinds, for $7,990. When I arrived, those very same homes, with limited updating, were selling for roughly $300,000, an increase of about 50 percent on what they had been fetching two years earlier. Richard Dallow, a Realtor whose family has been selling property there since 1951, showed me around town. He expressed surprise that home prices had defied the NASDAQ crash of 2000, the economic recession of 2001, and the aftermath of 9/11. "It has to impact at some point," he said. "But, then again, in the summer of 2000, I thought it was impacting, and then things came back."

By and large, the kinds of people buying houses in Levittown were the same as they had always been: cops, firefighters, janitors, and construction workers who had been priced out of neighboring towns. The inflation in home prices was making it difficult for these buyers even to afford Levittown. This "has always been a low-down-payment area," Dallow said. "If the price is three hundred and thirty thousand, and you put down five percent, that's a mortgage of three hundred and thirteen thousand five hundred. You need a jumbo mortgage. For Levittown." When I got back to my office in Times Square, I wrote a story for *The New Yorker* entitled "The Next Crash," in which I quoted Dallow and some financial analysts who were concerned about the real estate market. "Valuation looks quite extreme, and not just at the top end," Ian Morris, chief U.S. economist of HSBC Bank, said. "Even normal mom-and-pop homes are now very expensive relative to income." Christopher Wood, an investment strategist at CLSA Emerging Markets, was even more bearish: "The American housing market is the last big bubble," he said. "When it bursts, it will be very ugly."

Between 2003 and 2006, as the rise in house prices accelerated, many expressions of concern appeared in the media. In June 2005, *The Economist* said, "The worldwide rise in house prices is the biggest bubble in history. Prepare for the economic pain when it pops." In the United States, the ratio of home prices to rents was at a historic high, the newsweekly noted, with prices rising at an annual rate of more than 20 percent in some parts of the country. The same month, Robert Shiller, a well-known Yale economist who wrote the 2000 bestseller *Irrational Exuberance*, told *Barron's*, "The home-price bubble feels like the stock-market mania in the fall of 1999."

One reason these warnings went unheeded was denial. When the price of an asset is going up by 20 or 30 percent a year, nobody who owns it, or trades it, likes to be told their newfound wealth is illusory. But it wasn't just real estate agents and condo flippers who were insisting that the rise in prices wouldn't be reversed: many economists who specialized in real estate agreed with them. Karl Case, an economist at Wellesley, reminded me that the average price of American homes had risen in every single year since 1945. Frank Nothaft, the chief economist at Freddie Mac, ran through a list of "economic fundamentals" that he said justified high and rising home prices: low mortgage rates, large-scale immigration, and a modest inventory of new homes. "We are not going to see the price of single-family homes fall," he said bluntly. "It ain't going to happen."

As the housing boom continued, Nothaft's suggestion that nationwide house prices were unidirectional acquired the official imprimatur of the U.S. government. In April 2003, at the Ronald Reagan Presidential Library and Museum, in Simi Valley, California, Alan Greenspan insisted that the United States wasn't suffering from a real estate bubble. In October 2004, he argued that real estate doesn't lend itself to speculation, noting that "upon sale of a house, homeowners must move and live elsewhere." In June 2005, testifying on Capitol Hill, he acknowledged the presence of "froth" in some areas, but ruled out the possibility of a nationwide bubble, saying housing markets were local. Although price declines couldn't be ruled out in some areas, Greenspan concluded, "[T]hese declines, were they to occur, likely would not have substantial macroeconomic implications."

At the time Greenspan made these comments, Ben Bernanke had recently left the Fed, where he had served as governor since 2002, to become chairman of the White House Council of Economic Advisers. In August 2005, Bernanke traveled to Crawford, Texas, to brief President Bush, and afterward a reporter asked him, "Did the housing bubble come up at your meeting?" Bernanke said housing had been discussed, and went on: "I think it's important to point out that house prices are being supported in very large part by very strong fundamentals . . . We have lots of jobs, employment, high incomes, very low mortgage rates, growing population, and shortages of land and housing in many areas." On October 15, 2005, in an address to the National Association for Business Economics, Bernanke used almost identical language, saying rising house prices "largely reflect strong economic fundamentals." Nine days later, President Bush selected him to succeed Greenspan.

In August 2005, a couple of weeks after Bernanke's trip to Texas, the Federal Reserve Bank of Kansas City, one of the twelve regional banks in the Fed system, devoted its annual economic policy symposium to the lessons of the Greenspan era. As usual, the conference took place at the Jackson Lake Lodge, an upscale resort in Jackson Hole, Wyoming. Greenspan, who had, by then, served eighteen years as Fed chairman, delivered the opening address. Most of the other speakers, who included Robert Rubin, the former Treasury secretary, and Jean-Claude Trichet, the head of the European Central Bank, were extremely complimentary about the Fed boss. "There is no doubt that Greenspan has been an amazingly successful chairman of the Federal Reserve System," Alan Blinder, a Princeton economist and former Fed governor, opined. Raghuram G. Rajan, an economist at the University of Chicago Booth School of Business, who was then the chief economist at the International Monetary Fund, took a more critical line, examining the consequences of two decades of financial deregulation.

Rajan, who was born in Bhopal, in central India, in 1963, obtained his Ph.D. at MIT, in 1991, and then moved to the University of Chicago Business School, where he established himself as something of a wunderkind. In 2003, his colleagues named him the scholar under forty who had contributed most to the field of finance. That same year, he took the top economics job at the IMF, where he stayed until 2006.

He could hardly be described as a radical. One book he coauthored is entitled *Saving Capitalism from the Capitalists: Unleashing the Power of Financial Markets to Create Wealth and Spread Opportunity*. Bruce Bartlett, a conservative activist who served in the administrations of Ronald Reagan and George H. W. Bush, described it as "one of the most powerful defenses of the free market ever written."

Rajan began by reviewing some history. In the past couple of decades, he reminded the audience, deregulation and technical progress had subjected banks to increasing competition in their core business of taking in deposits from households and lending them to other individuals and firms. In response, the banks had expanded into new fields, including trading securities and creating new financial products, such as mortgage-backed securities (MBSs) and collateralized debt obligations (CDOs). Most of these securities the banks sold to investors, but some of them they held on to for investment purposes, which exposed them to potential losses should the markets concerned suffer a big fall. "While the system now exploits the risk-bearing capacity of the economy better by allocating risks more widely, it also takes on more risks than before," Rajan said. "Moreover, the linkages between markets, and between markets and institutions, are now more pronounced. While this helps the system diversify across small shocks, it also exposes the system to large systemic shocks—large shifts in asset prices or changes in aggregate liquidity."

Turning to other factors that had made the financial system more vulnerable, Rajan brought up incentive-based compensation. Almost all senior financiers now receive bonuses that are tied to the investment returns their businesses generate. Since these returns are correlated with risks, Rajan pointed out, there are "perverse incentives" for managers and firms to take on more risks, especially so-called tail risks—events that occur with a very low probability but that can have disastrous consequences. The tendency for investors and traders to ape each other's strategies, a phenomenon known as herding, was another potentially destabilizing factor, Rajan said, because it led people to buy assets even if they considered them overvalued. Taken together, incentive-based compensation and herding were "a volatile combination. If herd behavior moves asset prices away from fundamentals, the likelihood of large realignments—precisely the kind that trigger tail losses—increases."

Finally, Rajan added, there is one more ingredient that can "make the cocktail particularly volatile, and that is low interest rates after a period of high rates, either because of financial liberalization or because of extremely accommodative monetary policy." Cheap money encourages banks, investment banks, and hedge funds to borrow more and place bigger bets, Rajan reminded the audience. When credit is flowing freely, euphoria often develops, only to be followed by a "sudden stop" that can do great damage to the economy. So far, the U.S. economy had avoided such an outcome, Rajan conceded, but its rebound from the 1987 stock market crash and the 2000–2001 collapse in tech stocks "should not make us overly sanguine." After all, "a shock to the equity markets, though large, may have less effect than a shock to the credit markets."

As a rule, central bankers don't rush stages or toss their chairs; if they did, Rajan might have been in physical danger. During a discussion period, Don Kohn, a governor of the Fed who would go on to become its vice chairman, pointed out that Rajan's presentation amounted to a direct challenge to "the Greenspan doctrine," which warmly welcomed the development of new financial products, such as securitized loans and credit default swaps. "By allowing institutions to diversify risk, to choose their risk profiles more precisely, and to improve the management of the risks they do take on, they have made institutions more robust," Kohn went on. "And by facilitating the flow of savings across markets and national boundaries, these developments have contributed to a better allocation of resources and promoted growth."

The Greenspan doctrine didn't imply that financial markets invariably got things right, Kohn conceded, but "the actions of private parties to protect themselves—what Chairman Greenspan has called private regulation—are generally quite effective," whereas government "risks undermining private regulation and financial stability by undermining incentives." Turning to Rajan's suggestion that some sort of government fix might be needed for Wall Street compensation schemes, Kohn insisted it wasn't in the interests of senior executives at banks and other financial institutions "to reach for short-run gains at the expense of longer-term risk, to disguise the degree of risk they are taking for their customers, or otherwise to endanger their reputations. As a consequence, I did not find convincing the discussion of market failure that would require government intervention in compensation."

Lawrence Summers, who was then the president of Harvard, stood up and said he found "the basic, slightly lead-eyed premise of this paper to be largely misguided." After pausing to remark on how much he had learned from Greenspan, Summers compared the development of the financial industry to the history of commercial aviation, saying the occasional plane crash shouldn't disguise the fact that getting from A to B was now much easier and safer than it used to be, and adding, "It seems to me that the overwhelming preponderance of what has taken place is positive." While it was legitimate to point out the possibility of self-reinforcing spirals in financial markets, Summers concluded, "the tendency towards restriction that runs through the tone of the presentation seems to me to be quite problematic. It seems to me to support a wide variety of misguided policy impulses in many countries."

The reaction to Rajan's paper demonstrated just how difficult it had become to query, even on a theoretical level, the dogma of deregulation and free markets. As a longtime colleague and adviser of Greenspan's, Kohn might be forgiven for defending his *amour propre*. Summers, however, was in a different category. During the 1980s, as a young Harvard professor, he had advocated a tax on securities transactions, such as stock purchases, arguing that much of what took place on Wall Street was a shell game that added nothing to overall output. Subsequently, he had gone on to advise presidential candidates and serve as Treasury secretary in the Clinton administration. Along the way, he had jettisoned his earlier views and become a leading defender of the conventional wisdom, a phrase John Kenneth Galbraith coined for the unquestioned assumptions that help to frame policy debates and, for that matter, barroom debates. As Galbraith noted in his 1958 bestseller, *The Affluent Society*, the conventional wisdom isn't the exclusive property of any political party or creed: Republicans and Democrats, conservatives and liberals, true believers and agnostics, all subscribe to its central tenets. "The conventional wisdom having been made more or less identical with sound scholarship, its position is virtually impregnable," Galbraith wrote. "The skeptic is disqualified by his very tendency to go brashly from the old to the new. Were he a sound scholar . . . he would remain with the conventional wisdom."

But how does the conventional wisdom get established? To answer that question, we must go on an intellectual odyssey that begins in Glasgow in the eighteenth century and passes through London, Lausanne, Vienna, Chicago, New York, and Washington, D.C. Utopian economics has a long and illustrious history. Before turning to the flaws of the free market doctrine, let us trace its development and seek to understand its enduring appeal.

2. ADAM SMITH'S INVISIBLE HAND

n everyday language, a market is simply somewhere things are bought and sold. The convenience store on the corner is a market, as is the nearest branch of Walmart, Target, or Home Depot. Amazon.com is a market, so is the NASDAQ, and so is the local red-light district. Many towns and cities have organized street markets, including Leeds, in northern England, where I grew up. Every few days, my grandmother, who kept a boardinghouse, would go to Leeds market in search of cheap cuts of meat and other bargains. If Alan Greenspan is at one end of the spectrum when it comes to thinking about how markets work, she was at the other. An Irishwoman with little formal education but a wealth of personal experience, she regarded the shopkeepers and tradesmen she dealt with as "robbers," "villains," and "feckers," who were all out to cheat her in every way they could.

That is an extreme view to hold. So, too, is the idea that free markets invariably work to the benefit of all. Of course, when economists use the term "free markets," they are referring not to individual shopkeepers but to an entire system of organizing production, distribution, and consumption. Taking the economy as a whole, there are three markets of importance: the goods market, where shoppers purchase everything from Toyota Corollas to haircuts to vacations in Hawaii; the labor market, where firms and other types of employers hire workers; and the financial market, where individuals and institutions lend out or invest their surplus cash.

Each of these markets is distinct. Economists tend to obscure their differences, treating computer programmers and stock index futures in the same way as iPods and canned tomatoes—as desirable commodities. Generalizing like this obscures the fact that markets are social constructs, but it allows economists to focus on some underlying commonalities, such as the roles played by incentives, competition, and prices. Market systems have proved durable for several reasons. In allowing individuals, firms, and countries to specialize in what they are best at, they expand the economy's productive capacity. In providing incentives for investment and innovation, they facilitate a gradual rise in productivity and wages, which, over decades and centuries, compound into greatly improved living standards. And in relying on self-interest rather than administrative fiat to guide the decisions of consumers, investors, and business executives, markets obviate the need for a feudal overlord or omniscient central planner to organize everything.

One of the first economists to put these arguments together was Adam Smith, a bookish Scot who was born in Kirkcaldy, a town on the Firth of Forth, north of Edinburgh, in 1723. Smith's father, a lawyer and government official, died before his son's birth. After being brought up by his mother, Smith attended Glasgow University, where he studied philosophy under Francis Hutcheson, one of the great figures of the Scottish Enlightenment. He moved on to Oxford and Edinburgh universities, before returning to Glasgow, where from 1752 to 1764 he taught moral philosophy, a catchall subject that included ethics, jurisprudence, and political economy. Resigning his professorship to take a higher-paying job tutoring a wealthy young aristocrat, the Duke of Buccleuch, Smith began writing his great opus, *The Wealth of Nations*, which was eventually published in 1776, the same year as the American Declaration of Independence.

With a big nose, protruding teeth, and a slight stammer, Smith was far from an imposing figure. Famously absentminded, he often jabbered to himself as he walked the streets of Glasgow. But his metaphor of an unseen hand directing the economy is as powerful now as it was 230 years ago, and it remains central to any discussion of how markets operate. This is not just my opinion. "It is striking to me that our ideas about the efficacy of market competition have remained essentially unchanged since the eighteenth-century Enlightenment, when they first emerged, to a remarkable extent, from the mind of one man, Adam Smith," Alan Greenspan wrote in his 2007 memoir, *The Age of Turbulence*. "[I]n a sense, the history of market competition and the capitalism it represents is the story of the ebb and flow of Smith's ideas. Accordingly, the story of his work and its reception repays special attention."

Smith based his arguments not on abstract principles but on acute observation. He began by describing the operations of a pin (nail) factory. In the late eighteenth century, the process of mechanization was only beginning, and most factories in the British Isles were small; even the biggest of them had only three or four hundred employees. Already, though, each worker carried out a specialized task: "One man draws out the wire," Smith wrote, "another straights it, a third cuts it, a fourth points it, a fifth grinds it at the top for receiving the head; to make the head requires three distinct operations; to put it on is a peculiar business, to whiten the pins is another; it is even a trade by itself to put them into the paper; and the important business of making a pin is, in this manner, divided into about eighteen distinct operations, which, in some manufactories, are all performed by distinct hands, though in others the same man will perform two or three of them." Whereas one workman unacquainted with the methods and machines used in such establishments "could scarce, perhaps, with his utmost industry, make one pin a day," Smith went on, ten factory workers experienced and skilled in their individual tasks "could make among them, upwards of forty-eight thousand pins a day."

What applies to the making of pins applies to the production of many other items. Specialization, which Smith referred to as "the division of labor," generates "a proportionable increase of the productive powers of labor," first by increasing the dexterity of individual workers; second, in saving time moving from one task to another; third, in encouraging the invention of machines, which "enable one man to do the work of many." The result is what modern economists would refer to as a steady increase in productivity, or output per head. In a subsistence agricultural economy of the sort that had existed in Britain and elsewhere for centuries, most people struggled to feed and clothe their families. In a modern market system—Smith preferred the phrase "commercial society"—workers and tradesmen produce a surplus over and above their daily necessities, which they use to buy other, inessential goods, such as fashionable clothes and comfortable furniture. "It is," said Smith, "the great multiplication of the productions of all the different arts"—professions—"in consequence of the division of labor, which occasions, in a well-governed society, that universal opulence which extends itself to the lowest ranks of the people."

Considering that Smith was writing about a society in which bands of hungry laborers sometimes roamed the countryside, and in which cities such as Manchester and Leeds would soon be filling up with impoverished factory workers, many of them still children, his description of a capitalist economy may seem to our eyes rather uncritical. Still, as the industrialization of Britain continued and intensified over the ensuing century, wages and living standards did eventually increase, confirming Smith's point: free market capitalism raises living standards. The pattern has repeated itself in many other countries, with China and India providing recent examples. After decades of centralized control, both countries have opened up their economies and entered the global division of labor. As was the case in Great Britain and the United States, the development of the Chinese and Indian economies has involved sweatshop labor, rising inequality, and large-scale environmental degradation. But it has also created a great deal of wealth, at least some of which has already trickled down to "the lowest ranks of the people." Nobody would claim that the typical inhabitant of China or India is rich; but over the past couple of decades, many, many people have been raised from poverty. In China between 1981 and 2005, according to a recent study by researchers at the World Bank, the poverty rate fell from 84 percent to 16 percent, a drop of almost two-thirds. By the end of the period, more than 600 million Chinese had been lifted out of poverty.

As the division of labor proceeds, a fine and complex web of mutual trade and dependency comes into existence. Smith used the example of a day laborer's humble woolen coat, drawing attention to all the different professions that contribute to its manufacture: "The shepherd, the sorter of the wool, the wool comber or carder, the dyer, the scribbler, the spinner, the weaver, the fuller, the dresser, with many others, must all join their different arts in order to complete even this homely production. How many merchants and carriers, besides, must have been employed in transporting the material from some of those workmen to others who often live in a very distant part of the country!" That is just the first round of interconnections. What about all the steps that go into supplying, say, the dyer with his dye or the shearer with his shears? Smith listed another baker's dozen of them, invoking the merchant, the shipbuilder, the sailmaker, the rope maker, the sailor, the timber seller, the miner, the smelter, the brickmaker, the bricklayer, the millwright, the forger, and the smith. All this for a single cheap overcoat! If we also consider the laborer's other possessions, such as the contents of his home, Smith pointed out, and consider the labor that goes into them, we shall find that "without the assistance and cooperation of many thousands, the very meanest person in a civilized country could not be provided, even according to what we very falsely imagine the easy and simple manner in which he is commonly accommodated."

Today, of course, the division of labor is much more global and intricate than it was in Smith's day. Apple's iPod, of which more than 175 million have been sold, was conceived in Silicon Valley; most of the software it operates on was written in Hyderabad, India; and it is manufactured in China, where Apple has outsourced production to a number of Taiwanese companies. The music player contains 451 parts, including a hard drive made by Japan's Toshiba; two microchips produced by American companies, Broadcom and PortalPlayer; and a memory chip made by Samsung, a Korean firm. Each of these components, in turn, has a complicated global supply chain. The iPod is rightly seen as a triumph of American innovation and marketing. It is also a pocket-size emblem of the division of labor. (In June 2006, *The Mail on Sunday*, a British newspaper, revealed that many of the Chinese workers assembling iPods were young women who worked fifteen hours a day and lived in corporate dormitories, earning less than fifty dollars a month. Apple subsequently promised to improve the working conditions and hired a workplace standards auditing company.)

If a medieval monk were to descend on today's immensely complex global economy, which in 2007 produced about $55 trillion worth of goods and services, he would surely have some basic questions that we, blinded by familiarity, seldom stop to ponder: Who tells all the specialized producers what goods to supply, and in what quantities? Who prevents them from overcharging for their wares? Smith's answer was that no individual or authority has to carry out these tasks: the competitive market accomplishes them on its own. If, at any moment, demand for a particular commodity exceeds the amount presented for sale, its price will rise and existing suppliers will make excess profits, which will encourage others to enter the market. If the amount of a commodity offered for sale exceeds the demand, its price will fall and so will suppliers' profits, encouraging some of them to exit the market. In a market economy, these adjustments happen all the time.

In Smith's idealized version of the free market, competition forces businesses to supply what consumers want to purchase and to cut back on the production of less popular goods, while preventing them from profiteering. Prices gravitate toward a "natural price," at which suppliers just cover their outlays for labor, raw materials, and rent, as well as making an unexceptional rate of profit. The market system is efficient in that human and physical resources are directed to where they are most needed and prices are tied to costs. It is also self-correcting. If a shortage develops, prices rise and supply expands. If a glut occurs, prices fall and production contracts until supply and demand come into balance.

The technical phrase for this type of process is negative feedback, and it is found in most stable dynamic systems, such as thermostat-controlled heating systems and the body's hormonal system. When an initial disturbance occurs, price changes set in force offsetting movements, which restore equilibrium. (The opposite of negative feedback is positive feedback, which amplifies initial disturbances. Positive feedback helps to cause nuclear explosions, rapid population growth, and stock market bubbles.) It should be noted that none of these adjustments is imposed from above: in the language of systems analysis, they are all "emergent" properties, which result from a multiplicity of individual interactions. Each businessman "intends only his own gain," Smith wrote, "and he is in this, as in many other cases, led by an invisible hand to promote an end which was no part of his intention . . . By pursuing his own interest, he frequently promotes that of the society more effectually than when he really intends to promote it. I have never known much good done by those who affected to trade for the public good."

In the presence of this fantabulous market mechanism, what is left for a government to do? With a few exceptions, such as providing for national defense and making sure laws are properly enforced, Smith said it should confine itself to clearing away outmoded conventions that prevent competitive markets from operating, such as price controls and legal limits on entry to particular industries. "Every man, as long as he does not violate the laws of justice, is left perfectly free to pursue his own interest his own way, and to bring both his industry and capital into competition with those of any other man, or order of men."

This philosophy is often referred to as laissez-faire—a French phrase that means leave alone. In the eighteenth-century context, laissez-faire involved strengthening property rights, lowering tariffs on imported goods, and abolishing what remained of the medieval economy, with its feudal privileges, its restrictive labor guilds, its government-imposed local monopolies on the production and distribution of certain goods, its hostile attitude toward moneylenders, and its suspicion of novel production methods. If the economy were freed of artificial restraints, competition would ensure that employment and the utilization of resources evolved in the direction "most agreeable to the interests of the whole society," Smith wrote. Unlike some later economists, he didn't spend much time discussing the nature of societal interests, or whether they existed. He took it as self-evident that the ultimate goal of economic policy was maximizing a country's wealth, by which he meant the total value of the goods and services it produced on an annual basis, or what we now call the gross domestic product. Little "else is requisite to carry a state to the highest degree of opulence from the lowest barbarism but peace, easy taxes, and a tolerable administration of justice: all the rest being brought about by the natural course of things," Smith wrote in a 1755 paper.

With his espousal of free trade, limited government, and low taxes, it is easy to caricature Smith as the intellectual spokesman of the rising capitalist class, or bourgeoisie. Actually, he was deeply skeptical of businessmen's motives. Like my late grandmother, he suspected them of trying to diddle their customers at every opportunity. ("People of the same trade seldom meet together, even for merriment and diversion, but the conversation ends in a conspiracy against the public, or in some diversion to raise prices.") Here again, though, the free market comes to the rescue. Faced with actual and potential competition from rival suppliers, manufacturers and merchants have no choice but to trim their profit margins and invest in new production methods. In the Smithian world, competition cannot be avoided or circumvented. (Later economists would characterize it as a system of "perfect competition.") And the ultimate beneficiary of all this competing among firms is the shopper, who gets to buy better products at lower prices. In the words of Ludwig von Mises, a twentieth-century Austrian economist who greatly admired Smith, consumers are sovereign.

Before turning to the strengths and weaknesses of Smith's analysis, it is worth stepping back and admiring its scope. Starting out from the pin factory, he has characterized the entire economic organism, describing the workings of individual markets but also the outcome of countless households and businesses interacting in many, many markets. And what does this body look like? It is a self-regulating mechanism that stimulates technological innovation, satisfies human wants, minimizes wasteful activity, polices rapacious businessmen, and enriches the populace. Perhaps most remarkably of all, the fuel that keeps the mechanism humming is human selfishness: "It is not from the benevolence of the butcher, the brewer, or the baker that we expect our dinner, but from their regard to their own interest," Smith wrote in a famous passage. "We address ourselves, not to their humanity, but to their self-love, and never talk to them of our own necessities but of their advantages. Nobody but a beggar chooses to depend chiefly upon the benevolence of his fellow citizens."

The free market isn't merely an economic wonder: it is a godlike contraption that takes individual acts of egocentricity and somehow transforms them into socially beneficial outcomes. In the words of Milton and Rose Friedman: "Adam Smith's flash of genius was his recognition that the prices that emerged from voluntary transactions between buyers and sellers—for short, in a free market—could coordinate the activity of millions of people, each seeking his own interest, in such a way as to make everyone better off. It was a startling idea then, and it remains one today, that economic order can emerge as the unintended consequence of the actions of many people, each seeking his own interest." Small wonder that so many of Smith's followers have expounded their arguments with a quasi-religious fervor, castigating government intervention in the economy as not just unwise but morally wrong. Utopian economics goes beyond a scientific doctrine: it is a political philosophy, a secular faith.

Following Smith's death, in 1790, at the age of sixty-seven, the dual nature of his legacy became increasingly apparent. During the early and mid-nineteenth century, English "classical economists," such as David Ricardo, Nassau Senior, and John Stuart Mill, developed the scientific side of his analysis, spelling out the logic of free trade, and explaining how, through the interplay of market forces, the revenues that businesses generated were split among rents, profits, and wages. Like Smith, these men believed free markets had internal laws that governments sought to interfere with at their peril. John Stuart Mill, a childhood prodigy who by the age of seven was reading Plato, spelled this out in his book *Principles of Political Economy*, which appeared in 1848 and was for forty years the bible of British economics: "Laissez-faire, in short, should be the general practice," Mill wrote; "every departure from it, unless required by some greater good, is a certain evil."

During the reign of Queen Victoria, who acceded to the throne in 1837, Mill's prescription became the official doctrine of the British Empire. From Canada to the United Kingdom to India, free trade, limited government, and low taxes were the order of the day. Under the Poor Law Amendment Act of 1834, which Nassau Senior helped to devise, outdoor relief for paupers—a form of welfare that dated back to feudal times—was abolished. Henceforth, impecunious workers faced the choice of getting a job or entering the dreaded "workhouse," a jail-like institution where they would be provided with bread and gruel, but little else. Under the principle of "less eligibility," the explicit aim of the 1834 law was to stigmatize idleness and force the out-of-work to accept any position available, regardless of the wages it paid. After subjecting the landless laborers and urban poor to the harsh disciplines of the market, the Victorian free market reformers administered similar shock treatment to farmers. In 1846, following an epic political battle, the Corn Laws, which, through a system of tariffs, protected

British grain growers from foreign competition, were abolished, opening up the British market to cheaper foodstuffs produced in the American Midwest.

The classical economists justified their recommendations on economic grounds, but there was also a strong moral element to their teachings. Laissez-faire was the practical application of a philosophy that placed great emphasis on self-reliance and freedom of choice. "[T]he sole end for which mankind are warranted, individually or collectively, in interfering with the liberty of action of any of their number, is self-protection," Mill wrote in his most famous book, *On Liberty.* "That the only purpose for which power can be rightfully exercised over any member of a civilized community, against his will, is to prevent harm to others. His own good, either physical or moral, is not sufficient warrant."

For all their embrace of free market economics, and on occasion their righteous indignation, however, the classical economists were less dogmatic than many of their twentieth-century followers. Within confines, they saw a legitimate role for government programs. In *The Wealth of Nations,* Smith listed the three duties of government as defending the nation, administering justice, and "erecting and maintaining certain public works and certain public institutions, which it can never be for the interest of any individual, or small number of individuals, to erect and maintain; because the profit could never repay the expense to any individual or small number of individuals, though it may frequently do much more than repay it to a great society."

The third duty of government was defined broadly enough to admit a wide range of activities, such as building bridges and public parks, and operating public utilities, such as sewers and irrigation schemes. Smith's followers added to this list. David Ricardo, the great defender of free trade, called for the nationalization of the Bank of England, which in his time was privately operated; Nassau Senior, for all his heartless approach to able-bodied adult workers, advocated a national system of public education for children. Classical economists supported child labor laws, mandatory safety standards for workplaces and new products, and the expansion of the civil service. "The principle of laissez-faire may be safely trusted to in some things but in many more it is wholly inapplicable," wrote J. R. McCulloch, a prolific Scot who helped to popularize the doctrines of Smith and Ricardo. "[A]nd to appeal to it on all occasions savours more of the policy of a parrot than of a statesman or a philosopher." Even Mill, with his deep philosophical attachment to liberty, was an avid social reformer. "[T]he admitted functions of government embrace a much wider field than can easily be included within the ring-fence of any restrictive definition," he wrote in *Principles of Political Economy*, "and it is hardly possible to find any ground of justification common to them all, except the comprehensive one of general expediency."

Smith and his successors also believed that the government had a duty to protect the public from financial swindles and speculative panics, which were both common in eighteenth- and nineteenth-century Britain. The financial system was a two-tier one, consisting of a number of big banks based in London and dozens of smaller "country banks" located in other towns and cities. Many of these provincial banks issued their own promissory notes, which circulated as money. There was perennial concern that the banks would issue too much of this paper to unworthy borrowers, leaving them vulnerable to panics should concerned depositors try to withdraw their money. In book two of *The Wealth of Nations*, Smith cited the case of a Scottish bank that was established to provide loans to local entrepreneurs—"projectors," he called them—on more favorable terms than existing lenders, and which quickly ended up with many heavily indebted customers. "The bank, no doubt, gave some temporary relief to those projectors, and enabled them to carry on their projects for about two years longer than they otherwise would have done," Smith wrote. "But it thereby only enabled them to get so much deeper into debt, so that, when ruin came, it fell so much the heavier both upon them and upon their creditors."

To prevent a recurrence of credit busts, Smith advocated preventing banks from issuing notes to speculative lenders. "Such regulations may, no doubt, be considered as in some respects a violation of natural liberty," he wrote. "But these exertions of the natural liberty of a few individuals, which might endanger the security of the whole society, are, and ought to be, restrained by the laws of all governments, of the most free, as well as the most despotical. The obligation of building party walls, in order to prevent the communication of fire, is a violation of natural liberty, exactly of the same kind with the regulations of the banking trade which are here proposed."

Alan Greenspan and other self-proclaimed descendants of Smith rarely mention his skeptical views on the banking system, which were shared by many nineteenth-century economists who otherwise maintained a favorable view of the free market. J. S. Mill traced most economic downturns to disturbances that emerged from the financial system, as did Alfred Marshall, the late-Victorian economist whose *Principles of Economics* replaced Mill's textbook as the standard work. Marshall said "reckless inflations of credit" were "the chief cause of all economic malaise," and he called for vigorous action on the part of the monetary authorities to prevent them.

The notion of financial markets as rational and self-correcting mechanisms is an invention of the last forty years. Before that, most economists sympathized with Charles Mackay, the journalist and sometime colleague of Charles Dickens whose 1841 book, *Extraordinary Popular Delusions and the Madness of Crowds*, compared speculative manias, such as the "tulipomania" that gripped Holland in the 1630s and the South Sea bubble of 1720s London, to witch trials, millennialism, and other examples of collective insanity. The transition from Mackay's jaundiced opinion of finance to Greenspan's sunny view took a long time, and it was based, at least partially, on a misreading of the theory of the invisible hand, which Smith had never intended to be applied to finance. The transition began, ironically enough, in the 1930s and 1940s, when capitalism appeared to be floundering and many economists were looking favorably on replacing the price system with central planning.

3. FRIEDRICH HAYEK'S
TELECOMMUNICATIONS SYSTEM

Alan Greenspan first read Adam Smith shortly after World War II, a time, he recalls in his memoir, when "regard for [Smith's] theories was at a low ebb." To most survivors of the Great Depression and the war, the idea of the market economy as a benign, self-regulating mechanism was absurd. The laissez-faire regimen of free trade, small government, and low taxes was widely seen as responsible for the disasters of the early 1930s, when, in the United States, industrial production had fallen by half and the unemployment rate had reached one in four. Even among economists, especially the younger ones who had less of a professional stake in the old ideas, capitalism was widely viewed as inherently unstable. Most economists agreed with Keynes, the British economist and Treasury official, who had argued that the only way to prevent mass unemployment was for the government, through investing heavily in public works and other projects, to manage the level of demand in the economy.

On both sides of the Atlantic, governments had moved to protect people against the vagaries of the market, introducing unemployment benefits, Social Security, and much tighter regulation of the financial system. In the Soviet Union and its satellite territories, meanwhile, the effort to completely replace capitalism appeared to be having some success: Stalin's government boasted that it had eliminated unemployment and mass poverty. (The human costs of these achievements weren't yet clear to outsiders.) When, on October 4, 1957, the Soviet Union successfully launched *Sputnik I*, the first satellite to orbit the earth, some observers prematurely concluded that the Communist empire had moved ahead of the United States in the race for military and economic domination. "Chastened at home, Americans also felt humiliated abroad as they read of reports of foreign journalists claiming the USSR had overtaken the United States and was now the number one superpower," the historian John Patrick Diggins writes in *The Proud Decades*, his lively account of postwar America.

In such an environment, free market economists were relegated to the role of preachers in an obscure sect. They sustained themselves by offering eulogies up to Smith and the invisible hand. The two most important of these evangelists were Friedrich Hayek, a well-bred Austrian who was born in Vienna in 1899, and Milton Friedman, a voluble New Yorker who was born in Brooklyn in 1912. In the late 1940s, both Hayek and Friedman moved to the University of Chicago, where they helped to create the "Chicago School" of economics. Friedman, who died in 2006, remains a household name, but even among economists, Hayek, who died in 1992, is a much less well-known figure.

When I began studying economics at Oxford during the early eighties, Hayek was widely seen as a right-wing nut. True, he had received the Nobel Memorial Prize in 1974, but that was viewed within the economics profession as a political sop, with Hayek's name added to balance that of his co-winner, Gunnar Myrdal, a left-wing Swedish economist. (Myrdal later said that he wouldn't have accepted the award if he had known he would have to share it with Hayek.) Hayek's proposals to emasculate the trade unions and privatize the money supply seemed outlandish: he was regarded more as a libertarian political philosopher than a practical economist. I made it all the way through undergraduate and graduate school without reading any of his articles or books, and I wasn't unusual. Until recently, few economics textbooks mentioned Hayek's name, and there was no scholarly biography of him available.

Friedrich August von Hayek—his full Austrian name—was a distant cousin of the philosopher Ludwig Wittgenstein. His father was a doctor; his mother came from a family of wealthy government officials. After serving as an artillery officer in World War I, he enrolled at the University of Vienna, where he studied under a number of leading Austrian economists, including Ludwig von Mises, a fervent free-marketer who, as early as 1922, wrote a book, *Socialism: An Economic and Sociological Analysis*, that dismissed collectivist planning as impractical. When he wasn't teaching, von Mises worked at the Abrechnungsamt, a government office that dealt with Austria's postwar debts, and he hired Hayek as a research assistant. The young economist quickly abandoned the moderately left-wing views he had formed during the Great War, adopting a laissez-faire outlook similar to that of von Mises. Many of his fellow students would gather at the Kaffee Landmann to discuss Marxism and psychoanalysis, but Hayek found these fashionable disciplines "more unsatisfactory the more I studied them."

During the 1920s, Hayek worked on the causes of business cycles, formulating the view that slumps were the inevitable result of prior booms, during which growth had become "unbalanced," with investment in industrial capacity outstripping the supply of savings in the economy. Recessions, in this view, were a way of restoring the balance between savings and investment. Hayek's theory, which was eventually expostulated in a 1931 book, *Prices and Production*, attracted attention in England, where Keynes and his young Cambridge acolytes were developing the theory that it was a lack of overall demand in the economy that caused recessions, and that an increase in government spending could be used to restore prosperity. After World War II, governments all over the world adopted Keynesianism as their guiding policy framework, but in the early 1930s it was new and controversial. Lionel Robbins, a well-known professor at the London School of Economics, was one of the economists defending the traditional view that recessions were "nature's cure," and that the only way to forestall them was through wage cuts and government retrenchment. Robbins, who read German, spotted Hayek's work and saw a potential ally against Keynes. He invited Hayek to LSE in 1931 as a guest lecturer, and a year later as a full-time professor.

With Hayek's arrival in London, the stage was set for an epic intellectual debate. He got things going with a critical review of Keynes's 1930 book, *A Treatise on Money*, which identified too much saving as a cause of recessions, saying the book lacked a proper theory of capital investment and interest rates—an area Austrian economists considered the key to economic slumps. In 1931, Keynes returned fire, describing Hayek's *Prices and Production* as "one of the most frightful muddles I have ever read." It soon became clear that, despite the hopes Robbins had placed in him, Hayek, with his accented English and sometimes obscurantist prose, was no match for Keynes, an accomplished writer and debater. Hayek was an unknown; Keynes had been a public figure ever since the publication of his 1919 book, *The Economic Consequences of the Peace*, which correctly predicted that the punitive Treaty of Versailles would create great difficulties.

Rather than continuing to squabble publicly with Hayek, Keynes invited him to Cambridge, where they dined at King's College and talked with Piero Sraffa, a brilliant young Italian economist who had also written critically of Hayek's theories. One-on-one, the aloof Cambridge aesthete and the reserved Austrian enjoyed each other's company; among other things, they shared a passion for antiquarian books. "Hayek has been here for the weekend," Keynes wrote to his wife, Lydia, in March 1933. "I sat by him in hall last night and lunched with him at Piero's today. We get on very well in private life. But what rubbish his theory is."

Keynes won the great debate. Even before he wrote *The General Theory of Employment, Interest and Money*, which was published in 1936, most British economists had dismissed Hayek's theory of the business cycle, which failed to provide much guidance about how to end the Depression. Despite being bested by Keynes, Hayek greatly enjoyed his time in England. Endowed with the fastidious habits and elaborate manners of prewar Vienna, he fell in love with an educated British society that shared many of the same traits. He worked at home in the morning and went to LSE in the afternoon, often stopping for lunch at the Reform Club, on Pall Mall. The seminar that he ran with Robbins attracted many economists who later became famous, including John Kenneth Galbraith, John Hicks, and Nicholas Kaldor. Galbraith, who was visiting Cambridge from Harvard, and took the train to London every week to attend, later described Hayek as "one of the gentlest in manner, most scholarly and generally most agreeable men I have known," but added that his seminar was "possibly the most aggressively vocal gathering in all the history of economic instruction."

Finding his views on macroeconomics increasingly ignored, Hayek turned to other issues, such as the intensifying dispute between collectivists and supporters of the free market. As the Great Depression dragged on, some left-leaning economists argued that the adoption of central planning would enable resources to be directed to socially useful areas while avoiding the ups and downs of capitalism. Attempting to construct a middle way between laissez-faire and communism, these economists advocated a form of "market socialism," which would combine state ownership of major industries with a modified price system: the central planner would determine some prices; and the free market, others. Hayek, who had edited a book of essays on collective planning, was highly dubious of this idea. In the absence of genuine competition, how would the government know what prices to set, he asked, and how would factory managers know which goods to produce and in what quantities? "To assume that all this knowledge would be automatically in the possession of the planning authority seems to me to miss the main point," he wrote in a 1940 essay.

Hayek believed, with some justification, that many critics of the free market ignored the role it played in coordinating the actions of millions of individual consumers and firms, each with differing wants and capabilities. As early as 1933 he referred to the market as "an immensely complicated mechanism" that "worked and solved problems, frequently by means which proved to be the only possible means by which the result could be accomplished." In 1937, Hayek published a paper entitled "Economics and Knowledge." Although it attracted little attention at the time, it marked the first appearance of his most lasting contribution to economics: the suggestion that market prices are primarily a means of collating and conveying information. Centralized systems may look attractive on paper, Hayek argued, but they couldn't deal with the "division of knowledge" problem, which he described as "the really central problem of economics as a social science."

To understand what Hayek was getting at, imagine the task facing a central planner in a collectivized economy. Before he can decide where to direct the raw materials and workers that are available, he needs to know what goods people want to buy and how they can be produced most cheaply. But this knowledge is held in the minds of individual consumers and businessmen, not in the filing cabinets (or, later, computers) of a planning agency. Unless the central planner can find some way of eliciting this information, he won't be in any position to direct the workers and raw materials to their most productive uses, and great waste will result. In any economy, Hayek wrote in a 1945 paper, "The Use of Knowledge in Society," the central problem is "how to secure the best uses of resources known to any of the members of society, for ends whose relative importance only these individuals know. Or, to put it briefly, it is a problem of the utilization of knowledge which is not given to anyone in its totality."

The great advantage of organizing production in a market system, Hayek pointed out, is that firms don't need to go out and ask consumers what things to manufacture and how many to make: prices transmit that information. If consumers want more of a good—soap, say—than the market is supplying, its price will rise, signaling to business that they should step up production. If firms are already making more soap than consumers want to buy, its price will drop, signaling to businesses that they should cut back production. The same process applies to raw materials such as tin. If demand for tin increases, perhaps a new production process that uses it has been invented, and its price will rise, perhaps sharply. This will prompt existing users of tin to economize on its usage, and it will also encourage tin miners to supply more.

"We must look at the price system as . . . a mechanism for communicating information if we want to understand its real function," Hayek wrote. And he went on: "The marvel is that in a case like that of a scarcity of one raw material, without an order being issued, without more than perhaps a handful of people knowing the cause, tens of thousands of people whose identity could not be ascertained by months of investigation, are made to use the material or its products more sparingly; that is, they move in the right direction . . . I have deliberately used the world 'marvel' to shock the reader out of the complacency with which we often take the working of this mechanism for granted. I am convinced that if it were the result of deliberate human design . . . this mechanism would have been acclaimed as one of the greatest triumphs of the human mind."

Hayek's description of the free market as a coordination device echoed *The Wealth of Nations* but went beyond it. The invisible hand sounds like something unworldly and magical. Hayek's metaphor of the market as a "system of telecommunications" is more direct and specific. It helps explain how markets work—via the transmission of price signals—and why they are so difficult to replicate. "The most significant fact about this [market] system is the economy of knowledge with which it operates, or how little the individual participants need to know in order to be able to take the right action," Hayek wrote. "In abbreviated form, by a kind of symbol, only the most essential information is passed on and passed on only to those concerned."

The history of the Soviet bloc demonstrated what happens when governments replace market price signals with central planning and prices that are administratively determined. As a method of ramping up the production of basic goods, such as steel and wheat, collectivism proved pretty effective. But once the Communist economies moved beyond the stage of industrialization, they couldn't deal with the variegated demands of a consumer-driven society. Innovation was lacking, and information about consumer preferences got lost, or was ignored. Even after the Soviet government, under Mikhail Gorbachev, freed up some prices, shortages and surpluses were endemic, which confirmed Hayek's argument that attempts to create market socialism would founder.

In their 1990 book, *The Turning Point: Revitalizing the Soviet Economy*, Nikolai Shmelev and Vladimir Popov recall what happened when the government in Moscow increased the price it would pay for moleskins, prompting hunters to supply more of them: "State purchases increased, and now all the distribution centers are filled with these pelts. Industry is unable to use them all, and they often rot in warehouses before they can be processed. The Ministry of Light Industry has requested Goskomsten twice to lower purchasing prices, but the 'question has not been decided' yet. And this is not surprising. Its members are too busy to decide. They have no time: besides setting prices on these pelts, they have to keep track of another 24 million prices." None of this would have surprised Hayek. The idea of the free market as a spontaneously generated system for "the utilization of knowledge," he said to an interviewer later in his life, was "the basis not only of my economic but also much of my political views . . . the amount of information the authorities can use is always very limited, and the market uses an infinitely greater amount of information than the authorities can ever do."

Back in the 1940s, when Hayek formulated his ideas about information, there was no sign of communism collapsing: to most observers, it looked like laissez-faire was the ideology whose time had passed. In 1942, Joseph Schumpeter, another Austrian admirer of free markets, who taught at Harvard, published *Capitalism, Socialism, and Democracy*, in which he argued that capitalism itself was doomed and bureaucracy was its replacement. Hayek was equally fearful about the future, and he set out to write a popular text defending the values of free market liberalism. As with his intellectual heroes Smith and Mill, Hayek's support for laissez-faire extended far beyond a belief in its economic utility: he viewed the free market as the only effective guarantor of individual freedom, and he reacted viscerally to what he saw happening around him in Great Britain.

During World War II, Sir William Beveridge, a former colleague of Hayek's at LSE, published two influential papers—"Report on Social Insurance and Allied Services" and "Full Employment in a Free Society"—that laid the intellectual basis for the postwar welfare state. Like Keynes, Beveridge was a member of the Liberal Party rather than a socialist. He agreed with Keynes that capitalism needed adult supervision: left untended, it had produced a worldwide slump and, ultimately, fascism. Hayek never accepted the argument that fascism was a capitalist phenomenon. He saw Stalin and Hitler as two suits in the same closet, and the closet was marked "collectivism." He dedicated his book *The Road to Serfdom* "To the Socialists of All Parties," a clear reference to National Socialism.

Much of the book was devoted to central planning. Hayek repeated the arguments about prices and information that he had made in his academic papers, but his main concern was to develop their political implications. When the government has to decide how many pigs are to be raised or how many buses are to be run, these decisions cannot

be deduced purely from economic principles, Hayek said. The allocation of resources inevitably involves disputes between different communities and regions. The central planner has to choose among many
competing options, and in this role he acquires enormous power over
the economy and over people's lives. "In the end somebody's views
will have to decide whose interests are more important; and these
views must become part of the law of the land, a new distinction of
rank which the coercive apparatus of government imposes upon the
people," Hayek wrote. "[P]lanning leads to dictatorship, because dictatorship is the most effective instrument of coercion and the enforcement of ideals and, as such, essential if central planning on a large
scale is to be possible."

As far as the organization of Communist economies goes, Hayek's
argument was a penetrating one: so far, at least, all efforts to build a
fully centralized economy have involved one-party rule. But Hayek's
primary target wasn't the Soviet Union or China. His argument was
that Britain, France, and other European social democracies, and even
the United States, were only a step away from totalitarianism. "We are
rapidly abandoning not the views merely of Cobden and Bright, of
Adam Smith and Hume, or even of Locke and Milton, but one of the
salient characteristics of Western civilization as it has grown from
the foundations laid by Christianity and the Greeks and Romans," he
wrote. "[T]he basic individualism inherited by us from Erasmus and
Montaigne, from Cicero and Tacitus, Pericles and Thucydides, is pro-
gressively relinquished." In one passage, he even compared the Britain
of Churchill and Attlee to Nazi Germany. While "few people, if anybody, in England would probably be ready to swallow totalitarianism
whole," he said, "there are few single features which have not yet been
advised by somebody or other. Indeed, there is scarcely a leaf out of
Hitler's book which somebody or other in England or America has not
recommended us to take and use for our own purposes."

This was a strange way to portray the European welfare state and
Roosevelt's New Deal. From a purist perspective, health insurance,
Social Security, state-financed education, and regional development
programs were violations of laissez-faire, but none of them impinged
on the industrial and financial core of the free enterprise system. Alvin
Hansen, the dean of American Keynesians, had a point when he wrote
in *The New Republic*, "This kind of writing is not scholarship. It is see-

ing hobgoblins under every bed." In *The Road to Serfdom* and in his other works, Hayek neglected to account for some serious failures of the market system. In the 1930s and 1940s, it was already glaringly obvious that ordinary people needed decent medical care, breathable air, and money to retire on, and that the market had failed to provide these things. Why was that? Hayek didn't offer an answer; he didn't even seem particularly interested in the question.

The alarmist thesis of *The Road to Serfdom* didn't get much purchase in Britain, where there was widespread public support for the welfare state, but in the United States, where suspicion of government ran deep, Hayek was hailed as a visionary. In *The New York Times Book Review*, Henry Hazlitt, a conservative economic commentator, wrote a rave. *Reader's Digest*, then the voice of God-fearing conservatism, rushed out a condensed version of Hayek's tome, which the Book-of-the-Month Club published, selling six hundred thousand copies. By the time Hayek arrived in New York in early 1945, he was something of a celebrity. "The hall holds three thousand, but there's overflow," his publishing representative told him on the way to Town Hall, a theater in midtown Manhattan.

"My God. I have never done such a thing," Hayek replied. "What am I supposed to lecture on?"

"Oh, we have called the tune 'Law and International Affairs.'"

"My God, I have never thought about it. I can't do this."

"Everything is announced; they are waiting for you."

To his surprise, Hayek liked public speaking, and he traveled the country for five weeks. The book and book tour made his reputation in the United States, and in 1950 the University of Chicago's Committee on Social Thought, a newly formed interdisciplinary department, offered him a job. Feeling unappreciated in London, and having been recently divorced, Hayek accepted the invitation and moved to Chicago. Largely freed from the burden of teaching, he retreated from economics, devoting himself mainly to political and philosophical questions. His weekly seminar "The Liberal Tradition"—Hayek always used the word "liberal" in its nineteenth-century laissez-faire sense—covered a panoply of thinkers, from Locke, through Smith and Mill, to von Mises. One of the seminar's regular attendees was Milton Friedman.

In 1960, Hayek published what many consider his finest book, *The Constitution of Liberty*, a wide-ranging defense of individualism and the free market. He found the intellectual atmosphere at the University of Chicago congenial, but he missed Europe. In 1962, he accepted a post at the Albert-Ludwigs-Universität, in Freiburg, a small college associated with Ludwig Erhard, the founder of the West German "social market" economy. One reason for the relocation was financial: the Freiburg professorship offered a pension, something his job in Chicago didn't. Hayek loved the Black Forest scenery, but his return to Europe wasn't completely successful. During the late 1960s, he began to suffer from deep and paralyzing depression. "We used to talk on the telephone, and I could tell that he was depressed," Hayek's son, Dr. Laurence Hayek, told me in 2000, when I was researching an article about Hayek. "He couldn't summon up any energy to do anything." Hayek himself later attributed his mental problems to low blood sugar, which went undiagnosed by his doctors, but others thought differently. "He was depressed, I think, mostly because he saw the condition of the world as depressing, and he felt he wasn't receiving the kind of recognition he hoped for," Milton Friedman told me in 1999. After Hayek retired in 1968, he moved to the University of Salzburg, which didn't even have a proper economics department, but which was closer to his native Vienna.

Given the intellectual climate of the time, the 1974 Nobel Prize came as a complete surprise to Hayek, and it inspired him to start writing again. ("Some years ago, I tried old age but discovered I didn't like it," he later joked.) With belated academic recognition came political influence, especially in Great Britain, where Hayek's admirers included Margaret Thatcher, who, in 1975, became leader of the Conservative Party. During a visit to the party's Research Department, Mrs. Thatcher slammed a copy of *The Constitution of Liberty* on the table and declared, "This is what we believe." In 1988, at the age of eighty-nine, Hayek published *The Fatal Conceit*, an erudite book that stressed the evolutionary nature of capitalism. By gradually learning to follow a few rules, such as how to exchange goods for money, maintain respect for private property, and act honestly, man had "stumbled upon" a uniquely effective method of coordinating human activity, Hayek argued; socialism was a futile attempt to overturn the evolutionary process. A year later, the Berlin Wall came down and communism entered its death throes. Hayek didn't issue any public statements, but he greatly enjoyed watching the television pictures from Berlin, Prague, and Bucharest. "He would beam benignly," his son Laurence told me, "and the comment was, 'I told you so.'"

4. MARKETS AND WELFARE: WALRAS AND PARETO

ayek's vision of the free market as an information-processing system was one of the great insights of the twentieth century, but it also raised a tricky question: How can we be sure that the price signals the market sends are the right ones? Just because central planning failed, it doesn't necessarily follow that markets always get things right. The sheer scale of the pricing problem is breathtaking. A single Wal-Mart store contains tens of thousands of different items. In the economy as a whole, there are innumerable markets, many of them interconnected. When OPEC cuts its production quotas, and the price of heating oil rises, some moderate-income households will be forced to cut back on purchases of food and clothing; the demand for gas boilers, electric radiators, and window insulation will increase. Is there any reason to suppose that a set of market prices exists at which all of these goods will be supplied in exactly the quantities that people demand?

Yes, there is. As long as each industry contains many competing suppliers, and firms aren't able to lower their unit costs merely by raising output, it can be mathematically demonstrated that a market-clearing set of prices exists. Once these prices are posted, supply will equal demand in every industry, and no resources will be idle. There are two more bits of good news. At this "equilibrium" set of prices, labor, land, and other inputs will be directed to their most productive uses. It won't be possible, by rearranging production, to produce more output. Moreover—and this is the real kicker—it won't be possible to make anybody better off without making somebody else worse off. All such unequivocal gains from trade will already have been exploited.

A shorthand way to summarize these findings is to say that competitive markets are efficient. They ensure that businesses supply the products people want, in the right amounts, at the least cost. Consumers get to buy the goods they value most highly. They can't purchase everything they want—that really would be a utopia—but given their budgets, the market enables them to do the best they can. The only way to improve upon the market outcome is to provide the economy with more inputs, or to take resources from one person and give them to another who needs them more. But the latter type of transfer involves compulsion, which a market system based on voluntary exchange avoids.

The branch of economics that generated these findings is known as general equilibrium theory, and it is often interpreted as providing strong support for laissez-faire. Take the following passage from *Microeconomics*, a popular and generally first-rate college textbook by Robert S. Pindyck, of MIT, and Daniel L. Rubinfeld, of the University of California, Berkeley: General equilibrium theory, Pindyck and Rubinfeld write, "is the most direct way of illustrating the working of Adam Smith's famous invisible hand, because it tells us that the economy will automatically allocate resources efficiently without the need for governmental regulatory control."

A defining feature of equilibrium theory, and the source of its appeal to many economists, is its mathematical elegance. For a hundred years or so, following the publication of *The Wealth of Nations*, economics remained an informal discipline: most of its major figures expressed their arguments in prose. As the nineteenth century progressed, this began to change. In 1826, in Mecklenburg, in part of what would become Germany, Johann Heinrich von Thünen, a prominent landowner, devised an equation for the rent that land yielded. Twelve years later, the Frenchman Antoine Augustin Cournot invented a mathematical theory of monopoly and duopoly. These were isolated individual efforts. In Britain, in the second half of the century, scholars such as William

Stanley Jevons, Francis Ysidro Edgeworth, and Alfred Marshall began to apply the methods of calculus in a more systematic fashion, developing formal theories—or "models"—of how consumers and firms behave, many of which are still taught today.

Most of these theories applied to individual firms and businesses. Building on the *Tableau Economique* (Economic Table) that François Quesnay, the eighteenth-century philosopher, had constructed, Léon Walras and Vilfredo Pareto, who both taught at the University of Lausanne, set out to create a coherent mathematical theory of the entire economy. Walras was born in northern France in 1834 and died in 1910. After trying his hand at fiction, journalism, and mine engineering, he followed the advice of his father, an economist, and devoted himself to economics. During the 1860s, Walras published articles on various topics, but it was his 1874 treatise, *Elements of Pure Economics*, that established him as a major figure. (Joseph Schumpeter, in his *History of Economic Analysis*, described Walras as "the greatest of all economists.")

After reviewing previous economic doctrines, Walras began his formal analysis by considering how prices are determined in a barter economy where two people trade two items, such as bread and wine, for each other. Walras assumed that each person is aware of how much pleasure, or "utility," an item gives him, and that this pleasure gradually diminishes as he consumes more and more of the good. From there, it was relatively simple to show that the individual will consume each item up to the point where the last franc he spends on it yields the same amount of satisfaction. If this condition isn't met—if, say, another franc's worth of bread delivers more pleasure than another franc's worth of wine—the person will surely buy a bit more bread and a bit less wine. And he will keep adjusting in this way until the equality between satisfactions is established.

Walras referred to this argument as his "Theorem of Maximum Utility." Expressed algebraically, it implies the following equality: $U(Bread)/P(Bread) = U(Wine)/P(Wine)$. Here, $U(Bread)$ stands for the amount of satisfaction that the last piece of bread consumed yields, and $P(Bread)$ stands for the price of bread. Rearranging a bit gives the following: $U(Wine)/U(Bread) = P(Wine)/P(Bread)$. Economists know this equation as "the marginal condition," and it is probably the most important equation in the entire subject. The choice of bread and wine was purely for convenience. The marginal condition applies to clothes, CDs, sporting goods, outings to fancy restaurants, and pretty much anything else to which people attach value. If you aren't satisfying it, you can alter your spending patterns and improve your welfare.

As things turned out, Walras wasn't the only one to come up with the marginal condition. While he was working on his book, Stanley Jevons, in England, and Karl Menger, in Austria, independently derived the same condition. What set apart Walras was his recognition that individual markets can't be studied in isolation: they are all interconnected. The price of bread impacts the demand for butter. The Amtrak train service between New York and Washington affects the demand for flights between the two cities. On the supply side of the economy, there are other important linkages. Many manufactured goods serve as inputs for other goods. Bricks are used to build houses; glue is used to make furniture; paper is used to make books. Even you and I play a dual role in the economy. We generate income by selling our labor and, if we are rich enough, by investing our capital. Then we use our income to buy goods and services.

For each industry in the economy, Walras wrote down two equations: one for demand and another for supply. Then he asked if there was a set of prices that would satisfy this system of simultaneous equations. If such a solution existed, it would equate supply in every market and would therefore be a "general equilibrium." (Walras came up with the term.) After counting up the number of equations in his system and showing that it was equal to the number of prices to be determined, Walras claimed that such a solution did indeed exist and was unique. The price system worked!

As it happened, the mathematical "proof" Walras used to reach this conclusion wasn't as convincing as he thought it was. His achievement remains a considerable one, though. First and foremost, he demonstrated how in economics everything depends on everything else. The price of cars and trucks depends on the price of steel, but the demand for cars and trucks helps determine the price of steel. Given the ability of workers to change professions, the wages of bricklayers depend on the wages of carpenters, which depend on the wages of electricians, which depend on the wages of bricklayers. In Walras's grand schema, all prices are determined at the same time. The economy is an organic whole, not just a collection of individual parts. If there is a big disruption in one industry, it will inevitably spill over into others—a fact we have been reminded of lately.

Walras supported nationalization of land and other progressive causes: by no means was he a reactionary. However, he believed that many critics of capitalism had neglected its inner logic. On his retirement in 1893, Vilfredo Pareto, a disputatious Ligurian aristocrat, took his place. Walras and Pareto didn't get on well, but their names will forever be linked to the "Lausanne School" of economics. Like his predecessor, Pareto, who was born in 1848, took to economics late in life—in his case, after studying engineering, becoming a successful businessman, and dabbling in politics. Despite his wealthy background, he often sided with radical causes and railed against the power of the nobility. But Pareto, a former corporate director and a confirmed free-trader, was no ally of the Marxist left, which wanted to jettison the aristocracy and capitalism alike.

In his *Manual of Political Economy*, published in 1906, Pareto took up where Walras had left off, considering how the price system reconciles consumers' wants with the supply of raw materials and labor, as well as with the available production techniques. But where Walras concentrated on showing the feasibility of such a reconciliation, Pareto considered the deeper question of what it meant. In any economy, even one that satisfies all of Walras's equations, some people will fare better than others. How, then, do we decide which economic outcome is preferable? And, just as important, who gets to decide? You? Me? The government? In any nondictatorial system, there are going to be differences of opinion.

The British utilitarian philosophers, such as Jeremy Bentham and Mill, had proposed a solution to this conundrum. In Bentham's "hedonistic calculus," each person's welfare counts equally. The government's job is to maximize total happiness, defined as the arithmetic sum of individual happiness. This sounds like a reasonable idea, but it quickly ran into two practical difficulties: How is happiness to be measured? And how is it to be compared across people? Short of somebody inventing a happiness meter that could be inserted in people's brains, with the results being reported to the Ministry of Happiness, the first problem seems insoluble. In fact, it is another version of

Hayek's "division of knowledge" conundrum. The information that the government needs in order to promote social welfare is hidden from it: what is needed is some sort of mechanism to elicit people's feelings. But even if a happiness meter existed, would it settle things? Some people have a sunny disposition; others are depressive. Maximizing total happiness implies giving more money to the upbeat because they are more productive happiness machines. Is that just?

Pareto provided a way out of this thicket, or so it appeared to many of his successors. At the very least, he said, we can agree that outcome B is preferable to outcome A if in B nobody is worse off than he is in A and at least one person is better off. For example, let A be a situation in which you earn $500 a week and I earn $1,000 a week; and let B be a situation in which you earn $750 a week and I earn $1,000. Then, according to Pareto, B is superior to A, because your pay is higher and mine is the same. The same logic works the other way around. Let D be a situation in which you get a month's paid vacation each year and I get two weeks; and let E be a situation in which you still get a month's paid vacation but I get three weeks. E is superior to D: I am better off, and you are no worse off.

Modern economists refer to a shift from A to B, or from D to E, as a "Pareto improvement," and they define an economic outcome in which all such moves have been exhausted as "Pareto-efficient." If a situation is Pareto-efficient, it is impossible to make anybody better off without making somebody else worse off. Returning to the example involving wages, imagine there is another outcome, C, in which you get paid $800 a month, a $50 increase over your wage in B. But for that to happen, my wage has to fall from $1,000 to $975 a month. Moving from B to C would be good news from your perspective, but not from mine: it is not a Pareto improvement.

One way to think about Pareto efficiency is as a minimum requirement for any satisfactory economic outcome. It's obviously desirable because it means mutually advantageous options aren't wasted, but in other ways it doesn't take us very far. For one thing, Pareto-efficient outcomes are rarely unique. Going back to our original example, in which you earn $500 a week and I earn $1,000, any alternative that raises both our salaries is a Pareto improvement, but how would we choose between an option in which you got a raise of a hundred dollars and I got a raise of ten dollars, and another option in which your raise was ten dollars and mine was a hundred dollars? Pareto efficiency doesn't provide an answer.

Its inability to weigh gains and losses also means it can't rule out some very bad outcomes. If Bill Gates owned 99 percent of the world's wealth and everybody else owned 1 percent, the allocation could well be Pareto-efficient. If Gates objected to taking even $100 of his wealth and redistributing it to somebody poorer, forcing through such a change would hurt at least one person, Gates, and it wouldn't be a Pareto improvement.* Given the Pareto criterion's failure to deal with issues of equity, many liberal thinkers are understandably skeptical about using it as a policy guide. An economy can be Pareto-efficient "even when some people are rolling in luxury and others are near star- vation as long as the starvers cannot be made better off without cutting into the pleasures of the rich," the noted Indian economist Amartya Sen, now of Harvard, has pointed out. "In short, a society or an econ- omy can be Pareto optimal and still be perfectly disgusting."

Despite its shortcomings, however, Pareto efficiency remains a useful concept—if only to check on whether things are going wrong. If an eco- nomic outcome isn't Pareto-efficient, something is preventing mutually beneficial transactions from taking place. Let's say you and I sit down to discuss switching from A to B. If I am a selfish person, I might be reluctant because it will leave my wage unchanged at $1,000 a week. However, since your wage will increase from $500 to $750 a week, it's in your interest to persuade me to go along with the change. If you offered to give me an extra $100 a week out of your pay raise, for instance, we'd both be considerably better off, and I'd surely approve of the switch.

Perhaps the best thing about free markets is that they enable peo- ple to make these sorts of mutually advantageous deals. Indeed, from Pareto onward, some economists have argued that markets ensure that *all* such trades take place, which implies that every free market out- come is Pareto-efficient. This idea has been given a grand-sounding name: the first fundamental theorem of welfare economics. The rea- son it is fundamental is open to debate. To conservatives, it shows that free markets are fundamentally superior to any other system of social organization and are therefore inviolate; but that is stretching things.

---

* The existence of the Bill and Melinda Gates Foundation, to which Gates has donated billions of dollars, suggests this example is strictly illustrative.

What the theory actually demonstrates is that, under certain circumstances, market outcomes meet the minimum level of efficiency I mentioned earlier: they don't leave win-win deals on the table.

One more example, of the sort found in many economics textbooks, might help to make this clear. Imagine that I have six apples and you have six oranges. We both eat fruit, but you like apples twice as much as oranges, whereas I like them equally. A moment's thought suggests that you should trade some of your oranges for some of my apples, but how many? Since I'm indifferent to the merits of the two fruits, you could offer to exchange all six of your oranges for all six of my apples, in which case I would remain equally well off, but your welfare would double. Alternatively, I could offer you three of my apples for all six of your oranges. Your welfare would stay the same—three apples are as good as six oranges to you—but I would end up with six oranges plus three apples, so I'd be 50 percent better off. Both of these trades would clearly be Pareto improvements, but how can we be sure either one will take place? If you offer me the first deal, which doesn't do me any good, I might refuse it. If I offer you the second deal, which doesn't leave you any better off, you might turn it down.

Now let's imagine that a farmers' market opens nearby, where both of us can buy and sell fruit: in the market, apples cost $1.50 and oranges cost $1.00. How does this alter things? Well, at these prices you can sell your six oranges for $6.00 and use the proceeds to buy four apples. But since you like apples twice as much as oranges, which cost $1.00, those four apples will be worth $2.00 each to you, giving you a total value of $8.00 for your $6.00 outlay. Similarly, I can sell four of my apples for $6.00 and buy six oranges. Then I'll have two apples and six oranges, which together I value at $8.00. Now look at what has happened. We each started out with fruit—my six apples and your six oranges—that we valued at $6.00. By trading at market prices that differ from our private values, we have both gained the equivalent of $2.00.

The story may be contrived, but the principle is a general one. Markets facilitate mutually advantageous trading. Pareto was the first economist to spell all this out. Partly because much of his work wasn't translated into English, it took a long time for the rest of the economics profession to discover it. Ironically, a number of left-leaning economists were the first to realize its significance. In thinking through the economics of socialism, which Marx and Engels had largely neglected, these scholars were driven to explore the inner workings of the market system that they wished to replace. In doing so, something remarkable happened: they came to agree with Walras and Pareto that the free market has some highly desirable properties, which any rational form of socialism would seek to preserve.

In 1908, in a dense but very original article called "The Ministry of Production in the Collectivist State," Enrico Barone, another Italian economist, examined how industry should be organized in a state-run economy. Relying on a system of equations similar to those Walras had used, Barone came up with the counterintuitive answer that the ministry should direct state-owned enterprises to act as if they were capitalist firms, minimizing costs and relating prices to costs. Any attempt to deviate from these rules would be "destructive of wealth, in the sense that wealth which could have been produced with the available resources is not obtained," Barone concluded.

His article was published nine years before the October Revolution in Russia, which brought the Bolsheviks to power and established the first collectivized economy. In the 1920s, Stalin's ascent to power and brutal elimination of his rivals closed off much internal discussion of economic policy. In the West, though, discussion continued about the feasibility of combining state ownership with market determination of some prices. The most important proponents of market socialism, as it came to be known, were Abba Lerner, a Russian-born rabbinical student turned economist who grew up in London's East End, and Oskar Lange, a Polish-born economist who moved to England in 1934, and to the United States in 1936, where he taught at the universities of Michigan, Stanford, and Chicago.

Although Lerner and Lange were both leftists, neither of them displayed any affinity for Marxist economics, and its emphasis on labor as the source of all value. Like most modern economists, they assumed that prices reflected the interplay of supply and demand, and they were concerned primarily with how to combine equity and efficiency. In 1934, Lerner, who was then attached to LSE, published a paper in *The Review of Economic Studies*, in which he explored some of the mathematical conditions that were necessary for an economy to achieve a Pareto-efficient outcome. The rule he came up with was that the firms must set prices to cover their "marginal costs" of production. If it costs a sporting goods company ten dollars to manufacture another baseball bat, the bat should sell for ten dollars. (This doesn't mean firms shouldn't generate any earnings, but the profits they make, which can be regarded as part of their costs of production, shouldn't exceed the level needed to repay their debtors and investors.) In a competitive economy, Lerner showed, the fear of rivals stealing their market would force firms to follow the efficient-pricing rule. To the extent that firms charged prices that exceeded their marginal costs, and made excess profits, they were exploiting monopoly power, which wasn't consistent with Pareto efficiency.

Like Lerner, Lange also spent some time at LSE, which was a magnet for Eastern European emigres. In 1936, Lange published an essay in two parts that was entitled "On The Economic Theory of Socialism," in which he argued that a planned economy that utilized some market prices could be more efficient than a capitalist economy, because it would "avoid much of the social waste connected with private enterprise." In Lange's vision of market socialism, state planning boards would set the prices of basic inputs, such as coal and iron, by trial and error, raising them if shortages emerged and lowering them if gluts occurred. The managers of factories that produced consumer goods would be ordered to operate their facilities as cheaply as possible while trying to break even. This directive would lead them to economize on inputs, including labor, and to set prices that just covered their costs, which is what firms in competitive markets are driven to do.

This argument had clear echoes of Pareto and Barone, and even of Hayek, who had never doubted that laissez-faire capitalism was efficient. In many ways, Lange and Hayek had come to view the free market in a similar way: as a machine that solved allocation problems. (The big difference between them was over whether a socialist economy, even one with some freely determined prices, could replicate the market's efficiency.) Lange's 1936 essay included a clear verbal exposition of how competitive markets generate efficient outcomes. After moving to America in 1938, he developed this argument mathematically. In an article that appeared in the journal *Econometrica* in 1942, he applied the calculus methods of Joseph-Louis Lagrange to derive the conditions necessary to maximize the welfare of one person subject to the condition that everybody else's welfare was held constant.

In other words, Lange derived the mathematical conditions for Pareto efficiency. They turned out to bear a remarkable similarity to the conditions for competitive equilibrium. Wages had to be set in proportion to the productivity of workers; as in Lerner's paper, firms had to charge prices that covered their marginal costs; and consumers had to distribute their spending so they couldn't make themselves any happier by buying a bit less of one good and a bit more of another.

This result is worth dwelling on, at least for a moment. The leftist Lange had elucidated a striking correspondence between the equilibrium of an idealized free market economy and the outcome that a benevolent social planner would impose—always assuming, contrary to Hayek, the planner had at his disposal all the information he needed. There would be some differences, of course, in a socialist planned economy. Much of industry would be publicly owned, and any economic surpluses would be distributed more equitably than they are in a competitive system. But lots of things would be precisely the same as in a competitive market economy, including the allocation of labor and raw materials, the amount of the various goods to be produced, the production techniques used, and the prices to be charged for most goods and services. "Competition forces entrepreneurs to act much as they would have to act were they managers of production in a socialist system," Lange noted. "The fact that competition tends to enforce rules of behavior similar to those in an ideal planned economy makes competition the pet idea of the economist. But if competition enforces the same rules of allocating resources as would have to be accepted in a rationally conducted socialist economy, what is the use of bothering about socialism?"

Lange's answer was that capitalism fostered inequality and an assortment of other ills, such as poverty and recessions. Even after he became a U.S. citizen in 1943, he remained a socialist, and he retained strong ties to his native land. At the end of World War II, Lange gave up his post at the University of Chicago and joined the Soviet-sponsored coalition government that took over Poland, becoming its ambassador to the United States. After the Kremlin helped to engineer an overwhelming victory for the Polish Communist Party in the January 1947 elections, many Democrats fled. Lange, for whatever reason, remained loyal to the Communist regime. In 1947 he moved to Warsaw, where, until his death in 1965, he acted as a senior adviser to the government. "By all reports, he ended up a tragic figure, a willing puppet of the communist regime, never able to achieve in practice what he had preached in theory," Milton and Rose Friedman, who arrived in Chicago a year after Lange left, later wrote. "His personal life, also, was devastated. He abandoned his wife, who returned to the U.S. a sad and lonely figure. When he traveled abroad, it was with another woman, widely suspected of playing a dual role as companion and communist watchdog."

5. ARROW AND DEBREU'S FAMOUS PROOF

he revival of interest in the work of Walras and Pareto, which began in the 1930s, continued in the years after World War II. Until this stage, the various attempts to formalize the theory of the invisible hand had been scattered around. Some had emerged in the debate over market socialism; others still hadn't been translated into English. What was needed was for somebody to pull all these strands together and assess their significance. Lerner, Lange, and others had demonstrated the efficiency of an idealized free market, but how robust was this finding and how far could it be applied to the actual economy? These were the questions that consumed economic theoreticians in the decades after the war. Scholars associated with the Cowles Commission, a research institute that the wealthy investor Alfred Cowles had set up during the early 1930s, provided many of the answers.

Cowles, who owned a Colorado investment firm, was interested in whether the rapidly developing field of statistics could be used to provide useful investment advice. Enlisting Irving Fisher, of Yale, and several other prominent economists, he agreed to endow a research institute that would "advance the scientific study and development . . .

of economic theory in its relation to mathematics and statistics." Originally based in Colorado Springs, the Cowles Commission moved to the University of Chicago in 1936 and stayed there for twenty years. (It then moved to Yale.) Although, for a time, it occupied the same building as the Chicago Department of Economics, relations between the two organizations weren't always civil. In those days, Chicago Economics was known for its practical bent, and its reliance on simple economic concepts, such as supply-and-demand curves. Many of the scholars associated with the Cowles Commission were mathematicians and natural scientists who had turned to economics mainly because it provided interesting technical problems to study. In 1948, Tjalling Koopmans, a Dutchman and naturalized American who had started out in theoretical physics, became the research director at Cowles, and he gathered around him an assortment of brilliant young minds.

One belonged to Kenneth Arrow, who was born in New York City in 1921 to a family of European Jewish immigrants. During the Great Depression, Arrow's parents lost almost everything. Arrow graduated from City College in 1940 and enrolled in the graduate program in statistics at Columbia. After taking a class in economics with Harold Hotelling, a noted mathematical economist, he switched subjects and did his Ph.D. in economics. From 1942 to 1946, Arrow served in the research division of the Army Air Corps. In 1947 he went to Chicago to join the Cowles Commission, moving on to Stanford in 1949, but retaining an affiliation with Cowles.

At Columbia, Arrow had written his doctoral thesis on the problem of converting individual preferences over a set of possible outcomes— X, Y, and Z, say—into a consistent ordering for society as a whole, a problem with obvious applications to voting systems and other political questions. He was able to show that, in general, it simply isn't possible to construct a "social" ordering—a result that is today known as Arrow's impossibility theorem. Consider, for example, a government that is drawing up next year's budget and trying to decide among three alternatives, which I will label X, Y, and Z: spend more money on defense (X); spend more money on health care (Y); cut taxes (Z). One possibility would be to call up a random sample of voters and ask them to rank the three options in descending order of preference. However, as Arrow pointed out in his 1972 Nobel Prize lecture, it is quite possible that a third of the respondents would rank the alternatives XYZ, another third would rank them YZX, and the final third would rank them ZXY. In this case, a majority of voters prefer X to Y, a majority prefers Y to Z, and a majority prefers Z to X. What, then, is the social ranking?

At the Cowles Commission, Arrow turned his agile mind to the thorny issue of general equilibrium. He was armed with some recently developed mathematical tools, one of which—the study of convex sets—came in particularly usefully. In geometric terms, a convex set is a solid body without any holes or kinks in it. Think about a medicine ball. If you drew a straight line between any two points on or inside the ball, all of the points on the straight line would remain in the ball. That is the definition of a convex set. (A donut isn't convex, nor is a banana.) From the point of view of economists, convex sets provided a way of analyzing maximizing behavior that went beyond the old methods of curve sketching and calculus. With the aid of a few not-too-restrictive assumptions, the production possibilities of firms and the preferences of consumers could both be represented as convex sets. Similarly, the prices of inputs and outputs could be represented as the multidimensional analog of a line, a hyperplane.

What good did that do? In August 1950, Arrow presented a paper at Berkeley in which he proved rigorously that all competitive equilibriums are Pareto-efficient: at the equilibrium prices, the market will deploy the economy's resources in such a way that it is impossible to make a single person better off without making somebody else worse off. In one sense, this result merely restated the work of Pareto, Lerner, and others, but Arrow's proof was much more general. In constructing it, he used an important result in convex set theory, the separating hyperplane theorem. The paper showed the usefulness of the new mathematical methods. Once they were adopted, many of the complications that had bedeviled earlier researchers dropped away. Arrow's derivation took only a few pages, and his result became known as the first fundamental theorem of welfare economics.

In the second half of the paper, Arrow turned to the problem of equity. As I pointed out in the previous chapter, some Pareto-efficient outcomes are extremely unfair. If two people find $1,000 on the sidewalk and one of them keeps $990, giving the other just $10, that is a Pareto-efficient solution, since both individuals are better off than they were. In this case, however, there are also many Pareto-efficient outcomes that are much more equitable, such as dividing the money fifty-fifty, or fifty-one–forty-nine, and it is surely worth exploring if any of them is likely to be reached. In a general equilibrium context, things are much more complicated, because it is the entirety of the economy's resources that get divided up. Arrow, however, was able to prove a very neat result. As long as the government redistributes resources in an appropriate manner—by taxing some people and giving lump sum payments to others—society can select the specific Pareto-efficient solution it prefers, and the free market will generate the prices needed to support such an outcome. In Arrow's words: not just one but any "optimal point can be achieved by a suitable choice of prices under a competitive system." This result became known as the second fundamental theorem of welfare economics.

The first welfare theorem is a modern mathematical version of Smith's invisible hand argument: it says competitive free markets generate efficient outcomes. The second welfare theorem is more novel and intriguing. It raises the possibility of combining efficiency with equity within a free market system, something many economists had despaired of. Rather than being forced to accept gross inequality as an inevitable part of capitalism, Arrow's analysis suggests, a society can redistribute resources in a just manner and then rely on the market to ensure an efficient outcome. In theory, anyway, there is nothing to prevent the economy from achieving a "bliss point"—a phrase coined by Frank Ramsey, an English mathematical genius who died young.

Arrow's 1951 paper largely completed the task of exploring the properties of competitive free markets. But one big task remained: proving that there was a set of prices that equated supply and demand throughout the economy. If such a solution couldn't be found, then all of the work that had been done on general equilibrium theory wouldn't amount to much. By the 1930s, it was clear that Walras's method of proving the existence of an equilibrium, which involved counting equations and equating them to the number of price variables in his algebraic system, couldn't be relied on. Two parallel lines have two equations and two unknowns, but they don't have a common solution. Even if a solution to Walras's equations did exist, it wouldn't necessarily make any economic sense. Some of the prices that the equations generated could turn out to be negative ones, in which case tailors would have to pay people to wear their suits!

Lerner and Lange had both sidestepped these issues. They simply assumed that a general equilibrium existed, and they examined its properties. The first attempt to put the theory on a firmer footing emerged from prewar Vienna, where a talented group of mathematicians, philosophers, and scientists known as the Vienna Circle had assembled. Its members included the philosopher Moritz Schlick, the logicians Rudolf Carnap and Kurt Gödel, and the mathematician Karl Menger. Another member of this group was Karl Schlesinger, a wealthy businessman who had written an economics monograph that included an exposition of Walras's model. Schlesinger didn't have a solution to the existence problem, but in 1931 he took on as a math tutor Abraham Wald, a brilliant young Romanian Jew who had just obtained his doctorate at the University of Vienna under Menger's supervision.

Wald turned to Walras's equations, and before long he had solved them. To do this, though, he was forced to introduce some simplifications, such as assuming that the price of each commodity depended only on the quantities it was produced in, and not on the quantities of competing goods. Since the main point of Walrasian economics was to explore the connections between different markets, this wasn't entirely satisfactory, but it was the best Wald could do. There things rested until 1937, when John von Neumann, a Princeton mathematician who had taught in Berlin before moving to the United States, visited Vienna and presented a paper to Menger's Mathematical Colloquium that one leading historian of economic ideas has called "the single most important article in mathematical economics."

That judgment is debatable, but von Neumann, who was born in Budapest in 1903, was undoubtedly some sort of genius. The work he did in economics he considered a sideline to his other activities, which included formulating game theory and making significant contributions to logic, set theory, statistics, quantum mechanics, hydrodynamics, and computer science. A colleague of Albert Einstein's at Princeton's Institute for Advanced Study, von Neumann played an important role in the Manhattan Project, consulted for the CIA, and served on the U.S. Atomic Energy Commission. Loquacious and virulently anti-Communist, he drank heavily, told off-color jokes, was married twice, and died of cancer in 1957, when he was just fifty-three.

Von Neumann didn't have much time for the economics textbooks, or their authors, regarding them as mathematically challenged. "You know," he told one collaborator, "if those books are unearthed sometime a few hundred years hence, people will not believe they were written in our time. Rather they will think that they were about contemporary with Newton, so primitive is their mathematics." Nobody could accuse von Neumann of using primitive math. In the paper he presented in Vienna, he first complicated the problem of finding equilibrium prices by assuming that the economy expands every year at a constant rate. Then he developed a new result in pure mathematics and used it to demonstrate that his set of price equations, unlike those of Walras, could be guaranteed to have at least one set of nonnegative solutions.

The paper, which appeared under the forbidding title "On an Economic Equation System and a Generalization of the Brouwer Fixed Point Theorem," was difficult, very difficult. When von Neumann presented it to a graduate economics seminar at Princeton, most of those present scratched their heads. Adding to the bafflement factor, von Neumann's equations weren't strictly comparable to those of Walras: he had focused on production rather than consumption, and he had smuggled in a few restrictive assumptions of his own. In historical terms, though, none of that really mattered. In bringing to economics a number of abstract concepts that had recently been developed in higher mathematics—fixed-point theorems, convex sets, duality—von Neumann showed the way ahead to an entire generation of theoretically minded young economists.

In 1945, his paper was translated into English and published in *The Review of Economic Studies*, together with an explanatory essay by David Champernowne, of Cambridge University. It was also picked up in the United States, where the need for wartime planning and the influx of itinerant Europeans, many of them Jews fleeing the Nazis, had given a big boost to research in mathematical economics. Many of the European émigrés gravitated to the Cowles Foundation, where Koopmans was encouraging his colleagues to pursue the prewar work that Abraham Wald and von Neumann had done.

Arrow was one of the Cowles scholars who took up the challenge. He had first come across the existence problem of Walrasian equilibrium when he was studying at Columbia. Harold Hotelling, his thesis adviser, hired as a research assistant Wald, who had recently arrived in the United States on a fellowship from the Cowles Foundation. Arrow quizzed Wald about the theoretical work he and von Neumann had done, but the Romanian discouraged him from looking into it. "He felt the field was very difficult and did not encourage further work," Arrow subsequently recalled. "I did read the papers at the time, but in retrospect I feel my understanding was most imperfect. My German was . . . not very good, but I think it was the complexity of the argument that really put me off. I did not believe I was really the one capable of improving on the results."

In the early 1950s, Arrow returned to the task of generalizing Wald's and von Neumann's findings, this time in cooperation with Gérard Debreu, a top-notch French mathematician who, it transpired, had written a very similar paper to Arrow's 1951 article on Pareto efficiency. Debreu was a follower of Nicolas Bourbaki, the mythical French mathematician who, during the 1930s, had set out to recast the entirety of mathematics on the rigorous axioms of set theory. ("Bourbaki" was actually a pseudonym for a group of scholars connected to the École Normale Supérieure, in Paris.) A couple of years after arriving in the United States in 1948 on a Rockefeller Fellowship, Debreu joined the Cowles Commission. In late 1951, Arrow and Debreu learned that they were both working on the same problem. They decided to team up, and on December 27, 1952, at a conference in Chicago, they presented a paper titled "Existence of an Equilibrium for a Competitive Economy."

The article was long and involved. Unlike Wald's work from 1934, it didn't use any simplifying assumptions about the factors that influence demand, and unlike von Neumann's 1937 paper, it treated both consumers and firms extensively. Mathematically sophisticated, it eschewed calculus, which was rapidly becoming old hat, and instead made extensive use of convex sets, game theory, and fixed-point theorems—borrowing an application of the last from John Nash, the Princeton mathematician and game theorist. The Arrow-Debreu paper was nobody's idea of bedtime reading, but when their colleagues had made their way through it, they were agreed: Walras's problem had finally been solved, and the case for competitive markets had been placed on a sound analytical foundation, or so it seemed.

More than half a century later, the argument is still resting on the same support. The development of general equilibrium theory doesn't feature much in congressional debates or newspaper editorials, but whenever serious economists discuss the merits of free markets they invariably come back to it. "What is this idealized story telling us about the ecology of markets?" William Nordhaus, a professor at Yale, said in a presentation to scholars from other disciplines at the National Academy of Sciences. "It says that there is a coordinating mechanism at work above the level of the individual economic organism. That function is being performed by prices, which signal the marginal value of goods to consumers and the marginal cost of goods to producers. In a competitive market, there is no need for a supercomputer or central planner to try to optimize the entire system, accounting for all the trillions of interactions among the different economic organisms, for the prices are providing the appropriate signals."

Nordhaus's statement appears to confirm that Hayek was right, and there is no hope of improving on the efficiency of free market outcomes. Many introductory economics textbooks repeat this argument, sometimes by using a set of diagrams to illustrate how the free market economy generates a "bliss point." It is notable, however, that few of the theorists who created general equilibrium theory talked in these terms. Arrow and his colleagues rarely offered policy advice; when they did venture into public debates it was usually in advocating government interventions to correct shortcomings of the free market. The idea that general equilibrium theory amounts to a scientific endorsement of laissez-faire is a product of later popularizers.

The postwar theorists were perfectly open about the fact that their results depended on a number of restrictive assumptions, one of which is that economies of scale—the ability of firms to reduce their unit costs simply by ramping up production—are everywhere absent. In an industry such as cable television or computer software, this assumption clearly doesn't apply. Bigger firms can undercut smaller ones. Absent government regulation, a few giants will come to dominate the industry. And once these giants have tamed the competition, there will be nothing to prevent them from setting prices well above their marginal costs, violating the marginal condition and reaping hefty profits. The free market outcome will be inefficient, and quite possibly scandalous.

Even if the technical assumptions of the general equilibrium models are satisfied, there is no guarantee that the economy will settle down to a Pareto-efficient rest point—a finding that emerged in the period from 1953 to 1973, as economic theorists sought to extend the findings of Arrow and Debreu. The work that was done in this period is technically demanding even to mathematically trained economists, and much of it hasn't made it into the textbooks. This is a pity, because it bears directly on the question of whether general equilibrium theory can serve as a useful guide to policy, and the answer it provided was a negative one.

To begin with, there can be no assurance that the economy's equilibrium is unique: there may be dozens of solutions to the equations defining supply and demand. Without relying on some extreme assumptions about preferences, the most that can be said is that the number of solutions is probably finite. To make things worse, orthodox theory doesn't provide any guidance about which one of the possible equilibriums the economy will settle on. In many cases, the outcome is indeterminate.

Second, there is the problem of time, which Arrow and Debreu's original article didn't deal with. In another influential paper, which appeared in French in 1953, Arrow divided the future into a set of distinct periods and assumed that markets existed for the delivery of each commodity at every future date, in every possible contingency. For example, Arrow assumed consumers could order a picnic hamper to be delivered this day next week if it is sunny, or this day next year, and that such contingent orders could be placed for every good and service. Having made this heroic assumption, he was able to prove the existence of a set of prices that would equate supply and demand in all possible future states. The fertility of Arrow's mind in this period is a thing of wonder, but this particular piece of mental gymnastics proved a little too clever. Setting aside the obvious fact that many such futures markets don't exist, the mental requirements that such an economy would place on human beings are simply enormous.

Take a forty-five-year-old investor wanting to hedge his 401(k) stock portfolio against the vagaries of the market when he retires. He would need a mental list of all the possible states of the economy in 2030, the likelihood of each occurring, and the impact each would have on the stock market. If his beliefs differed from those of other people, as surely they would, he would have to take into account all of their deliberations, and how their actions would affect the market. In the late 1960s, Roy Radner, an economist who is now at New York University, wrote down a formal model along these lines. To make such an economy work, he concluded, people would need access to an infinite amount of computational capacity. Not just a lot—an infinite amount! The general equilibrium model "breaks down completely in the face of limits on the ability of agents to compute optimal strategies," Radner concluded.

This was a discouraging finding for economic theorists, and worse was to follow. The theory of the invisible hand says that market economies are stable. When a shock hits, such as a fall in the supply of oil, prices adjust to restore balance. Prices don't veer off in one direction and keep going. Or do they? In the early 1970s, a series of papers demonstrated that an economy in which all the firms and consumers followed the conditions specified in the Arrow-Debreu model could, nonetheless, behave in all sorts of bizarre ways. The economy might exhibit a stable pattern, sticking close to its equilibrium position; it might act chaotically, veering off to extremes; its path might lie somewhere in between. The axioms of individual rationality and perfect competition simply weren't sufficient to determine what would happen.

The authors of these papers were Hugo Sonnenschein, who later went on to become the president of the University of Chicago; Rolf Mantel, an Argentine who did his Ph.D. at Yale; and Gérard Debreu himself. The implications of their findings are nihilistic in the extreme. From Walras onward, general equilibrium theorists had sought to start out with individual consumers and firms, each of them following a simple set of rules, and to build up a theory of how the economy as a whole behaves. Sonnenschein, Mantel, and Debreu essentially said this wasn't possible: the whole could not be derived from the parts. "In the aggregate, the hypothesis of rational behavior has in general no implications," Kenneth Arrow wrote in a 1986 article reviewing general equilibrium theory. The authors of a high-level textbook for Ph.D. students made the same point in a more lighthearted manner, entitling their section that deals with this body of research "Anything Goes: The Sonnenschein-Mantel-Debreu Theorem."

Some researchers are still trying to rescue the general equilibrium approach, but they face at least two formidable issues. In an Arrow-Debreu world, the only restrictions that people face on their consumption patterns is that they can't spend more than their lifetime incomes, they can't make blatantly inconsistent choices, and, eventually, they get satiated. Given these minimal guidelines for individual behavior, the set of possible outcomes for the economy as a whole is simply vast, and pinning down one of them, or even a set of them, is extremely difficult. Copycat behavior, such as buying a new car because you want to keep up with your neighbor, can impart some more structure to the combinatorial problem, but that doesn't help with economic stability. If a rise in demand generates more demand, markets can be prone to wild ups and downs of varying lengths and amplitudes, which mathematicians refer to as chaos. "Economics so effortlessly offers the needed ingredients for chaos that, rather than being surprised about exotic dynamics, we should be suspicious about models which are always stable," comments Donald G. Saari, a mathematical economist at the University of California, Irvine.

As I have already noted, few of these theoretical findings have made it into teaching curriculums, let alone the policy sphere, but in the world of mathematical economics they are well established. In a lecture on general equilibrium that I attended at the New School for Social Research a few years ago, Duncan Foley, a noted economic theorist who did his Ph.D. at Yale during the 1960s, recalled how the findings of Sonnenschein et al. came as a terrible shock to mathematically minded economists of his generation, many of whom were building their careers on exploring the intricacies of Arrow and Debreu's legacy. Once they had assimilated the negative result and realized its implications, Foley said, many of the brightest young scholars gave up on general equilibrium and switched to game theory.

And that is a story you won't find in the economics textbooks.

6. THE MARKET EVANGELIST: MILTON FRIEDMAN

ilton Friedman didn't sweat the math. Slight, quick-witted, and irascible, he viewed the tortuous derivations of general equilibrium theory as largely a waste of time and effort: to him, the efficacy of free markets was self-evident. Martin Anderson, one of Ronald Reagan's economic advisers, has described Friedman as "the most influential economist since Adam Smith." That may be an exaggeration, but nobody did more than Friedman to resurrect laissez-faire ideas. In academic venues, in his long-running column in *Newsweek*, and in two much-read books, *Capitalism and Freedom*, first published in 1962, and *Free to Choose*, which he and his wife, Rose, put out in January 1980, just as Ronald Reagan was beginning his successful run for the White House, Friedman furnished conservative politicians with a consistent and well-articulated set of ideas and policy proposals. After Friedman's death in 2006, even Paul Krugman, the liberal *New York Times* columnist, who was then at Princeton, saluted his achievements, writing, "I regard him as a great economist and a great man."

Broadly speaking, Friedman made four major contributions to the rehabilitation of free market economics. He championed individual measures, such as cutting government programs, reducing taxes, and deregulating industries; he provided a revisionist explanation of the Great Depression, describing it as an example of government failure rather than market failure; he critiqued Keynesian demand management and supplied an alternative policy framework, monetarism; and he reminded Americans of the connection that John Stuart Mill, one of his heroes, had stressed between economic freedom and political freedom.

Like many of the leading American economists of his generation, Friedman hailed from a family of Jewish immigrants: his mother and father moved from eastern Hungary to the United States in the 1890s. In 1913, when Friedman was one, the family moved from Brooklyn to the equally blue-collar locale of Rahway, New Jersey. Young Milton proved a precocious and opinionated schoolboy: he started high school two years early, played on the chess team, and won a medal in a national public speaking contest on the Constitution. Entering Rutgers University, in nearby New Brunswick, in 1928, at the age of sixteen, he studied mathematics and economics. One of his economics teachers was Arthur Burns, who many years later served as chairman of the Federal Reserve. On graduating Phi Beta Kappa, Friedman received offers of graduate scholarships to Brown University for math, and to the University of Chicago for economics. "Put yourself in 1932 with a quarter of the population unemployed," he later recalled to his biographer, Lanny Ebenstein. "What was the important, urgent problem? It was obviously economics and so there was never any hesitation on my part to study economics."

Surprisingly, perhaps, Friedman didn't do his best-known work until he was approaching middle age. After doing graduate work at Chicago and Columbia, he struggled to find an academic job, something he later attributed partly to anti-Semitism. Eventually, he moved to Washington, where he worked for the National Resources Committee, one of the new agencies that had been set up under FDR's New Deal. He also got married, to Rose Director, another economist, whom he had met in Chicago. "In later years, Rose and I came to be among the best-known critics of the growth in centralized government that the New Deal initiated," Friedman noted in a 1998 memoir that he and his wife wrote jointly. "Yet, ironically, the New Deal was a lifesaver for us personally." During World War II, Friedman worked for the

Treasury Department, dealing with tax issues, and then for the Statistical Research Group, a government-funded entity headquartered at Columbia University. When the war finished, he taught for a year at the University of Minnesota. In 1946, he finally got a full-time academic job, at Chicago. There he stayed for thirty years, enthusiastically combining the roles of academic researcher and policy advocate.

As early as 1946, Friedman and George Stigler, another noted critic of government interventionism who for many years taught at Chicago, published a pamphlet in which they argued that rent controls, rather than shortage of building space or greedy landlords, were responsible for the lack of affordable apartments in New York. The article shared two attributes with many of Friedman's subsequent publications. It took a simple economic concept—the law of supply and demand—and applied it to a practical problem; and it proved popular with business interests. The National Association of Real Estate Boards circulated half a million copies.

In 1947, Friedman and Stigler went to Switzerland for the first meeting of what became the Mont Pelerin Society, an international association of conservative and libertarian academics. (Hayek attended the meeting, too.) During the 1950s, Friedman took part in a series of conferences organized by the right-leaning William Volker Fund, at which he lectured groups of impressionable young scholars. These talks formed the basis for *Capitalism and Freedom*, which inspired an entire generation of conservatives. At the time of the book's publication, though, few people outside of the economics profession heard about it. "It was not reviewed by any American publication other than *The American Economic Review*," Friedman later recalled. "I was a full professor at the University of Chicago. I was very well known in the academic world—it is inconceivable that a book on the other side by someone in that same position would not have been reviewed in every publication, the *New York Times*, the *Chicago Tribune*."

In many ways, *Capitalism and Freedom* was an American version of Hayek's *Road to Serfdom*. Like Hayek, Friedman portrayed the choices facing democratic societies in stark and simplistic terms. "Fundamentally, there are only two ways of coordinating the economic activities of millions," he wrote. "One is central direction involving the use of coercion—the technique of the army and of the modern totalitarian state. The other is voluntary co-operation of individuals—the technique of the marketplace." To Friedman, the choice between the two systems of organization was an easy one. "Our minds tell us, and history confirms, that the great threat to freedom is the concentration of government power," he wrote on page 2; and he went on: "[T]he scope of government must be limited."

Citing Adam Smith, Friedman conceded the need for some government activities, such as national defense and law enforcement. Unlike Smith, though, he questioned the government's involvement in public projects, such as highway construction and the provision of public education, which he argued the market could supply. Nothing if not specific, he listed fourteen unnecessary government interventions, including tariffs on imported goods, price support programs for farmers, minimum wage rates, Social Security, public housing, the U.S. mail's monopoly, limits on the ownership of radio and television stations, and regulation of the banking system. "The list is far from comprehensive," Friedman added.

Moving on to other areas, he argued that the problem of monopoly had been exaggerated. He called for the legalization of unlicensed medicine, the establishment of privately run schools to compete with public schools, the replacement of the progressive income tax code with a flat tax, and the abolition of national parks such as Yellowstone and the Grand Canyon, noting, "If the public wants this kind of activity enough to pay for it, private enterprises will have every incentive to provide such parks." Some of Friedman's recommendations were economically sound; others weren't. (Absent the government's power to acquire property and rezone land, the practical difficulties of setting up a national park are insurmountable.) He opposed almost all types of regulation, and his attitude toward government was one of almost unremitting skepticism: "The great advances of civilization, whether in architecture or painting, in science or literature, in industry or agriculture, have never come from centralized government," he wrote. "Columbus did not set out to seek a new route to China in response to a majority directive of parliament, though he was partly financed by an absolute monarchy. Newton and Leibniz; Einstein and Bohr; Shakespeare, Milton, and Pasternak; Whitney, McCormick, Edison, and Ford; Jane Addams, Florence Nightingale, and Albert Schweitzer; no one of these opened new frontiers in human knowledge and understanding, in literature, in technical possibilities, or in the relief of human misery in response to governmental directives."

Although much of the book was taken up with discussion of specific economic issues, Friedman started and finished it with broad philosophical and political speculations. "On the one hand . . . economic freedom is an end in itself," he wrote. "In the second place, economic freedom is also an indispensable means towards the achievement of political freedom." Although he didn't go as far as Hayek in suggesting that the United States and other Western countries were on the verge of becoming totalitarian states, he insisted that the expansion of government posed a fundamental threat to Americans' civil liberties, noting, "Historical evidence speaks with a single voice on the relation between political freedom and a free market." "I know of no example in time or place of a society that has been marked by a large measure of political freedom, and that has not also used something comparable to a free market to organize the bulk of economic activity."

In his professional life, Friedman was primarily a macroeconomist. Here, too, his work had a political edge. Arguably, the most urgent task facing conservatives in the postwar world was confronting the consensus that unregulated capitalism had failed during the global slump of the 1930s. Before laissez-faire policies could be taken seriously again, something (or somebody) else would have to be blamed for the Great Depression. Friedman's candidate was the Federal Reserve Board, which had been founded in 1913 with a mandate to stabilize the economy and prevent financial panics.

Prior to the 1963 publication of *A Monetary History of the United States*, which Friedman coauthored with Anna J. Schwartz, an economist at the National Bureau of Economic Research, most scholars had blamed the Great Depression on an irresponsible speculative binge during the 1920s, the stock market crash of 1929, the Smoot-Hawley Tariff Act of 1930, the budget-balancing orthodoxies of Herbert Hoover, or some combination of the above. Friedman and Schwartz, drawing on an impressive trove of statistical evidence, argued that the real culprit was a sharp decline in the country's money stock, which was supposedly under the Fed's control. Between the summer of 1929 and the spring of 1933, the total amount of currency in circulation and demand deposits at banks fell by almost a third. If only the Fed had pumped more money into the economy, Friedman and Schwartz argued, disaster could have been avoided: "The Great Depression, like most other periods of severe unemployment, was produced by government mismanagement rather than by any inherent instability of the private economy. A governmentally established agency—the Federal Reserve System—had been assigned responsibility for monetary policy. In 1930 and 1931, it exercised this responsibility so ineptly as to convert what otherwise would have been a moderate contraction into a major catastrophe."

This isn't the place for a lengthy discussion of Friedman and Schwartz's hypothesis, which, actually, wasn't totally original. (As early as 1933, the Yale economist Irving Fisher criticized the Fed for not reacting aggressively enough to the economic downturn of 1930–32.) Among mainstream economists, there was until recently general agreement that Friedman and Schwartz were broadly correct. In 2002, at a conference organized to celebrate Friedman's ninetieth birthday, Ben Bernanke, who was then a governor at the Fed, ended a favorable look back upon A Monetary History of the United States with these words: "I would like to say to Milton and Anna: Regarding the Great Depression. You're right, we did it. We're very sorry. But thanks to you, we won't do it again."

Unlike some of his modern followers, Friedman was well aware of the dangers that can arise in an unregulated financial system. In A Monetary History, he and Schwartz devoted quite a bit of space to the banking crises of 1873, 1884, 1890, 1893, and 1907, which led to the formation of the Fed. In Capitalism and Freedom, he explained how a bank faced with demands for money from its depositors and creditors "will put pressure on other banks by calling loans or selling investments or withdrawing its deposits, and these other banks will in turn put pressure on still others. The vicious cycle, if allowed to proceed, grows on itself as the attempt of banks to get cash forces down the prices of securities, renders banks insolvent that would otherwise have been entirely sound, shakes the confidence of depositors, and starts the cycle over again." This is a succinct description of what is today called contagion. However, Friedman argued that the best way to stabilize the financial sector, and indeed the entire economy, was not by beefing up regulation or strengthening the discretionary powers of the central bank. Rather, he said that Congress should pass a law instructing the Fed to achieve a specified growth rate of the money stock—somewhere between 3 and 5 percent a year was his preferred range—and leave things at that. Targeting the money supply would both keep inflation in check and maintain economic stability: thus the doctrine of "monetarism."

It is difficult today to convey the intensity of the debate that surrounded Friedman's espousal of monetary targets and his attacks on the Keynesian idea of managing the economy through changes in taxes and government spending. The participants appeared to be talking past each other, using completely different frames of reference: Friedman liked to invoke the ancient "quantity theory of money," which many of his critics considered hopelessly out of date. Setting aside obscure monetary debates, he was basically reviving the laissez-faire view of the economy as a self-correcting mechanism that, left to its own devices, would quickly gravitate to a state in which most available resources, including most workers, were productively employed. The Keynesians regarded the economy as at best sluggish and at worst downright unstable. Without active supervision—"fine-tuning," it was then called—unemployment could remain elevated for considerable periods of time, and there was even the possibility of another Great Depression.

In December 1967, in a presidential address to the American Economic Association, Friedman set out his views. Couching his argument in the language of general equilibrium theory, which he rarely used, he said there would always be some people out of work. Some might have lost their jobs due to plant closures, others may have quit to look for better-paying jobs, or moved to another city. This "natural rate of unemployment" was unavoidable. If the government sought to reduce or eliminate it by cutting taxes, say, it would only create more inflation.

In making this argument, Friedman correctly identified a weak point in the Keynesian consensus. During the 1960s, many Keynesian economists, relying on data first collated by A.W.H. ("Bill") Phillips, of LSE, came to believe that there was an inverse relationship between unemployment and inflation. The Phillips Curve, as it came to be known, appeared to imply that if policymakers were willing to put up with a bit more inflation, they could reduce unemployment. Friedman begged to differ. If the government brought unemployment down to below its natural rate, he argued, workers would bid up wages and firms would raise prices, which would cause inflation to pick up. In seeking to prevent an inflationary spiral, the government would eventually have to allow unemployment to rise back to its natural rate. "There is always a temporary trade-off between inflation and unemployment," Friedman said. "There is no permanent trade-off."

In 1967, and for a few years after, Friedman's argument didn't go anywhere. Fine-tuning appeared to be working pretty well. In 1971, Richard Nixon described himself as "a Keynesian in economics." But as the 1970s progressed, the Phillips Curve broke down. The inflation rate jumped into the double digits, but unemployment didn't fall; it went up—a phenomenon that became known as stagflation. Mainstream Keynesians were at a loss to explain what was happening. Friedman and the Columbia economist Edmund Phelps, who had helped to pioneer the concept of a natural rate of unemployment, looked like visionaries. "Friedman and Phelps had no way of foreseeing the inflation of the 1970s," Robert Lucas, a colleague of Friedman's at Chicago, later commented, "but the central forecast to which their reasoning led was a conditional one, to the effect that a high-inflation decade should not have less unemployment on average than a low-inflation decade. We got the high-inflation decade, and with it as clear-cut an experimental discrimination as macroeconomics is ever likely to see, and Friedman and Phelps were right. It really is as simple as that."

The stagflation of the 1970s discredited Keynesian fine-tuning and paved the way for the revival of conservative economics. In 1976, the same year that Friedman won the Nobel Prize in economics, James Callaghan, the Labour prime minister of Great Britain, told his party's annual conference, "We used to think that you could spend your way out of a recession and increase employment by cutting taxes and boosting government spending. I tell you in all candor that that option no longer exists, and insofar as it ever did exist, it only worked on each occasion since the war by injecting a bigger dose of inflation into the economy, followed by a higher level of unemployment as the next step . . . You cannot now, if you ever could, spend your way out of a recession."

Actually, there was nothing in Friedman's work to suggest that, during a slump, the traditional Keynesian remedy of boosting government spending wouldn't work. Rather, natural rate theory contended that the economy was self-equilibrating, so lengthy recessions couldn't occur and Keynesian pump priming was unnecessary. In this sense, Friedman didn't defeat Keynesianism so much as define it out of existence. But in the tumult of the seventies, with inflation raging and labor unrest widespread, few paid attention to the subtleties of economic theory: Keynesianism was in disgrace, and Friedman was enjoying his moment of triumph. When *Free to Choose* came out in January 1980, he was inarguably the world's most famous economist. The book, accompanied by a ten-part television documentary, was translated into seventeen languages, not including samizdat editions in the Soviet Union and Poland. The hardcover alone sold four hundred thousand copies; the paperback and foreign editions sold another million.

Friedman wrote the book with his wife, Rose. Eighteen years after the publication of *Capitalism and Freedom*, it was another antigovernment manifesto. The Friedmans attacked the Food and Drug Administration, the Consumer Product Safety Commission, the Securities and Exchange Commission, the Environmental Protection Agency, the Federal Trade Commission, and the antitrust division of the Department of Justice for stifling innovation and burdening industry with unnecessary costs. "By now considerable evidence has accumulated that indicates that FDA regulation is counterproductive," they wrote, "that it has done more harm by retarding progress in the production and distribution of valuable drugs than it has done good by preventing the distribution of harmful or ineffective drugs."

The only workable type of regulation, Friedman insisted, was self-regulation. "If one storekeeper offers you goods of lower quality or higher price than another, you're not going to continue to patronize his store," he wrote. Drug companies, if left alone, would refrain from distributing dangerous products because to do so would be "very poor business practice—not a way to develop a loyal and faithful clientele." Similarly, industrial companies such as General Electric and General Motors would not risk sullying their brand names by distributing faulty or unsafe products. "The consumer is protected from being exploited by one seller by the existence of another seller from whom he can buy and who is eager to sell to him. Alternative sources of supply protect the consumer far more effectively than all the Ralph Naders of the world."

If Friedman had been known solely as a defender of big business, and a proponent of monetarism, he wouldn't have exercised as much influence as he did. But he cleverly wrapped his proposals to emasculate government programs and cut taxes in the language of rugged American individualism. What would come of American ingenuity, he and Rose asked, "if we continue to grant ever more power to government, to authorize a 'new class' of civil servants to spend ever larger fractions of our income supposedly on our behalf. Sooner or later—and perhaps sooner than many of us expect—an even bigger government would destroy both the prosperity that we owe to the free market and the human freedom proclaimed so eloquently in the Declaration of Independence."

In short, firing federal regulators, slashing welfare programs, and cutting taxes on the rich didn't just represent a return to sound economics; they were a moral imperative. "The two ideas of human freedom and economic freedom working together come to their greatest fruition in the United States," the Friedmans wrote on the final page. "Those ideas are still very much with us. We are all of us imbued with them. They are part of the very fabric of our being. But we have been straying from them. We have been forgetting the basic truth that the greatest threat to human freedom is the concentration of power, in the hands of government or anyone else . . . Fortunately, we are waking up."

In bringing out *Free to Choose* at the start of 1980, the Friedmans displayed perfect timing. Two months before the publication date, Ronald Reagan announced his presidential candidacy. The two conservative icons were old friends. During the 1960s, when Reagan was governor of California, Friedman had supported his efforts to cut taxes. In 1976, when Reagan made his first presidential bid, Friedman had endorsed him. Now he served as an economic adviser to Reagan's campaign. After the Republican triumph, Friedman was appointed to the President's Economic Policy Advisory Board, a panel of independent economists who met with the Gipper regularly and encouraged him to stick to his conservative principles. "Reagan was especially taken with Milton Friedman," Martin Anderson wrote in *Revolution*, his account of the Reagan years. "He could just not resist Friedman's infectious enthusiasm and Reagan's eyes sparkled with delight every time he engaged in a dialogue with him."

Friedman's influence wasn't confined to the United States. In the United Kingdom he had a lengthy association with the Institute of Economic Affairs, a free market think tank that kept up an unceasing attack on the Keynesian policies that the British government pursued in the 1960s and '70s. Friedman published a number of articles for the IEA, most of them about monetary policy. Many of Mrs. Thatcher's economic advisers, including Sir Keith Joseph and Sir Alan Walters, an LSE professor who later moved to Johns Hopkins, were strongly influenced by Friedman's ideas. In 1980, a year after Mrs. Thatcher became prime minister, she invited Friedman to Downing Street, where she asked him to instruct some of the "wets" (moderates) in her cabinet.

The most famous and controversial example of Friedman influencing events overseas came in Chile, where, in March 1975, he spent six days giving lectures and meeting with members of Augusto Pinochet's military regime, including the dictator himself, who had toppled Salvador Allende's Democratic Socialist government, many supporters of which were rounded up and murdered. General Pinochet had embarked on a series of sweeping free market reforms, some of which had been devised by a group of young Chilean economists who had studied at the University of Chicago. Arnold Harberger, a Chicago professor who spoke Spanish and married a Chilean, was the primary mentor of the "Chicago Boys," and he accompanied Friedman to Santiago.

When the two professors arrived, inflation was running at more than 500 percent a year, and some of Pinochet's colleagues were advising him to abandon the free market experiment. Friedman encouraged the Chileans to accelerate the reform process: addressing a group of students, he said the country's problems were "due almost entirely to the forty-year trend toward collectivism, socialism, and the welfare state." On returning to Chicago, he wrote Pinochet a long letter, beginning "Dear Mr. President," in which he advised him to adopt a "shock program," which would include controlling the money supply, slashing government spending by a quarter in six months, and removing "as many obstacles as possible that now hinder the private market."

Pinochet took Friedman's advice. His government abolished price and wage controls, sold off hundreds of state-owned firms, privatized the pension system, liberalized trade, and deregulated the financial sector. For a time, things worked out well. The inflation rate came down to less than 10 percent, foreign investments poured in, and GDP rose sharply. But in 1982, the Chilean economy went into a deep slump and financial scandals erupted, discrediting the architects of the boom. In 1985, a second wave of economic reformers took office. Vigorous growth resumed, continuing after Pinochet's replacement, which came in 1990, by the democratically elected Patricio Aylwin. Since the early 1990s, the Chilean economy has had its share of ups and downs, but, generally speaking, it has outperformed most other economies in Latin America. In his 1998 memoir, Friedman defended his visit to Chile and claimed that the country's experience had demonstrated beyond doubt the efficacy of free market policies. "From 1973 to 1995, real income-per-capita multiplied more than two and a half fold, inflation fell from 500 percent per year to 8 percent, the infant mortality per 1,000 live births fell from 66 to 13, and life expectancy at birth rose from 64 years to 73 years. And authentic political freedom has been restored with the turnover of power by the junta to a freely elected government."

Some experts on the Chilean economy would quibble with Friedman's historical account, but there is no doubting the significance of the Chilean free market experiment. Following the collapse of the Soviet Union, Russia, Poland, and many other transition economies adopted "shock therapy" programs, which, in some cases, were explicitly modeled on the Chilean example. A new generation of American economists, such as Jeffrey Sachs, who now heads the Earth Institute at Columbia University, helped to organize these controversial exercises in social engineering. Many of them, Sachs included, hailed from Harvard and MIT, longtime strongholds of Keynesian economics. By the early 1990s the traditional distinction between monetarists and Keynesians had been blurred. Many economists who were nominally associated with the Keynesian tradition were strong supporters of the free market ideas that Friedman had devoted his life to espousing. "What's the single most important thing to learn from an economics course today?" Lawrence Summers asked an interviewer during the late 1990s, when he was deputy secretary of the Treasury. "What I tried to leave my students with is the view that the invisible hand is more powerful than the hidden hand. Things will happen in well-organized efforts without directions, controls, plans. That's the consensus among economists. That's the Hayek legacy. As for Milton Friedman, he was the devil figure in my youth. Only with time have I come to have large amounts of grudging respect. And, with time, increasingly ungrudging respect."

7. EUGENE FAMA AND THE EFFICIENT MARKETS HYPOTHESIS

ne of the striking things about the development of modern economics is how long it took for finance to be taken seriously. Stock markets have existed since Roman times, when state-chartered companies known as *publicani*, which carried out many of the functions of the empire—collecting taxes, building temples, and dredging rivers—issued stocks (*partes*) and bonds. It wasn't until the 1960s and '70s, however, that the study of financial markets started to be integrated with the rest of economics. This slow progress can partly be explained by the fact that the financial industry used to be a lot smaller than it is today. Until the development of mutual funds and 401(k) plans, Wall Street and the City of London were largely the preserve of rich people, gamblers, and crooks. Economists tended to share the common man's view that financial markets simply weren't that important. What determined a country's prosperity was how effectively it mobilized its natural resources, the commitments it made to educating its workers, and the fruits of its investments in science and technology. The financial system was merely a "veil" covering the real economy. Monetarists and Keynesians alike shared this way of looking at things. In the standard textbook model that many policymakers relied on, the entire financial sector was subsumed in one equation.

In analyzing how policy changes affect the economy from quarter to quarter, this neglect of finance was a defensible simplification. Taking a longer-term view, it didn't make much sense. Economic development is a process of capital accumulation, and financial markets play a key role in distributing investment capital among competing projects. At the risk of overusing a now familiar metaphor, financial markets are the central processor of Hayek's telecommunications system. They take in information about the future prospects of individual companies and the economy at large, and spit out prices for stocks, bonds, and other financial assets. If financial markets work properly, they help the economy to prosper: if they fail to provide financing for worthwhile capital projects, if they divert money to the worthless objects of speculative bubbles and fads, they are a hindrance to the economy.

During the 1960s and '70s, a group of economists, many of them associated with the University of Chicago, promoted the counterintuitive idea that the central processor works perfectly, and that speculative bubbles don't exist. The efficient market hypothesis, which Eugene Fama, a student of Friedman, popularized, states that financial markets always generate the correct prices, taking into account all of the available information. What does this mean? In the case of an individual company, it implies that the stock price accurately reflects the best guesses of analysts, investors, and even the firm's management about its future earnings prospects. In the case of a commodity, such as crude oil or gold, spot prices take into account everything that is known about resource stocks, future demand, and the development of potential substitutes, such as biofuel. Similarly, the price of bonds issued by the Brazilian or Russian government reflects the likelihood of Brasilia or Moscow defaulting on its obligations.

In short, financial prices are tied to economic fundamentals: they don't reflect any undue pessimism or "irrational exuberance"—the famous phrase that Alan Greenspan introduced to the American lexicon in December 1996. If markets rise above the levels justified by fundamentals, well-informed speculators step in and sell until prices return to their correct levels. If prices fall below their true values, speculators step in and buy. It is easy to see how a free market economist could fall in love with this logic, which Milton Friedman spelled out in a 1951 essay about currency exchange rates, because it suggests that the theory of the invisible hand works on Wall Street just as effectively as it works on Main Street.

For somebody lacking the benefit of a higher degree in economics or finance, it may be difficult to accept that the daily lurches of the Dow and S&P 500 reflect a calm and rational processing of new information on the part of investors; that the tripling of home values in some parts of the country between 1996 and 2006 was nothing untoward; and that crude oil was correctly priced at roughly $50 a barrel in January 2007, was equally reasonably valued at $140 a barrel in June 2008, and was also accurately priced at $40 a barrel in February 2009. But such is the message of the efficient market hypothesis. If the price of a stock changes, it means that somebody somewhere has uncovered some pertinent information. Perhaps one of the firm's divisions is doing badly; or maybe a competitor has developed an exciting new product. Once investors have reacted to the news, and the adjustment process is assumed to be almost instantaneous, prices once again reflect fundamental values.

Like other aspects of free market dogma, the efficient market hypothesis is based on some sensible observations. As anybody who has tried his or her hand at investing will readily testify, predicting what financial markets will do next is extremely difficult. Much of the time, it is impossible. Unlike many of the theorems in this book, this one can be demonstrated without any Greek symbols but instead using a method that logicians refer to as proof by contradiction. Assume, for a moment, that there is a reliable way to predict the stock market. Given all the physical and human resources that are devoted to the financial industry, somebody somewhere is pretty sure to find it. This genius, or group of geniuses, will make a lot of money. But the financial industry is extremely competitive, and there are no patents on smart ideas. Before too long, other investors will hear about the geniuses' methods and copy them. When this happens, the market will incorporate the new information, and the juicy returns that the geniuses were making will be arbitraged away. Prediction will no longer work, and the market will return to a state of being unfathomable.

The first person to develop this type of logic was Louis Bachelier, a

French mathematician who, way back in 1900, wrote a doctoral dissertation entitled "The Theory of Speculation." Take an individual stock. At any moment in time, Bachelier observed, some optimists think it will go up; some pessimists think it will go down. If there are more of the former than the latter, their purchases will bid the price up. If there are more pessimists, their sales will bring the price down. The stock price will keep moving until the optimistic and pessimistic expectations cancel each other out, at which point, since there is no reason to suppose that either group has superior information, the speculator has an equal chance of winning or losing. There is a 50 percent chance that the stock's next move will be up and a 50 percent chance that it will be down. Taking these possible outcomes together, Bachelier concluded, "[t]he mathematical expectation of the speculator is zero." What this means is that investing in the market is just like tossing a coin for money: a speculator may win or he may lose—if he plays the market repeatedly, he might even rack up a string of gains or losses. But the outcomes will be governed by luck rather than skill, and, moreover, they will be subject to precise probability laws. If a person repeatedly tosses a fair coin, the odds that he will get three heads in a row are one in eight. The odds that he will get six heads in a row are one in sixty-four.

The coin-tossing view of finance that Bachelier pioneered today goes under the name of the "random walk" theory, because it implies that the prices of stocks and other speculative assets will wander about aimlessly like an inebriated person. Benoit Mandelbrot, another eminent French mathematician, described the theory this way: "Suppose you see a blind drunk staggering across an open field. If you pass by again later on, how far will he have gotten? Well, he could go two steps left, three right, four backwards, and so on in an aimless jagged path. On average—just like the coin-toss game—he gets nowhere." If you were asked to predict where the drunk will end up in an hour's time, the best guess you could make would be to say he will be where he is now. Similarly, the best forecast of where Citigroup's stock will be trading this time next week is the current price.

For fifty years, Bachelier's thesis was largely unread. In 1954 or 1955, nobody seems to recall for sure, Jimmy Savage, a statistician at the University of Chicago who had coauthored several important papers about risk with Milton Friedman, happened across a book that Bachelier had written in 1914. He sent a note to a number of people he knew, including Paul Samuelson, the famous MIT economist, ask-ing if they had heard of the Frenchman. Samuelson dug a copy of Bachelier's thesis out of the MIT library, and it impressed him. The coin-tossing model was resurrected: by the early 1960s, Samuelson and a number of other economists were publishing papers claiming that stock prices followed a random walk.

One of these authors was Eugene Fama, an Italian American from Boston who was still in his early twenties. After paying his way through Tufts, Fama went to the University of Chicago, where he did his Ph.D. thesis on the behavior of stock prices, using the school's spiffy new IBM mainframe to analyze data covering the period from 1926 to 1960. After providing a critical survey of previous research that had purported to find some predictability in stock returns, Fama reported details of his own statistical tests, which supported the random walk model. What made Fama's paper especially distinctive was the criti-cism it contained of "fundamental analysis"—the type of stock research that many Wall Street professionals relied on, which involved decon-structing companies' earnings reports, visiting factories, and so on. The usefulness of this methodology hadn't been subjected to rigorous test-ing, Fama noted, and there was always the possibility that even the most successful analysts had simply gotten lucky: in the coin-tossing view, he pointed out, any analyst has a 50 percent chance of being right, "even if his powers of analysis are completely non-existent." Given the evidence supporting the random walk model, Fama concluded, "fun-damental analysis is a fairly useless procedure both for the average analyst and the average investor."

Fama's thesis attracted a lot of attention. In January 1965, *The Journal of Business*, which is based at Chicago's Graduate School of Business, published it in its entirety—a rare accolade for a twenty-five-year-old scholar. Later in the year, the *Financial Analysts Journal* ran a shorter version of the paper, and in 1968 the magazine *Institu-tional Investor* reprinted it again and organized a big conference at the New York Hilton to discuss the random walk model. Many people who worked on Wall Street saw Fama's dismissal of stock research and professional investment advice as an outrage. To economists, however, the key innovation in his article was the claim that the stock market was "efficient," in the sense that prices reflected all of the available information.

In a follow-up paper that appeared in the prestigious *Journal of Finance* in 1970, Fama developed this idea further, proposing three separate versions of the efficient market hypothesis: the weak form, the semistrong form, and the strong form. A market was weakly efficient, Fama said, if it wasn't possible to predict prices on the basis of past movements: that is, there were no recognizable patterns. Semistrong efficiency meant that prices reflected all publicly available information, such as a company's SEC filings, and any coverage it had received in the media. Strong-form efficiency meant that prices reflected all information, even if it was private. For example, if a consulting firm had carried out an in-depth analysis of the company, the contents of its report would be reflected in the stock price before it was even published. After reviewing the evidence, Fama claimed that the first two types of efficiency were clearly confirmed by the data, and he said there was only "limited evidence" contradicting the strongest form of the theory.

The efficient market hypothesis was up and running. Three years later, Burton Malkiel, a Princeton economist who had worked on Wall Street, brought it to the masses in his book *A Random Walk Down Wall Street*, which turned into one of the bestselling business books of recent decades. In addition to referencing Fama, Malkiel reported the results of research that he and others had carried out, which showed that most Wall Street earnings forecasts were hopelessly off the mark, and that the majority of mutual funds failed to outperform the market. "The past history of stock prices cannot be used to predict the future in any meaningful way," Malkiel wrote. "Technical strategies are usually amusing, often comforting, but of no real value."

The efficient market hypothesis transformed Wall Street. Most immediately, it raised the popularity of "index funds"—mutual funds that bought large baskets of stocks, seeking to replicate the performance of the overall market. If fundamental analysis doesn't work and most fund managers routinely fail to outperform the market, there can be no justification for the hefty fees that actively managed mutual funds charge investors. Investing in index funds, which keep their fees at minimal levels, is much more sensible. By 2000, tens of millions of Americans had taken Malkiel's advice and placed much of their retirement money in these types of savings vehicles. (For many years, Malkiel served as a director of the Vanguard Group, which pioneered index funds. Fama joined another firm that manages index funds, Dimensional Fund Advisors.)

The rise of efficient market theory also signaled the beginning of quantitative finance. In addition to the random walk model of stock prices, the period between 1950 and 1970 saw the development of the mean-variance approach to portfolio diversification, which Harry Markowitz, another Chicago economist, pioneered; the capital asset pricing model, which a number of different scholars developed independently of one another; and the Black-Scholes option pricing formula, which Fischer Black, an applied mathematician from Harvard, and Myron Scholes, a finance Ph.D. from Chicago, developed. Some of the mathematics used in these theories is pretty befuddling, which helps explain why there are so many physicists and mathematicians working on Wall Street, but the basic ideas underpinning them aren't so difficult. Many of them originated with Bachelier and his coin-tossing view of finance.

Imagine tracking the daily movements in a stock over a year, or two years, and plotting them on a bar chart. Most of the movements would be roughly similar in size, and they would cluster together in the middle of the chart. Very big movements and very small movements would be much less common, and they would be located at either end of the chart, in its tails. Bachelier's insight was that the resultant chart would look like the famous bell curve, which describes the distribution of many naturally occurring phenomena, from human IQs, to the height of giraffes, to the strength of metal girders, to the movement of tiny solid particles suspended in liquid. Invoking the bell curve, which statisticians refer to as the normal distribution, doesn't make individual random events any easier to forecast, but it does allow you to make some predictions about their overall rate of occurrence.

Let's say you want to know the likelihood of Google's stock making a big move tomorrow. The first step is to log on to a financial website and call up the closing prices of the stock over the past year. Next, figure out the average daily change in the price and its standard deviation—a simple measure of how spread out something is. Once you have worked out the mean price movement and the standard deviation, which is usually referred to as the Greek letter sigma, you are almost done: the normal distribution does the rest of the work. It will tell you that the chances of the stock rising or falling by more than the sigma you worked out is roughly one in three; the odds of the stock moving by more than two sigma is about one in twenty; and the probability of it moving by more than three sigma is about one in three hundred.

Note the economy of this procedure, which can be applied to Treasury bonds, mortgage bonds, currencies, commodities, or any other asset that is subject to random movements in prices. On the basis of one sample and two simple statistics—the mean and standard deviation—it is possible to make precise statements about the likelihood of extreme outcomes. But what is the likelihood of extreme outcomes if not a measure of risk? The implications of being able to capture risk in this manner are enormous. For an individual investor or a big financial institution, it points to the possibility of designing a portfolio to minimize the possibility of a big loss, or to maximize returns given a certain willingness to accept losses. Take, for instance, a bank with large holdings of mortgage securities and other financial assets. By looking at how its portfolio has zigzagged up and down during the last year or two, and assuming that movements follow the bell curve, it should be able to work out the odds of a big fall in its value over a certain time period—a day, a month, a year. And if a bank can put a figure on the risks it is taking, it will be able to take the necessary precautions, in the form of capital reserves and other financial hedges. Risk can be managed scientifically, or so it appears.

On Wall Street, this is done in various ways, almost all of which rely on the coin-tossing view of finance, and its application via the bell curve. One of them, known as the value-at-risk (VAR) methodology, involves doing precisely what I outline in the previous paragraph: using statistical methods to put a dollar value on the risks of certain adverse outcomes, and holding enough capital in reserve to meet such a contingency. Another way to hedge against bad things happening is to buy insurance, which, in the financial industry, comes in the form of futures and options. An option is simply a security that puts a price on risk. The most common types of options are "puts" and "calls," which give the owner of them the right to sell or buy a stock on a certain date in the future at a specified price. For example, a December 2011 put on IBM with a "strike" of $100 gives you the right to sell a share in IBM for $100 in December 2011. If you write (sell) a put, you are insuring the buyer against the possibility that the value of the stock will fall below the strike price. But how much should you charge for this insurance policy? In the 1950s and '60s, many eminent economists and mathematicians tussled with this problem without meeting any success. Finally, in the early 1970s, Black, a man of few words, and Scholes, a voluble Canadian, derived a simple formula that related the price of an option to the volatility of the underlying stock.

By coincidence, the paper that contained the Black-Scholes option pricing formula was published in May 1973, a month after the opening of the Chicago Board Options Exchange. To compute the value of an option using the Black-Scholes formula all you needed, in addition to the strike price, the current price, and the duration of the option, was the interest rate on government bonds, the standard deviation of the stock, and a table of the normal distribution. By the end of 1973, you didn't even need a pen and paper to do the calculation: Texas Instruments had introduced a calculator that did it for you. That was only the beginning. In the following three decades, an enormous "risk management" industry developed, based on the idea of using options and other optionlike securities, known as derivatives, to guard against extreme outcomes. Mutual funds were able to insure themselves against the risk of corporations defaulting on their bonds, banks could insure themselves against some of their lenders defaulting, and insurance companies could insure against the chances of a freak hurricane leaving them with enormous claims from their policyholders. In each of these areas, the key was the development of mathematical methods to price risk. Almost all of these methods relied, to some extent, on the Black-Scholes formula and the bell curve. Simply by invoking the ghost of Louis Bachelier, it was possible to take much of the danger out of finance.

Or was it? As far back as the 1960s and '70s, some academics and Wall Street practitioners didn't buy into the coin-tossing view of finance. Many old-school bankers and traders were put off by the mathematical demands it came with, but numbered among the skeptics were also some technically adept economists, including Sanford Grossman, of Wharton, and Joseph Stiglitz, who is now at Columbia. In 1975, Grossman and Stiglitz published a brief paper in which they claimed that the efficient market hypothesis was based on a logical inconsistency. If stock prices at every moment reflected all of the available information about the economic outlook and other factors pertinent to individual companies, investors wouldn't have any incentive to search out information and process it. But if nobody finds and processes information, stock prices won't reflect that information, and the market won't be efficient. For the market to work at all, there must be some level of inefficiency! Grossman and Stiglitz entitled their paper "On the Impossibility of Informationally Efficient Markets." Other economic theorists admired its terse logic, but it didn't have much immediate impact on Wall Street.

The aforementioned Benoit Mandelbrot, who is perhaps best known as one of the founders of chaos theory, was another skeptic of the efficient market hypothesis. In the early 1960s, when he was working in the research department at IBM, Mandelbrot got interested in some of the new theories that were being developed to explain how financial markets worked, and he started to gather evidence on how they performed. The Harvard economist Hendrik Houthakker, whom he met while giving a talk in Cambridge, gave him the records of daily movements in the prices of cotton and cotton futures going back more than a century, which he had obtained from the New York Cotton Exchange. Mandelbrot plotted the changes in prices on a computer and quickly saw that they didn't look anything like a smooth bell curve. The charts showed a great many small movements and some very large ones, but relatively few intermediate changes. "If the cotton-price changes fit the standard theory, they would be like sand grains in a heap: somewhat different sizes, but all sand grains, nonetheless," Mandelbrot and a coauthor, Richard Hudson, recalled in their 2004 book, The (Mis)Behavior of Markets. "But the cotton research showed something different . . . Some days, cotton prices hardly budged from the previous close; those are the small sand grains . . . Other days—perhaps word of a drought in Missouri finally reached New York—the news was big: wild price moves, statistical boulders."

Mandelbrot's evidence was confined to an obscure corner of the financial market, but other researchers subsequently found similar discrepancies in the behavior of many other speculative assets, including stocks, bonds, and currencies. "In fact, the bell curve fits reality very poorly," Mandelbrot and Hudson note. "From 1916 to 2003, the daily index movements of the Dow Jones Industrial Average do not spread out on graph paper like a simple bell curve. The far edges flare too high; too many big changes. Theory suggests that over that time there should be 58 days when the Dow moved more than 3.4%; in fact, there were 1,001. Theory predicts six days of index swings beyond 4.5%; in fact, there were 366. And index swings of more than 7% should come once every 300,000 years; in fact, the 20th century saw 48 such days."

On Wall Street, the tendency for big moves to occur more often than the bell curve says they should became known as the phenomenon of "fat tails." It raised serious questions about many applications of the coin-tossing view of finance, including the efficient market hypothesis and the Black-Scholes option pricing formula. Both of these theories depend on the notion that movements in the prices of speculative assets are (a) independent of each other—what happens to the Dow on Tuesday doesn't affect what happens on Wednesday or Friday—and (b) random. (It is these assumptions that justify the use of the normal distribution.) Mandelbrot's research implied that the first of these assumptions wasn't justified. It suggested that what happened yesterday in financial markets influences what happens today, and what happens today influences what happens tomorrow. The data showed that markets are characterized by long periods of relative calm, during which prices don't move very much, interspersed with short periods of frantic activity, when prices zigzag dramatically. In Mandelbrot's words, "[L]arge changes tend to be followed by more large changes, positive or negative. Small changes tend to be followed by more small changes."

This pattern, which became known as "volatility clustering," suggests that financial markets contain an element of predictability. However, it also raises the possibility that the causal relationships that determine market movements aren't fixed, but vary over time. Maybe because of shifts in psychology or government policy, there are periods when markets will settle into a rut, and other periods when they will be apt to gyrate in alarming fashion. This picture seems to jibe with reality, but it raises some tricky issues for quantitative finance. If the underlying reality of the markets is constantly changing, statistical models based on past data will be of limited use, at best, in determining what is likely to happen in the future. And firms and investors that rely on these models to manage risk may well be exposing themselves to danger.

The economics profession didn't exactly embrace Mandelbrot's criticisms. As the 1970s proceeded, the use of quantitative techniques became increasingly common on Wall Street. The coin-tossing view of finance made its way into the textbooks and, with the help of Burton Malkiel, onto the bestsellers list. By the 1980s, many M.B.A. students were being taught that the efficient market hypothesis was a description of reality, and Mandelbrot's strictures had been largely forgotten. "Modern finance was the official religion," Mandelbrot later recalled. "My hypothesis contradicted it; and I was about as welcome in the established church of economics as a heretical Arian at the Council of Nicene."

8. ROBERT LUCAS AND THE TRIUMPH OF UTOPIAN ECONOMICS

Robert Lucas, yet another Chicago economist, and the winner of the 1995 Nobel Memorial Prize, isn't nearly as well known as Milton Friedman. Among his peers, however, Lucas is widely regarded as one of the most influential economists since World War II. During the early 1970s, he and some collaborators developed a new way of thinking about economic policy issues that, effectively, extended the efficient market approach to the entire economy. Calling on some clever mathematics and an appeal to ultra-rationality, the Lucasians purported to show that government attempts to manage the economy were unnecessary, counterproductive, or both. Although one or two of Lucas's individual theories were quickly discredited, his overall approach came to dominate economic theorizing in the same way that Keynesian thinking had dominated the subject during the decades after World War II. In 1980, Lucas wrote, "One cannot find good under-forty economists who identify themselves or their work as Keynesian . . . At research seminars, people don't take Keynesian theorizing seriously anymore: the audience starts to whisper and giggle to one another."

Lucas was born in Yakima, a modest city in the apple-growing country of Washington state, in 1937. As an undergraduate at the University of Chicago, he majored in history. After spending a year as a graduate student in the history department at Berkeley, he moved back to Chicago and enrolled in the Ph.D. program in economics. In preparation for his classes with Friedman and his colleague George Stigler, whom Chicago students knew as "Mr. Macro" and "Mr. Micro," Lucas read Paul Samuelson's *Foundations of Economic Analysis*, which had first appeared in 1947, and which presented economics as a branch of applied mathematics. "I loved the *Foundations*," Lucas later recalled. "Like so many others in my cohort, I internalized its view that if I couldn't formulate a problem in economic theory mathematically, I didn't know what I was doing. I came to the position that mathematical analysis is not one of many ways of doing economic theory: it is the only way. Economic theory is mathematical analysis. Everything else is just pictures and talk."

The thrust of Samuelson's book was that economic decision-makers could be treated as rational automatons who attempt to maximize mathematical functions. (In the case of firms, it is a profit function; in the case of consumers, it is a happiness, or "utility," function.) The decision-makers face some restrictions on their choices: consumers are limited in how much they can spend; firms are limited in the technologies they can use. Using this basic setup, it is possible to derive a set of "optimal" choices for everything from how much to save for retirement, to what stocks to invest in, to how many hours to work, to the types and quantities of products that firms should manufacture. In the 1950s and '60s, Samuelson's methods were applied to many areas of economics, including industrial organization, finance, and trade. (In many cases, the person who did the applying was Samuelson himself!)

But one area remained largely beyond the purview of rationality and individual choice: economic policy. In *The General Theory*, Keynes had emphasized that the logic of individual behavior often doesn't apply to the entire economy, as evidenced by the "paradox of thrift." For a single person, it often makes sense to cut back on spending and save money. But if everybody tries to save more at the same time, the overall level of spending will fall; firms will cut back on production and lay off workers. Ultimately, incomes will be reduced, and so, quite possibly, will total savings. To avoid this type of problem, Keynes focused on aggregate concepts, such as the economy-wide level of consumption, investment, and government spending. Using this framework, he was able to explain how economies could get stuck in a depressed state, and, along the way, he invented macroeconomics as a field separate from microeconomics. Particularly in the United States, though, some economists remained uncomfortable with the failure to integrate the two sides of their subject. Lucas was one of these dissidents. He was determined to develop Samuelson's idea of constructing theories from the ground up.

Once he tried to do this, though, Lucas immediately ran into some of the problems that had plagued general equilibrium theory. A modern economy is immensely complicated, and aggregate outcomes, such as the rate of unemployment and inflation, emerge from decisions made by countless individuals and firms. The American economy, for example, is made up of roughly 300 million people, 110 million households, and about 30 million companies. Other important players include the federal government, which accounts for about a fifth of GDP, fifty state governments, and numerous municipalities. In deciding how much to spend and save, each of these entities has to think about the future. A family has to form a view of what its income is likely to be over the coming year or two. A government has to make an assumption about tax revenues. Firms have to forecast their own sales, which in turn involves taking a view about how the overall economy will be doing. Will the economy be growing next year? What will be the level of unemployment?

Without some way of pinning down how these expectations are formed, there is no way to say how much money firms will invest, consumers will spend, or governments will take in. Traditionally, economists had addressed this problem by assuming that economic decision-makers extrapolated from the past: if the inflation rate is 5 percent this year, they predict it will be 5 percent next year as well. In the early 1970s, however, inflation unexpectedly spiked, and models of the economy that incorporated backward-looking, or "adaptive," expectations performed badly.

Lucas's idea was to assume that everybody knows exactly how the economy works. People aren't merely aware that unemployment is somehow linked to inflation, which is linked to interest rates: they all have the same (correct) mathematical model of the economy in their heads, which they use to form expectations of wages, prices, and other variables. This is the "rational expectations hypothesis," which an economist at Carnegie Mellon, John Muth, had introduced in 1961. By invoking the rational expectations hypothesis, Lucas could simply write down some equations to describe how workers, firms, and the government behave, put a mathematical expectation operator in front of them, and derive a solution that was consistent with the decision rules of everybody in the economy. Clearly, this wasn't very realistic, but to a Chicago economist, that is not a valid criticism: the test of an economic model is its explanatory power. "[T]he relevant question to ask about the 'assumptions' of a theory is not whether they are descriptively 'realistic,' for they never are, but whether they are sufficiently good approximations for the purpose in hand," Milton Friedman wrote in a famous 1953 essay. "And this question can be answered only by seeing whether the theory works, which means whether it yields sufficiently accurate predictions."

One of Lucas's predictions was that anticipated changes in monetary policy wouldn't have any impact on output or employment. Another way of putting this is to say that money is "neutral"—it doesn't affect real variables, only financial variables, such as inflation. If the Fed announces that it is going to expand the money supply, or cut interest rates, to boost growth, workers and businesses will be able to predict the results of this increase, Lucas said, and their responses will exactly offset the policy change. The only way for the Fed to affect job creation and growth is by varying the money supply, or changing interest rates, in ways that people weren't anticipating.

This "policy ineffectiveness proposition"—a phrase coined by Thomas Sargent and Neil Wallace, two of Lucas's followers—turned on its head the Keynesian paradigm, in which the government stabilizes the economy by altering monetary and fiscal policy. Another of Lucas's followers, Robert Barro, now at Harvard, purported to show that changes in taxes, a favored Keynesian tactic, wouldn't be any more effective than changes in the money supply. If the government cuts taxes to stimulate spending, consumers will assume that taxes are destined to go back up later, and they will save extra to pay for them, thus negating the impact of the policy change. Even by the standards of Chicago economics, these were controversial arguments, which took Friedman's skepticism about the usefulness of fine-tuning to its logical (or illogical) extreme. According to the rational expectations theorists, the government was either powerless or a source of trouble.

Insofar as it behaved in a predictable manner, its policies wouldn't make any difference. Insofar as it adapted to this reality by continually surprising the markets, it would destabilize the economy.

The rational expectations approach was so novel that it took the economics profession quite a while to figure out what it really meant. For a long time, its critics and defenders focused almost exclusively on the issue of rationality, assuming this was the key to the stark policy conclusions. In fact, the assumption of rational expectations, by itself, has few definitive policy implications: everything depends on the economic framework in which it is embedded. By using different auxiliary assumptions from the ones Lucas and his followers adopted, it is perfectly possible to write down models in which people have rational expectations and the government can successfully stabilize the economy.

The economic framework Lucas used was the idealized general equilibrium world of Arrow and Debreu. Lucas assumed that all of the conditions necessary for the attainment of general equilibrium were satisfied, and, further, that the equilibrium was unique and stable. In such a setup, supply always equals demand throughout the economy, which means unemployment is always at or close to Friedman's "natural rate." If in one period an external shock knocks the economy out of kilter, at the start of the next period it jumps right back to the equilibrium.

Arrow and Debreu had never intended for their work to be used in policy analysis: it was a purely theoretical analysis that explored the conditions under which a free market economy would display Pareto efficiency. Lucas and his followers claimed that a slightly modified version of the Arrow-Debreu model could be used to represent reality. It is in this sense that Lucas adopted the efficient market hypothesis to the entire economy. Eugene Fama and others had depicted the stock exchange and other financial exchanges as perfectly functioning markets. Lucas assumed that the market for consumer goods, the market for workers, and practically every other market were equally efficient and stable. The only imperfection in the entire economy that Lucas allowed for was a somewhat implausible one: he assumed that, for short periods, individual workers couldn't distinguish between rises in their own wages and increases in the overall price level. By working longer hours in response to a general inflation, or working shorter hours in response to a fall in inflation, they could temporarily move the economy away from its equilibrium.

That was the only source of economic volatility in Lucas's model. There was no place for stupidity, ignorance, or herd behavior. Economic slumps and mass joblessness were ruled out by assumption. In a Lucasian economy, unemployment is a matter of choice. If a quarter of the labor force were jobless during the Great Depression, then most of them must have been unwilling to work at the prevailing wages and chosen to stay at home. Had workers been more willing to accept wage cuts, unemployment would have remained at normal levels. One liberal economist accused Lucas of doing fascist economics. A fairer criticism, which also emerged, was that his theory resembled the philosophy of Voltaire's Dr. Pangloss, a professor of "métaphysico-théologo-cosmolonigologie" who taught his pupils the maxim "All is for the best in the best of all possible worlds."

Another peculiarity of Lucas's work is that he created a model of capitalism without any capitalists. In the world of Arrow-Debreu, firms are merely shells that react to market prices by transforming inputs into outputs. There is no room for innovation. There are no monopolists, such as Microsoft, and no oligopolists, such as Exxon Mobil and Chevron, Citigroup and Goldman Sachs. Financial markets exist, but only in a very abstract form. People are assumed to plan ahead for every possible state of the world and make contingency plans for each of them. There is no place for stock market bubbles, banking crises, or lending crunches. The typical ups and downs of a modern credit-driven economy are nowhere to be seen.

When I interviewed Lucas in 1996, he was engagingly modest about his achievements, perhaps because he could afford to be. (The preceding year, he had visited Stockholm to pick up his Nobel.) "I write down a bunch of equations, and I say this equation has to do with people's preferences and this equation is a description of the technology," he said. "But that doesn't make it so. Maybe I'm right, maybe I'm wrong. That has to be a matter of evidence." As it happens, the evidence hasn't been kind to the rational expectations theory. There is now an overwhelming body of statistical evidence that anticipated changes in monetary policy *do* affect unemployment and output. Unanticipated policy changes also have an impact, but their role is a lesser one. Even Lucas himself has accepted this point. "Monetary shocks just aren't that important: that's the view I've been driven to," he told me. "There's no question, that's a retreat in my views."

Academic studies are one thing, but the rational expectations approach was also subjected to a fascinating real-world test. Between 1979 and 1982, Paul Volcker, the then Fed chairman, made clear his intention to wring inflation out of the system by restricting the growth of the money supply, which is just what Friedman and other Chicago economists had advocated. If workers and firms had formed rational expectations along the lines Lucas suggested, they would have anticipated a big drop in inflation and reduced their wage demands, allowing the economy to jump to a new low-inflation equilibrium, without much of a change in output or unemployment. Instead, the economy plunged into a deep recession, which is precisely what happens in mainstream Keynesian models when the money supply is drastically reduced. Short-term interest rates jumped from 10 percent to 19 percent. The unemployment rate rose to 9.5 percent—which was then its highest level since the Great Depression.

Although they had failed the test of reality, Lucas's theories remained extremely influential within the academy. During the 1980s and '90s, his followers extended the rational expectations approach in various ways and marketed it under a new name: new classical economics. The high point of this research was the construction of "real business cycle" models of the economy, which retained the assumptions of individual optimization and rational expectations, but added some richer dynamics. Since shocks to the money supply had been found wanting as an explanation of economic ups and downs, the economists working in this area, who included one of Lucas's earliest collaborators, Edward C. Prescott, the winner of the 2004 economics Nobel, were forced to come up with some alternatives. Their main candidate was random fluctuations in productivity growth. When a new invention or an influx of skilled workers raises the productivity rate, people work harder and businesses invest more. For a time, output and employment expand. Eventually, the productivity rate falls back, and so does GDP. That explains upswings. What about downturns? Random falls in productivity growth, perhaps due to bad weather or stifling new regulations, cause them. When productivity growth is unusually low, firms invest less and pay less, and people choose to work fewer hours. Output and employment fall.

If you think all this sounds like hocus-pocus, you are not alone. The empirical evidence has proved no kinder to real business cycle theory than it was to the original rational expectations theory. One of the advantages of the second-generation models was that they could easily be "calibrated" and run on computers. But when this was done, they had great difficulty generating the sort of booms and recessions that many countries have experienced over the past ten or twenty years. The only way the models could mimic the actual data was by invoking implausibly large productivity shocks. In the face of such difficulties, some supporters of real business cycle theory resorted to saying that it was too subtle to be judged by standard statistical methods—an argument that smacked of desperation.

By the mid-1990s, many economists who were forced to deal with the real world, rather than construct mathematically elegant theories about it, had virtually given up on Lucasian economics, and the young economists who were schooled in it. In 1996, when I set out to research an article for *The New Yorker* about the state of economics, I came across a lot of unhappiness and criticism. The economics department at Morgan Stanley, for example, was refusing to hire any economics Ph.D.s unless they had experience outside of academe. "We insist on at least a three-to-four-year cleansing experience to neutralize the brainwashing that takes place in these graduate programs," Stephen S. Roach, the firm's chief economist, told me. "Academic economics has taken a very bad turn in the road," Mark Dadd, who was then the top economist at AT&T and the chairman of the National Association for Business Economics, said. "It's very academic, very mathematical, and it really doesn't—I want to choose my words carefully here: it is nothing like as useful to the business community as it could be." The Columbia economist Joseph Stiglitz, who was acting as chairman of the White House Council of Economic Advisers, said, "It's very clear that new classical economics is irrelevant. You can't begin with the assumption of full employment when the President is worried about jobs—not only this President but any President."

I would like to report that my article changed economics: it didn't. I got some letters from (mostly elderly) economists complimenting me for pointing out the emperor's naked state, but the reaction of the profession as a whole was one of denial. The following year, at its annual meeting, the American Economic Association held a series of panel discussions highlighting the relevance and practicality of economics. In many areas, of course, the subject was vital and useful: I had merely highlighted the state of macroeconomics, which is what most people associate with economics. And in that area, the Lucasian methodology remained dominant. Even today, more than a decade later, most first-year Ph.D. students start their macroeconomics training by learning the "dynamic optimization" methods that Lucas helped to popularize and applying them to models based on the rational expectations hypothesis.

The problem is not the mathematics per se, but how it is used (and abused). During the past ten years, many economists working at central banks and finance ministries have embraced so-called New Keynesian models. Despite the name attached to them, these models owe at least as much to Lucas as they do to Keynes: they are self-correcting equilibrium models, built on the foundations of efficient financial markets and rational expectations. The only thing that distinguishes them from Lucas's own models is that they contain one or two more "rigidities," which allow unemployment to deviate from its natural rate for a time. "The assumption of 'rational expectations' as a modeling device is now entirely orthodox," Michael Woodford, one of the leading New Keynesians, wrote in 1999.

The third-generation rational expectations models can be useful for exploring the old question of how central banks should set interest rates to achieve a low and stable rate of inflation, but they have virtually nothing to say about what policymakers should do to maintain financial stability. As in the original Lucas models, there is no role in them for stock market bubbles, credit crunches, or a drying up of liquidity. Indeed, recognizable financial markets don't really exist. The illusions of harmony, stability, and predictability are maintained, and Hayek's information processing machine does its job perfectly: at all times, prices reflect economic fundamentals and send the right signals to economic decision-makers.

Even the creators of these models concede that they don't provide any guidance for policymakers in times of financial turbulence. "In the wake of the October 1987 stock market crash, for example, most economists supported the decision of the Federal Reserve Board to reduce interest rates," three of the most prominent New Keynesians wrote in a review article. "This support was based largely on instinct, however, since there is virtually no formal theoretical work that rationalizes this kind of intervention." No "formal theoretical framework" perhaps, but there is more than a century's worth of well-thought-out justifications for the central bank slashing interest rates and pumping more money into the system during a crisis. Walter Bagehot, the English journalist who was one of the first editors of *The Economist*, detailed some of them in his 1873 book, *Lombard Street*. Unfortunately, though, many economists educated in the past forty years have little time for history, and still less for the history of ideas. Like Lucas, they believe that economic theory is mathematics, and anything else is just talk.

The great attraction of rational expectations theorizing was that it appeared to have succeeded in Samuelson's quest of building theories on the basis of individual decisions, and thereby reunited microeconomics and macroeconomics. Ultimately, however, the rational expectations approach was just another incarnation of utopian economics. Behind all the posturing and fancy mathematics, it relied on the ancient notion of the free market economy as a stable, self-equilibrating mechanism, and ignored many of the problems and pathologies that the history of capitalism had thrown up. In the middle part of the twentieth century, the most important of these appeared to be mass unemployment: Keynesian economics was explicitly designed to prevent a repeat of the 1930s. During the 1970s, inflation emerged as a major problem, and the Keynesian models faltered, presenting the opportunity that Friedman, Lucas, and others had been looking for. Chicago School economics, and its ultimate expression in the form of the efficient market and rational expectations theories, could never have achieved the success it did if its promulgation hadn't coincided with a period of economic turmoil. Once the counterrevolution had taken place, history continued to run in favor of the heirs to Adam Smith. Following the steep recession of 1981–82, the U.S. economy went twenty-five years without entering another prolonged downturn. When things are going well, it is much easier to sell people on the latest exposition of the invisible hand, and to ignore inconvenient issues, such as rising inequality, chronic budget deficits, gaps in the health care system, and the potential for financial instability. Such problems take a long time to emerge. As long as the vast majority of the population remains employed, healthy, and sheltered, there is little support for reforming the private enterprise system, which, as Friedman understood so well, can be marketed as the economic manifestation of some very attractive ideals. In such circumstances, the deregulators and government-bashers, financed as they are by business interests, will inevitably retain the initiative.

As the long expansion continued, Lucas turned away from economic fluctuations and started thinking about other issues, such as the sources of long-term growth. In 2002, he was elected president of the American Economic Association, and at its annual meeting, which took place in January 2003, he explained why his intellectual pursuits had changed: "Macroeconomics was born as a distinct field in the 1940s, as a part of the intellectual response to the Great Depression. The term then referred to the body of knowledge and expertise that we hoped would prevent the recurrence of that economic disaster. My thesis in this lecture is that macroeconomics in this original sense has succeeded: Its central problem of depression-prevention has been solved, for all practical purposes, and has in fact been solved for many decades."

PART TWO

REALITY-BASED ECONOMICS

9. CLIMATE CHANGE, SPILLOVERS, AND PROFESSOR PIGOU

n the fall of 2004, a team of surveyors from the U.S. government's Minerals Management Service, which is part of the Department of the Interior, set out to count the number of bowhead whales in the Beaufort Sea, northeast of Alaska's Prudhoe Bay. Some of the ocean is permanently covered with ice; parts of it are revealed in the summer months, when the icecap retreats. During their flights across the open water in search of whales, the researchers came upon the floating carcasses of four polar bears. The animals appeared to have drowned while they were attempting to swim to land that was more than a hundred miles away.

Polar bears come onshore only when they have to. They prefer to live on the ice, rearing their young and hunting seals, which are particularly abundant in the shallow seas off the Alaska coast. For centuries, this area has been home to large concentrations of bears, which hunt near the edge of the icecap, preying on the seals when they make holes in the ice to breathe. Since the 1950s, average temperatures in the region have increased by two or three degrees centigrade, and the summer limit of the icecap has shifted well to the north, taking it beyond the edge of the continental shelf, which is about forty miles offshore. In

2004, the ice had retreated about a hundred and sixty miles to the north, to an area where seals are much less plentiful. Deprived of their staple food, the bears had apparently set out for the coast and got caught in a storm. Although polar bears are strong swimmers, these four had been unable to make landfall.

The researchers were shocked. During surveys carried out in the same area between 1986 and 2003, few bears had been seen in open waters, and not a single drowning had been documented. But in September 2004, more than ten bears had been spotted swimming, on top of the four that had perished. "We speculate that mortalities due to offshore swimming . . . may be an important and unaccounted source of natural mortality given the energetic demands placed on individual bears engaged in long-distance swimming," one of the survey partici-pants, Charles Monnett, a marine ecologist, and Jeffrey Gleason, a wildlife biologist, subsequently reported in a research paper. "We fur-ther suggest that drowning-related deaths of polar bears may increase in the future if the observed trend of regression of pack ice and/or longer open water periods continues."

The drowned bears made headlines around the world, heightening public worries about global warming. Pressure for an aggressive policy response increased in 2006 with the release of Al Gore's documentary, *An Inconvenient Truth*, which included animated footage of a polar bear struggling to pull itself onto a block of ice. "It's not a political is-sue," Gore said of climate change. "It's a moral issue." These develop-ments presented a challenge to orthodox economists, particularly in the United States, who for years had been downplaying the need for rapid steps to avert an environmental catastrophe. An even bigger threat to their complacency came in October 2006, when Sir Nicholas Stern, a respected English scholar who had previously served as chief economist at the World Bank, issued an official report on the econom-ics of global warming, which raised the specter of "major disruption to economic and social activity, later in this century and in the next, on a scale similar to those associated with the great wars and the economic depression of the first half of the 20th century."

Citing the increased risks of flooding, droughts, famines, and forced migrations on a massive scale, Stern warned that climate change "threatens the basic elements of life for people around the world— access to water, food production, health, and use of land and the environment." He called for immediate and coordinated policy action, including the imposition of hefty taxes on the burning of carbon and a major commitment to investing in alternative energy sources; he dismissed the wait-and-see attitude favored by many economists. "Climate change presents a unique challenge for economics," Stern concluded. "It is the greatest and widest-ranging market failure ever seen."

Until the publication of the Stern Report, most people had regarded global warming as a scientific problem, a political problem, or an ethical problem. It is all of these things, but at root it is an economic problem. Two hundred and fifty years ago, the stock of carbon dioxide in the atmosphere was equivalent to about 280 parts per million. Today, the level is about 430 parts per million, and by 2050, if current trends persist, it will be about 550 parts per million. When the gas builds up in the atmosphere, it acts like a greenhouse, trapping heat: in terms of average global temperatures, the ten warmest years on record all occurred between 1995 and 2007. The most important source of rising carbon dioxide levels is the emissions of power plants, factories, motor vehicles, and other man-made burners of carbon fuels. Now, contrary to the claims of some eco-activists, there is nothing particularly venal about managers of power plants, factory owners, or SUV buyers. Like most people in the economy, they pursue their self-interest, reacting to the signals that the market provides them. The key to global warming, and the source of the market failure that Stern was talking about, is the presence of something that economists call negative "spillovers" or "externalities."

When a power station burns coal to create electricity, the carbon dioxide it creates is a by-product that spills over into the atmosphere. The power station suffers little penalty for its polluting actions, so it doesn't have any incentive to stop them. In fact, market incentives are usually what drive a firm to become a polluter in the first place: producing electricity from coal is a lot cheaper than building vast windmill farms or erecting solar panels. Another way of saying this is that the *social* costs of burning coal and other forms of carbon diverge from the *private* costs. "In common with many other environmental problems, human-induced climate change is at its most basic level an externality," the Stern Report stated. "Those who produce greenhouse-gas emissions are bringing about climate change, thereby imposing costs on the world and on future generations, but they do not face directly, neither via markets nor in other ways, the full consequences of the costs of their actions." It is in this sense, the Stern Report went on, that climate change is a market failure—and "one that is not 'corrected' through any institution or market, unless policy intervenes."

The publication of the Stern Report prompted a vigorous debate. Some economists, led by Yale's William Nordhaus, accused Stern of exaggerating the costs of climate change; others defended his calculations. The dispute is still raging, but nobody can diminish Stern's achievement in bringing the concept of market failure to public attention, and in pointing out the need for politicians to factor it into their actions.

I well remember the first economics lecture I ever attended. The instructor, an eminent Oxford don, introduced a Robinson Crusoe figure living on a desert island, where he has to decide how to allocate his time and energy to maximize his well-being. Should he spend more time on hunting or fishing, on building a shelter or making clothes? The Walras/Jevons marginal condition, which the lecturer derived with the aid of a diagram, provides a simple answer: he should carry on each activity until the additional benefit yielded by another hour devoted to any one of them is the same. If it is easier to catch fish than capture deer, he should head for the shore. If his roof is leaking in rain, he should repair the roof. Next, the instructor introduced Man Friday, who is also living on the island. Crusoe and Friday trade with each other to their mutual benefit, but otherwise they don't have much interaction. The smoke from Friday's fire doesn't bother Crusoe, and neither does the fact that Friday has a bigger hut. All that Crusoe cares about is his own possessions.

This is the economist's ideal of atomistic competition. But humans are social animals who live together in groups, breathe the same air, share the same buildings, and jostle with one another for resources, prestige, and mates. In this environment, spillovers are endemic. Once you start thinking about them, you can spot them everywhere—even in your own home. If your roommate smokes heavily, you run a higher risk of getting lung cancer; if he plays loud music late at night, you will lose sleep. Then there is the workplace. If the person working in the cubicle next to you gets the promotion that you thought you deserved, you will be miffed; you might even get sick. (According to a famous study of seventeen thousand British civil servants, low-ranking workers develop more health problems and experience higher rates of heart disease than do people in senior positions.)

The first economist to examine spillovers in modern terms was Arthur Cecil Pigou (1877–1959), a prolific and somewhat tragic English scholar who, for many years, was the forgotten man of economics. In the early decades of the twentieth century, it was Pigou, rather than his colleague Keynes, who dominated British economics. He published authoritative texts, served on expert commissions, and helped to define a pragmatic middle ground between laissez-faire and collectivism. After Pigou clashed with Keynes during the Great Depression, however, his reputation suffered a precipitous decline, and he ended his life as a reclusive and sadly diminished figure. Only lately has his work been rediscovered. The Stern Report cited two of Pigou's books. And in 2006, Greg Mankiw, a well-known Harvard economist who served as chairman of the White House Council of Economic Advisers from 2003 to 2005, launched a "Pigou Club" for economists and pundits who supports the imposition of higher taxes on gasoline and other sources of carbon dioxide.

Pigou grew up on the Isle of Wight, off the south coast of England. His father was an army officer descended from French Huguenots; his mother was of Irish extraction. After attending Harrow, an exclusive private school also attended by Winston Churchill, he went to King's College, Cambridge, where he studied history and economics, winning a series of academic prizes. His tutor, the legendary Alfred Marshall, regarded him as a budding genius and helped him get a series of teaching jobs, including the Cambridge Chair in Political Economy, which Marshall himself vacated in 1908. Pigou ascended to that position, which was then the most prestigious post in all of economics, at the age of just thirty. "Tall and handsome as a Viking," in the words of a contemporary, he was known as "the Prof." On top of his intellectual pursuits, he was a keen sportsman, playing cricket, tennis, and golf, and touring the United Kingdom on his bicycle. "Pigou carried himself as if on parade," Robert Skidelsky, the biographer of Keynes, wrote. "Morals in his mind were inextricably linked with physical exertion, and he was never so happy as when taking parties of handsome, athletic young men on climbs to Switzerland or the Lake District."

Inspired by his mentor Marshall, Pigou regarded economics as a "machinery or method of thinking," rather than a set of ethical precepts or a political philosophy. He was no radical or malcontent. Generally speaking, he supported private enterprise and limited government. Still, like most of the great British economists, from Smith to Mill to Marshall, he believed that careful analysis of the economy revealed a number of areas where a policy of laissez-faire couldn't be justified. "[E]ven in the most advanced States there are failures and imperfections . . . there are many obstacles that prevent a community's resources from being distributed . . . in the most efficient way," Pigou wrote in *The Economics of Welfare*, which was published in 1920. "The study of these constitutes our present problem . . . its purpose is essentially practical. It seeks to bring into clearer light some of the ways in which it now is, or eventually may become, feasible for governments to control the play of economic forces in such ways as to promote the economic welfare, and through that, the total welfare, of their citizens as a whole."

Pigou's great intellectual contribution was to take some of the "failures and imperfections" of the market and develop them into a systematic case for public intervention. The key step in his argument was the distinction he drew between the private value and social value of economic activity. "Industrialists are interested, not in the social, but only in the private net product of their operations," Pigou pointed out. In some areas of the economy, this distinction doesn't matter, because private costs and social costs coincide. But where the two differ because of the presence of spillovers, markets can no longer ensure an ideal allocation of resources, and "certain acts of interference with normal economic processes may be expected, not to diminish, but to increase" overall welfare.

To explain what he meant, Pigou discussed the building of a new railway, which facilitates the transportation of people and goods across long distances. The savings in time and money that users of the railway enjoy are private benefits, and their existence will be reflected in the fares the users are willing to pay. Similarly, the railway company's expenditures on laying track, acquiring rolling stock, and paying its employees are private costs, which will show up in the prices it charges. From the perspective of traditional economic theory, so far all is well and good. But it may well happen, Pigou went on, that with the opening of the railway, "costs are thrown upon people not directly concerned, through, say, uncompensated damage done to surrounding woods by sparks from railway engines." These social costs don't enter the calculations of the railway company, but in tallying up the ultimate social value of its operations, Pigou insisted, "all such effects must be included."

Pigou's point is fundamental. As I explained in Part I, the essence of utopian economics is that the free market, by generating a set of prices at which firms and consumers equate private costs and private benefits, produces an efficient outcome. But from the point of view of society, what is needed is a balancing of *social* costs and *social* benefits. Free markets don't lead to such a balancing. Whenever spillovers are present, the prices that Hayek's supercomputer spits out reflect only private costs and benefits, and the overall outcome that the market economy produces is neither efficient nor socially desirable. The market fails, and fails in a very specific and predictable sense.

Pigou didn't use the precise phrase "market failure," but *The Economics of Welfare* was, essentially, the first economics book devoted to the subject. To correct the market failure that spillovers cause, Pigou advocated the use of taxes and subsidies. Where the social value of an activity was lower than its private value, as in the classic case of a factory pumping toxic waste into a river, it was appropriate for the government to restrict the activity by imposing a tax—a policy Pigou referred to as introducing "extraordinary restraints." On the other hand, Pigou pointed out, some activities have a social value that exceeds their private value. For example, the providers of lighthouses, parks, and streetlamps have difficulty charging people for using their services, even though the social benefits they provide are clearly substantial. Pigou warned that the market wouldn't supply enough of these types of goods, which later become known as public goods. The government, therefore, was justified in using subsidies—"extraordinary encouragements"—to correct this market failure and ensure their adequate provision.

Unlike with some later textbook authors, Pigou's analysis of spillovers and other market failures went beyond the important but straightforward case of firms damaging their surrounding environments. In a modern society, he pointed out, there are all sorts of economic interdependencies. Among the examples he cited were the crimes induced by the sale of alcoholic drinks; the damage done to road surfaces by private motor vehicles; the harm done to unborn babies caused by the practice of pregnant women working in factories; and the casualties suffered in military campaigns designed to protect a country's foreign investments—at its height, the British Empire carried out many such exercises in "gunboat diplomacy." By invoking these sorts of problems, Pigou was able to justify a whole range of government policies, such as temperance laws, zoning laws, progressive taxation, slum clearance, and state-financed maternity leaves.

Almost a century after the publication of *The Economics of Welfare*, the clarity and ambition of Pigou's vision remains striking. As the historian of economic thought Mark Blaug has commented, "no-one can continue to believe in the spontaneous co-ordination of private and social interests who has digested Pigou's insistence on the possible interdependence of firms and households." In introducing the concept of social cost, Pigou pinpointed a central problem with the invisible hand that many free market economists had deliberately obscured or ignored. He also proposed some simple ways of correcting the market's shortcomings, sometimes through the tax system, but also by the provision of public services and the introduction of regulations. Moreover, he accomplished all this using the same tools of "marginal analysis" that Walras, Pareto, and others had used to extol the virtues of the invisible hand. The defenders of free market orthodoxy could hardly dismiss Pigou's conclusions as the product of an inappropriate methodology: his method was theirs!

Still, as time went on, economic conservatives launched a sustained and partially successful effort to discredit Pigou's work—a task in which they found an unlikely ally. In 1933, when the British unemployment rate reached 15 percent, Pigou published another book, *The Theory of Unemployment*, in which he repeated the orthodox argument that the root cause of mass joblessness was that wages were too high. Keynes was outraged. Three years later, in *The General Theory*, he portrayed Pigou as the leading exponent of the outmoded "classical" school of economics and poured scorn on *The Theory of Unemployment*, commenting that it "is not capable of telling us what determines the actual level of employment; and on the problem of involuntary unemployment it has no bearing." In a critical review of *The General Theory*, Pigou tried returning fire. "Einstein actually did for Physics what Mr. Keynes believes himself to have done for Economics," he wrote. "He developed a far-reaching generalization, under which Newton's results can be subsumed as a special case. But he did not, in announcing his discovery, insinuate, through carefully barbed sentences, that Newton and those who had hitherto followed his lead were a gang of incompetent bunglers."

The damage to Pigou's reputation had been done, however. The success of *The General Theory* turned its author into an international celebrity and Pigou, once a great prodigy, into something of a museum piece. Thereafter, he retreated into pure theory, publishing articles and books at regular intervals, but largely withholding public comment on the progress of the Keynesian revolution. In 1943, Pigou gave up his university professorship, retaining his fellowship at King's. Thereafter, he retreated to his rooms and books, emerging rarely.

In 1960, a year after Pigou's death, Ronald Coase, a conservatively inclined British economist who had moved to the University of Chicago, questioned whether the presence of spillovers justified government intervention. In a paper entitled "The Problem of Social Cost," Coase pointed out that, in most cases, the problem came down to an issue of conflicting property rights. If a chemical factory releases noxious fumes into a nearby housing development, the factory's "right" to carry out its legitimate business is ranged against the "right" of the people who live nearby to breathe clean air. Providing that property rights were well specified and laws were enforced effectively, Coase argued, private bargaining between the affected parties would ensure an economically efficient outcome.

Coase cited the example of a cattle farmer with livestock that tended to wander onto a neighboring arable farm, destroying some of the crops being grown there. As long as the two farmers could put a dollar figure on the crop damage, and the law of trespass was clearly defined, they would both have an incentive to reach a financial agreement about future incursions. Who paid whom would depend on the law. If the statute held the cattle farmer legally liable for damage done by his straying animals, it would be his responsibility to fence in his land, cut back his herd, or pay the arable farmer an agreed sum to overlook the occasional incursion. If the law didn't hold the cattle farmer liable for the actions of his animals, money could end up going in the opposite direction. It would be in the interest of the arable farmer, if he valued his crops highly enough, to pay for the construction of his neighbor's fence. As long as the law was clear, Coase argued, it didn't really matter which side it came down on. Either way, the final pattern of production would be efficient in the Pareto sense; that is, it wouldn't be possible to make one of the farmers better off without making the other one worse off.

Coase's reasoning was novel and ingenious. When he first presented it to a roomful of his Chicago colleagues that included Milton Friedman and George Stigler, twenty of them disagreed with him and only one agreed with him. However, after a couple of hours of discussion, the crowd unanimously accepted Coase's argument that, regardless of the initial law, private bargaining would generate an efficient outcome. Other conservative economists quickly seized on this result, which Stigler dubbed the "Coase theorem." To supporters of laissez-faire, its appeal was obvious: if Coase was right and Pigou was wrong, there were solid grounds for questioning a whole litany of government policies.

As the free market revival gathered strength, Coase emerged as one of its intellectual leaders. In 1974, he published an article suggesting, contrary to Pigou, that the private sector could provide many "public goods." Hundreds of years ago, he pointed out, many English lighthouses financed themselves by levying charges on ships and shipping companies. Along with two of his colleagues at the University of Chicago Law School, Richard Posner and Frank Easterbrook, Coase also played a prominent role in an organized and successful conservative effort to educate judges and other lawyers about free market economics, serving as the longtime editor of *The Journal of Law and Economics*. In 1991, he was awarded the Nobel Prize.

Today, many Chicago-leaning economists argue that the only policy necessary to deal with spillovers is the adequate spelling out and enforcement of property rights. According to one of Coase's followers, "We should expunge the concept of externality." Coase himself didn't go this far. In his 1960 article, he acknowledged that when an activity inflicted harm on many different people, getting all the interested parties to agree on an efficient solution might be difficult and costly. Economists refer to the costs of negotiation as transaction costs: in his Nobel lecture, Coase acknowledged that the theorem named after him applied only when these were negligible. "I tend to regard the Coase Theorem as a stepping stone on the way to an analysis of an economy with positive transactions costs," he said. And he went on: "[I]t does not imply, when transaction costs are positive, that government action . . . could not produce a better result than relying on negotiations between individuals in the market. Whether this would be so could be discovered not by studying imaginary governments but what real governments actually do."

Pigou wouldn't have disagreed with much of this statement. As I said, he was no radical. But when it came to large-scale spillovers, such as industrial pollution or the existence of urban blight, he believed that private bargaining was impractical, given the highly complex "inter-relations of the various private persons affected." In cases like these, he said, government intervention, even though it might create some problems of its own, was often the best option available.

Pigou was surely right. For three decades after World War II, two factories operated by General Electric dumped more than a million pounds of carcinogenic polychlorinated biphenyls (PCBs) into the Hudson River, polluting a two-hundred-mile stretch of the famous waterway. In 1976, New York State stopped all fishing in the worst-affected region, and the next year the federal government banned the use of PCBs. GE vigorously resisted efforts to force it to repair the damage it had done. Finally, in 2002, the Environmental Protection Agency ordered the firm to dredge parts of the river and clean up what's left of the PCBs. The Hudson Valley is now the biggest Superfund site in the country, but as of the start of 2009, dredging still hadn't begun. (In May 2009, the work finally started.)

The GE episode illustrates the folly of relying on the Coase theorem to prevent environmental disasters. Property rights were hardly the issue. Even had GE been willing to strike an efficient bargain, providing compensation to some of the fishermen and bathers downstream from its plants so it could continue to use the Hudson as a dump, how could it have done this? Millions of people inhabit the Hudson Valley, and as history has demonstrated, PCBs linger in a riverbed for decades. Calculating all the individual costs and benefits would have been impractical, as would one-to-one negotiations. In cases of large-scale pollution, such as this one, government action is the only way to provide some sort of balancing of social costs and social benefits.

The same issues arise, to an inestimably greater extent, in dealing with global warming. The Coase theorem clearly has little relevance—most of the interested parties haven't been born yet. From a Pigovian perspective, the central problem is that carbon is too cheap: the market prices people pay for carbon products, such as gasoline and electricity generated from fossil fuels, don't reflect the environmental impact of greenhouse gases. In the language of modern economics, a stable climate is a public good. We all enjoy its benefits, but none of us gets charged for them.

The most straightforward way to bring the private cost of carbon closer to its social cost is to impose a "Pigovian tax" on products such as coal and gasoline, with the size of the tax proportional to how much greenhouse gases the products emit. (Pound for pound, coal produces more carbon dioxide than oil, which, in turn, is dirtier than natural gas.) For example, imposing a levy of $100 per ton of carbon emissions would translate into an additional tax on gasoline of about $0.20 a gallon. Recently, even some Republican economists have expressed support for the introduction of a carbon tax. The members of Greg Mankiw's informal Pigou Club include Gary Becker and Posner, both of the University of Chicago; Alan Greenspan; and the former secretary of state George Shultz. According to Mankiw:

The Pigou Club wants to move beyond the rhetorical syllogism, all too common in Republican circles, that: (1) Taxes are bad; (2) Pigovian taxes are taxes; (3) Pigovian taxes are bad. Such a simplistic mindset makes it impossible for people to discuss in a responsible way the relative merits of different tax systems. Instead, we Pigovians acknowledge: (1) There will be some government spending; (2) This spending will be funded with taxes; (3) Government should use the least bad taxes it has available. In fact, Pigovian taxes are not only least bad—

they are good. They correct market failures when transaction costs are too high to expect the forces of the Coase theorem to fix the problem.

An alternative method of dealing with global warming is for the government to impose a cap on total carbon emissions. A variant of this idea, which the Obama administration is pursuing, is to distribute a limited number of "emission rights," which can be traded in a secondary market. "Cap and trade" schemes of this type have already been used successfully to reduce emissions of sulfur dioxide and nitrogen oxide, which cause acid rain, and they form the basis of the Kyoto Protocol, the international climate change treaty, from which the United States withdrew in 2001. In the environmental economics literature, there is much debate on the merits of Pigovian taxes versus cap and trade. But as long as emissions rights are auctioned off to the highest bidders, rather than being handed out for free, the two approaches aren't very different. Both aim to correct the divergence between private costs and social costs at the heart of global warming, and both raise revenues, which can be used to cut other taxes or finance clean-energy policies.

Unfortunately, the cap-and-trade bill that the House of Representatives approved in June 2009, and which seeks to reduce carbon emissions to considerably below 2005 levels by 2020, didn't meet the necessary economic standards. The legislative draft stripped the auction provision and endorsed giving away 85 percent of the emissions rights. Still, the growing bipartisan recognition that markets don't function well in the presence of spillovers represents intellectual progress. Until fairly recently, the influence of free market ideology was such that most Republicans, and even some Democrats, weren't even willing to discuss the idea of market failure. There remains little consensus on how far to restrict future greenhouse gas emissions, or—and this comes to the same thing—how high to set the carbon tax, but the crucial conceptual breakthrough appears to have been made.

Still, in both intellectual and practical terms, there is a long way to go. Global warming is just one of many damaging spillovers, and spillovers are just one of many types of market failure. Other important failures include anticompetitive behavior on the part of big companies exploiting monopoly power; the refusal of health insurers to offer insurance to some of those who need it most (the sick); and the repeated emergence of speculative bubbles in financial markets. Fortunately, some economists have been working on these issues, and others like them, for decades. In the rest of Part II, I describe some of their work. As I say in the introduction, reality-based economics isn't as unified as utopian economics, but that is an advantage rather than a disadvantage, because it means that different theories can be used to explain different market failures. Pigou, in the early pages of *The Economics of Welfare*, compared economists to doctors, who are interested in scientific knowledge "for the healing that knowledge may help to bring." To a doctor, the key thing about treating a disease is not the elegance and internal consistency of the analysis underpinning the diagnosis he makes, but whether the treatment he recommends works. Reality-based economists have the same outlook.

10. FRANCIS BATOR'S TAXONOMY OF
MARKET FAILURES

s far as I can tell, the first economist to use the phrase "market failure" was Francis Bator, who is now an emeritus professor of economics at Harvard's John F. Kennedy School of Government. Between 1964 and 1967, Bator served as a deputy national security adviser to President Lyndon Johnson. He also worked as a consultant for the departments of Treasury and State, and he was the founding chairman of the Kennedy School's public policy program. Bator's major contribution to economics came in the late 1950s, when as a young member of the MIT faculty he wrote a pair of memorable articles on the limits of free market economics. The first one, which appeared in the March 1957 issue of *The American Economic Review*, provided a clear and digestible exposition of general equilibrium theory. Even for economists with strong mathematical training, the original work of Arrow and Debreu was heavy going. Bator distilled it into forty pages of English. With the aid of some fairly simple diagrams, he showed how, under certain conditions, a free market system generated a Pareto-efficient outcome. Fifty years after its publication, the article remains perhaps the most painless introduction to the pure theory of the invisible hand.

Bator's second paper appeared in *The Quarterly Journal of Economics* in August 1958. Entitled "The Anatomy of Market Failure," it examined the circumstances in which the theories he had previously outlined didn't apply—cases where the free market allocation system would fail "to sustain 'desirable' activities or to stop 'undesirable' activities." Bator began by pointing out that the world is full of things that violate the assumptions of the Arrow-Debreu model: "imperfect information, inertia and resistance to change, the infeasibility of costless lump-sum taxes, businessmen's desire for a 'quiet life,' uncertainty and inconsistent expectations, the vagaries of aggregate demand, etc." Some of these phenomena, such as inertia and the desire for peace and quiet, might seem a bit arbitrary, but uncertainty and imperfect information are fundamental features of any economy. They emanate from the second law of thermodynamics, commonly referred to as "time's arrow." Since time doesn't run backward, the future is unknown and businesses, investors, and consumers are compelled to make decisions on the basis of best guesses about what might happen. Sometimes these guesses turn out to be fairly accurate. Often, they don't, and when this happens resources tend to get misallocated. (In adopting the rational expectations hypothesis, the members of the Chicago School sidestepped this problem.)

Having raised the issues of uncertainty and information, which pose fundamental problems for any economic theory, Bator turned to areas that are more amenable to traditional analysis. Even in a world of perfect foresight, he argued, there would be at least three other sources of market failure. One is monopoly or oligopoly power. In the free market model, each industry consists of large numbers of competing firms, none of which can capture more than a small share of the market. The survival of atomized competition depends on the assumption of diminishing returns to scale: if any individual firm tries to ramp up output, its costs will rise and it won't be able to compete with smaller firms. Clearly, this is not very realistic. Most manufacturing industries are organized on a production line basis, which ensures that unit costs fall as production rises. Ford or Toyota can operate a plant making a thousand cars a week almost as cheaply as one making eight hundred cars a week. As noted earlier, in mass production industries, big firms can almost always undercut smaller ones, and over time a handful of them will come to dominate the market. With competition restricted to a few big players, firms will be able to set prices above costs, which violates the conditions necessary for economic efficiency.

The second market failure that Bator identified is that businesses may have little incentive to produce some things that people value highly, such as bridges, hospitals, parks, and fire departments, because they can't charge enough for them to make it worthwhile. This is the problem of "public goods" that Smith and Pigou addressed, but which the schools of Lausanne and Chicago glossed over. Public goods have two unusual characteristics. First, one person's use of them doesn't prevent others from using them: if I go sailing on Long Island Sound, there will be plenty of space for you to do the same thing. The second distinguishing characteristic of public goods is that it is very difficult to prevent people from using them for nothing. If the authorities decided to charge small boats for using Long Island Sound, they would have to patrol hundreds of miles of coastline, which would be prohibitively expensive.

The final source of market failure that Bator mentioned was the phenomenon of spillovers or "externalities." (The latter term was another of his inventions.) He updated Pigou's analysis, pointing out exactly how the presence of these effects violated the marginal conditions of classical economic theory. Like Pigou, he also pointed out that spillovers aren't always negative. He gave the example of a beekeeper located next to an apple orchard, which James Meade, a renowned British economist, had originally developed. By pollinating the flowers on the apple trees, the bees help the orchard owner to grow more fruit; by providing the bees with nectar, the apple trees help the beekeeper to produce more honey. But neither the orchard owner, in deciding how many trees to grow, nor the beekeeper, in deciding how many hives to maintain, takes account of these positive spillovers. Consequently, the market doesn't produce as much as it's capable of.

After Bator published his taxonomy of market failures, it didn't take long for other economists to recognize its usefulness. Most modern textbooks contain chapters on uncertainty, imperfect information, monopoly, public goods, and spillovers. However, these topics are usually treated as addendums to the main body of analysis, which is devoted to the classical free market model. This ordering has the effect, welcome to many economists, of relegating market failure to a special case of the Platonic ideal—one to be treated at the end of the course, time permitting. If economics is to be regarded as a reality-based science, the order of presentation should be reversed.

Market failures range from "micro" problems that afflict particular markets to "macro" malfunctions that affect the entire economy. Often, though, the dividing line isn't very clear. Traffic congestion is clearly a microlevel issue—although no less annoying for it. Abuses of monopoly power by large corporations and excessive CEO pay are microfailures, and yet they have a systemic impact on the economy. Pollution and destruction of the environment is a global problem that results from micro spillovers. The subprime crisis started out as a microfailure: it developed into a global recession. Slumps of this nature are obviously macrolevel market failures, but they have their roots in uncertainty and coordination problems at the micro level, especially in the financial sector.

The problem of monopoly is as old as economics. Many people are introduced to the subject as children when they play the popular board game of the same name, the object of which is to buy up as many properties as possible and charge your opponents exorbitant rents. Parker Brothers, a unit of Hasbro, has marketed Monopoly since the 1930s, but the game's origins can be traced back to the Landlord's Game, which Lizzie Magie, a young Quaker woman from Virginia, invented in 1904 to demonstrate the evils of private land monopolies. Around the turn of the twentieth century, there was also a great deal of public concern about the formation of vast commercial monopolies, known as "trusts," which had come to dominate many industries, such as sugar, tobacco, railroads, and beer. The best known of these behemoths were John D. Rockefeller's Standard Oil Company, and the United States Steel Corporation, which the financier J. P. Morgan put together after buying out Andrew Carnegie's business empire.

Worries that the new combines were squeezing out smaller competitors and bilking customers led to the introduction of antitrust laws. The Sherman Antitrust Act of 1890 outlawed restraints of trade by existing monopolies and any attempt to create a new monopoly. The Clayton Antitrust Act of 1914 proscribed price discrimination, exclusive dealing contracts, and other predatory tactics that the trusts had used to boost their profits. During the same era, President Theodore Roosevelt

(1901–1909) and his successor, William Howard Taft (1909–1913), issued lawsuits to break up more than a hundred of the trusts, including Standard Oil.

On paper, the antitrust laws, which remain on the books, were strong pieces of legislation. In practice, the federal courts have generally been accommodating toward big companies, often adhering to Judge Billings Learned Hand's dictum: "The successful competitor, having been urged to compete, must not be turned upon when he wins." The rise of the Chicago School provided opponents of antitrust with new arguments to hurl at judges and would-be regulators. George Stigler insisted that markets populated by a few big firms were more competitive than they appeared. Friedman and Arnold Harberger—the same Arnold Harberger who would later accompany Friedman to Pinochet's Chile—backed him up. (According to one of Harberger's studies, the economy-wide efficiency losses from monopoly amount to just one-tenth of 1 percent of GDP.) Later on, even some moderate economists, such as NYU's William Baumol, argued that monopolies didn't need to be exposed to actual competition in order to curb their predatory behavior: the mere threat of competition would do the job. During the administration of George W. Bush, antitrust policy was relaxed to favor big companies. In 2008, the Justice Department published guidelines making it much harder to sue big companies for predatory or anticompetitve behavior.

There is no doubt that some liberal economists of the postwar generation overstated the market power that sheer size conferred on corporations. In his 1967 book, *The New Industrial State*, John Kenneth Galbraith argued that companies such as General Motors, Exxon, and General Electric had effectively usurped the role of the free market. "[W]e have an economic system which, whatever its formal ideological billing, is in substantial part a planned economy," Galbraith declared. "The initiative in deciding what is to be produced comes not from the sovereign producer who, through the market, issues the instructions that bend the production mechanism to his ultimate will. Rather, it comes from the great producing organization which reaches forward to control the markets that it is presumed to serve and, beyond, to bend the consumer to its needs."

Galbraith's analysis proved poorly timed. Subsequent decades saw the rise of globalization and the removal of import restrictions, which left much of American manufacturing—from autos to textiles to toys to furniture to steel to chemicals—struggling to fend off foreign competition. Meanwhile, the rise of corporate raiders such as Carl Icahn and T. Boone Pickens, and leveraged buyout conglomerates such as Kohlberg Kravis Roberts and Texas Pacific, created an active market in the ownership of blue-chip companies. The cosseted top executives of Fortune 500 companies found their positions and perquisites of office under threat.

The demise of the megacorporation shouldn't be overstated, though. Of the top ten companies on the 1967 *Fortune* list—General Motors, Exxon, Ford, General Electric, Chrysler, Mobil, Texaco, U.S. Steel, IBM, Gulf Oil—eight were still on the 2007 list, as independent companies or as divisions of even bigger conglomerates. In many parts of the economy, such as oil, autos, and finance, giganticism remains a basic fact of economic life. Then there is the high-technology sector, where monopoly power is endemic.

One of the first people to point this out was W. Brian Arthur, a soft-spoken applied mathematician who grew up in Northern Ireland and fell into economics almost by accident. Back in the mid-1980s, Arthur, who was then at Stanford, presented a paper at Harvard in which he argued that chance events and network effects can enable inferior technologies to beat out superior products and take over entire markets. A Harvard economist, Richard Zeckhauser, stood up afterward and said, "If you are right, capitalism can't work." A few months later, Arthur presented the same paper in Moscow, where an eminent Russian economist said, "Your argument cannot be true!"

The essence of Arthur's paper was that with some types of goods, the utility they provide to people depends not just on their intrinsic merits but on how many other people are using them. If you buy a new dishwasher or refrigerator, it doesn't really matter whether your friends and neighbors have bought the same model. But if you are considering switching to a new video game console or a new social networking site, the number of people already using these products is crucial. If the network of established users is large, you will have plenty of games to play and many friends to contact; if the console or site is new, or has failed to take off, the value it can offer you will be strictly limited.

The additional benefit that each new user of a product incidentally delivers to all the other users is called a "network externality." As the number of users expands, these externalities increase in size, making the product even more attractive. Before very long, markets of this nature tend to "tip" in the direction of a single product, which acquires a monopoly, or near-monopoly, position. Once this has happened, even rival goods that are cheaper or offer better features struggle to find a foothold. In the phrase that Arthur used in his original paper, the maker of the inferior product "locks in" to a position of great power.

When I interviewed Arthur in 1998, he recounted the early opposition to his theory with wry amusement. "I was saying all this during the Cold War, so ideology got in the way," he said. "I spent about ten years in the wilderness." Eventually, some other economists began to take Arthur's ideas seriously, and so did some senior figures in business and government. "At first people said, 'Your theory may be theoretically valid, but there's no actual evidence of it in the economy,'" Arthur recalled. "I thought about that and said, 'No, no, no. The whole high-tech sector operates in this way.' When I started to say that, I found it had a lot of resonance in Silicon Valley. People I talked to there just nodded wisely, grinned, and said, 'This is how we see it, too, but we've never seen it written down and formalized.'"

I came across Arthur and his work in the late 1990s, when I was reporting on the Clinton administration's antitrust suit against Microsoft. Then, as now, Microsoft's Windows operating system and Office software suite dominated the PC industry, with about 90 percent of the market. Many computer experts considered Apple Macintosh a far superior product to Windows, but neither Apple nor anybody else had been able to stop Bill Gates and his company. Rivals accused Microsoft of entrenching its position with a variety of abusive practices, such as issuing restrictive contracts to PC manufacturers, tying its products together in a way that forced customers to buy things they didn't want, and refusing to make its products compatible with those of its rivals. In 1994, under pressure from the Justice Department, Microsoft agreed to make its product licenses somewhat less restrictive and to avoid tying other products to Windows. Three years later, the Justice Department sued Microsoft for violating this decree by forcing computer manufacturers to include a copy of its Internet Explorer Web browser with each copy of Windows.

In a historic finding of fact issued in November 1999, Judge Thomas Penfield Jackson, of the D.C. district court, ruled that Microsoft's dominance of the operating system market constituted a monopoly. Jackson subsequently ruled that the firm's anticompetitive practices had violated the Sherman Act, and he recommended that Microsoft be split in two, with one unit manufacturing Windows and another producing the Office software. In 2001, the D.C. Circuit Court of Appeals overturned Jackson's rulings, and the Justice Department, which by then was under the control of the Bush administration, dropped the threat to break up Microsoft. The case was settled with Microsoft agreeing to share some proprietary information with other companies, and the government effectively dropping most of its demands. Although the antitrust suit ended indecisively, it provided plenty of evidence of how dominant companies use predatory behavior to smother competition. During the trial, one senior Microsoft executive was quoted as saying the firm intended to "smother" the rival Netscape browser and to "cut off Netscape's air supply" by giving away Internet Explorer.

In some ways, the high-tech version of monopoly is more difficult to deal with than sugar and oil combines. Even if the government had broken up Microsoft, the two halves of the company would almost certainly have retained their strangleholds on the markets for operating systems and consumer software. The subsequent rise of Google and Facebook has only added to concerns about monopolization. Google's grip on the Internet search market gets tighter every year, and Facebook may be on its way to establishing a similar position in social networking. While both companies market themselves as cool Silicon Valley do-gooders, some of their recent actions belie their public image. Google's attempts to digitize entire libraries without getting any copyright approval and Facebook's repeated efforts to assert ownership rights over the information that people post on their profiles both smack of old-fashioned abuse of market power.

In April 2009, the antitrust division of the Justice Department announced it was investigating Google's book initiative, and some reports suggested it might eventually launch a Microsoft-style antitrust suit. A month later, the Obama administration formally abandoned the Bush administration's antitrust guidelines, indicating that it intended to look particularly closely at the high-tech and Internet sectors. Quite what this reversal amounts to remains to be seen, but it seems to mark a return to the approach of the Clinton administration, which Berkeley's Daniel Rubinfeld, who was chief economist at the antitrust division during the Microsoft case, explained to me thus: "In these kinds of markets, it is just not right that leaving it to the market is always going to get an efficient outcome. There is still an honest debate about exactly what role government ought to play, and people are going to differ, but there are very few economists I have talked to who would argue that leaving it to the market is always the best solution. We are just not in that world anymore."

The modern treatment of public goods begins from the recognition that capitalism is a system of property rights. In some cases, these rights are clearly defined and easily enforceable. American Airlines owns planes, which it flies to cities all over the world. For a certain fee, you or I can buy the right to occupy a seat on one of these flights. If we can't afford the fee, we can't get on the plane: that is the basis of free enterprise. Now consider the U.S. Air Force. It, too, owns a big aircraft fleet, which it uses to patrol the skies and protect Americans from attack. The air force provides a valuable service, which, theoretically, it could market to individuals. Why doesn't this happen?

Some free market fanatics might claim the answer is politics. A more realistic explanation is that national defense, like the construction and operation of national parks, doesn't lend itself to private enterprise. If you buy the last two seats on the American Airlines red-eye from Los Angeles to New York, that is the end of the matter: there isn't any space left for me. In that sense, we are rivals for consumption of the good. However, the fact that the air force is defending you doesn't affect the services it is supplying to me. To the contrary, it is virtually impossible to exclude me or anybody else from sheltering under its protection. If the air force were privatized and it offered to sell me an air defense policy for $1,000 a year, I'd say no thanks, knowing full well that its planes and missiles would be protecting my neighbors anyway. This sort of behavior is known as "free riding." Short of issuing a list of free riders that the country's foreign enemies were free to bomb, a for-profit Defense Department could do little to prevent it. The only practical way to get people to pay for the armed forces is to force them to do it through the tax system.

To adopt the ugly terminology of contemporary economics, flights from JFK to LAX are "rival" and "excludable"; hence they are private goods. National defense is "nonrival" and "nonexcludable"; it is the prototypical public good. Other obvious cases include irrigation systems, streetlights, and clean air. Less obviously, but equally important, many public services, such as education and health care, are essentially public goods—a point Galbraith emphasized in his 1958 bestseller, *The Affluent Society*, which contrasted the abundance of consumer durables, such as cars and televisions, in postwar America with the dearth of many collectively provided services. "[T]here are large ready-made needs for schools, hospitals, slum clearance and urban redevelopment, sanitation, parks, playgrounds, police and other pressing public services," Galbraith wrote. "Of these needs, almost no one must be persuaded. They exist because, as public officials of all kinds and ranks explain each day with practiced skill, the money to provide for them is unavailable . . . The economy is geared to the least urgent set of human values. It would be far more secure if it were based on a range of need."

Galbraith's analysis, which has often been reduced to the phrase "private affluence, public squalor," still rings true. Despite repeated efforts on the part of conservatives to encourage private enterprise to build schools, provide low-cost housing, and redevelop run-down areas, governments continue to bear the financial burden in these areas, and in many others. Indeed, for all the efforts of Margaret Thatcher and Ronald Reagan, the role of the state has continued to expand. To be sure, other factors have played a role in this process, such as a concern about equity, interest-group activity, and pork barrel spending. Still, Galbraith's main point stands: "[T]o a far greater degree than is commonly supposed, functions accrue to the state because, as a purely technical matter, there is no alternative to public management."

In the domain of goods and services that are nonrival and nonexcludable, public provision isn't just inevitable; it is necessary on classical economic grounds to secure a Pareto-efficient outcome. Relying on the market to provide both private and public goods will always lead to underprovision of the latter. Similarly, in monopolistic industries, producers will produce too little and charge too much. "We need not pursue the fine detail," Bator wrote in 1960. "The point is clear enough—public goods and decreasing cost phenomena cause private market decisions to go wrong. Market prices will fail to approximate true scarcity values in terms of wants; they will be loaded with misinformation, and producers' profit calculations will leave out of account much of the private benefit associated with public goods. The 'invisible hand' will fumble: people's decentralized market choices will not efficiently cater to their tastes."

A highly important public good that largely escaped the attention of economists until pretty recently is scientific knowledge. Back in the 1950s, Robert Solow, an economist at MIT, calculated that between 1909 and 1949, technical progress accounted for about 51 percent of the annual growth in U.S. GDP, which meant it had made a bigger contribution to American prosperity than population growth and the accumulation of capital combined. Subsequent studies confirmed that the application of scientific knowledge, in the form of new inventions and new methods of organizing production, is central to the growth process, but for many years economists had little to say about where this technological advancement came from and whether it could be speeded up. Solow joked that it was "manna" from heaven.

Things started to change in the early 1980s, when Paul Romer, a Stanford economist whose father, Buddy Romer, was once the governor of Colorado, turned his attention to the forces that drive technical change. Romer quickly realized that knowledge is a lot like national defense in that it is nonrival and largely nonexcludable. If Firm A's research and development division comes up with a good idea, such as making tennis rackets out of lightweight graphite composites, Firm B can exploit the same idea without wearing it out. Once a piece of technical knowledge has been invented, preventing other firms from copying it, and perhaps improving on it, is extremely difficult, which means that the originators of new technologies often don't end up benefiting from them—as Netscape Communications and many other innovative companies have discovered. IBM and AT&T are both notorious for having created technologies that other companies exploited. "After the transistor was invented at Bell Laboratories"—which was then part of AT&T—"many applied ideas had to be developed before this basic science discovery yielded any commercial value," Romer noted. "By now, private firms have developed improved recipes that have brought the cost of a transistor down to less than a millionth of its former level. Yet most of the benefits from those discoveries have been reaped not by the innovating firms, but by the users of the transistors."

Romer's work inspired a huge if not universally enlightening literature. Its main importance was that, starting out from a perfectly orthodox position—Romer did his Ph.D. at Chicago, where Robert Lucas was one of his teachers—it ended up undermining Adam Smith's argument that unfettered competition is always the most effective vehicle for promoting economic growth. In an encouraging sign, at least some textbook writers have recognized this point. "That knowledge is both nonrivalrous and nonexcludable creates substantial problems for a market economy," David Miles and Andrew Scott, the authors of *Macroeconomics: Understanding the Wealth of Nations*, note. "Because the output of R&D activity is both uncertain and, largely, nonexcludable, firms would prefer to let other firms discover successful new technologies and then copy them. But this means that no firm will want to spend money on R&D because as soon as they are successful the technology will be stolen, and the firm that spends money will be unable to make any profit. As a result, market economies with competitive firms will not produce enough R&D."

One way of tackling this problem is by strengthening patents, which give inventors and innovators a temporary monopoly on their brainwaves. Another option is for the government to fund scientific research. During the past twenty-five years, the U.S. government has combined both these methods in a strategy designed to maintain the country's technological leadership. By giving universities and other publicly funded research institutes the right to patent their inventions, the Bayh-Dole Act of 1984 created financial incentives for academic researchers to team up with businesses and venture capitalists. According to one study, since the act became law, U.S. universities have created more than 4,500 companies and signed more than 40,000 licensing deals. In research-intensive areas such as information technology and biotechnology, the development of this public-private framework has helped the United States maintain its dominant position.

This strategy recognizes that the key to creating a successful economy is finding a middle ground between laissez-faire and state control. Two of the biggest success stories in the U.S. economy are commercial aircraft production and the rise of online commerce. At first glance, the two industries don't seem to have much in common, but they share a common heritage: the technologies they are based on—the jet engine and the Internet—were both developed by the government. Scientists working for Hitler's Luftwaffe built one of the first high-speed jets, the Messerschmitt ME-262. In the United States, Boeing built a number of prototype jets for the Pentagon, culminating in two long-range jet bombers, the B-47 Stratojet and the B-52 Stratofortress, which formed the basis of the company's first commercial jetliner, the Boeing 707. Then there is the Internet. In the early 1960s, Paul Baran, a computer scientist at the Pentagon-financed RAND Institute, which is based in Santa Monica, invented the concept of packet switching on which it is based. A few years later, the Pentagon's own Advanced Research Projects Agency (ARPA) financed construction of the network, which for the first eleven years of its life was called the ARPANET.

These stories aren't untypical. The list of commercial products that originated in research financed by the Pentagon or NASA includes satellite television, titanium golf clubs, GPS navigation systems, water filters, cordless power tools, smoke detectors, ear thermometers, and scratch-resistant spectacles. It can even be argued that the Department of Defense, through its finance of research into integrated circuits during the 1950s and '60s, was primarily responsible for the rise of the personal computer industry. The Pentagon's Republican defenders would never admit it, but one of its main contributions to the strength and well-being of the United States has been in providing it with a surrogate industrial policy. Freed from the threat of free riders and the imperatives of short-term profit maximization, scientists and companies working for the U.S. military have created many of the technologies on which the country's prosperity is now based. Whether by design or accident, the military-industrial complex, which President Eisenhower warned his countrymen about half a century ago, has arguably done more to encourage scientific research than the entire private sector of the U.S. economy.

Although it is more than a half century old, Bator's taxonomy of market failures remains useful. Increasing returns to scale, monopoly power, and the issue of providing public goods aren't just arcane economic concepts. They are essential elements of twenty-first-century capitalism, and they play an important role in reality-based economics. But Bator, writing in the mid-1950s, couldn't address all of the problems that plague modern economies. Some hadn't become manifest; others hadn't been subjected to productive analysis.

One common problem arises when two or more parties to a given transaction have different incentives. The senior executives of a corporation, for example, may be more interested in ramping up the value of their stock options before they retire than in preserving the long-term interests of the stockholders. The problem, in this case, is designing an incentive package that aligns the two sets of interests.

Another class of problems emerges when the parties on either side of a transaction have different amounts of information. An important issue in health reform, for example, is that individuals know more about their health than insurance companies do, so the insurers are understandably wary about taking on individual new clients with preexisting conditions. I use the word "understandably" because, today, almost all health insurers are profit-making concerns with a shareholder base that demands a certain level of earnings. From the perspective of an individual insurer, it is perfectly rational to turn away sick people. From the perspective of society as a whole, it is inhumane and inefficient. Sick people who don't get treated tend to get worse, at which point, often, they end up in the emergency room, where somebody has to pay for their care. This is an example of what I call rational irrationality. In the coming chapters, we will come across many more examples of it.

11. THE PRISONER'S DILEMMA AND RATIONAL IRRATIONALITY

s the problems of pollution and free riding make clear, many types of market failure come down to the fact of human interdependence. What I do affects your welfare; what you do affects mine. The same applies in business. When General Motors cuts its prices or offers interest-free loans, Ford and Chrysler come under pressure to match GM's deals, even if their finances are already stretched. If Merrill Lynch sets up a hedge fund to invest in collateralized debt obligations or some other newfangled securities, Morgan Stanley will feel obliged to launch a similar fund so its wealthy clients don't defect. Now, the chairmen of the Big Three automakers, despite all the criticism they have received recently, are presumably fairly rational, intelligent fellows who would rather coexist peaceably than get into damaging competition. (For now, we will set aside the mental capacities of Wall Street CEOs.) Isn't there some way they can get together and work out solutions that are beneficial to each of their companies and to their customers, too? Often the answer is no.

Consider the following example. Two firms, each of which owns a coal-burning power plant, are competing to supply electricity to a small town. As things stand, they split the market and each of them makes $20 million in annual operating profits. However, the local residents' association is pursuing a long-running lawsuit to try to stop their smoke emissions, which often blow into residential areas. Defending the suit and paying some high-priced publicity consultants costs the firms $10 million a year each, reducing their net profits to $10 million. At an individual cost of $5 million a year, the power plants could each install a filtering system that would capture most of their damaging emissions. If the two firms introduced the filters, the residents' association would drop its lawsuit, and the firms would each make net profits of $15 million.

At first glance, it seems obvious that the two plants should quit fighting the lawsuit, install the filters, and raise their net profits by $5 million. Things aren't so simple, however. The estimated cost of operating the filters assumes that the two firms introduce them simultaneously and raise the price of the electricity they produce, which brings them some extra revenue. Explicit price fixing of this sort is illegal in most countries: in the United States, it constitutes a violation of the Sherman Antitrust Act. This means that each of the firms has to reach its decision independently, taking into account what the other might do. If one of them installs the filters and the other one doesn't, the laggard will be able to supply power at a lower price, and its market share will increase, perhaps dramatically. For sake of argument, let's assume its annual net profits rise to $20 million, and that the profits of the other firm, the one that installed the filters, fall to $5 million. Now what should the firms do?

A convenient way of depicting the situation is to present both of the firms' options and payoffs in the same diagram. (See Table 11.1.) In each entry, the profits in millions of dollars of Firm A appear first and the profits of Firm B appear second. For example, in the upper-right-hand corner, Firm A makes $5 million and Firm B makes $20 million.

The way to think about this situation is that Firm A chooses a row and Firm B chooses a column. For example, if Firm A picks the first row and Firm B picks the first column, it means that both firms decide to install the filters: the outcome is shown in the top-left-hand corner, with both firms making $15 million in profits. If Firm A installs the filters and Firm B doesn't, the outcome is the top-right-hand corner, with profits of $5 million for Firm A and $20 million for Firm B.

TABLE 11.1: THE INSTALLATION GAME

		FIRM B	
		INSTALL	DON'T INSTALL
FIRM A	INSTALL	15, 15	5, 20
	DON'T INSTALL	20, 5	10, 10

There are at least two ways to figure out what is the best strategy for the firms to follow. The first one, which I mistakenly followed when I was presented with a problem of this nature in my college entrance interview, is to fixate on the top-left corner, which is clearly the most desirable outcome, and to try to rationalize why the two firms would select it. Initially, this doesn't seem very hard. The total payout if both firms installed the filters would be $30 million, which is higher than any of the other outcomes. Surely, the two firms would realize this. Being rational, they would gladly agree to install the filter systems, earning $15 million each. Everybody would win, the local town included.

To see what is wrong with this reasoning, place yourself in the shoes of the CEO of Firm A and imagine that you have just convinced yourself that installing the filters is the right thing to do. Since your counterpart at Firm B is almost as smart as you are, it is only safe to assume that he has reached the same conclusion, which means Firm B will also be installing the filters. In that case, however, your firm ought to renege on its conversion plans, thereby increasing its putative profits from $15 million to $20 million—bravo! Before congratulating yourself on your fiendish cunning, take a breath. The process doesn't end there. If you can figure out this logic, so can the head of Firm B, which means he, too, might well end up deciding not to approve the new filter system. And if that is a real possibility, you certainly shouldn't go ahead with your plans for installation, lest you end up seeing your firm's profits reduced to just $5 million!

This type of logic—"If I do this, he'll do that; if he does that, I'll do this"—might seem a little perverse to those uninitiated in game theory, but if you mull it over for a while, you will realize it is inexorable. The only sustainable outcome is the one in which Firm A and Firm B both continue to pump out toxic emissions and make profits of $10 million, just half of what they could have earned by installing the filters. The firms would like to settle on that cooperative outcome, in which they would both earn $15 million, but the temptation of trying to steal extra market share, and the threat of the other firm doing the same thing, are too great.

The situation that Firms A and B find themselves in is known as the prisoner's dilemma. In many cases, it is the basis of what I call rational irrationality, by which I mean a situation in which the application of rational self-interest in the marketplace leads to an inferior and socially irrational outcome. When the prisoner's dilemma was first introduced, back in the early 1950s, many people refused to accept that the two firms wouldn't be able to reach the cooperative solution. Economists and mathematicians were excitedly exploring the new science of game theory that John von Neumann and Oskar Morgenstern had invented in their 1944 treatise *Theory of Games and Economic Behavior*. Many smart people held out great hope for game theory, imagining it could solve many of the outstanding problems in the social sciences. The key to this process was thought to lie in extending the solution methods that von Neumann and Morgenstern had introduced, most of which applied to zero-sum games, such as coin-tossing and poker. In games of that nature, the players compete against one another, and one player's winnings are another player's losses. But many types of economic activity, such as international trade and investing in the stock market, involve the possibility of cooperation and mutual gains: they are positive-sum games. During the late 1940s, some progress was made in tackling this broader category of problems when John Nash, a Princeton mathematician, introduced a general method for solving non-zero-sum games, but much remained unclear.

Merrill Flood and Melvin Dresher were two mathematicians working at the RAND Corporation, which the Pentagon had founded in the aftermath of World War II to engage in scientific research "for the public welfare and security of the United States of America." Much of the work undertaken at RAND had military implications, but it was also an important center of operations research and other applications of mathematics. Flood got interested in how people actually played the sorts of non-zero-sum economic games that von Neumann and Nash

had theorized about: Did they cooperate and reach a mutually beneficial solution? Or did they lapse into cutthroat competition? One of
Flood's first experiments involved his three teenage children. He offered them a babysitting job and arranged an informal reverse auction,
asking each of the teenagers to submit the lowest wage they would
accept to do the job, with the bidding starting at $4.00. Despite ex-
plicit encouragement from Dresher to get together and avoid a bidding
war, the young Dreshers ended up submitting competing bids, and the
winning bid, which landed the job, was just $0.90. If the three teen-
agers had agreed to submit a single bid of four dollars, they could have
divided the work and money among them, with *each* receiving $1.33.

That was how children behaved; what about supersmart adults?
In January 1950, Flood and Dresher recruited a couple of friends,
another RAND scholar named John D. Williams and a UCLA economist named Armen Alchian, to play a game similar to the one involving
Firm A and Firm B, and they had them play it a hundred times in a
row. At this stage, Flood and Dresher didn't have a name for their
game; in their research they simply called it "a Non-cooperative Pair."
The outcome of the exercise was inconclusive. Alchian chose the cooperative strategy (the equivalent to "Install") sixty-eight times out of
a hundred, and he selected the self-seeking strategy (the equivalent to
"Not Install") thirty-two times. Williams picked the cooperative strategy seventy-eight times and the self-seeking strategy twenty-two times.
The results could be read as providing evidence that cooperation was
feasible, after all; but they could also be interpreted as demonstrating
that even experts in game theory sometimes couldn't resist the self-
seeking strategy that would lead to an inferior outcome.

The prisoner's dilemma received its name a few months later. Albert
Tucker, a Princeton mathematician who had an affiliation with RAND,
was asked to give a talk on game theory to a group of psychologists at
Stanford. To make the concepts underlying Flood and Dresher's experiment easier to understand, he invented a story about two men who,
having been arrested and charged with jointly carrying out a crime, are
held and questioned separately, with no means of communicating.
Both men have reason to believe that if they both deny the charge they
will be cleared, or charged with a lesser crime. If they both confess
they will face a heavy fine. But if one confesses to the crime and the
other doesn't, the one who confesses will be given a reward and the

one who sticks to his denial will be punished severely. The question is: Should the men confess or deny?

The setup is logically identical to the power plant game, and it can be represented with the same type of diagram. (See Table 11.2.) The only difference I will make to Tucker's original story is to substitute specific prison sentences for fines as the punishments. Each number in the table refers to the number of years in jail that the players will serve. If both men confess to the crime, they each get five years. (This outcome is shown in the lower-right-hand corner.) If they both stick to their denials, they get a year each on a lesser charge. If one confesses and the other denies, the one who confesses gets off free and the other gets fifteen years.

TABLE 11.2: THE PRISONER'S DILEMMA

		PRISONER 2	
		DENY	CONFESS
PRISONER 1	DENY	1, 1	15, 0
	CONFESS	0, 15	5, 5

As in the power plant game, the most desirable outcome appears to be the top-left-hand entry (Deny, Deny), which involves total time in jail of just two years. But what are the chances of the two prisoners achieving that solution? This time, let's tackle the problem in a slightly different manner—the way somebody schooled in game theory would attack it. Assume you are Prisoner 1. The key to analyzing any game is to figure out what your opponent is likely to do and then select your best option in response. Prisoner 2 has two options: If he sticks to his denial, the game is reduced to the elements of the first column. Your choices are to deny and face a year in jail, or confess and get discharged: clearly, confessing is the better option. Now, let's examine what happens if Prisoner 2 selects his other option and confesses. The game is reduced to the elements of the second column. If you stick to your denial, you will get fifteen years in prison; if you confess, you will get five years. Once again, confessing is the better option. The peculiar twisted logic of the game should now be clear: whatever Prisoner 2 does, Prisoner 1 is better off confessing, and the same reasoning applies to Prisoner 2's choice. In the language of game theory, confessing is a "dominant strategy," even though it leads to a bad outcome for both players.

Many people find the prisoner's dilemma infuriating; their instinctive reaction is that there must be some way out of it. According to William Poundstone, the author of an illuminating account of early game theory, from which I have taken some historical details, the founders of the problem felt the same way. "Both Flood and Dresher say they initially hoped that someone at RAND would 'resolve' the prisoner's dilemma," Poundstone writes. "They expected Nash, Von Neumann, or someone to mull over the problem and come up with a new and better theory of non-zero-sum games. The theory would address the conflict between individual and collective rationality typified by the prisoner's dilemma. Possibly it would show, somehow, that cooperation is rational after all. The solution never came."

One criticism that is often made of the prisoner's dilemma is that the noncooperative solution (Confess, Confess) can't possibly be the rational outcome, because rational decision-makers would never choose an inferior outcome. This would be true if the two prisoners were deciding jointly what to do. However, collusion is ruled out by assumption: the essence of the game is that the two players have to choose independently. Another argument sometimes made is that since either Confess or Deny must be the best strategy to follow, both players, being rational, will end up choosing the same strategy. That narrows the possible list of solutions to "Confess, Confess" and "Deny, Deny." Since "Deny, Deny" is clearly the better choice for both players, it must be the logical solution. The problem with this reasoning is that it ignores the element of conflict that is key to the game. If Prisoner 1 believes that Prisoner 2 will deny, it doesn't matter how he reaches that conclusion: it always makes sense for him to confess.

Another objection to the prisoner's dilemma is that it is a one-shot game, whereas many types of economic interactions occur repeatedly: you go to work for the same company every day; Morgan Stanley and Merrill Lynch compete against each other every quarter. If economic decision-makers take into account the long-run gains from cooperation, isn't it sensible to cooperate in the short run, too? This turns out to be a deep question. On a theoretical level, it can be shown that as long as the game is repeated many times and the players don't know when it will end, the cooperative outcome ("Deny, Deny"/"Install, Install") is a rational solution, but so is the noncooperative solution ("Confess, Confess"/"Don't Install, Don't Install")!

Unlike in the case of the one-shot game, where "Confess, Confess" is the single dominant strategy, in the repeated game there are many rational strategies to follow. Another one, for instance, is to flip a coin before each round, confessing if it comes up heads and denying if it comes up tails. In 1980, Robert Axelrod, of the University of Michigan, organized a prisoner's dilemma tournament in which game theorists from around the country submitted fifteen different strategies for playing the repeated game. Axelrod then matched the strategies against one another in a computer tournament. Each match consisted of two hundred rounds, with points awarded according to a payoff box that looked very much like the one in Table 11.2. The winner was a simple version of tit for tat. The exact strategy was: "Cooperate on the first round and then in each consecutive round copy what your opponent did in the previous round." As long as the opponent cooperates, such a strategy can sustain cooperation indefinitely.

Axelrod's findings have received a lot of attention, and they may well help to explain how cooperation is sustained in many areas of human society and even in the animal kingdom. Playing tit for tat signals to other players that you are willing to cooperate, but you aren't a sap. If your opponent plays nasty, he gets punished, which gives him an incentive to revert to cooperating. Applying Axelrod's results to economics is dangerous, though. In many business situations, players don't have the luxury of taking a longer view, which makes the environment more akin to the one-shot game. If you are CEO of a company and you follow a cooperative strategy, only to have a rival CEO double-cross you, the mistake could well cost you your job. On Wall Street, traders are judged on a quarterly basis; if they have one bad quarter, the consequences can be disastrous. Even in journalism, the logic of cutthroat competition can be difficult to overcome. At the offices of one British tabloid, there used to be a sign hanging in the newsroom that read, "Do it to them before they do it to you!" Sadly, that is what most of us learn to do. Experiments with ordinary people playing one-shot prisoner's dilemmas show that many of them start out by denying their guilt and hoping that the other player does the same thing. However, they rapidly discover that cooperating with somebody whose actions they can't control doesn't pay off. By the tenth trial, about 90 percent of the players choose the self-preserving strategy of confessing.

The prisoner's dilemma can crop up in any situation that involves elements of conflict and cooperation. In many industries, firms would like to restrict supply and raise prices, but such a strategy of tacit collusion is difficult to sustain, because each of the players has an incentive to cheat and raise its output. This is especially true in industries that produce a homogenous good, such as oil, where cheating is difficult to detect.

A typical production game is shown in Table 11.3. Here, again, the numbers represent millions of dollars in profits. Each player has a choice of two strategies. "Low" means low output and "High" means high output. The mutually preferred outcome is "Low, Low," with both firms restricting their output and making profits of $100 million. But if either firm plays "Low," the other one has an incentive to play "High." If this happens, the firm that plays "Low" makes only $25 million in profit. Therefore, the dominant strategy for both firms is to play "High," which results in them each making profits of $50 million.

TABLE 11.3: A PRODUCTION GAME

		FIRM 2	
		LOW	HIGH
FIRM 1	LOW	100, 100	25, 200
	HIGH	200, 25	50, 50

Prisoner's dilemmas aren't necessarily a bad thing. In some industries, such as oil and airlines, they help prevent cartels from operating effectively and keep prices down. OPEC, the association of oil-producing countries, is notoriously unstable. Every few months its members get together and make noise about cutting their output quotas to raise prices, but it rarely happens. The governments of many oil-rich nations are so dependent on oil revenues that they can't resist opening the spigots, and the result is widespread cheating on the production quotas. For Western oil consumers, this is a good thing. Much of the time, it ensures a ready supply of cheap gasoline and heating oil. (Whether it is in the long-term interest of Western consumers to run down energy supplies rapidly is another question.)

With some products, however, an increase in output isn't necessarily socially desirable, and the prisoner's dilemma can lead firms to oversupply the market. The residential mortgage may well be such a product. At any given time, a limited number of households have the income and employment security necessary to service a mortgage to maturity. But when house prices are rising and interest rates are low, banks and other financial companies lower their credit standards in search of quick profits, lending to borrowers who are one piece of bad news away from defaulting. Initially, some of the more responsible financial companies hold back—in terms of Table 11.3, they play "Low"—but as they see their opponents gaining market share, the pressure to switch strategies becomes irresistible. Eventually, almost all the firms in the industry adopt a high-output strategy, with deleterious consequences for one and all.

To capture the essential logic of the prisoner's dilemma, I have described the two-person game. In reality, banks and other lenders have to take into account the actions of many rivals: they are facing an "n-person" prisoner's dilemma. With just two people playing the game, it is difficult to sustain a cooperative outcome. When there are ten, or twenty, or a hundred players, it is virtually impossible—a fact highly germane to the overexploitation of natural resources, such as tropical rain forests, the fish in the sea, and the sub-Saharan plains. In 1968, Garrett Hardin, a Texan ecologist who died in 2003, tackled this problem in a famous article, "The Tragedy of the Commons." The example Hardin used was that of a pasture shared by local herders. The pasture is limited in size, and all the herders know that overgrazing will render it useless for everybody. At the same time, though, the herders' incomes are determined by the size of their herds, which gives them an incentive to add more animals to the pasture.

As Hardin pointed out, each herdsman is interested primarily in his own welfare. In deciding whether to add another animal to his herd, he carefully considers the likely consequences of such a step. The upside is that once the animal is grown, he can sell it and keep all of the proceeds for himself. The downside is that adding to his herd increases the dangers of overgrazing, which damages the pasture. However, since all the farmers together will share the costs of overgrazing, the prospect of selling another animal will loom larger in the mind of the individual herdsman. "Adding together the component partial utilities, the rational herdsman concludes that the only sensible course for him to pursue is to add another animal to his herd," Hardin wrote. "And another; and another . . . But this is the conclusion reached by each and every rational herdsman sharing a commons. Therein is the tragedy. Each man is locked into a system that compels him to increase his herd without limit—in a world that is limited. Ruin is the destination toward which all men rush, each pursuing his own best interest in a society that believes in the freedom of the commons."

The story of the herdsman is just a parable, but it illustrates some vital issues relating to the sustainability of economic development. In each country, rivers, lakes, aquifers, mountains, and wilderness regions are part of the commons. The earth's atmosphere is part of the global commons, as are the oceans and oil and gas reserves. Biodiversity in the plant and animal kingdoms is another element of the global commons. Every time a species becomes extinct, the stock of natural resources is irreversibly depleted. Inevitably, the question becomes one of figuring out how to preserve the commons for future generations, or, where that is not possible, how rapidly to deplete it.

Free market economists often argue that privatizing common resources would ensure that they were used more responsibly. In some cases, this may be true—many historians believe the enclosure of common lands in fifteenth- and sixteenth-century England helped to raise agricultural productivity and stimulate economic growth. But privatization doesn't remove the conflict between private benefits and social benefits that defines the commons problem. In the United States, logging companies have decimated parts of the California redwood region, while in New York, Florida, and many other states, rampant real estate development threatens the supply of natural drinking water. On a global level, pollution, congestion, overfishing, and deforestation remain chronic problems, which are only likely to get worse as the global population continues to expand, globalization intensifies, and the demand for natural resources increases. Specifying property rights may well be a necessary part of tackling these enormously complex issues, but blind reliance on self-interest and the market is a recipe for further environmental catastrophes.

The first step in preventing such outcomes is recognizing the pervasive nature of rational irrationality and how difficult it is to overcome. "Game theorists get a lot of stick for denying that the individual behavior that leads to such disasters is irrational," Ken Binmore, one of the world's leading game theorists, notes in a recent book.

> Our critics ask how can it possibly be rational for a society to engineer its own ruin. Can't we see that everybody would be better off if everybody were to grab less of the common resource? The error in such reasoning is elementary. A player in the human game of life isn't some abstract entity called "everybody." We are all separate individuals, each with our own aims and purposes. Even when our capacity for love moves us to make sacrifices for others, we each do so in our own way and for our own reasons. If we pretend otherwise, we have no hope of ever getting to grips with the Tragedy of the Commons.

12. GEORGE AKERLOF'S MARKET FOR LEMONS

In the late summer of 1966, significant things were happening in California's Bay Area. In Haight-Ashbury, a run-down neighborhood of cheap apartments and vacant buildings just east of Golden Gate State Park, a vibrant subculture was developing around marijuana, LSD, and the psychedelic music of Jefferson Airplane and the Grateful Dead, two local bands; in Candlestick Park, out near the airport, which was then home to the San Francisco Giants football team, the Beatles played what turned out to be their final concert before paying fans; across the water in Oakland, Bobby Seale and Huey P. Newton were founding the Black Panther Party.

In nearby Berkeley, George Akerlof, a twenty-six-year-old graduate of MIT's prestigious Ph.D. program in economics, was starting his teaching career. From early childhood, Akerlof had appeared destined for academia. His father, who emigrated from Sweden to the United States in the 1920s, was a chemistry professor. His mother, who met his father while she was in graduate school, came from a bookish family of German Jews. Akerlof was a bright and studious kid. In high school, he later recalled, "I belonged to a small group of students, who in today's terminology would be called nerds . . . Socially, I was a misfit. I failed to understand why my classmates spent the typical free afternoon watching *American Bandstand*."

At MIT, Akerlof studied under Paul Samuelson and Robert Solow, two of the leading figures of postwar economics. By the early 1960s, the subject had been divided into several mutually antagonistic camps. The high theorists were busy debating the intricacies of general equilibrium and game theory. Out in Chicago, Friedman and his followers were pursuing their own libertarian path. At MIT and most other American universities, a pragmatic, if not wholly consistent, mélange of Marshallian microeconomics and Keynesian macroeconomics held sway. (In the textbooks, it became known as the "neoclassical-Keynesian synthesis.") Akerlof wrote his thesis on mathematical theories of economic growth, but he was more interested in the causes of economic fluctuations.

Shortly after arriving in Berkeley, he went to dinner with a colleague, who asked him what he was working on. Akerlof said he was thinking about information problems in the used car market and how they affected overall vehicle sales, which moved up and down in irregular cycles. To say this wasn't a matter of common discussion among professional economists would be an understatement. One of the defining features of economic theory was its abstraction from reality. Neither the general equilibrium people nor the members of the Chicago School paid much attention to the institutional structure of the economy: although their methods varied, both groups pictured the world in terms of Adam Smith's model of perfect competition.

For a bright young economist from a top university to show an interest in something as mundane as the used car market was highly unusual. Still, Akerlof's colleagues encouraged him to keep going, and he did. The nub of his research was the fact that sellers of secondhand cars know a lot more about the trustworthiness of their vehicles than potential buyers, which makes buying a used car a risky proposition. The seller has an incentive to say the car is in good shape, but if that were true, why would he be getting rid of it? To the buyer, the true condition of the car is uncertain. Akerlof believed that "a major reason as to why people preferred to purchase new cars rather than used cars was their suspicion of the motives of the sellers of used cars."

Horse traders and other dealers in secondhand goods of questionable quality have been dealing with this type of dilemma for centuries.

Economists now refer to it as the problem of "adverse selection," but "hidden information" is equally accurate and less off-putting. Within a year or so of arriving in Berkeley, Akerlof had written a paper showing how in some circumstances the presence of "lemons" in the used car market could drive out sellers of higher-quality vehicles, even though there are some customers willing to pay a premium for reliability. "[M]ost cars traded will be 'lemons,' and good cars may not be traded at all," Akerlof wrote. "The bad cars tend to drive out the good."

It is fairly easy to see how this happens. Everybody knows that some, perhaps many, sellers are trying to offload troublesome wheels. Consequently, many buyers of used cars won't pay the prices that sellers of good cars are demanding. Since there is no way for sellers of reliable vehicles to convince potential buyers that their cars aren't faulty, too, many of these sellers will end up taking their cars off the market. When this happens, the only used vehicles available will be cheap duds.

Akerlof entitled his paper "The Market for Lemons: Quality Uncertainty and the Market Mechanism." In 1967, he sent it off to *The American Economic Review*, the leading economics journal in the country. Not long after, he received a rejection letter in which an editor said the *Review* didn't publish articles on subjects of such triviality. Akerlof next tried *The Review of Economic Studies* and *The Journal of Political Economy*, two slightly lesser journals, only to obtain essentially the same reply. Eventually, he got to see a couple of referees' reports, which said the information problem couldn't be as severe as the article claimed, because goods of all qualities did get sold. If the author was correct, one referee said, economics would be very different. A dismayed Akerlof sent out his paper once again: this time to *The Quarterly Journal of Economics*, which published it in 1970. Four decades later, it has become one of the most widely referenced articles in all of economics.

The problem of hidden information arises in many areas other than the market for used cars. In the labor market, employers know much less about the skills and diligence of job applicants than the applicants themselves. In banking, lenders know less about borrowers' ability to repay their loans than the borrowers do. In health care, the providers of medical insurance know less about the health of their customers than the customers do. These examples show that hidden information can exist on either side of a market. In the used car business, sellers have more information than buyers. In the insurance and banking industries, buyers have more information.

Akerlof pointed out that hidden information "was potentially an issue in any market where the quality of goods would be difficult to see by anything other than casual inspection. Rather than being a handful of markets, the exception rather than the rule, that seemed to me to include most markets." The free agent market in sports provides an intriguing case study. Under baseball's laws, any player who has served six years on a major-league team has the right to demand another contract or become a free agent and sign with another club. The hidden information is the player's true state of fitness: many baseball players develop nagging injuries, which plague them later in their careers. A player's original team knows more about his health than a potential acquirer, and the decision to release him to free agency rather than keeping him may be a sign that it has concerns about his health. Acquiring teams therefore face a dilemma. Often, they address it by examining a free agent's medical records and subjecting him to rigorous fitness tests supervised by their doctors; but the evidence suggests that these tests are far from foolproof. Kenneth Lehn, a financial economist who was then at the Washington University School of Business, examined a large sample of players who had signed multiyear deals, dividing them into those who re-signed with their original teams and those who became free agents. In subsequent seasons, the first group averaged fewer than ten days a season on the disabled list, whereas the free agents averaged more than seventeen days on the list. These findings strongly suggest that many free agents are lemons.

Clearly, hidden information doesn't always prevent a market from operating. This is partly because of product warranties, money-back guarantees, and other measures devised to mitigate the problem. In offering warranties, used car dealers signal to potential customers that they have confidence in the quality of their vehicles. On eBay and other retail websites, money-back guarantees are a way of dealing with the fact that, unlike in regular stores, buyers can't physically inspect the goods they purchase. Brand names are another way to reassure customers about quality. When somebody buys a can of Diet Coke or a McDonald's Quarter Pounder, they know what they are getting. Coca-Cola and McDonald's have invested heavily in their brands, and they have every incentive not to sully them by selling goods that don't match people's expectations.

In some venues, though, the problem of hidden information is so acute that it causes serious problems. Unemployed people often discover, to their cost, that the labor market is one such area. There is an old saying that it's a lot easier to get a job when you've already got one than when you are out of work. The reason is hidden information: potential employers don't know you personally, and the fact that you are unemployed indicates that you might be a lemon. Even if you were let go from your previous job through no fault of your own, unemployment carries a stigma. The longer you are out of work, the more serious this problem becomes. Research shows that the odds of getting a new job fall steadily as the duration of unemployment continues. Eventually, many out-of-work people become so despondent that they stop actively looking for work, or drop out of the labor force completely. (In March 2009, according to the Bureau of Labor Statistics, about 2.1 million people were "marginally attached" to the workforce, which means they were out of work but hadn't searched for a job in the previous month.)

Many free market theories ignore this sort of problem. They assume that if people are out of work for lengthy periods, they are choosing to spend time "searching" for a suitable position. In fact most unemployment is strictly involuntary. What the out-of-work need is some way of signaling to employers that they are able and hardworking. Letters of recommendation are often insufficient: too many job applicants can provide them. A signaling device, if it is to really impress employers, has to be hard to obtain. In 1974, Michael Spence, a young economist at Harvard, published a book called *Market Signaling*, in which he argued that higher degrees are particularly effective on this score. Employers are interested in a person's productivity on the job, but productivity at work is often correlated with productivity in other areas of life, such as education. By getting an M.B.A. or a Ph.D., a person can signal to future employers his or her productivity in a way that less-able and less-productive people find it tough to match. Consistent with this theory, highly educated people tend to have lower unemployment rates and shorter spells of joblessness than less-educated people.

Health insurance is another area where the problem of hidden information reaches chronic proportions. The people who need medical coverage the most are the elderly and the infirm; in a market system, they are precisely the ones who have the hardest time obtaining it. The fact that members of these groups develop more serious illnesses than the rest of the population explains the lack of cheap plans targeted at them, but it doesn't explain why no coverage at all is available. In a properly functioning free market, premiums for the elderly should rise to reflect the higher costs of care, but insurers should always provide coverage to people willing and able to pay high prices.

A big reason why commercial insurers are so reluctant to insure high-risk groups, such as the elderly, is that insurance is a lemons market. Think about what would happen if insurers started to offer plans with higher rates for, say, people over fifty-five. (For now, imagine that Medicare doesn't exist.) As people got older and their premiums rose, many of the healthier folk would start to drop out of the plans, leaving the insurers to deal with the frail and the already sick. The insurers' revenue would fall relative to their costs, forcing them to raise prices further, which would encourage even more relatively healthy people to drop out of the system. Eventually, just as in the used car market, only the lemons would remain, and the insurers would suffer big losses.

The only reason most seniors have health coverage today is because of Medicare, which President Lyndon Johnson founded in July 1965. Hidden information creates a market failure that only government intervention can correct. As Akerlof pointed out, "it is quite possible that every individual in the market would be willing to pay the expected cost of his Medicare and buy insurance, yet no insurance company can afford to sell him a policy—for at any price it will attract too many 'lemons.'" Today, Medicare is part of the national fabric, and the same argument that justifies its existence can be made for universal health insurance.

Most Americans obtain coverage from their employers. Since good health is generally a precondition for employment, the group plans skim off many of the healthiest citizens, leaving the self-employed, the unemployed, and workers whose employers don't offer health benefits to seek coverage of their own alongside the sick and the indigent. Inadvertently, the existence of group health plans has helped turn the market for individual insurance into a lemons market. It should be no surprise that individual health care plans are expensive and difficult to obtain, or that some insurers simply refuse to provide coverage to people with preexisting conditions. In any private insurance market, insurers will seek to take on good risks and avoid bad ones. Doing otherwise would hit their profits.

By introducing universal coverage, the federal government could effectively eliminate the lemons problem. If every adult were obliged to obtain coverage of some sort, healthy people would be prevented from dropping out of the risk pool, and insurers would be more willing to take on people with a history of medical problems. Precisely how to manage the transition to universal coverage remains a subject of legitimate debate. During the 2008 campaign, Senator Obama suggested forcing companies that don't offer insurance to pay some of their employees' health care costs; providing tax breaks to make insurance more affordable; and proscribing the practice of refusing people coverage because of preexisting conditions. After getting elected, rather than proposing a reform plan of his own, President Obama laid out a few general principles for such a program, such as expanding coverage to the uninsured, and left it up to Congress to fill in the details.

Whether this approach will work remains to be seen. The key is to acknowledge that health care doesn't operate like the soap industry or the leisure business: leaving things to the "market" isn't realistic. That policy has been tried for more than fifty years, and it has left almost fifty million Americans without health coverage. As is now well known, the American health care system is chronically inefficient. Despite the fact that the United States spends roughly twice as much per person on health care than Canada, the United Kingdom, and France, life expectancy in this country is considerably lower than it is in those three nations. (According to the CIA World Factbook, America ranks about fiftieth among all countries in terms of life expectancy.)

In 2006, total spending on health care topped $2 trillion—that's $2,000,000,000,000. Health care spending already accounts for about a sixth of U.S. GDP, and by 2020 a quarter of the economy could be devoted to it. This isn't necessarily a bad thing: people are living longer, and they value their health more than almost anything else. However, the combination of massive expenditures and poor health outcomes strongly suggests the possibility of reorganizing the system to get more value for money without harming anybody. In the language of orthodox economics, Pareto improvements should be available.

Curiously, a big reason why spending on health care is so astronomical is that most people *are* insured, which means that when they use medical services, they don't pay the costs directly; the insurer foots the bill. One of the first economists to point out how this setup perverts incentives was none other than Kenneth Arrow, the American economist who provided the definitive proof that competitive economies are efficient. But as Arrow frequently pointed out, his work on equilibrium theory didn't take information problems into account. One of the key assumptions of the free market model is that everybody has all the information they need to make the right decisions.

In an article published in *The American Economic Review* in 1963, Arrow detailed many of the ways that the health care industry departed from the textbook model: "The most obvious distinguishing characteristic of an individual's demand for medical services is that it is not steady in origin as, for example, for food or clothing, but irregular and unpredictable. Medical services, apart from preventative services, afford satisfaction only in the event of illness, a departure from the normal state of affairs." Moreover, Arrow went on, "the cost of medical care is not completely determined by the illness suffered by the individual but depends on the choice of a doctor and [the] willingness to use medical services. It is frequently observed that the widespread medical insurance increases the demand for medical care." Insured people with minor ailments invariably seek medical attention. Doctors, who have even less incentive to economize on spending, order too many tests and refer too many patients to specialists. "Insurance removes the incentive on the part of individuals, patients, and physicians to shop around for better prices for hospitalization and surgical care," Arrow noted.

Following Arrow's example, economists now refer to the phenomenon of insurance changing people's behavior as "moral hazard." Ultimately, this is another problem of hidden information: insurers can't fully monitor the behavior of their policyholders, so they try to influence it in other ways. In the cases of hurricane and earthquake insurance, moral hazard is a minor concern, because the policyholders can't affect the probability of a payout. In other areas, they can. Motorists with car insurance tend to drive less carefully and leave their vehicles unattended, which means they are more likely to crash and have their vehicle stolen; drivers with seat belts tend to drive faster; and property owners with fire insurance are less apt to install fire alarms and fire extinguishers.

As Arrow suggested, medical insurance encourages people with migraines to have brain scans and people with mild arthritis to get knee replacements. Insurers try to mitigate this costly behavior by introducing deductibles and co-payments. They also insist on precertification for visits to specialists, limit the choice of doctors whom patients can see, and investigate suspect claims. But such measures add to the insurers' already substantial administrative costs, and they haven't proved sufficient to keep down costs. One way to banish moral hazard would be to do away with health insurance, but that would also eliminate the benefits of risk sharing, which are substantial. Alternatively, insurers could refuse to pay for superfluous tests and treatments that don't offer much prospect of curing the patient. In a competitive environment, however, holding the line is difficult. For any individual insurer, there is always a temptation to offer more services in order to attract more customers.

Arrow and many other economists who have studied the health care industry believe that the only effective way to control escalating medical costs is to move to a single-payer system, where the government could address the problem of moral hazard by imposing some limits on the consumption of medical services. In a 2005 interview, Arrow, who at the age of eighty-three was still cycling into his office at Stanford on a regular basis, said the argument about health care reform "really comes down to the fact that the government is better than the private sector at keeping costs down for insurance purposes. This isn't true in any other industry. If, for example, you are trying to produce electronics, you could hardly do worse than have the government run such an industry. But, in an insurance program, it's a different matter."

Outside of health care, the financial industry is perhaps the area of the economy most subject to information problems. Indeed, hidden information is the primary reason why banks exist in the first place. To reiterate what I said earlier, the financial sector exists to funnel funds from people saving for retirement, and others with surplus cash, to entrepreneurs and firms that need money to pursue business projects. If information were perfectly accurate and free, there wouldn't be any need for intermediaries such as banks: businesses could borrow directly from savers. But the fact of the matter is that banks and other financial institutions provide more than half of the financing for American businesses. (The rest comes from the financial markets and from funds that corporations generate internally.)

A quick mental experiment might help to explain the principle of financial intermediation. Imagine that you had $100,000 of surplus funds that you wanted to loan out at a reasonable interest rate, say 5 percent a year. If you placed an ad in the local newspaper, or on Craigslist, you would surely get plenty of responses, but would you trust your money to any of the people who replied? Probably not—and for two good reasons. The first one is the lemons problem. All of the potential borrowers who showed up at your door would have business ideas for which they wanted money, but you would have no way of telling which ones were genuine opportunities and which were likely to fail. That information would be hidden from you. The second problem is moral hazard. Let's say one of the entrepreneurs' schemes struck you as safe and sound, and you lent him the $100,000 to pursue it. Once he had taken your money, how could you prevent him from investing it in a much riskier venture that might make him rich but would also make him more likely to default on the loan? With great difficulty, is the answer.

By far the wiser course of action is to put your money in a CD, accept a slightly lower rate of return, and let the bank handle the information problem: after all, that is what it is there for. By cultivating long-term lending relationships with businesses, banks are able to mitigate the lemons issue and moral hazard. A properly run bank doesn't extend a loan before it examines the borrower's credit history and convinces itself of the soundness of his or her business plan. Even if the bank decides to extend a loan, it will take additional steps to safeguard its money. If it's a real estate loan, the bank will demand the property as collateral. If the loan is uncollateralized, the bank will charge a higher interest rate and make the borrower agree to a series of covenants, restricting his or her ability to enter new businesses or engage in other risky behavior. As time passes, a bank can monitor its clients' actions by inspecting their checking accounts and demanding regular consultations. Even with all of these measures, banks don't always get repaid. In normal times, though, the precautions they take to deal with hidden information are sufficient to make them profitable, while also ensuring a fairly free flow of credit.

When the economy enters a downturn, however, things change. As firms' revenues and people's incomes fall, many of them try to borrow more money to tide them over. Banks and other lenders can't immediately tell which of these borrowers are good risks or bad risks. All they know is that those who have been hardest hit by the downturn will be those most eager to take out more credit. This creates a serious lemons problem. Fearing that new borrowers will be more likely to default, banks have strong incentive to curtail lending. But if they do this, businesses will be deprived of credit; the economic downturn and the problem of adverse selection will only get more acute. In extreme circumstances, the entire lending market might freeze up.

In solving one set of information problems, banks create others, of which the possibility of a credit crunch is but one example. Since banks don't publish a list of all the loans they have made, the typical bank customer doesn't really know if his bank is sound. If his deposits aren't guaranteed, he has every incentive to withdraw his savings at the first sign of trouble. Since each depositor is in the same position, the possibility of a "run" on the bank is very real. Between 1929 and 1932, more than five thousand banks went out of business, and in early 1933, there was another big wave of failures as depositors in many states rushed to get out their money. The panic was stemmed only when FDR, the new president, declared a bank holiday, during which he introduced a federal system of deposit insurance. Since then, bank runs have been rare.

Deposit insurance provides an effective means of dealing with the problem of hidden information, but it creates moral hazard. If a bank gets into serious trouble, the government will make good the deposits of all its customers up to an agreed limit, which was recently raised to $250,000. Having this backstop gives the managers and owners of banks an incentive to act irresponsibly. In the words of two leading banking experts, "Banks can offer high interest rates to depositors and in turn try to earn the money to pay those high interest rates by making high-risk loans. In this manner, both banks and depositors can engage in imprudent banking practices, secure in the knowledge that if the high-risk loans do not pay off, deposit insurance protects their principal."

There is now a wealth of evidence from all around the world that the existence of deposit insurance encourages banks to take bigger risks, and raises the probability of financial crises occurring. In the United States, the savings-and-loan scandal of the late 1980s and early '90s is Exhibit A. Originally, most S&Ls, or thrifts, were local firms that focused on providing residential mortgages to middle-class families. In the 1970s, many of these thrifts struggled to find depositors, because of competition from bank money market accounts, which yielded higher rates of interest. (For decades, Congress had limited the deposit rates thrifts could offer.) Under pressure from local thrift owners and their allies on Capitol Hill, Ronald Reagan deregulated the S&L industry, allowing thrifts to offer higher interest rates and to expand their lending to riskier areas, such as commercial real estate and junk bonds. At the same time, the limit on insured deposits at S&Ls was raised from $40,000 to $100,000.

In signing the Garn-St. Germain Depository Institutions Act of 1982, Reagan said it would provide "a long-term solution for troubled thrift institutions." What it produced was reckless lending, poor judgment, and outright fraud, much of it linked to a real estate boom and bust across the Sunbelt. By the mid-1980s, many of the thrifts were insolvent and should have been closed down. For several years, they used their lobbying power to prevent this from happening. In 1989, Congress finally stepped in and set up the Resolution Trust Corporation, giving it the power to take over troubled thrifts, fire their managers, and sell off their assets. In just a few years, more than seven hundred S&Ls went out of business. None of the thrifts' depositors lost any money, but the total cost to U.S. taxpayers of cleaning up the mess was about $125 billion.

In many ways, the S&L scandal was a rehearsal for the subprime crisis. The latter, because it included the major commercial banks as well as specialized mortgage companies, was much larger. But the central causes of the two financial calamities were the same: a misguided faith in the free market, deregulation that was heavily influenced by industry lobbyists, and an unsustainable real estate boom. Reviewing the S&L debacle some years later, L. William Seidman, who was head of the Federal Deposit Insurance Corporation from 1985 to 1991, pointed to another important lesson it taught regulators, which would later be forgotten: orthodox economics couldn't be applied to banks and other financial institutions. "As Adam Smith recognized, banking is different," Seidman said. "[F]inancial systems are not and never will be totally free market systems."

Following the pioneering work by Akerlof and Arrow, other economists extended the study of hidden information to many other parts of the economy. One of them was Joseph Stiglitz, who shared with Akerlof and Michael Spence the 2001 Nobel Prize in economics. Like Paul Samuelson, one of his mentors at MIT, Stiglitz grew up in Gary, Indiana, a steel town on Lake Michigan. His parents were FDR supporters, and Stiglitz from his earliest years had liberal views. In high school, he was on the debate team; at Amherst, a liberal arts college in Massachusetts, he served as president of the student council. Moving on to MIT, where he was a class behind Akerlof, Stiglitz quickly established himself as something of a boy genius, editing Samuelson's scientific papers and concocting new mathematical models. (Much later, Samuelson would refer to him as "Joe Stiglitz, who exudes theorems from every pore.")

In a publishing career that dates back to the late 1960s, Stiglitz has contributed to many areas of economics, but his most lasting contribution was to show how information issues are key to many different types of market failure, such as unemployment, credit rationing, and financial blowups. His key insight was that information isn't, as Hayek suggested, fully revealed by market prices. Nor is it, as George Stigler and other Chicago economists suggested, just another input to the productive process, akin to labor or capital. Information is more like air: its adequate provision is a precondition for other things to happen. And when information is lacking, or hidden, the standard theories of economics, such as those of Arrow and Debreu, often don't apply.

In his Nobel lecture, Stiglitz, who is now at Columbia, put the point this way: "In effect, the Arrow-Debreu model had identified the single set of assumptions under which markets were (Pareto) efficient. There had to be perfect information." Working with Bruce Greenwald, who is also at Columbia, Stiglitz published a series of important papers in which he showed that economies with imperfect information—that is, economies that exist outside of economics textbooks—are, in general, *never* Pareto-efficient. In theory, at least, there is always a potential policy intervention that could improve the welfare of at least one person while leaving nobody worse off. Without getting bogged down in technical details, the basic reason why many real-world markets can't be efficient is that the hidden information acts like one of Pigou's spillovers, such as congestion and atmospheric pollution. Spillovers lead Hayek's telecommunications system to issue the wrong price signals. So does hidden information.

By the late 1980s, the new paradigm of hidden information had been widely accepted in the economics profession. It complements and extends the older analyses of market failure provided by Pigou, Francis Bator, and others, which covered problems such as monopoly power, spillovers, and public goods. By their nature, information problems aren't as visible as extortionate prices, smog, and crumbling schools, but in some ways they present even more of a challenge to the free market gospel. "The older market failures were, for the most part, easily identified and limited in scope, requiring well-defined government interventions," Stiglitz wrote in his 1994 book, *Whither Socialism?* in which he discusses the consequences of communism's collapse. "Because . . . information is always imperfect—moral hazard and adverse selection problems are endemic to all market situations—the market failures are pervasive in the economy."

Stiglitz is, of course, a well-known liberal Democrat. By today's standards, he might even be called left-wing. As Milton Friedman's ghost would surely point out, the fact that markets are imperfect doesn't mean that governments can do a better job, or that all markets need close government oversight. In those parts of the economy devoted to the production of consumer goods and the provision of personal services—babysitting, beauty treatments, that sort of thing—private enterprise does a highly effective job of providing what people want to buy. Generally speaking, where brand names and reputations are important, they can serve to mitigate some of the problems caused by hidden information. So can product warranties and money-back guarantees. In areas such as these, the precautionary principle and the experience of the planned economies would suggest leaving well enough alone.

In many areas of the economy, however, the hidden information problem is acute. Pharmaceuticals, finance, and health care provide three important examples. Friedman, as I mention earlier, advocated doing away with the FDA and relying on the drug companies to police themselves. Alan Greenspan, until recently anyway, acted as if he would have been happy to see the SEC and other regulatory agencies closed down, leaving Wall Street to its own devices. Some Republican congressmen and cable television hosts still advocate a fully private system of health insurance. The reality-based economics that Akerlof, Stiglitz, and others helped to develop tells us quite clearly that these are bad ideas. Yes, proposed government solutions to market failures need to be examined critically and monitored carefully, but as Stiglitz noted, the ubiquity of hidden information should "remove the widespread presumption that markets are necessarily the most efficient way of allocating resources. There is, to repeat, no general theorem on which one can base that conclusion."

13. KEYNES'S BEAUTY CONTEST
THEORY OF INVESTING

or almost four decades, Harry's at Hanover Square has been a popular Wall Street gin mill. Opened in 1972 by Harry Poulaka-kos, a Greek immigrant who previously had been a headwaiter at the nearby Delmonico's, it closed for a time some years ago but is now operating again, under Harry's son, Peter. On the evening of Monday, October 19, 1987, I rushed downtown from my apartment in the Village, expecting to find some Wall Street types crying into their glasses: that day, the Dow had plummeted 508 points, from 2,246.73 to 1,738.74, its biggest percentage fall in history—22.6 percent. The selling had been so intense that the New York Stock Exchange's trading systems had buckled. Many brokers had stopped answering their phones, and executed orders had been reported up to an hour late, leaving investors unable to tell where stocks were trading.

To my surprise, Harry's was packed, and there was a carnival atmosphere. Traders and brokers were busy regaling journalists with details of the crash; white-shirted waiters were ferrying trays of champagne and whiskey; glamorous women of uncertain origin were on hand. As a young reporter who had been covering Wall Street for only a couple of months, I sought out one of the older-looking revelers and asked him what the heck was going on. Most of these people worked on commission, the man explained, and with all the panic selling—trading volume on what came to be known as "Black Monday" reached a level never before seen—they had enjoyed one of the most rewarding days of their careers. That evening taught me a couple of lessons about Wall Street I haven't forgotten: things aren't always what they seem; and the interests of financial insiders often differ from those of regular investors.

In retrospect, the size of the fall in the market wasn't very surprising, only its rapidity. The Dow had more than doubled in three years, prices had shot well ahead of earnings, and a number of commentators, such as Elaine Garzarelli, of Shearson Lehman, and Robert Prechter, of *The Elliott Wave Theorist* newsletter, had issued sell warnings. To the economics profession, though, the crash came as a thunderbolt. According to the efficient market hypothesis, which was then at the zenith of its popularity, big market moves happen only in response to news that has major implications for corporate earnings. There was no such news on or before Black Monday. The previous week, Congress had moved to eliminate a tax break for corporate takeovers, and the August trade deficit came in higher than expected, adding to worries that the Fed might raise interest rates, but neither of these things could conceivably have accounted for a 22.6 percent fall in the value of corporate America.

By far the most pertinent news going into Black Monday concerned the market itself. During the previous week, stocks had dropped almost 10 percent; on Friday alone, the Dow fell 108 points. The story I filed that Friday night was headlined "Wall Street Bedlam as Bulls Turn Tail," and it began: "Above the block-trading desk at Shearson Lehman Brothers, situated in the grand new World Financial Center in downtown Manhattan, traders have hung a metal sign bearing a directional arrow that points 'To the lifeboats.'" I quoted Bob O'Toole, a managing director at Shearson, who said, "The bull is dead. I've been in the business thirty-three years, and it's one of the worst corrections I have ever seen."

On Monday morning, millions of investors sought to get out of the market simultaneously, creating an old-fashioned stampede. Computer programs that generated more sell orders as the Dow and S&P 500 slumped below certain levels greatly accentuated the panic. Subsequent research confirmed the theory that the crash was internally generated. In response to a survey from Yale's Robert Shiller asking them what had been occupying their minds on October 19, institutional and private investors ranked highest the news that the Dow had fallen 200 points at the opening; the second most important story the investors mentioned was news of the previous week's declines. Shiller also asked the investors whether they thought economic fundamentals or investor psychology had been responsible for the crash: more than 60 percent of respondents cited investor psychology. "Thus it appears that the stock market crash had substantially to do with a psychological feedback loop among the general investing public from price declines to selling and thus further price declines," Shiller wrote in his 1999 book *Irrational Exuberance*. "The crash apparently had nothing to do with any news story other than the crash itself, but rather with theories about other investors' reasons for selling and about their psychology."

One economist who would not have been in the least bit surprised by the 1987 stock market crash, or by Shiller's explanation for it, was John Maynard Keynes, himself a keen investor. Every day in his rooms in King's College, Cambridge, and later, at his house in London's Bloomsbury district, Keynes perused the newspapers and latest brokerage reports from his bed. During the early 1920s, Keynes speculated on currencies, running up big gains before losing them along with his original stake. In later years, he played the stock market, making considerable sums for his own account and for the King's College investment fund, parts of which he managed. Between 1924 and 1946, the college fund grew from £30,000 to £380,000, an annual return of more than 12 percent during a period in which the world's financial markets were ravaged.

In a book full of annoyingly smart fellows, Keynes, who was born in 1883, has strong claims to be considered primus inter pares. The son of a prominent Cambridge economist, John Neville Keynes, he won a scholarship to Eton, England's poshest school, where he purchased a violet waistcoat, joined the debating team, and distinguished himself in many subjects. After acing the scholarship examination to Cambridge, he studied mathematics, dabbled in economics, and joined the Apostles, a secret society of bright upper-class men who devoted themselves to witty conversation, philosophic contemplation, and same-sex romance. After graduating with a first-class degree, Keynes started reading economics seriously; he also began a graduate thesis on the underpinnings of probability theory. In 1906, he took a break from academia, joining the India Office, the British government department that administered the subcontinent. After a couple of unhappy years in the civil service, he returned to Cambridge, where Alfred Marshall had helped to secure him a lectureship in economics. There he stayed, on and off, until his death in April 1946.

Throughout his career, Keynes applied the lessons he learned in the financial markets to his economic theorizing. The most important was that investing and many other economic activities are carried out on the basis of information that is limited and unreliable. "The outstanding fact is the extreme precariousness of the basis of knowledge on which our estimates of prospective yield have to be made . . . ," Keynes wrote in *The General Theory*. "If we speak frankly, we have to admit that our basis of knowledge for estimating the yield ten years hence of a railway, a copper mine, a textile factory, the goodwill of a patent medicine, an Atlantic liner, a building in the City of London amounts to little and sometimes to nothing." Keynes was not talking about periods of turmoil and crisis, when it might be expected that accurate information would be hard to come by; in his view, a state of near ignorance was the normal course of affairs.

In such an environment, Keynes argued, investors would seek to reassure themselves that the current situation would continue, all the while knowing that at any moment the outlook could be transformed. "A conventional valuation which is established as the outcome of the mass psychology of a large number of ignorant individuals is liable to change violently as the result of a sudden fluctuation of opinion due to factors which do not really make much difference to the prospective yield," he wrote, "since there will be no strong roots of conviction to hold it steady." Keynes went on: "[T]he market will be subject to waves of optimistic and pessimistic sentiment, which are unreasoning, and yet in a sense legitimate where no solid basis exists for a reasonable calculation."

This portrait of financial markets flailing around, with no firm foundation, could hardly be more different from the rational-expectations/efficient-market hypothesis, wherein reliable information about the future is assumed to exist. Individual events can't be predicted, but investors know the probability distributions that determine them, and they can form accurate mathematical expectations. Keynes was writing well before the development of the modern theory of finance, but he refuted it in advance, pointing out that the future wasn't merely uncertain in a statistical sense: it was unknowable. As the author of a doctoral thesis on probability, and as a director of an insurance company, Keynes was well versed in the mathematics of probabilistic risk, which he was careful to distinguish from intrinsic uncertainty.

Insurance companies can't predict the future health of every person who buys a life insurance policy from them, but they are able to price their policies on the basis of actuarial tables that show the overall distribution of human mortality with remorseless accuracy. Unfortunately, Keynes pointed out, many economic decisions are of a one-off nature, and they are taken in situations where "our existing knowledge does not provide a sufficient basis for a calculated mathematical expectation." In 1937, replying to some reviewers of *The General Theory* who had failed to understand the fundamental importance that Keynes attributed to this point, he wrote, "[W]e have, as a rule, only the vaguest idea of any but the most direct consequences of our acts," and he went on: "By 'uncertain knowledge,' . . . I do not mean merely to distinguish what is known for certain from what is only probable . . . The sense in which I am using the term is that in which the prospect of a European war is uncertain, or the price of copper and the rate of interest twenty years hence, or the obsolescence of a new invention, or the position of private wealth holders in the social system in 1970. About these matters, there is no scientific basis on which to form any calculable probability whatsoever. We simply do not know."

Keynes also gave short shrift to the Chicago idea that when prices of financial assets depart from economic fundamentals, professional speculators can be relied on to restore the correct prices: a more likely outcome, he argued, was that they would add to the mispricing. Rather than putting money to work on the basis of what they perceive as the fundamentals, many professional investors concentrate on "foreseeing changes in the conventional basis of valuation a short time ahead of the general public" in order to make a quick profit, Keynes wrote. "They are concerned, not with what an investment is really worth to a man who buys it 'for keeps,' but with what the market will value it at, under the influence of mass psychology, three months or a year hence."

(If he had been writing in today's world of day traders and momentum funds, Keynes might well have written "three hours or a day hence.")

Like John von Neumann, the Hungarian genius who invented game theory, Keynes believed that simple parlor games have much to teach economists: they feature the sort of strategic interactions that are largely absent from orthodox economics, but that play such an important role in reality. On Wall Street, Keynes pointed out, investing is a "battle of wits," the primary aim being "to outwit the crowd, and to pass the bad, or depreciating, half-crown to the other fellow." Translated into today's language, this is the "Greater Fool" theory of investing, which attracted a lot of attention during the Internet stock bubble of 1998–2000. On any conventional valuation basis, there was no justification for the prices at which stocks of companies such as America Online, TheGlobe.com, and Priceline.com were changing hands, but for a couple of years it appeared that there would always be another willing buyer.

Adding a note of specificity, Keynes compared investing to newspaper competitions in which "the competitors have to pick out the six prettiest faces from a hundred photographs, the prize being awarded to the competitor whose choice most nearly corresponds to the average preferences of the competitors as a whole; so that each competitor has to pick, not those faces which he himself finds prettiest, but those which he thinks likeliest to catch the fancy of the other competitors, all of whom are looking at the problem from the same point of view." The basic principle for giving yourself a chance to win such a contest is straightforward: withhold your own opinions and try to select the outcome on which others will converge. "It is not a case of choosing those which, to the best of one's judgment, are really the prettiest, nor even those which average opinion genuinely thinks the prettiest," Keynes explained. "We have reached the third degree where we devote our intelligences to anticipating what average opinion expects the average opinion to be. And there are some, I believe, who practice the fourth, fifth, and higher degrees."

One objection to the Beauty Contest theory is that while investing with the crowd might work over short periods, in the long run, true value will surely assert itself, rewarding investors who concentrate on the fundamentals. Keynes, a skeptic to his bones, presented several reasons why such a fine and just outcome couldn't be relied upon to materialize. Given the near impossibility of predicting the future, investing based on the calculation of cash flows and other economic fundamentals "is so difficult to-day as to be scarcely practicable." Furthermore, many professional investors operate on borrowed money. When the market takes a tumble, as it invariably does from time to time, investors who hold on to their positions in the belief that they are fundamentally sound face the prospect of margin calls from their lenders. If they can't raise the cash to meet these demands, their positions are liquidated. Finally, and perhaps most important, there is peer pressure. The genuine long-term investor who eschews fads and tries to seek out real value will run into criticism from his colleagues and bosses, Keynes said: "For it is the essence of his behavior that he should be eccentric, unconventional and rash in the eyes of average opinion. If he is successful, that will only confirm the general belief in his rashness; and if in the short run he is unsuccessful, which is very likely, he will not receive much mercy. Worldly wisdom teaches that it is better for reputation to fail conventionally than to succeed unconventionally."

Keynes's professional investors are rationally irrational: in their position, aping each other's moves makes sense. If they purchase out-of-favor stocks, they risk lagging behind the market until sentiment changes, which could take some time. In the short run, prices may move further out of line with fundamentals, causing them to make even bigger losses. Following the herd, even when you believe prices have become disconnected from reality, cannot be described as "wrong-headed," Keynes insisted, "For it is not sensible to pay 25 for an investment of which you believe the prospective yield to justify a value of 30, if you also believe that the market will value it at 20 three months hence."

Keynes's jaundiced view of the financial world was consistent with his overall attack on utopian economics. In arguing that individual acts of self-interest led to socially desirable outcomes, believers in the invisible hand had fallen victim to a fallacy of composition—confusing the sum with the parts—Keynes argued. As early as 1907, when he was working at the India Office, Keynes provided an interesting example of this sort of reasoning. At the time, India enjoyed a lucrative near monopoly in the trading of jute, a stringy vegetable fiber that can be strung into sack. Some dishonest merchants were threatening this business by covertly marketing a cheap and inferior form of jute that didn't last. It was theoretically possible, Keynes noted, that as overseas buyers turned away from Indian jute, the mendacious merchants would be forced out of business, and the free market would correct the prob-lem. More likely, though, competitive pressures would force other Indian merchants to mimic the dishonest ones, lest they lose market share. "[W]hile adulteration"—the adding of impurities—"is plainly opposed to the interests of the trade as a whole, it is nevertheless to the interest of every individual to practice it," Keynes wrote. The only solution, he concluded, was for the Indian government to pass legislation to protect the buyers of jute.

The paradox of thrift, which I mentioned earlier, is based on another fallacy of composition. If at the first sign of an economic downturn people start saving more—putting off kitchen renovations, going out to eat less often, and postponing the purchase of new cars—the construction, hospitality, and auto industries will be forced to lay off workers. Unemployment will rise. People will become even more concerned about the future, and even more reluctant to spend. When these knock-on effects are taken into account, an initial rise in saving of, say, $100 can generate a fall in spending of $200 or $300. This is Keynes's famous "multiplier," and it helps to explain how relatively small shocks to the economy can lead to recessions.

In contemporary language, Keynes was pointing out that market economies are subject to positive feedback: downturns have a tendency to feed on themselves and get amplified, with the level of spending spiraling down. The only way to reverse this process is for somebody, somewhere, to spend more. Since consumers and firms are unwilling to do this, for reasons that make sense to them, the burden has to fall on the government, in the form of increased outlays on public works and other programs. Thus the central policy tenet of Keynesianism: the most reliable cure for a deep recession is a big government "stimulus" package.

In Keynes's time and today, some economists have argued that using fiscal policy is unnecessary because the central bank can cut interest rates and revive the economy that way. Keynes was dubious of this argument. When the economy enters a slump, he noted, people of wealth tend to flee from risky financial paper, such as stocks, switching their portfolios into cash. This rise in the "propensity to hoard" short-circuits the free market recovery mechanism, which involves a fall in interest rates and a rise in business and residential investment. Even if the central bank prints more money, the typical response to a downturn, people and businesses will simply hold on to the extra cash rather than spending it. The economy will get stuck in a "liquidity trap," with further increases in the money supply having little or no impact on interest rates or spending. Keynes conceded that liquidity traps were rare, but he claimed that one had occurred in the United States during the financial crisis of 1932, when a large number of banks failed and "scarcely anyone could be induced to part with holdings of money on any reasonable terms."

Whenever the economy is humming, as it was in the United States for much of the period from 1982 to 2007, conservative economists dismiss Keynes's argument for countercyclical spending programs as confused and outmoded. But when hard times reappear, as they inevitably do, governments, regardless of their ideological predilections, almost always administer the Keynesian medicine. The Reagan administration introduced a stimulus package in 1981; George W. Bush's government introduced stimulus packages in 2001 and 2008; Barack Obama introduced one in 2008. In other advanced countries, such as the United Kingdom and Japan, the record is similar.

Despite his dark view of the financial world, Keynes was no socialist or radical. A faithful member of the Liberal Party and longtime adviser to the UK Treasury, he accepted a life peerage to the House of Lords. In his spare time, he was more likely to be found at the Royal Opera House than on the picket lines. Keynes's critique of capitalism was based on reason rather than animus. In switching the level of economic analysis from the individual to the economy as a whole, and in discrediting, at least for a time, some extremely misleading free market doctrines, he made a major contribution not just to economics but to history. "The idea that supply creates its own demand disappeared," wrote Roy Harrod, an eminent Oxford economist who was Keynes's official biographer, "so also did the idea that unemployment is primarily due to unwillingness to work for sufficiently low rewards."

Harrod's biography came out in 1951. He had no inkling that Milton Friedman and other Chicago economists would revive many of the old laissez-faire nostrums, and that some economists who identified themselves as Keynesians would adopt many of the misconceptions Keynes had railed against. Following Keynes's death in 1946 at the relatively young age of sixty-two, bitter disputes arose over his legacy, which continue to this day. The textbook Keynesian model, for which Sir John Hicks (1904–1989) and Franco Modigliani (1918–2003) were primarily responsible, captured some of Keynes's arguments in succinct form, and it dominated policy discussions for more than forty years. But in translating the four hundred pages of *The General Theory* into a handful of linear equations and two simple diagrams, the Hicks-Modigliani model also did Keynes something of a disservice.

In examining the immediate impact of changes in fiscal and monetary policy, not much is lost in adopting the Hicks-Modigliani framework, and much is gained in terms of clarity. But when it comes to analyzing the dynamics of capitalist economies over periods of several years, or more, this "bastard Keynesianism"—the phrase comes from Joan Robinson, one of Keynes's colleagues at Cambridge—won't do at all, because it largely ignores the financial sector. The only financial assets the model admits are money and risk-free government bonds. This excludes many areas where potential instabilities arise, such as the stock market, the commodities market, and the mortgage market. The mainstream model reduced Keynesian economics to a special case of the free market model in which, for some unexplained reason, prices and wages don't adjust to ensure full employment. But Keynes, as he stressed in his 1937 paper, was primarily concerned not with wage rigidity, which he used mainly as an analytical device, but with how the economy operates in an environment of irreducible uncertainty about the future, populated by individuals who don't know very much and are, therefore, susceptible to peer pressure and other inchoate factors such as psychology.

As every economics major knows, and as George Akerlof and Robert Shiller have recently reminded us, Keynes said that "animal spirits," or the "spontaneous urge to action rather than inaction," play an important role in economic behavior. Seizing on these statements, critics of Keynes have suggested that his theories depend on mass irrationality. That is mistaken: they pivot on rational irrationality, rationality that is rational at the individual level but that leads to socially irrational outcomes.

Rationality isn't a binary variable; it exists on a continuum. At one extreme, there is the ultrarationality of the human supercomputers that inhabit the models of Lucas and his followers; at the other extreme, there is unthinking behavior. Most people occupy the middle ground, a realm of purposeful but constricted decision-making, of limited information, of actions motivated by careful forethought *and* rules of thumb. That is the realm of Keynesian economics, and of some of the more recent reality-based economics that he inspired, which I will discuss in the next few chapters. "We should not conclude from this that everything depends on waves of irrational psychology," Keynes wrote in an often-overlooked passage of *The General Theory*. "We are merely reminding ourselves that human decisions affecting the future, whether personal or political or economic, cannot depend on strict mathematical expectation, since the basis for making such calculations does not exist; and that it is our innate urge to activity which makes the wheels go round, our rational selves choosing between the alternatives as best we are able, calculating where we can, but often falling back for our motive on whim or sentiment or chance."

14. HERD BEHAVIOR AND
THE DOT-COM BUBBLE

Black Monday reignited interest in Keynes's view of finance, which had been largely forgotten, at least in the United States. In June 1990, two young economists from MIT and Harvard, David Scharfstein and Jeremy Stein, published an article in *The American Economic Review* entitled "Herd Behavior and Investment," which began by citing Keynes's quip "Worldly wisdom teaches that it is better for reputation to fail conventionally than to succeed unconventionally." Scharfstein and Stein went on to construct a mathematical model, demonstrating that in some circumstances it was an optimal strategy for investment managers to mimic the actions of others rather than trust their own judgments. The setup of the Scharfstein-Stein model was somewhat different from the Beauty Contest, but the reasoning that motivated it was the same: if an investment manager goes with the crowd and things turn out badly, he gets to share the blame with everybody else; if he follows a contrarian strategy, he bears sole responsibility for his mistakes.

"The underlying idea is that if you do something dumb, but everybody else is doing the same dumb thing at the same time, people won't think of you as stupid, and it won't be harmful to your reputation,"

Stein explained to me in an interview some years ago. "We first got motivated by the 1987 crash. The conventional wisdom leading up to it was everybody thought the market was overvalued, but all the fund managers said, 'Gee, all the other guys are in equities, so I ought to be in equities, too. If it goes down, we'll all go down together. If I bail out, I may be the one guy who bailed out too soon.' If you believe this story is true, it means the market is more fragile and unstable. If everybody acts on their own opinion, you'd have a diversity of opinion in the marketplace, whereas this way everybody is following the group. If the group shifts, then everybody shifts."

Following the publication of the Scharfstein and Stein paper, other researchers provided empirical evidence that supported it. After analyzing the hiring and firing of fund managers at mutual fund firms such as Fidelity, Franklin Templeton, and T. Rowe Price, Judith Chevalier, who is now at the Yale School of Management, and Glenn Ellison, of MIT, concluded that young fund managers who followed investment strategies that deviated significantly from their peers were more likely to lose their jobs, regardless of how their funds performed. The threat of being fired gave the fund managers a strong incentive to invest in popular sectors even if they believed they were overvalued, Chevalier and Ellison concluded. In another paper that supported the rational herding model, Harrison Hong, of Princeton, Jeffrey D. Kubik, of Syracuse University, and Amit Solomon, who was then at Salomon Smith Barney, found a similar pattern in the hiring and firing of Wall Street securities analysts—the folks who produce quarterly earnings forecasts that investors rely on. Looking at the period from 1983 to 1996, the researchers found that inexperienced analysts who produced forecasts that differed significantly from the industry consensus tended to lose their jobs at higher rates. Not surprisingly, most young analysts tended to stick close to the consensus forecasts. In a wry conclusion, Hong, Kubik, and Solomon noted that "being bold and good does not significantly improve an analyst's future career prospects."

These findings, and others like them, put some dents in the efficient market hypothesis. Ultimately, though, it was the stock market boom of the late 1990s, culminating in the dot-com bubble, which discredited the idea that rational investors would never invest in stocks they considered overvalued. An early casualty of the rising market was Jeffrey Vinik, the manager of what was then the biggest mutual fund in the country, Fidelity's Magellan Fund. At the end of 1995, Vinik shifted some money out of the market and into bonds, citing "euphoria" among investors. During the first quarter of 1996, stock prices continued on their upward course, and Magellan lagged its rivals. In May 1996, Vinik resigned from Fidelity. "It sent a message that you had better be right or your job is on the line," Barton Biggs, a Wall Street veteran who was then a market strategist at Morgan Stanley, said of Vinik's demise. "He was early, and there's no difference between being early and being wrong."

The mania for Internet stocks can be traced to the August 1995 initial public offering of Netscape, the maker of the first commercial Web browser. The bubble began in earnest in the summer and fall of 1998, when companies such as GeoCities, eBay, and TheGlobe were floated on Wall Street. To begin with, institutional investors shied away from dot-com stocks, citing a chronic lack of revenues and profits, and it was mainly individual investors who bought them. This divergence didn't last long. As many technology stocks doubled, tripled, and quadrupled, those investment managers who had shunned them struggled to keep pace with the market averages. "[I]f they want to beat their benchmarks this year," fund managers "will either have to own Internet stocks or be very proficient in picking other stocks," Brian E. Stack, manager of the MFS New Discovery Fund, told *BusinessWeek* in February 1999.

Some mutual fund companies set up funds specifically to buy Internet stocks; others bought them through existing funds. One of the converts to investing in dot-com stocks was Vinik's successor at Magellan, Robert Stansky. Toward the end of 1998, Stansky sharply increased Magellan's exposure to technology: America Online became the $90 billion fund's fourth-biggest holding, behind only General Electric, Microsoft, and MCI. "I simply can't analyze the Internet sector the same way I analyze other sectors," Stansky said in an investment report to clients. "I do use some traditional fundamental analysis. At the same time, I evaluate investor psychology when it comes to Internet stocks." In the short term, Stansky's Beauty Contest strategy paid off. AOL's stock price rose about 90 percent in the first quarter of 1999, helping Magellan to outpace the S&P 500 handily, and prompting Donald Dion, Jr., the publisher of the *Fidelity Independent Adviser* newsletter, to comment: "Time has come today to add Bob Stansky to the list of mutual fund manager heroes for the four million Americans who are Magellan shareholders . . . During 1999, the money will pour into Magellan because assets follow performance." When the dot-com bubble burst in 2000, Magellan suffered along with other mutual funds, but Stansky retained his job, thus confirming the Scharfstein-Stein model. Despite the fund's lagging the S&P 500 for a number of years, Stansky ended up running it until late 2005.

The notion that rational behavior on the part of individual investors can lead to a collectively irrational outcome—a bubble—goes back a long way. In his 1841 book, *Extraordinary Popular Delusions and the Madness of Crowds*, the Scottish journalist Charles Mackay gave a pointed account of the famous South Sea bubble of 1720, which was based on the promise of unbounded riches to be garnered from trade with Spain's colonies in Latin America. Many of the investors who took part in the bubble knew full well that the South Seas trade had been exaggerated, and that many of the bubble companies that issued stock in the London market were fraudulent, but they seized on the chance to make some quick money anyway. "When the rest of the world is mad, we must imitate them in some measure," said a banker whom Mackay quoted.

The same twisted but persuasive logic applied during the dot-com bubble. Mutual fund managers weren't the only institutional investors who got caught up in it. In May 1999, *Barron's*, the weekly investment newspaper, published the results of its annual "Big Money Poll," in which it had asked a cross-section of professional money managers, "Is the stock market in a speculative bubble?" Seventy-two percent of the managers said yes; 28 percent said no. At the height of the market, even public pension funds, which are traditionally some of the most conservative investors around, started to purchase bubble stocks. In March 2000, the California Public Employees' Retirement System owned almost $3 billion worth of Internet stocks; the New York State Common Retirement Fund owned more than $1 billion worth.

It is now clear that many hedge funds also played a significant part in the bubble. Research by Markus Brunnermeier, of Princeton, and Stefan Nagel, of Stanford, demonstrates that some of the biggest funds, such as George Soros's Quantum Fund and Paul Tudor Jones II's Tudor funds, were heavily invested in technology stocks during the period from 1998 to 2000. In the third quarter of 1999, the fifty-three hedge funds for which Brunnermeier and Nagel obtained records raised their portfolio weightings in dot-coms and other high-priced technology stocks from 16 to 29 percent. By March 2000, when the NASDAQ peaked at 5,132.52, the hedge funds had devoted almost a third of their portfolios to the Internet and technology sector. (The weighting of these stocks in the market as a whole was about a fifth.) "From an efficient markets perspective, these results are puzzling," Brunnermeier and Nagel noted. "Why would some of the most sophisticated investors in the market hold these overpriced technology stocks? And why would they devote a larger share of their portfolio to these stocks than other investors?"

One possibility is that the hedge fund managers genuinely believed AOL was worth more than Time Warner, and that Webvan was going to challenge Wal-Mart. This notion can be safely discounted. During 1999, several prominent fund managers, including Stanley Drucken-miller, the chief investment officer at Soros Fund Management, said publicly that the rise in Internet stocks was a bubble. Evidently, hedge fund managers were playing a version of Keynes's Beauty Contest, trying to surf the bubble and get out before it burst. According to Brunner-meier and Nagel's research, which appeared in *The Journal of Finance* in October 2004, some of them succeeded: "We find that hedge funds in our sample skillfully anticipated price peaks of individual technology stocks. On a stock-by-stock basis, they started to cut back their hold-ings before prices collapsed, switching to technology stocks that still experienced rising prices. As a result, hedge fund managers captured the upturn, but avoided much of the downturn."

In the efficient market view of finance, you may recall, speculators play a stabilizing role, purchasing undervalued assets and selling short overvalued ones; it is this arbitrage activity that keeps prices tied to economic fundamentals and prevents bubbles from developing. Dur-ing the dot-com era, though, speculators played a destabilizing role, buying overvalued stocks and pushing prices farther and farther away from the fundamentals. In the words of Brunnermeier and Nagel, "Hedge funds were riding the bubble, not fighting it."

The sight of sophisticated investors knowingly helping to pump up a bubble was doubly destructive to the efficient market hypothesis, and to the Chicago project generally. Tens of billions of dollars' worth of investment capital was diverted into flimflam schemes that ultimately came to nothing. (At the same time, some of the dot-coms, such as Amazon and eBay, did eventually develop into profitable companies.) Chicago School economics is premised on the idea that rationality and competition prevent bad outcomes: in this case, rationality actually aggravated the market failure. "Our findings are consistent with the view that investor sentiment driving the technology bubble was predictable to some extent, and that hedge funds were exploiting this opportunity," Brunnermeier and Nagel wrote. "Under these conditions, riding a price bubble for a while can be the optimal strategy for rational investors."

As it happened, this result had been formally demonstrated a number of years before the Internet bubble, in a series of papers that put forward what came to be known as the "noise trader" approach to financial markets. According to this theory, which also reflects the influence of Keynes, investing is essentially a game played between sophisticates and boobs. The sophisticates are assumed to be fully rational, with access to reams of information and an ability to sift significant news from irrelevant ephemera, which statisticians refer to as noise. The boobs are naive and mentally limited. In the description of Andrei Shleifer, a Harvard professor who played a leading role in developing the noise trader model, they "follow the advice of financial gurus, fail to diversify, actively trade stocks and churn their portfolios, sell winning stocks and hold on to losing stocks, thereby increasing their tax liabilities, buy and sell actively and expensively managed mutual funds, follow stock price patterns and other popular models." In short, the boobs react to noise—hence the phrase "noise trader."

While Scharfstein and Stein provided a formal model of the Beauty Contest approach to investing, they didn't convincingly explain why, in the midst of a bubble, it doesn't pay for hedge funds and other sophisticated investors to short overpriced stocks, which will eventually fall back to more reasonable valuations. The noise trader approach answered this question. It showed how in the presence of naive investors, some of whom may react to rising prices by buying more stocks, selling overpriced stocks is risky. Instead of trying to counteract the activities of noise traders, and pushing prices back toward fundamental levels, it may well pay to trade alongside them. "[R]ational arbitrage can destabilize security prices," Shleifer wrote in his 2000 book, *Inefficient Markets*. "Rather than bucking the trends, smart investors might rationally choose to jump on the bandwagon."

Shleifer was born in Russia in 1961, and he arrived in the United States as a teenager. After attending Harvard as an undergraduate, he got his Ph.D. at MIT. In expounding the noise trader approach, he and his colleagues provided reams of algebraic and statistical data, but the essence of their argument can be conveyed with the help of a simple hypothetical example. Imagine it is 1999 and you are a hedge fund manager considering whether to speculate against Amazon.com's stock by shorting it. (The stock quintupled in 1998 and was, to all appearances, grossly overvalued.) To carry out the short trade, you will first have to find somebody willing to lend you as many Amazon shares as you want to short. (That is how short-selling works: the speculator sells a stock he doesn't own by borrowing some stock to give to the buyer. Then he buys back the stock in the market, hopefully at a lower price, and delivers it to the party he borrowed from.) Finding a lender won't be easy. In 1999, Amazon and many other Internet companies, being new to the market, didn't have very many shares outstanding.

Apart from this practical issue, you face "noise trader risk." Let's say you go short ten thousand Amazon shares. Since the speculative fever is raging, and more people are entering the market every day, there is every possibility that Amazon's stock, rather than falling back toward its fundamental value, will go up further, causing you to take heavy losses. And, in fact, this is what happened. By April 1999, the stock had risen another 80 percent, which means the short trade would have been down 80 percent. To be sure, if you have a long enough time horizon, this won't necessarily be a problem. You could maintain your short position until Amazon's price finally tumbles, which it did in 2000.

Patient hedge fund managers, or even mutual fund managers, are a rarity. Most of them get judged every three months. If they have a bad quarter, they can face a slew of investor redemptions. Moreover, most hedge funds operate on leverage, which makes them subject to margin calls if their trades go wrong. As Keynes pointed out, the difficulty of financing a losing position is a significant disincentive to speculating on the basis of fundamentals. Shleifer elucidated this point: "This risk comes from the unpredictability of the future resale price or, put differently, from the possibility that the mispricing gets worse before it disappears," he wrote. "[E]ven an arbitrage that looks nearly perfect from the outside is in reality quite risky and therefore likely to be limited."

Surfing the bubble, on the other hand, is relatively straightforward, at least in theory. In one paper, Shleifer and his colleagues developed a model of the stock market divided into four time periods. During the first period, not much happens. In the second period, rational speculators bid up prices, hoping to entice noise traders into the market. The strategy works. At the start of the next period, noise traders, having seen prices rising, start buying, which pushes prices up even further. Meanwhile, the speculators sell out at higher prices than they paid. In the fourth period, prices collapse, and the boobs suffer losses.

The model is neat—too neat, probably. As the Internet bubble demonstrated, knowing when to get in and out of the market can be a major challenge. The experience of Stanley Druckenmiller, the much feted manager of Soros's Quantum Fund, was particularly illuminating. In early 1999, Druckenmiller decided to sell many of his technology holdings. During the ensuing months, Quantum lagged its rivals, and in the summer of 1999, Druckenmiller reversed course, making new bets on Cisco Systems and other Internet-related stocks. "We were too early in calling the bursting of the Internet bubble," he told *The Wall Street Journal*. The way things turned out, Druckenmiller would have done better sticking to his original judgment. When the bubble burst, in March and April 2000, the Soros funds lost close to $2.5 billion; soon after that, Druckenmiller resigned.

If rational herding is a big factor in financial markets, the prices of stocks and other securities should display some predictable patterns. As I explain in Part I, Eugene Fama and other defenders of the efficient market hypothesis claimed that stocks moved randomly, but during the 1980s and '90s, strong evidence emerged that this wasn't the case. Researchers showed that stocks did better in January than in other months, and did better on Mondays than on other days of the week. They also showed that small cap stocks outperform large cap stocks; and that value stocks—those with a low price-to-dividend ratio or price-to-earnings ratio—outperform growth stocks. Confirming the point Benoit Mandelbrot made as early as 1963, researchers also demonstrated that successive movements in the market are correlated. Upward moves tend to come in clumps, and so do downward moves. And it isn't just price changes that display this pattern: trading volumes and volatility are clustered, too.

Fama himself coauthored two revisionist papers. In one of them, which *The Journal of Finance* published in June 1992, he and Kenneth French, of Dartmouth, showed that between 1963 and 1990, stocks that traded at low prices relative to the value of the physical and intellectual assets of the company (value stocks) systematically outperformed stocks that traded at high prices relative to book value (growth stocks). In another paper, using monthly data from 1941 to 1986, Fama and French found that more than a quarter of the variability in total market returns could be explained by examining the initial dividend yield alone. Roughly speaking, when the dividend yield was low, stocks tended to do badly in subsequent years; when the dividend yield was high, stocks did well in subsequent years.

The suggestion that the market does, after all, follow some predictable patterns sparked an academic debate that kept financial economists busy for more than a decade. Amid the welter of claims, counterclaims, and counter-counterclaims, two findings stand out. On a short-term basis—days, weeks, and months—stocks do tend to follow trends: winners keep winning; losers keep losing. But over the longer term— several years, say—the high fliers tend to fall back to earth, and the dogs get up and bark. Statistically speaking, stocks display short-term momentum and long-term mean reversion.

Rational herd behavior can help to explain some of these patterns. In an exercise using data from 1965 to 1989, Narasimhan Jegadeesh, of the University of Illinois, and Sheridan Titman, of the University of Texas, Austin, examined how a fund manager would have done who edited his investment portfolio every month, buying stocks that had risen in the previous three to twelve months and selling stocks that had fallen in that period. "The strategy of chasing the winners did much better than the average, and this was true for every single three-year period over the past thirty years," Titman explained to me. "Fund managers that were buying stocks whose prices were going up looked a lot better than the ones which didn't." This finding, and others like it, has not gone unnoticed. Many hedge funds now have "momentum funds," which buy stocks that appear to be going up and hold on to them for short periods, maybe as short as a few hours or days. These funds don't even pretend to estimate the fundamental values of the securities they buy. They simply follow the crowd, figuring that many other investors will do the same thing.

The revival of interest in Keynes's Beauty Contest didn't occur in a vacuum: it coincided with a series of speculative manias. After the Japanese real estate and stock bubble of the late 1980s, the technology stock bubble in the United States, and the housing bubble of 2002–2006, it is hard to say with a straight face that asset prices always reflect economic fundamentals, and that herding isn't a major problem. The efficient market hypothesis has finally been discredited; even some of its original promoters admit it was oversold. In an article that appeared in *The Journal of Economic Perspectives*, Burton Malkiel, the author of *A Random Walk Down Wall Street*, wrote, "[P]ricing irregularities and even predictable patterns in stock returns can appear over time and even persist for short periods." During the dot-com bubble, Malkiel allowed, "the stock market may have temporarily failed in its role as an efficient allocator of capital." Fortunately, Malkiel added, such episodes were "the exception rather than the rule." Malkiel's timing was a little off. His article was published in 2003, just as the housing bubble was getting going.

The proliferation of speculative bubbles also revived economists' interest in psychology, particularly crowd psychology. While the rational irrationality of Wall Street insiders, in the form of Beauty Contest behavior, plays an important role in creating and sustaining bubbles, it doesn't explain the behavior of the millions of ordinary investors—the noise traders—who buy in at the top of the market. To understand what went through the mind of somebody who invested some of her 401(k) in Internet stocks during 1999, or borrowed heavily to buy a new home in 2006, it is necessary to consider a variety of psychological factors that economists long neglected, such as myopia, overconfidence, and peer pressure. In experimental psychology, the study of these phenomena has a long history.

In the early 1950s, a psychologist at Swarthmore College, Solomon Asch, invited some male students to take part in what he described as a "vision test." When the young men had gathered in a classroom, seven to nine of them at a time, an instructor told them they would be comparing the lengths of straight lines, and he showed them two big white cards. On one, there was a single vertical line; on the other, there were three vertical lines, one of which was the same length as the line on the first card. The instructor went around the room, asking each student in turn to identify which of the three lines on the second card matched the line on the first card. The exercise was repeated eighteen times, each time with a different pair of cards.

The sight test was easy. The lines had been drawn so that it was immediately clear which line on the second card matched the line on the first card. But in each of the groups, just one of the students was a genuine volunteer. Unbeknownst to this person, Asch had recruited all the others and told them how to answer the questions. In six of the eighteen trials, they selected the line on the second card that was the same length as the line on the first card. But in the other twelve trials, Asch's stooges all gave the same wrong answer, picking a line that clearly wasn't of the same length. This setup placed the genuine subject in an awkward spot: "Upon him we have brought to bear two opposed forces: the evidence of his senses and the unanimous opinion of a group of his peers," Asch noted. "Also, he must declare his judgments in public, before a majority which has also stated its position publicly."

The experiment was conducted with more than a hundred volunteers, at three different colleges. Roughly one in four of the subjects maintained their independence, picking the right line every time. The rest yielded to the majority in at least one of the trials, selecting the wrong line. Some subjects gave the wrong answer virtually every time, completely ignoring the evidence of their eyes. In normal sight tests of this type, the error rate is about one in a hundred. When Asch varied the length of the lines to make the right answer even more obvious, it didn't make much difference. "Even when the difference between the lines was seven inches, there were still some who yielded to the error of the majority," Asch reported.

In follow-up interviews with Asch, the subjects who had given wrong answers greatly underestimated the number of times they had done so, suggesting that they were kidding themselves or that being in a minority of one had actually impaired their eyesight. Some said they had suspected that the other people in their groups had been acting like sheep, copying the answer of the first responder, but despite these suspicions, they also copied their answers. Others said they quickly came to the conclusion that the majority was right, and then attempted to hide their own shortcomings by merging with the crowd. "[C]onsensus, to be productive, requires that each individual contribute independently out of his experience and insight," Asch concluded. "That we have found the tendency to conformity in our society so strong that reasonably intelligent and well-meaning young people are willing to call white black is a matter of concern."

Recently, the urge to join the crowd has been shown to have a neurological basis. A team of researchers led by Gregory S. Berns, a neuroscientist at Emory University, carried out a version of Asch's experiment in which they asked a group of volunteers, all but one of whom were stooges, to look at pairs of three-dimensional objects and say whether they were the same or different. Some of the objects were shown from different angles, so the answers weren't quite as obvious as in Asch's experiment, but when the genuine subjects were questioned without first being shown the responses that others in the group had given, they almost always gave the right answers. However, when the subjects were informed of the incorrect answers the others had given, they often followed the crowd and gave the wrong response: in fact, their error rate jumped to 41 percent.

The evidence of conformity confirmed Asch's findings. What was different in this case was that the subjects were inside MRI machines, whereas the other participants' answers were shown to them on a small screen. Some of the imaging data from these experiments were striking. When subjects submitted to the group and gave the wrong answer, their brains exhibited substantially more activity in the visual cortex and another area of the brain associated with spatial awareness and perception, the right intraparietal sulcus. When subjects resisted the temptation to follow the herd, there was heightened activity in the amygdala, which are associated with heightened emotions. These results, which appeared in *The Journal of Biological Psychiatry* in 2005, seemed to suggest that when people go along with a group they aren't merely making an expedient decision: peer pressure makes them actually perceive the world differently.

On the basis of experiments such as these, it is tempting to view the participants in speculative bubbles as lemmings headed for a cliff. But even lemmings aren't as stupid as they appear. (Recent research suggests that they don't commit suicide en masse, as was once commonly believed.) In 1953, two psychologists from NYU, Morton Deutsch and Harold Gerard, repeated Asch's vision test but with a slightly different setup. This time the subjects didn't meet the other members of their group, and they didn't have to answer publicly: they just pushed a button. However, before they gave their responses, the instructors told them the (often mistaken) answers that other people in the group had given. If the pressure to conform was the primary reason for Asch's results, the subjects in this experiment, who were under no such pressure, should have given the right answer. In fact, many of them also gave the wrong answer. Compared to Asch's experiment, the error rate fell, but not by very much. (It was 23 percent. In Asch's trials, the figure was 37 percent.)

What is the explanation? Deutsch and Gerard concluded that many of their subjects had deliberately given the wrong answers because they simply couldn't believe that everybody else was wrong. Rather than trusting the evidence of their own eyes, they had relied on the mistaken judgments of others. "It is not surprising that the judgment of others (particularly when they are perceived to be motivated and competent to judge accurately) should be taken as evidence to be weighed in coming to one's own judgment," Deutsch and Gerard wrote. "From birth on, we learn that the perceptions and judgments of others are frequently reliable sources of evidence about reality. Hence, it is to be expected that if the perceptions by two or more people of the same objective situation are discrepant, each will tend to re-examine his own view and that of others to see if they can be reconciled."

Economists refer to the tendency to infer information from the actions of others as "social learning." Consider the options facing a hungry person who happens by two restaurants that have just opened next to each other, neither of which has attracted any customers. The person doesn't know which one to pick, so he flips a coin. Now consider the next hungry passerby. He, too, has little information of his own to go on, but he sees somebody sitting in one of the restaurants. Assuming that person knows what he is doing, the second person follows him in. Now there are two customers in one restaurant and none in the other. The next potential customer has a strong incentive to follow the prior two. Ditto the fourth, fifth, and sixth customers, and so on. Given the logic of social learning, one of the restaurants, through pure luck, will end up packed, and the other one will stay empty.

This example is somewhat unrealistic. In selecting from alternatives, an individual usually has at least some reliable information of his own to go on. However, in an article published in *The Journal of Economic Perspectives* in 1998, Sushil Bikhchandani, of UCLA, David Hirshleifer, of the University of California, Irvine, and Ivo Welch, of Brown, demonstrated that this doesn't necessarily matter. As long as private information isn't wholly reliable, rational decision-makers will take into account other people's actions, and the possibility that they have access to better intelligence. Consequently, in many cases, everybody will end up doing the same thing.

Economists refer to this process as an "information cascade." In the real world, whether a cascade forms depends largely on the perceived accuracy of public and private information. In many industries, such as the market for new cars, private information is pretty informative: before purchasing a car, the buyer can take it out for a test drive. The sight of somebody else driving a particular vehicle is suggestive, but nothing more than that. In markets such as this, cascades are unlikely to occur. Speculative markets are another matter. In assessing the value of stocks or commodities, say, the average investor is pretty much at sea. When he sees the price of technology stocks or energy stocks rising, it is hardly surprising if he infers that other investors know more than he does.

The theory of information cascades provides yet another example of how deliberate and purposeful behavior on the part of individuals can lead to collectively irrational results. As Hayek stressed, the primary role of a free market price system is to encode information and signal it to buyers and sellers. But in an information cascade, this signaling process breaks down. Once a cascade begins, "public information stops accumulating," Bikhchandani, Hirshleifer, and Welch pointed out. "An early preponderance towards adoption or rejection" of a single option "causes subsequent individuals to ignore their private signals, which thus never join the pool of public knowledge." In such a situation, economic outcomes are essentially arbitrary. Good products might win out in the marketplace, but so might inferior ones. Stock markets and other financial markets may adhere to economic fundamentals; it is more likely that they will be subject to frequent bubbles and crashes. And all of this is the product of individual rationality.

15. PSYCHOLOGY AND ECONOMICS:
KAHNEMAN AND TVERSKY

n eighteenth- and nineteenth-century Britain, economics and psychology were two branches of the same subject: moral philosophy. As professor of moral philosophy, Adam Smith ranged widely over finance and matters of the mind. Prior to writing *The Wealth of Nations* he published another important book, *The Theory of Moral Sentiments*, in which he argued that human decision-making can be divided into two realms, one involving the emotions, such as fear, anger, and love, which Smith referred to as "the passions," and the other involving reason, "the impartial spectator." Much of daily life reflects a mental struggle between the emotional desire for immediate satisfaction and the practical need for longer-term planning, Smith said. "There are some situations which bear so hard upon human nature that the greatest degree of self-government . . . is not able to stifle, altogether, the voice of human weakness, or reduce the violence of the passions to that pitch of moderation, in which the impartial spectator can entirely enter into them."

The idea of the divided self goes back, at least, to the Greek philosopher Plato. As well as expounding it, Smith identified several other mental traits that later economists overlooked, including an inability to focus on long-term outcomes; a concern for the well-being of others; a tendency to overrate one's own abilities; and an inclination to underestimate risks. Myopia was a basic element of the human condition, Smith believed. "The pleasure which we are to enjoy ten years hence interests us so little in comparison with that which we may enjoy today . . . that the one could never be any balance to the other, unless it was supported by the sense of propriety," he wrote in *The Theory of Moral Sentiments*.

The Wealth of Nations also contains numerous discussions of how psychology affects the economy. In exploring the determinants of wages and profits, Smith referred to the "overweening conceit which the greater part of men have of their abilities," adding, "The chance of gain is by every man more or less over-valued, and the chance of loss is by most men undervalued." He cited the rise of state lotteries, which were so popular in his time that tickets were resold on the black market. "The vain hope of gaining some of the great prizes is the sole cause of this demand," Smith wrote. "The soberest people scarce look upon it as a folly to pay a small sum for the chance of gaining ten or twenty thousand pounds; though they know that even that small sum is perhaps twenty or thirty percent more than the chance is worth." By contrast, people dislike paying insurance premiums so much that "[t]aking the whole kingdom on average, nineteen houses in twenty, or rather perhaps ninety-nine in a hundred, are not insured from fire."

Smith's nineteenth-century followers also displayed a keen interest in psychology. J. S. Mill wrote at length on the subject, putting forward a theory of "mental chemistry," which compared creative thinking to combining chemical elements in compounds. Later in the century, when Francis Ysidro Edgeworth applied the calculus to economic decision-making, he entitled his treatise *Mathematical Psychics*. Alfred Marshall discussed the impact of social conventions on the demand for prestige goods such as silk hats and big houses. Arthur Pigou reiterated Smith's point that people prefer instant satisfaction to deferred pleasure, noting "our telescopic faculty is defective."

It was in the aftermath of World War II that economists began to focus almost exclusively on *Homo economicus*, elevating rationality to a near-sacred principle. By the 1970s, economists had locked themselves in straitjackets, and it took external help to liberate them. Assistance arrived in the unlikely form of two Israeli experimental psychologists, Daniel Kahneman and Amos Tversky, who were studying how people choose between uncertain outcomes, a subject that most economists regarded as having been settled in the 1940s, when John von Neumann and Oskar Morgenstern, the founders of game theory, put forward the "expected utility hypothesis." According to this theory, decision-makers weigh possible outcomes according to how likely they are. If a bachelor has to choose between a definite date tonight with his pals for a beer, or a possible but by no means certain movie date tomorrow night with his girlfriend, he will take the sure thing and head for the bar.

Many choices involving numerous uncertain options are a lot more complicated than this one. Von Neumann and Morgenstern assumed people could formulate probabilistic views of the world and carry out the calculations necessary to make the right decisions. In a series of papers published in the 1970s, Kahneman and Tversky demonstrated the folly of this view. Their experiments showed that when people are faced with problems involving uncertain outcomes, most of them don't even attempt the von Neumann–Morgenstern math, but instead fall back on rules of thumb ("heuristics") and unsubstantiated beliefs ("biases"). To the proverbial man on the street, this view of human behavior might seem like merely acknowledging the obvious, but it challenged the very foundations of orthodox economics.

Kahneman was born in 1934 and grew up in occupied France, moving to what was then Palestine in 1946. Tversky was born in Haifa in 1937 and died in 1996, of skin cancer. As young men, both of them did military service in the Israel Defense Forces: Tversky served his time as a paratrooper, receiving a medal for bravery after leaping on top of a colleague and dragging him to the ground just as an explosive charge was about to detonate next to him; Kahneman worked in the IDF's psychology branch, helping to design screening programs for future officers. After leaving the service, Kahneman got his Ph.D. in psychology at Berkeley; Tversky moved to the United States and did a doctorate at the University of Michigan. It was in the late 1960s, when they were both working at the Hebrew University of Jerusalem, that they began collaborating on research into how people make choices.

Tversky was nocturnal. He worked till dawn and then met Kahneman for a long lunch, at which point they tried out ideas on each other. "We spent hours each day just talking," Kahneman would later recall. "We were not only working, of course; we talked of everything under the sun, and got to know each other's mind almost as well as our own." In experimental psychology, ideas weren't taken seriously unless they had been confirmed in controlled human trials. Kahneman and Tversky carried out a series of these experiments, often using their students as subjects. In 1974, they published an article in the journal *Science* that laid out many of the mental shortcuts, or "heuristics," people use when confronted with complex decisions.

The first, and arguably most important, was the "representativeness heuristic"—the tendency to generalize on the basis of insufficient evidence. Confronted with a given piece of evidence, or sample, people usually assume it is representative of reality. For example, if a person tosses a coin five times and gets heads every time, he or she may well decide that the coin is unfair. But it is more likely that the coin is fair and the string of heads is merely the product of random chance. (If you repeat thousands of times the exercise of tossing a fair coin five times, heads will come up every time about once in every thirty-two trials.) Given the laws of probability, extreme outcomes are much more likely to occur in small samples than in large ones, but even people familiar with statistics tend to ignore this fact. Kahneman and Tversky cited evidence that many of their fellow research psychologists had, on occasion, "put too much faith in the results of small samples and grossly overestimated the replicability of such results."

The tendency to jump to conclusions isn't confined to decisions involving explicit probabilities. In one of the experiments Kahneman and Tversky described, an instructor read out a description of a man called Steve, which he said came from a former neighbor: "Steve is very shy and withdrawn, invariably helpful, with little interest in people or in the world of reality. A meek and tidy soul, he has a need for order and structure, and a passion for detail." The instructor then read out a list of professions—"farmer, salesman, airline pilot, librarian, physician"—and asked the subjects to identify the one Steve was most likely to be in. Statistically, the most likely answer by far is farmer or salesman: there are many more farmers and salesmen than there are pilots or librarians. But because the description of Steve appeared representative of a librarian, many respondents chose that as their answer. (In later experiments along the same lines, Kahneman and Tversky made a point of informing the subjects about the true proportions of each profession in the population, but this information had virtually no impact on their choices.)

The representativeness heuristic is sometimes referred to as the "law of small numbers," and it crops up in many areas. In sports, fans underestimate the chances of a good team suffering a string of losses. In New York, for example, whenever the Yankees or Mets get swept in a three-game series, sports radio is full of people calling for the team's manager to be fired. But baseball is a long season, and one three-game series isn't really representative of anything. Conversely, when an indifferent team or athlete has a string of successes, fans tend to assume it will continue because the team or individual has a "hot hand." Often, they are disappointed. In 1985, Tversky coauthored a study contesting the existence of the "hot hand" in basketball. After analyzing every shot taken by the Philadelphia 76ers in the 1980–81 season, he concluded that a basketball player is less likely to make a shot if he made the last one than if he missed the last one. (Of all Tversky's studies, that one probably got the most publicity.)

In finance, the representativeness heuristic leads people to predict that short-term trends in the market will continue and to underrate the prospects of a major reversal. This can lead to very bad outcomes, especially when it is combined with one of the mental traits that Adam Smith identified and which Kahneman and Tversky confirmed: overconfidence. Once people are convinced that a small sample is representative of reality, they place unwarranted faith in their ability to forecast the future, "with little or no regard for the factors that limit predictive accuracy," Kahneman and Tversky noted. In particular, people often ignore the fact that outliers in one period—be they shooting guards, baseball teams, or stocks—are likely to fall back into the pack during subsequent periods, a phenomenon known to statisticians as "regression to the mean."

Another trap that people fall into is putting too much weight on their own experiences. If asked about the risk of having a heart attack, they answer differently depending on whether somebody they know has suffered a coronary. If asked about the danger of getting mugged in a certain neighborhood, their answers depend on whether they know any mugging victims. And it isn't just their personal histories that cloud people's judgment. Dramatic and salient events of any kind stick in their minds, whereas they are apt to downplay everyday happenings. Since 9/11, for example, many Americans fret more about being killed in a terrorist attack than in a road accident, even though in advanced countries the latter outcome is roughly four hundred times more likely. Kahneman and Tversky refer to this sort of thing as the "availability heuristic." When thinking about the dangers we face, getting blown up comes to mind more readily than getting run over: it is more available.

Kahneman and Tversky also pointed out that people have a general inclination to judge things relative to arbitrary reference points. When the status quo is their reference point, people tend to assume that things won't change very much—the bias of conservatism. There are odder cases. In an oft-recalled experiment, Kahneman and Tversky asked people to estimate what percentage of countries in the United Nations were African. Before the subjects answered, the questioner spun a roulette wheel in their presence, with numbers between zero and a hundred, and asked them if their answer was higher or lower than the number that came up. When the roulette ball landed on ten, the median answer was 25 percent; when the ball landed on sixty-five, the median answer was 45 percent. "Payoffs for accuracy did not reduce the anchoring effect," Kahneman and Tversky noted drily.

Experiments suggest that once a person gets "anchored" on a certain number, or argument, he may well try to cling to it by mistakenly interpreting any evidence that is presented to him as supportive, even if it is actually contradictory. (In the literature, this is known as the "confirmation bias.") In the aftermath of the latest Columbine-style mass shooting, supporters of gun control invariably say, "I told you so," but so do supporters of maintaining an armed citizenry.

In 1977–1978, Kahneman and Tversky spent the academic year at Stanford, where they became friends and collaborators with Richard Thaler, a young economist who had done his Ph.D. at Rochester, a bastion of mathematical orthodoxy. During his graduate training, Thaler had developed a list of anecdotes that seemed to contradict the theory he'd been taught, such as people's reluctance to part with minor possessions—mugs, pens, those sorts of things—and their tendency to divide their expenditures into separate mental accounts (one for leisure, another for rent, and so on). Thaler thought these types of behaviors might be linked to the mental shortcuts and biases that Kahneman and Tversky had identified. In 1980, he published a paper outlining some of his ideas in a reputable but somewhat obscure publication, *The Journal of Economic Behavior and Organization*, and in 1987 he began writing a regular column entitled "Anomalies," in the much more influential *Journal of Economic Perspectives*. The latter series of articles introduced to the rest of the economics profession what would become known as behavioral economics.

In the past twenty years, the field has expanded in many directions. Led by pioneers such as Thaler, Colin Camerer of Caltech, and George Loewenstein of Carnegie Mellon, it has attracted some of the brightest young economists, such as Berkeley's Matt Rabin, Harvard's David Laibson, and MIT's Esther Duflo. In the fast-growing field of behavioral finance, researchers have used the mental quirks that Kahneman and Tversky identified to help explain trend following, speculative bubbles, poor corporate decision-making, and many other phenomena that violate the efficient market hypothesis. The progress that behavioral finance has made is reflected in the fact that Thaler, once the enfant terrible of financial economics, is now a professor at the University of Chicago Booth School of Business. In 2002, Kahneman became the first non-economist to be awarded the Nobel Prize in Economics, which he shared with Vernon Smith, of George Mason University, who pioneered the use of economic experiments modeled on those used in experimental psychology. In announcing the prize, the Nobel committee said that Kahneman and Tversky's work "inspired a new generation of researchers in economics and finance to enrich economic theory using insights from cognitive psychology into intrinsic human motivation."

Often echoing the insights of Keynes and other economists of earlier generations, the best papers in behavioral economics start with a seemingly minor psychological quirk and examine how, in a competitive setting, it can scale up into a significant market failure. For example, Richard Roll, an economist at UCLA, addressed the growing popularity of corporate takeovers. Many empirical studies have shown that these arranged marriages rarely deliver the financial benefits that bidders hope to reap, but that hasn't prevented ambitious CEOs from going ahead with them. In a paper entitled "The Hubris Hypothesis of

Corporate Takeovers," Roll suggested that overconfidence on the part of top executives was the driving force of many mergers; despite all the evidence to the contrary, CEOs kid themselves they are getting a bargain. "[T]he average individual bidder/manager has the opportunity to make only a few takeover offers during his career," Roll wrote. "He may convince himself that the valuation is right and that the market does not reflect the full economic value of the combined firm."

Hubris comes in many forms. Especially when the economy is doing well, businesses and individuals find it increasingly difficult to imagine that anything very bad could happen—a phenomenon known as "disaster myopia." The representativeness heuristic obviously plays a role here, but so does the availability heuristic. By definition, low-probability events such as stock market crashes and credit crunches occur rarely, which means that many people don't have any personal experience of them to draw on. After the 1981–82 recession, it was almost twenty years before the stock market underwent another lengthy downturn. (After the 1987 crash, the market rebounded rapidly.) With the market going up, a lot of money was made. As memories of the past bear markets faded, investors found it difficult to conceive of another lengthy fall in stock prices. Implicitly, they assigned lower and lower probabilities to such a possibility. Eventually, many of them assigned it a zero probability—the so-called "threshold heuristic."

Disaster myopia isn't confined to investors. In 1996, two professors at Wharton, Jack Guttentag and Richard Herring, published an article entitled "Disaster Myopia in International Banking," which was based on the troubled experience of money center banks such as Citibank and Bank of America, which lent heavily to developing countries during the 1970s and early 1980s, only to suffer big losses. In the normal course of their domestic business, bankers experience regular defaults on credit card bills, car loans, home mortgages, and other credit products. They know how to track these defaults, and they do a reasonable job of setting aside reserves to meet them. But Guttentag and Herring pointed out that the banks tend to underestimate the chances of a systemic shock that could render many of their borrowers simultaneously unable to repay their loans, such as the American economy plunging into a deep recession, or a sovereign government defaulting on its loans. When the economy is growing strongly, such a possibility is difficult to imagine (the availability heuristic), and bankers downplay it. Eventually, the danger comes to be seen as so remote that it is ignored (the threshold heuristic), and banks take on too much lending exposure relative to their capital.

Myopia is another mental trait that behavioral economists have examined. In the late 1990s and early 2000s, the U.S. personal savings rate fell sharply. Eventually, it turned negative, meaning Americans were spending more than they were earning, and were running up debts. To an orthodox economist, this wasn't necessarily a point of concern. If people take the rational decision to spend more now and pay off their financial obligations later, that is their concern. But was that really what was going on? In a series of papers, David Laibson and some colleagues argued that many Americans were falling victim to shortsightedness and an inability to plan for the future. Many of them were ignoring the offer of free money, in the form of employer matches to their 401(k) contributions. Even in retirement plans that allowed withdrawals at any time without penalty, about 50 percent of those eligible were failing to contribute up to the maximum matching threshold. "For these employees, contributing below the match threshold is an unambiguous mistake," Laibson wrote in 2005. "Nevertheless, half of employees with such clear-cut incentives *do* contribute below the match threshold, forgoing match payments that average 1.3 percent of their annual pay."

In many cases, it appears, procrastination and laziness play a bigger part in people's savings decisions than economic calculus. At companies where employees have to opt into their retirement plans, only about half of those eligible bother to do so within the first year. At companies where employees are automatically enrolled, with an option to opt out, some nine in ten employees accept the automatic enrollment and make their monthly contributions. This acute form of "status quo" bias extends to the investment choices people make in their 401(k) plans. In plans that offer a default asset allocation— a mixture of stocks and bonds, usually—about three quarters of all participants accept it. Similarly, if a plan's default option involves investing in the parent company's stock, many people accept that, too. "[T]his pattern of investment was unaffected by the prominent bankruptcies of Enron, WorldCom, Global Crossing, and many other firms in the aftermath of the collapse of the technology bubble," Laibson notes. "Employees who lost their entire life savings in the Enron debacle were frequently discussed in the media at the time of the Enron bankruptcy, but American workers have not generalized that message."

Evidently, economic reasoning is not something that comes naturally to people. Maybe this is because of the way the human brain is wired. In recent years, many behavioral economists have adopted Plato's idea that human beings have two distinct decision-making systems, one intuitive and the other deliberative. In a 2003 interview, Kahneman elaborated on this idea. "There are some thoughts that come to mind on their own," he said. "Most thinking is really like that, most of the time. That's System One. It's not like we're on automatic pilot, but we respond to the world in ways that we're not conscious of, that we don't control . . . There is another system, System Two, which is the reasoning system. It's conscious, it's deliberate, it's slower, serial, effortful, and deliberately controlled, but it can follow rules. The difference in effort provides the most useful indicator of whether a given mental process should be assigned to System One or System Two."

To illustrate what Kahneman is getting at, try answering this brainteaser as quickly as you can: The combined cost of a bat and a ball is $1.10, and the bat costs $1.00 more than the ball: What is the price of the bat?

If your answer was $1.00, consider yourself as smart as the vast majority of people who take this test. The actual answer is $1.05. But something about the way the question is phrased makes the answer appear immediately obvious. Your System One urges you to say $1.00, and it takes a deliberate effort to override this automatic response. If you take the time to think about the question carefully, the answer isn't hard to come up with. However, there is definitely an extra level of mental effort involved, which suggests that a different cognitive mechanism is involved. That would be System Two.

Recently, economists and neuroscientists have provided evidence supporting Kahneman's two-system model in the form of brain scans. As blood pumps through the brain, it causes minor changes in the magnetic field, which powerful magnetic resonance imaging machines can pick up, enabling researchers to tell which structures in the brain are particularly active when people are trying to solve various problems. This burgeoning field is often referred to as neuroeconomics. The studies suggest a distinct pattern in brain function. When people are engaged in complicated thought processes, such as working out a mathematical problem, most of the activity takes place in the prefrontal cortex, an area at the front of the brain that is much larger in humans than in other animals. When people get anxious or excited or emotional, there is a lot more activity in the limbic region, which is located deep inside the brain, and which evolved earlier. The limbic region is sometimes called the reptilian brain.

In one demonstration of this effect, Colin Camerer and some colleagues devised an experiment to study "ambiguity aversion"—a mental trait that Keynes identified in his 1921 book, *A Treatise on Probability*, and Daniel Ellsberg, a Harvard economist and government official who later became famous as the man who leaked *The Pentagon Papers*, popularized in a 1961 paper. Imagine that there are two decks of cards, Deck A and Deck B, on a table in front of you. Deck A contains ten black cards and ten red cards; that much you know. Deck B also contains twenty red and black cards, but you aren't told anything else; the number of red versus black cards is kept ambiguous. If you had to pick a black card to win twenty dollars, which deck would you choose from? Most people choose Deck A, which gives them a fifty-fifty chance of winning. That seems reasonable, but now let's change the rules a bit, so the twenty-dollar prize is awarded for picking a red card. Now which deck would you pick? In choosing Deck A last time, you seemingly indicated a suspicion that Deck B contains more red cards than black cards. If that is true, it surely makes sense to switch to Deck B. Or does it? In test after test, people choose Deck A for a second time. The most plausible explanation for this pattern is that people have an intense dislike of ambiguous situations: rather than plunging into the unknown, they opt for the gamble with known odds.

Camerer and his researchers scanned the brains of a group of volunteers while they were playing a similar game to the one I have just described. In an initial set of trials, the players were told how many red cards and black cards were in a given deck, and they had to predict whether the next card would be red or black. In a second set of trials, they were also asked to predict the color of the next card, but without being given any information about the makeup of the deck. The imaging data showed that the subjects reacted differently depending on how much information they had. In the second set of trials, their brains exhibited much more activity in the amygdala, a pair of almond-shaped structures deep in the limbic region. "The brain doesn't like ambiguous situations," Camerer told me. "When it can't figure out what is happening, the amygdala transmits fear to the orbitofrontal cortex."

In some circumstances, it appears, the brain's limbic system can even override its more evolved regions, prompting people to make myopic decisions. In an experiment that Laibson and Loewenstein carried out with two psychologists, Princeton's Jonathan Cohen and Stanford's Samuel McClure, some instructors asked a group of student volunteers to choose one of two gifts: a fifteen-dollar Amazon gift voucher they could use immediately, or a twenty-dollar Amazon gift voucher that they could use in two weeks or a month. The results of the study, which were published in *Science* in 2004, showed that both gift options triggered activity in the prefrontal cortex, but the immediate option also caused a rush of activity in the limbic region. And the more activity there was in the limbic area, the more likely the subject was to pick the voucher that was immediately available but worth five dollars less.

Imaging studies such as this one may well help to explain a number of phenomena that have puzzled economists, such as the popularity of Christmas savings accounts, which people contribute to throughout the year. "Why would anyone put money into a savings account that offers zero interest and imposes a penalty if you withdraw the cash early?" Cohen asked when I interviewed him for an article that appeared in *The New Yorker* in 2006. "It simply doesn't make sense in terms of a traditional, rational economic model. The reason is that there is this limbic system that produces a strong drive. When it sees something it likes, it wants it now. So you need some type of pre-commitment device to make people save."

The rise of behavioral economics and neuroeconomics has presented a direct challenge to the concept of rationality that underpins much of economics. Even among the pioneers in these fields, though, there are differences of opinion as to how far they should go in jettisoning *Homo economicus*. Some, such as Camerer and Loewenstein, believe that the entire rational choice paradigm needs replacing. Others are more cautious. "It isn't a wholesale rejection of the traditional methodology," David Laibson told me. "It is just a recognition that decision-making is not always perfect. People try to do the best they can, but they sometimes make mistakes."

My own view is close to Laibson's. People aren't stupid, but they don't necessarily know what they really want or where their best interests lie. The problem is internal and external. The efficient market/rational expectations approach assumes transparent self-knowledge: in order to maximize our self-interests, we must know what they are. But people are often subject to rival impulses. Their System Two brain tells them to plan ahead, save for retirement, and act cautiously, but their System One brain screams at them to enjoy the moment, make a quick buck, and get ahead of the other fellow. At the same time, as Keynes emphasized, people's knowledge about the outside world, especially knowledge about the future, is often strictly limited. Even if they sit down and try to calculate all the pros and cons of a certain purchase, or investment, the figures rarely give an unequivocal answer.

In this sort of environment, otherwise known as reality, it is hardly surprising that rational irrationality is often a problem. Rather than carefully considering all the options and possible permutations, people tend to react to immediate and obvious financial incentives. If a hedge fund can make a quick return by buying into the industrial sector or foreign market of the moment, it will go ahead and do it. If a stockbroker can earn a bigger bonus by selling more Internet stocks to gullible investors, he will make the sale. And if a homeowner with some spare cash sees the chance to make a quick killing by buying and flipping a condo in a new building that just went up across the street, he'll be around there tomorrow morning to see the Realtor handling sales.

16. HYMAN MINSKY AND PONZI FINANCE

n August 2007, shortly after the beginning of the subprime crisis, a story on the front page of *The Wall Street Journal* said, "The recent market turmoil is rocking investors around the globe. But it is raising the stock of one person: a little-known economist whose views have suddenly become very popular." The economist concerned was Hyman Minsky, an avowed Keynesian who taught for many years at Washington University in St. Louis. From the early 1960s until shortly before his death in 1996, Minsky advanced the view that free market capitalism is inherently unstable, and that the primary source of this instability is the irresponsible actions of bankers, traders, and other financial types. Should the government fail to regulate the financial sector effectively, Minsky warned, it would be subject to periodic blowups, some of which could plunge the entire economy into lengthy recessions. "At a time when many economists were coming to believe in the efficiency of markets," the *Journal*'s Justin Lahart noted, "Mr. Minsky was considered somewhat of a radical." Now, however, many Wall Street economists and at least one former governor of the Fed were eagerly poring over his articles and books, most of which were out of print. "We are in the midst of a Minsky moment, bordering on a Minsky meltdown," Paul McCulley, a managing director at Pacific Investment Management Company, the world's biggest manager of bond mutual funds, told Lahart.

Minsky was born in Chicago on September 23, 1919. He came from a left-wing background: his mother was a trade union activist and his father a member of the Socialist Party. (According to family legend, the two met at a party to celebrate the hundredth anniversary of Karl Marx's birth.) As with Paul Samuelson, Milton Friedman, and many others of his generation, it was the Great Depression that inspired Minsky's interest in economics. In high school he joined the youth section of the Socialist Party, and during his second year at the University of Chicago, which he entered in 1937, he attended a series of lectures on the economics of socialism. The lecturer was Oskar Lange, the Polish economist and technocrat who helped to formalize the concept of market efficiency. Minsky had been majoring in mathematics, but he decided to switch to economics, attending classes taught by Lange and Henry Simons, a true Chicago man who nonetheless was critical of several aspects of capitalism. In the summer of 1942, Minsky spent a summer at Harvard working with Wassily Leontief, one of the pioneers of mathematical economics. After three years serving in the U.S. Army, he returned to Harvard to complete his graduate work and serve as a teaching assistant to Alvin Hansen, who was the leading American Keynesian of his day.

With this admirably catholic education, it was perhaps not surprising that Minsky failed to adhere to the increasingly rigid orthodoxy that took hold of economics during the postwar decades. In some ways, he was a throwback. He expressed his thoughts in clear English, used equations sparingly, and made little attempt to keep up with intellectual fashion. But what Minsky lacked in modernity, he more than made up for in insight. Although he rarely made explicit reference to concepts such as the prisoner's dilemma, asymmetric information, or disaster myopia, his analysis displayed an acute awareness of the various sources of market failure. A keen student of Keynes's *Treatise on Probability* as well as *The General Theory*, he had never accepted that financial markets aggregated economic data efficiently, or that decisions involving the future could be represented as a process of taking mathematical expectations of known probabilities. "To businessmen, portfolio managers and bankers, uncertainty means that decisions are made in the absence of firm knowledge," Minsky wrote in 1986. "For both the doubting scientist and the skeptical businessman, 'I don't know' is often the most appropriate answer to questions relevant to decision-making."

Minsky regarded himself as a "post-Keynesian." Although Keynes, in *The General Theory*, succeeded in his central aim of demonstrating how a free market economy could get stuck in a slump, he didn't explain how booms and busts developed in the first place. His mainstream followers, such as Alvin Hansen and Paul Samuelson, also largely ignored this problem. Their brand of Keynesianism concerned itself mainly with exploring how monetary and fiscal policy could be used to stabilize the economy in the face of exogenous shocks, such as a rise in oil prices or a collapse in exports. The mainstream Keynesian framework treated the financial sector in a cursory manner. It had no place for stock market bubbles, credit crunches, or other Wall Street pathologies. That was the lacuna that Minsky set out to fill. "[T]he Wall Streets of the world are important," he wrote in his 1986 book, *Stabilizing an Unstable Economy*, copies of which were reportedly selling for hundreds of dollars on eBay in the summer of 2007; "they generate destabilizing forces, and from time to time the financial processes of our economy lead to serious threats of financial and economic instability, that is, the behavior of the economy becomes incoherent."

Minsky's analysis of financial capitalism began from the observation that it usually involves the advancing of money today in return for the promise of money in the future. The cash advanced is used to finance the production of investment goods, such as factories, machines, and commercial properties. If all goes well, the new investments will generate enough cash to provide the provider of the initial money with a stream of profits or interest payments, as well as repayment of his principal. However, because the future is inherently uncertain, there is no way to predict if such a favorable outcome will materialize, or if the creditors will default. Therefore, Minsky pointed out, the expansion of the economy depends on the willingness of people and institutions with money "to speculate on future cash flows and financial market conditions."

In a capitalist system, much of this speculation takes place through the banking system, which acts as the primary allocator of capital. During times of prosperity, banks' appetite for risk-taking increases at the same time as businesses and entrepreneurs are seeking more money to finance their expansion plans. In fact, banks and other financial institutions compete with one another to supply additional capital, both by expanding existing forms of credit and by inventing what Minsky described as "'new' forms of money"—by which he meant new types of loans. With borrowed money increasingly easy to come by, investment spending rises, and so do stock prices and corporate profits. This reinforces businesses' demand for credit and the willingness of bankers and other lenders to supply it.

Minsky stressed that this process doesn't depend on any external precipitating event, such as the invention of an exciting new technology or an easing in monetary or fiscal policy, although such things would reinforce the upward momentum. The primary initiative came from the competitive forces at work within the financial sector. Any period of economic stability "leads to an expansion of debt-financing—weak at first because of the memories of preceding financial difficulties," Minsky wrote. The period of calm is "a transitory state because speculation upon and experimentation with liability structures and novel financial assets will lead the economy to an investment boom."

At the risk of oversimplifying, Minsky's argument can be reduced to three words: stability is destabilizing. In the early stages of the cycle, banks will lend only to businesses that are generating enough cash to meet regular interest payments and repay the principal on an amortized basis. Minsky referred to this form of lending as "hedge finance." (Before the rise of hedge funds, to "hedge" meant to take precautions.) As the boom proceeds, competition between lenders increases, and their innate sense of caution gets diminished. Many of them make loans to borrowers who can meet only the interest payments: repaying the principal would be beyond them. Loans of this nature have to be rolled over at regular intervals; Minsky called them "speculative finance."

Eventually, banks start extending credit to people and firms that can't even afford to make regular interest payments. On each payment date, the portion of the interest due that these borrowers are unable to pay gets added to their principal, meaning the longer the loan lasts, the more they end up owing. Technically, loans with this feature are called "negative amortization" loans. Minsky referred to them as "Ponzi finance," because their repayment depends on the borrower somehow getting access to a new source of income. If such a source doesn't materialize, the borrower will be forced to default.

Negative amortization loans are particularly prevalent in the real estate industry. During an economic boom, land and property values tend to rise sharply. This facilitates a big expansion in dubious lending to real estate developers and other speculative entrepreneurs, who pledge the projects they are working on as collateral. Sometimes, banks agree to issue a loan and defer any interest payments until a particular building or development is completed, reflecting a belief that it will be sold at a price that covers the principal and the accrued interest. But there is always a danger that the real estate market will turn before the project is sold, leaving the creditor unable to repay in full. "Such loans impart a Ponzi flavor to the financial structure," Minsky wrote.

No credit boom lasts forever. At some point, lenders get nervous about all the dubious credit they have already extended. This prompts them to call in some existing loans and restrict the issuance of new ones. Where money was flowing freely, it is suddenly much harder to obtain, even for financially sound creditors. This is a "Minsky moment" of the type that Paul McCulley and other Wall Street economists identified in August 2007. Struggling to meet their financial commitments, some shaky borrowers are forced to sell off whatever assets they can liquidate. "This," Minsky noted drily, "is likely to lead to a collapse of asset values," which, in turn, can lead to "a spiral of declining investment, declining profits, and declining asset prices." Unless the financial authorities intervene, lending public money freely to whoever needs it, the ultimate result could well be "a traumatic debt deflation and deep depression."

In what was perhaps a poke at the efficient market hypothesis, Minsky described his thesis that capitalist economies inevitably progress from conservative finance to reckless speculation as the "financial instability hypothesis." Minsky described it as an interpretation of Keynes's *General Theory*, and he also credited the Austrian economist Joseph Schumpeter for influencing his views. "The first theorem of the financial instability hypothesis is that the economy has financing regimes under which it is stable, and financing regimes in which it is unstable," he explained in 1992. "The second theorem of the financial instability hypothesis is that over periods of prolonged prosperity, the economy transits from financial relations that make for a stable system to financial relations that make for an unstable system."

Although Minsky didn't state it as such, the financial instability hypothesis is a theory of rational irrationality, with the individually rational actions of banks and other financial firms serving to destabilize the entire system. "In a world with capitalist finance it is simply not true that the pursuit by each unit of its own interest will lead an economy to equilibrium," Minsky wrote. "The self-interest of bankers, levered investors, and investment producers can lead the economy to inflationary expansions and unemployment-creating contractions. Supply and demand analysis—in which market processes lead to an equilibrium—does not explain the behavior of a capitalist economy, for capitalist financial processes mean that the economy has endogenous destabilizing forces."

Minsky's knowledge of banking wasn't confined to what he had read in books. For years he served as a consultant to and director of the Mark Twain Bank in St. Louis, taking a keen interest in all aspects of its business. In the traditional banking model, which dates back centuries, banks take in money from their customers and lend most of it out to businesses and other borrowers, keeping a small amount in reserve to meet depositors' demands for cash. The source of banks' profits is the "spread" between the interest rate they pay depositors and the rate they charge borrowers. In this version of banking, the banking sector's role is essentially passive: it acts as an intermediary between savers and borrowers, and its activities don't have much impact on the overall level of economic activity.

Minsky pointed out a number of deficiencies in this analysis, beginning with the fact that when a bank extends a loan it creates a very special commodity: money. When banks lend more together, the total supply of money in the economy grows, which means total spending power increases. Similarly, when banks call in loans and refuse to make new ones, the money supply contracts and overall spending power falls. Apart from the government, banks are the only institutions in the economy with the ability to create money, and that is what makes them so important.

Unfortunately, there is nothing in a typical banker's employment contract that says he should take into account the impact of his actions on the economy as a whole, which is another type of Pigovian spillover. As an employee of a public company, his only obligation is to maximize profits, which involves expanding lending when he thinks the outlook is good and refusing to lend when he is worried about the future. But the level of bank lending that makes sense for individual banks doesn't necessarily make sense for the country.

A similar point applies to bank leverage, or borrowing. It may seem strange to think of banks and other financial companies as borrowers; after all, their traditional role is to act as lenders. But in addition to securing money from depositors that they then lend out, banks borrow money in a variety of ways. They issue long-term bonds and short-term bonds; they take out overnight loans from one another in the interbank market; occasionally, they borrow from the Fed. What do the banks do with all this money they borrow? Some of it they lend to individuals and businesses; the rest they invest in financial assets, such as Treasury bonds and mortgage securities. If the returns a bank receives on its financial investments exceed its own borrowing costs, it makes money.

Like any other investor, a bank can increase its returns by increasing its leverage. Take a bank with $100 million in equity and $400 million in customer deposits, on which it pays an annual interest rate of 3 percent. If the bank maintains a 10 percent capital reserve and lends out the rest of its funds at an interest rate of 8 percent, it earns $24 million a year. Now consider the same bank, but imagine that it borrows another $500 million at a rate of 4 percent, raising its total borrowing to $900 million, and lends that money out at 8 percent, too: its profits will jump to $40 million. Simply by applying the magic of leverage, the bank will have increased its return on capital employed by two-thirds.

Where is the catch? In leveraging up, the bank takes on more risk. If some of its borrowers default, or some of its investments sour, much of its capital can quickly get wiped out, leaving it vulnerable to a collapse. To prevent banks from getting themselves into this predicament, regulators examine their loan books at regular intervals and insist on their maintaining adequate reserves of capital. However, banks often find ways to circumvent regulatory guidelines. At the end of

1983, Minsky reported, some of the biggest banks in the country, such as Bank of America and Bankers Trust, were borrowing about ninety-seven cents of every dollar they lent out and invested. Even supposedly conservative institutions such as the Mellon Bank had debts equivalent to more than 90 percent of their assets. The increase in bank leverage ratios "was part of the process that moved the economy toward financial fragility," Minsky wrote. In addition to leaving banks more vulnerable to economic shocks, it generated a lot of irresponsible lending. To employ all the money they had borrowed, banks had to search out marginal customers and extend themselves into new, riskier areas. As Minsky put it, "[T]he leverage ratio of banks and the import of speculative and Ponzi financing in the economy are two sides of a coin."

Another shortcoming in the traditional view of banking that Minsky highlighted was its failure to take adequate account of financial innovation. "Like all entrepreneurs in a capitalist economy, bankers are aware that innovation assures profits," Minsky wrote. "Thus, bankers, whether they be brokers or dealers, are merchants of debt who strive to innovate in the assets they acquire and the liabilities they market." One quick way for a bank to expand its revenues is by extending credit to people and firms that previously it would have turned down for loans because of doubts about their ability to repay. In the era when banks ordinarily held on to the loans they issued until they matured, pursuing such a risky lending strategy generally didn't make sense: the extra income from the new loans wasn't enough to cover the increased probability of defaults. But, beginning in the 1970s, a series of financial innovations transformed the incentive structure that banks faced.

The key development was the rise of "securitization." In 1970, the Government National Mortgage Association (Ginnie Mae), one of three government-sponsored agencies that guarantee certain types of home loans—the other two are the Federal National Mortgage Association (Fannie Mae) and the Federal Home Loan Mortgage Corporation (Freddie Mac)—issued a new type of bond known as a residential mortgage-backed security (RMBS). A bond is simply a loan. It is a piece of paper that promises its bearer (the lender) a set of interest payments over a certain period, together with full repayment of the principal at a certain date. In theory, any economic entity that generates a reliable set of cash flows can issue a bond. Prior to 1970, the biggest issuers were governments, which generate taxes, and corporations. Ginnie Mae's idea was to take a number of home loans, pool the monthly payments they generated, and use that cash flow as the backing for a bond. As long as most of the homeowners kept making their monthly payments, it wouldn't matter very much if a few defaulted or repaid the principal early: there would still be enough cash to pay the bondholders the interest they were owed. Since the individual home loans that underpinned these mortgage bonds were government-guaranteed, the credit risk attached to them was greatly reduced. They received high credit ratings, and they paid an interest rate that was only slightly higher than Treasury bonds.

After a slow start, mortgage bonds proved popular with institutional investors, such as mutual funds and pension funds. Seeing the success of Ginnie Mae, Fannie Mae and Freddie Mac followed its lead, and the number of outstanding mortgage bonds expanded rapidly. Once the principle of securitization had been established, Wall Street firms looked around for other cash flows that could be transformed into sellable paper. In 1977, Salomon Brothers and Bank of America managed the first securitization of home loans that weren't government-guaranteed. During the 1980s, new securitized products and acronyms came thick and fast. In 1983, Freddie Mac marketed the first collateralized mortgage obligation (CMO)—a sort of bond mutual fund in which the cash flows from a pool of mortgages and mortgage-backed securities were divided into a number of different layers, or "tranches." The purchasers of the senior tranches got first claim on the underlying cash flows; the buyers of the mezzanine tranches got second dibs; the holders of the junior tranches were entitled to whatever was left. Two years later, a company called Sperry Lease Finance Corporation created the first asset-backed security (ABS) when it issued a set of bonds backed by the cash flows from a pool of computer equipment leases.

With the development of a secondary market in mortgages and other types of credits, banks were able to sell many of the loans they made. The "originate-to-distribute" model of banking gradually replaced the "originate-to-hold" model. If a mortgage holder whose loan has been securitized falls behind on his monthly payments, it is the buyers of the mortgage securities who lose out rather than the bank that issued the loan.

Unlike many economists, Minsky took a keen interest in these developments, and he didn't view them as wholly negative. In a 1987 paper, he pointed out that the purchase of mortgage bonds and other securitized products enabled investors to diversify their holdings across asset classes and geographic boundaries. (In 2007, it would transpire that some of the biggest holders of U.S. mortgage securities were obscure European banks.) Minsky also noted that the banking industry's eager embrace of securitization was a reflection of the increased competition it was facing for deposits and borrowers. Mutual fund companies and other nonbank financial companies were providing interest-bearing checking accounts, and S&Ls, which previously had been tightly controlled, were offering depositors attractive interest rates. At the same time, many big corporations that needed working capital were bypassing banks. Rather than taking out loans from the likes of Citibank and Wells Fargo, they issued short-term bonds of their own, which were called commercial paper.

Securitization enabled banks to move many of their loans off their balance sheets. This meant they didn't have to keep as much capital in reserve to satisfy the regulators, which boosted their profits. To help this process along, many banks, following the lead of Citigroup, set up special-purpose vehicles (SPVs)—also known as structured investment vehicles (SIVs) and conduits—which became heavy purchasers of RMBSs, CMOs, and other securitized products. (The buyers also included mutual funds, hedge funds, and wealthy endowments.) Thus conceived, the so-called shadow banking system would grow to elephantine proportions while remaining largely beyond the purview of regulators, bank stockholders, and journalists.

Minsky didn't realize the full implications of securitization—nobody did—but he was one of the few economists to draw attention to it. After his death in 1996, some of his colleagues in the small but dedicated post-Keynesian school pursued his interest in financial innovation. In his 2002 book, *Financial Markets, Money and the Real World*, Paul Davidson, of the University of Tennessee, pointed out that almost half the loans that U.S. banks initiated in 2001 had subsequently been transferred to nonbank entities, mostly through securitization. "The downside aspect of this shift in the source of bank profits from interest earnings to originating and servicing fees is that bank loan officers do not worry as much about the creditworthiness of borrowers as long as there is a strong market for these loans," Davidson wrote. "There is therefore an incentive for bank loan officers to become 'loan pushers' and loan traders rather than investigators of the soundness of the borrower's use of loan money."

A confirmed worrywart, Minsky never fell victim to the illusion of stability. As early as the mid-1980s, he perceived a rising threat of financial chaos. Referring to the collapse of the Penn Square Bank in 1982, the federal bailout of Continental Illinois Bank in 1984, and the first inklings of the savings-and-loan crisis, he pointed out that countering financial instability was becoming a "major task" of economic policy. Most economists, including some supposedly liberal ones at places such as the Brookings Institution, supported the efforts by the White House and Congress to deregulate the banking industry: Minsky argued that finance couldn't be treated like other sectors that had been freed of government supervision, such as airlines and trucking. "For a new era of serious reform to enjoy more than transitory success," he wrote, "it should be based on an understanding of why a decentralized market mechanism—the free market of the conservatives—is the efficient way of handling the many details of economic life," twinned with an acceptance that the "financial institutions of capitalism . . . are inherently disruptive. Thus, while admiring the properties of free markets we must accept that the domain of effective and desirable free markets is restricted."

With most mainstream economists still in thrall to the efficient market hypothesis, interest in and sympathy for Minsky's arguments was largely confined to the fringes of the economics profession. During the 1980s and '90s, a diminishing band of Marxist economists, centered around *The Monthly Review*, a small New York journal that had been eking out an existence since the 1940s, focused on what they termed the "financialization" of U.S. capitalism, pointing out that employment in the financial sector, trading volumes in speculative markets, and the earnings of Wall Street firms were all rising sharply. Between 1980 and 2000, financial industry profits rose from $32.4 billion to $195.8 billion, according to figures from the Commerce Department, and the financial sector's share of all domestically produced profits went from 19 percent to 29 percent.

Paul Sweezy, a Harvard-trained octogenarian who had emerged from the same Cambridge cohort as Galbraith and Samuelson, and who wrote what is still the best introduction to Marxist economics, was the leader of these left-wing dissidents. To a free market economist, the rise of Wall Street was a natural outgrowth of the U.S. economy's competitive advantage in the sector. Sweezy said it reflected an increasingly desperate effort to head off economic stagnation. With wages growing slowly, if at all, and with investment opportunities insufficient to soak up all the profits that corporations were generating, the issuance of debt and the incessant creation of new objects of financial speculation were necessary to keep spending growing. "Is the casino society a significant drag on economic growth?" Sweezy asked in a 1987 article he cowrote with Harry Magdoff. "Again, absolutely not. What growth the economy has experienced in recent years, apart from that attributable to an unprecedented peacetime military build-up, has been almost entirely due to the financial explosion."

Minsky and Sweezy didn't agree on everything, but their highly developed critical faculties enabled both of them to see, well before many mainstream economists, that a new model of financially driven capitalism had emerged. In this type of economy, they agreed, the only way to prevent rampant instability was for the government to play a more active role—a subject that Minsky, in particular, spent a lot of time examining. In addition to staunchly opposing efforts to weaken the financial statutes that had been created during the Great Depression, he favored much stricter supervision of financial institutions by the Federal Reserve—another idea that would become popular only well after his death. (He died in 1996.)

As we have recently been reminded, the failure of a big bank or investment bank can lead to a catastrophic panic. It is up to the central bank to prevent such an outcome by lending to the stricken institution, so it can meet its financial commitments, and, if necessary, by organizing a government takeover. Minsky pointed to the Fed's October 1974 closure of the Franklin National Bank of New York, which was the twentieth-biggest bank in the country, as a textbook case of how to handle a failing bank, but he argued that, in the future, the central bank needed to act more proactively to prevent financial crises from developing in the first place. "[T]he Federal Reserve must broaden its scope and take initiatives to prevent the development of practices conducive to financial instability," he wrote in *Stabilizing an Unstable Economy*. "The Federal Reserve needs to guide the evolution of financial institutions by favoring stability-enhancing and discouraging instability-augmenting institutions and practices."

Minsky wrote these words not merely as an economist but as a banking industry insider. Paul Volcker, the chairman of the Federal Reserve from 1979 to 1987, was another banking veteran: before going into public service, he worked at Chase Manhattan. There was little in what Minsky wrote that Volcker would have disagreed with. During his time as Fed chairman, the early years of which were largely taken up with fighting inflation, "Tall Paul"—he is six foot seven—consistently opposed efforts by the White House and Congress to weaken financial regulations. But in 1987, Volcker retired from the Fed and was succeeded by a fellow New Yorker who had a very different worldview.

PART THREE

THE GREAT
CRUNCH

17. ALAN GREENSPAN SHRUGS

peculative bubbles present an extreme case of the financially driven boom and bust cycles that Minsky identified. Citing his influence, the late economic historian Charles P. Kindleberger, who taught at MIT for many years, divided the evolution of a typical bubble into five stages: displacement, boom, euphoria, peak, and bust. The displacement is what gets the speculative process started: it could be the beginning or end of a war, the invention of a transformative technology, or a change in economic policy. Whatever it is has to be sufficiently important to alter how investors and other financial players conceive of the future.

In the case of the housing and credit bubble, the displacement came in the form of a drastic reduction in interest rates. From a peak of 6.5 percent in 2000, the Federal Reserve cut the federal funds rate—the rate at which banks lend to one another—to 1.25 percent in November 2002. There the rate stayed for the next eight months. On June 24, 2003, the twelve members of the Fed's Open Market Committee (FOMC) gathered in the central bank's vast boardroom, which overlooks Constitution Avenue in Foggy Bottom, Washington, D.C., for a two-day policy meeting. In the winter of 1941–1942, FDR and Churchill met in this same grand setting to plan the Allied war against Hitler. Since the summer of 1987, the room had been the preserve of Alan Greenspan, who was now in his sixteenth year at the helm of the Fed and dominated it utterly.

The meeting began with a presentation by the Fed's economic staff about the possibility of a Japanese-style deflation, in which prices would fall and the economy would stagnate for a prolonged period despite extremely low interest rates. In the previous few months, the annual rate of consumer price inflation had dipped toward 2 percent, payrolls had fallen, and GDP growth had been weak, partly because of fears of a war in Iraq, which had duly arrived in March. The stuttering economy had left the Fed in a bind. With the funds rate already at its lowest level since the 1960s, there were doubts about how much further the central bank could go to stimulate spending.

Greenspan was sitting in his usual chair at the forty-foot-long mahogany table that dominates the boardroom. He didn't seem overly concerned about the Japan comparison. After listening to Vincent Reinhart, the head of the Fed's Division of Monetary Affairs, suggest several ways the Fed could try to revive the economy if interest rate changes could no longer be used, he dismissed the discussion as "premature" and described the possibility of a prolonged deflation as "a very small probability event."

The discussion turned to the immediate issue of whether to keep the funds rate at 1.25 percent. Since the committee's previous meeting, Congress had approved the Bush administration's third set of tax cuts since 2001, which was expected to give spending a boost. The Fed's own statistical model of the economy was predicting a vigorous upturn later in 2003, suggesting that further rate cuts would be unnecessary and that some policy tightening might even be needed. "But that forecast has a very low probability, as far as I'm concerned," Greenspan said curtly. "It points to an outcome that would be delightful if it were to materialize, but it is not a prospect on which we should focus our policy at this point." Rather than raising rates, Greenspan proposed reducing the funds rate to 1 percent and including a sentence in the postmeeting press release saying that the risk of an upturn in inflation remained very low. "We need to convey the notion that we may not have completed our easing, and that we are still watching ongoing developments in that regard," he said.

In theory, the twelve-member FOMC operates democratically: in practice, Greenspan's word was law. His six fellow Fed governors, who worked alongside him in Washington, routinely voted with him, guaranteeing him a majority. (The presidents of the Fed's regional reserve banks, which are spread out across the country, hold the other five seats.) When the roll call was taken, Greenspan's proposal was passed 11–1. Immediately after the meeting, the Fed issued a press release announcing its new target level for the funds rate of 1 percent—the lowest rate since July 1958, when Dwight Eisenhower was in the White House. With inflation running at roughly 2 percent—or even less, according to one of the Fed's favored measures—the real (inflation-adjusted) cost of short-term borrowing was now well below zero, and there it would remain for another two years. The Fed wouldn't start to raise rates to more normal levels until June 2004, and even then it would move very cautiously, in a series of quarter-point increments.

There are many interest rates in the economy. Some of the most important are the prime lending rate, which banks charge businesses; the corporate bond rate, which big companies pay to issue their own debt; and the mortgage rate, which homeowners pay to banks and mortgage companies. The Fed doesn't set any of these rates, but by altering the federal funds rate, it can influence them indirectly. When the funds rate goes up, other rates usually go up with it. When the funds rate is reduced, other rates tend to follow it down.

By keeping the funds rate below 2.5 percent from November 2001 to February 2005, the Fed ensured that most other rates fell to record, or near-record, lows. The result, not surprisingly, was a borrowing binge on the part of homeowners, consumers, businesses, and speculators. Between the end of 2002 and the end of 2006, the total amount of debt outstanding in the United States went from $31.84 trillion to $45.32 trillion, an increase of 42.3 percent. Numbers of this magnitude are difficult to visualize. The $13.5 trillion increase in debt amounted to about $43,000 for every person in the country, including children and senior citizens, or about $128,000 for each household. By 2006, the country's total indebtedness amounted to 350 percent of GDP—see Figure 17.1.

Most accounts of the credit crunch have focused on the rapid growth in mortgage debt, especially subprime loans, but the rise in mortgage lending was just part of a much larger credit boom. Of the overall rise in indebtedness between 2002 and 2006, households were responsible for about a third—some $4.4 trillion—and that figure includes all types of household debt, not just mortgages and home equity loans. Another $2 trillion, or thereabouts, came in the form of increased borrowing on the part of federal, state, and local governments. The balance of the $13.5 trillion increase was debt taken out by businesses. Some of the borrowers were in the nonfinancial sector, which includes big industrial corporations such as Caterpillar and 3M and privately owned businesses of all kinds. But by far the biggest rise in borrowing came in the financial sector. As interest rates tumbled, banks, investment banks, mortgage finance companies, real estate in-

FIGURE 17.1: RISING DEBT LEVELS

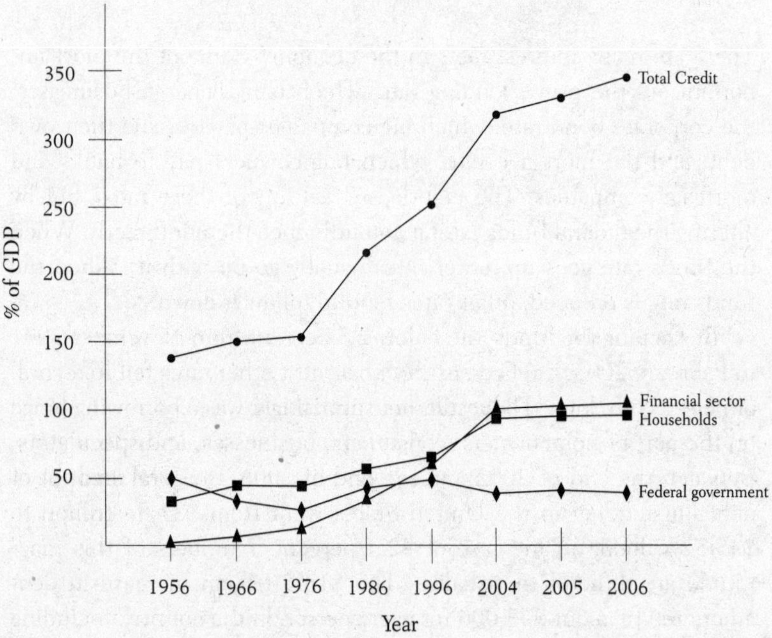

(Sources: Federal Reserve System, Flow of Fund Accounts of the United States; Bureau of Economic Analysis, National Economic Accounts Data)

vestment trusts, private equity companies, hedge funds, and financial companies of other types leveraged up their balance sheets in a manner that would have stunned even Minsky. In four years, the financial sector's indebtedness jumped by $4.2 trillion.

There is no mystery why financial institutions were so eager to borrow. When interest rates are low, the cost of taking on additional debt is modest, and the positive effect of leverage on bank earnings, which I discussed in the previous chapter, gets magnified. During much of 2003 and 2004, a bank could take out a twelve-month loan of $100 million from another bank at a cost of less than $2 million. (Overnight loans were even cheaper.) With this extra $100 million in hand, the bank could lend more money to businesses that needed financing, such as real estate developers, pocketing the "spread" between its own low funding cost and the considerably higher rates it charged its borrowers.

Between the end of 2002 and the end of 2006, the indebtedness of the financial sector went from about $10.1 trillion to $14.3 trillion. Subsequently, it increased even further—to some $16 trillion at the end of 2007. By then, the financial sector's debts came to a mountainous 117 percent of GDP. (See Figure 17.1. again) This wholesale gearing up of the financial sector was unprecedented in U.S. history, and it made the banking system much more fragile. Any economic entity with high borrowings—be it a homeowner, a pizza restaurant, or Bank of America—is vulnerable to negative shocks. If a bank with capital of $50 million borrows another $50 million, lends out $100 million, and then sees 10 percent of its clients default because of a recession, it loses a fifth of its capital. If the same bank borrows $450 million and lends out $500 million, a 10 percent default rate wipes out its entire capital. The magic of leverage works in both directions.

The rapid expansion of the financial sector amounted to a giant credit bubble, which accompanied, and in some ways overshadowed, the housing bubble. For a long time, however, it passed largely unnoticed. Some of the institutions raising money were mortgage finance and consumer lending companies, such as New Century Financial and American General Finance, which attracted little public attention. When well-known firms, such as Citigroup and Merrill Lynch, borrowed money, the additional liabilities they took on often didn't appear on their books because they were parked in SIVs and other shell companies that constituted the shadow banking system. However, even the published accounts of firms such as Citi and Merrill indicated that their borrowings were expanding very rapidly. At the end of 2002, Merrill's balance sheet showed total liabilities of $422 billion; four years later, the firm's liabilities were roughly $800 billion. Other Wall Street firms geared up in the same way. Their actions amounted to a remarkable increase in leverage and risk taking, but neither Greenspan nor anybody else in authority expressed any concerns.

The Fed chairman must have been aware of what was happening. The Fed's flow of funds accounts, which are released every three months, recorded the enormous expansion in the financial sector's debts, and Greenspan was justly famous for his detailed knowledge of obscure economic statistics. The Fed's banking division was the ultimate supervisor of virtually all the large banks in the country. It knew that many of them were busy setting up SIVs and conduits, but it didn't do anything about it. Some officials did register concerns. As early as 2002, the Bank for International Settlements (BIS), a sort of central bank for central banks, which is based in Basel, Switzerland, issued a discussion paper that pointed out that a big rise in the percentage of debt outstanding relative to GDP—that is, precisely what the United States was experiencing—often presaged a financial crisis. As the credit boom grew larger and larger, BIS repeated its warnings about excessive leverage and risk-taking on a regular basis. In the U.S. economics establishment, nobody listened, least of all Greenspan. "In the field of economics, American academics have such a high reputation that they sweep everything before them," William White, a former chief economist at BIS, recalled. "If you add to that the personal reputation of the 'Maestro,' it was very difficult for anybody else to come in and say there were problems building."

The Fed chairman had fallen victim to disaster myopia and the illusion of stability. In January 2004, he acknowledged that there had been cases in the past when excessive leverage had "brought down numerous, previously vaunted banking institutions, and precipitated a financial crisis that led to recession or worse," but he dismissed the possibility of another such calamity. "[R]ecent regulatory reform coupled with innovative technologies has spawned rapidly growing markets for, among many other products, asset-backed securities, collateral loan obligations, and credit derivative default swaps," he said. "These increasingly complex financial instruments have contributed, especially over the recent stressful period, to the development of a far more flexible, efficient, and hence resilient financial system than existed just a quarter-century ago."

7

Greenspan hadn't always sounded like such a naïf. During his first ten years at the Fed, he was a successful and fairly orthodox chairman. With the aid of E. Gerald Corrigan, the flinty head of the New York Fed at the time, he dealt adroitly with the 1987 stock market crash; during the run-up to the 1992 election, he refused to be cowed by the White House of George H. W. Bush, which wanted him to cut interest rates more rapidly; and later on in the 1990s, he was one of the first economists to spot a surge in productivity growth, which enabled the U.S. economy to expand more rapidly without generating inflation. The latter part of Greenspan's tenure was disastrous. Between 1998 and 2006, he presided over two of the biggest speculative bubbles in American history, one of which he bequeathed to his successor, along with a negative personal savings rate and a dangerously overextended financial system. In its entirety, Greenspan's eighteen-and-a-half-year tenure at the Fed provides a classic confirmation of Minsky's financial instability hypothesis: the forces of leverage and financial innovation gradually built up until they were on the verge of overwhelming the system.

If Washington insiders had viewed Greenspan as a free market ideologue, he wouldn't have survived for half as long as he did. His political career began in 1968, when he advised Richard Nixon on his successful presidential bid, and it didn't end until January 31, 2006, when he retired from the Fed. Of the prominent Republican public officials of his generation—George H. W. Bush, James Baker, Bob Dole, Howard Baker, Donald Rumsfeld—he outlasted almost all of them. (The only person who has rivaled Greenspan's longevity in Washington is Dick Cheney, his colleague in the Ford administration.)

For many years, Greenspan cultivated the image of a detached technocrat. In 1974, when Gerald Ford was considering him for the post of chairman of the White House Council of Economic Advisers, Greenspan told L. William Seidman, who was then one of Ford's aides, that he was a pure economist and not a politician. "It turned out that he was a better politician than any of us thought," Seidman later told me. When Ronald Reagan came to office, Greenspan distanced himself from the "supply side" economists who surrounded the new president, refusing to endorse the idea that tax cuts would pay for themselves. During the Clinton administration, he worked closely with Democrats, particularly Robert Rubin and Larry Summers, at times in opposition to senior members of his own party.

As a professional economist, too, Greenspan demonstrated flexibility. For more than thirty years, he ran a successful consultancy, which had a client list that included Alcoa, U.S. Steel, and J.P. Morgan. The senior executives of these companies weren't interested in theoretical disputes within the economics profession; they wanted to know what would happen to their industries and the rest of the economy over the coming months. Greenspan's method of analysis was inductive: he ingested as many figures as he could, from as many sources as he could find, then tried to fit them together into a coherent pattern. When I visited Greenspan at his office one day in 2000, I discovered him knee-deep in figures. He explained that he was trying to revamp a forty-year-old statistical model that his consulting firm had used to estimate realized capital gains on home sales.

What made Greenspan such an interesting and important figure is that his empiricism was accompanied by a fervent belief in the efficiency and morality of the free market system. The conclusion that untrammeled capitalism provides a uniquely productive method of organizing production Greenspan took from his own observations and his reading of Adam Smith. The notion that markets also foster trustworthiness, integrity, and personal freedom he took from Ayn Rand, with whom he maintained a long-running intellectual relationship. (Rumors of a physical relationship are unfounded.) Greenspan has openly acknowledged his debt to the Russian American novelist and philosopher. When I was writing a lengthy profile of him some years ago, the one quote of his that he agreed to place on the record related to her achievements: "She did things in her personal life which I would not approve of, but ideas stand on their own. What was a syllogism back then is a syllogism today."

During the 1950s, famously, Greenspan attended the weekly meetings of Rand's "Collective," which met at her apartment on East Thirty-fourth Street in New York City. In the early 1960s, he contributed articles to *The Objectivist Newsletter*, in which he called for the antitrust laws to be scrapped, and described the welfare state as "nothing more than a mechanism by which governments confiscate the wealth of productive members of society." Although he rarely voiced them in public, Greenspan's libertarian, antigovernment instincts stayed with him throughout his long career. In a 2000 conversation with a fellow economist, he insisted that his general view of the world had changed hardly at all since the 1950s. But he also instructed his interlocutor to distinguish carefully between his personal views and his actions at the Fed, a point he repeated in his 2007 memoir, *The Age of Turbulence*. "As Fed chairman, I decided, my personal views on regulation would have to be set aside," he wrote. "After all, I would take an oath of office that would commit me to uphold the Constitution of the United States and those laws whose enforcement falls under the purview of the Federal Reserve. I planned to be largely passive in such matters and allow other Federal Reserve governors to take the lead."

As the years went on, Greenspan honored this pledge mainly in the breach. During the 1990s, he played a key role in the dismantling of the Glass-Steagall Act, the Depression-era legislation that prevented depository institutions, such as Citigroup and Wells Fargo, from taking part in investment banking activities, such as peddling stocks, bonds, and mortgage securities. In 1990, the Fed allowed J.P. Morgan to become the first commercial bank to underwrite securities. Six years later, the Fed allowed banks to acquire investment banking affiliates, with some restrictions, which were then gradually eliminated. Finally, in November 1999, Congress, with Greenspan's encouragement, passed the Gramm-Leach-Bliley Act, which formally repealed most of Glass-Steagall, and President Clinton signed the legislation. Appearing before the Senate Banking Committee in February 1999, Greenspan described the Glass-Steagall regulations as "archaic," adding that failure to repeal them "could undermine the competitiveness of our financial institutions, their ability to innovate and to provide the best and broadest possible services to U.S. consumers, and ultimately, the global dominance of American finance."

When critics pointed out that deregulation increased the level of systemic risk within the financial system, Greenspan countered that many financial transactions didn't need regulating. Adopting Milton Friedman's argument that fear of alienating buyers of medicines and cars would prevent auto and drug companies from marketing unsafe products, Greenspan said that purchasers of financial products, even the most complicated ones, would regulate Wall Street. "Risks in financial markets, including derivatives markets, are being regulated by private parties," he said on Capitol Hill in 1994. "There is nothing involved in federal regulation per se which makes it superior to market regulation."

The 1990s was the decade of derivatives—securities whose value is derived from the price of something else. (The value of a stock option depends on the price of the stock; the value of a dollar-yen futures contract depends on the value of the dollar.) In 1994, Orange County was forced into bankruptcy after its treasurer, Bob Citron, took the county's $7.6 billion investment pool, borrowed more money from Wall Street firms, and invested it in some derivative securities known as "inverse floaters." A year later, the misplaced bets of a single derivatives trader, Nick Leeson, brought down the venerable Barings Bank. In 1998, the giant (and unregulated) hedge fund Long-Term Capital Management, which was a big player in many derivatives markets, had to be propped up and then wound down by a consortium of Wall Street banks, with the Fed playing a coordinating role.

The demise of Long-Term Capital, which had two economics Nobel winners as partners—Robert Merton and Myron Scholes— demonstrated the limitations of counterparty regulation. When the secretive firm opened its books to its Wall Street lenders and counterparties, many of them were astonished to discover that its leverage ratio was close to thirty to one, and that its derivatives exposures totaled about $1.4 trillion. The lesson was clear: in a world of hidden information, there is often no way for financial firms to know what risks their counterparties have taken on—be they hedge funds, banks, investment banks, or subsidiaries of industrial companies such as GE Capital.

Greenspan later acknowledged that the fall of Long-Term Capital, which prior to its troubles had been lionized in the media, was "a major failure of counterparty surveillance." However, it didn't prevent him, in the period after 1998, from repeating his previous arguments to head off efforts to regulate derivatives trading. Brooksley E. Born, the then-head of the Commodity Futures Trading Commission (CFTC), tried to bring credit default swaps, which offered investors protection against the possibility of a bond defaulting, under the regulatory jurisdiction of the CFTC. Such a move would have involved establishing some minimal capital requirements for Wall Street firms that bought and sold credit default swaps, and forcing them to disclose more information. "Recognizing the dangers . . . was not rocket science, but it was contrary to the conventional wisdom and certainly contrary to the economic interests of Wall Street at the moment," Born told *Stanford Magazine* in early 2009. Despite the warnings of Born, Warren Buffett, and others, the Fed chairman simply wouldn't accept the idea that concentrating large amounts of ill-defined risk in a handful of derivatives dealers constituted a danger to the system. "Greenspan told Brooksley that she essentially didn't know what she was doing and she'd cause a financial crisis," Michael Greenberger, a former colleague of Born, told *The New York Times* in 2008. In November 1999, Greenspan, along with the Treasury, called on Congress to bar the CFTC from regulating credit default swaps and other derivatives—a proposal that was passed into law the following year. "I certainly am not pleased with the results," Born commented in 2009. "I think the market grew so enormously, with so little oversight and regulation, that it made the financial crisis much deeper and more pervasive than it otherwise would have been."

There was a striking parallel between Greenspan's attitude to derivatives and his approach to speculative bubbles. In both cases, he adamantly refused to take seriously the concept of market failure. During the late 1990s, as the NASDAQ headed skyward, he argued that it wasn't possible to distinguish between a stock market bubble and a rise in prices that was justified by economic fundamentals. And even if it were possible to make such a distinction, raising interest rates to burst the bubble wouldn't necessarily be the right thing to do: it could end up causing the very recession you were seeking to avoid. In testimony to the Senate Banking Committee that he delivered in July 1999, Greenspan said that, rather than taking drastic actions with unpredictable consequences, such as pricking bubbles, the Fed should focus on policies designed "to mitigate the fallout when it occurs, and, hopefully, ease the transition to the next expansion."

The problem with this hands-off approach is that bubbles tend to feed on themselves, and their consequences can be severe. When the NASDAQ bubble finally burst, in March 2000, it destroyed more than $2 trillion in paper wealth; by the end of 2001, further market declines had brought the total cost to about $7 trillion. Much of this money had been imaginary, but its sudden disappearance unleashed powerful deflationary forces throughout the economy, prompting Greenspan and his colleagues to "mitigate the fallout" by slashing interest rates. Cheap money helped to ensure that the recession of 2001 lasted only eight months, but consumption and business investment remained sluggish, prompting the Fed to cut the funds rate by another half point in November 2002, bringing it down to 1.25 percent.

It was in this context that the June 2003 decision to reduce the funds rate yet again, this time to 1 percent, was taken. Based on the circumstances of the time, it appeared to be a reasonable step, and together with the effects of the Bush tax cuts and a revival of business and consumer confidence following the rapid end of full-scale combat in Iraq, it produced a rapid turnaround in the economy. In the third quarter of 2003, GDP expanded at an annualized rate of 7.5 percent. Speaking to the American Economic Association on January 3, 2004, Greenspan gave himself a little pat on the back. "There appears to be enough evidence, at least tentatively, to conclude that our strategy of addressing the bubble's consequences rather than the bubble itself has been successful," he said. "Despite the stock market plunge, terrorist attacks, corporate scandals, and wars in Afghanistan and Iraq, we experienced an exceptionally mild recession—even milder than that of a decade earlier."

A month later, Ben Bernanke, who was then a Fed governor, gave Greenspan and himself another pat on the back, arguing that "improvements in monetary policy" had been an important source of the extended period of relative economic calm dating back to the 1980s, which economists referred to as the Great Moderation. Bernanke said he was "optimistic for the future" because policymakers were unlikely to forget the lessons they had learned.

In reality, the Fed, by keeping interest rates artificially low, was in the process of substituting one bubble for another. John B. Taylor, a well-known Stanford economist, has put forward a simple equation that shows what interest rate the Fed should set depending on the level of inflation and unemployment. For the period from 1983 to 2002, the "Taylor rule" tracks the funds rate pretty accurately. But throughout much of 2003, 2004, and 2005, the rate was at least 2 percent lower than the Taylor rule would have predicted. Taylor is a Republican who between 2001 and 2005 served as an undersecretary of the Treasury. In a recent paper, he held Greenspan and his colleagues directly responsible for the financial crisis of 2007–2008, saying the Fed "caused it by deviating from historical precedents and principles for setting interest rates which had worked well for 20 years." Even some Fed officials have suggested that under Greenspan the central bank followed a misguided policy. In November 2006, Richard Fisher, the admirably plainspoken president of the Dallas Fed, said the funds rate "was held lower longer than it should have been," which "amplified speculative activity in the housing and other markets."

Critics such as Taylor and Fisher have singled out Greenspan's overly loose monetary stance; others have focused on his support for deregulation. But it was the twinning of the two policies that was to prove so disastrous. In a modern economy with a large financial sector, the combination of cheap money and lax oversight, if maintained for years on end, is sure to lead to trouble. But this was something that Greenspan, trapped in the world of utopian economics, never accepted. "In many respects, the apparent stability of our global trade and financial system is a reaffirmation of the simple, time-tested principle promulgated by Adam Smith in 1776," he wrote shortly before the subprime crisis began.

> People must be free to act in their self-interest, unencumbered by external shocks or economic policy. The inevitable mistakes and euphoria of participants in the global marketplace and the inefficiencies spawned by those missteps produce economic imbalances, large and small. Yet even in crises, economies seem inevitably to right themselves (though the process sometimes takes considerable time).

This ode to the invisible hand failed to mention that what usually enables modern economies to "right themselves" is prompt government action. Greenspan wasn't presiding over a free market nirvana; he was chairman of a central bank that had been set up, in 1913, specifically to deal with a series of glaring market failures that the great Bankers' Panic of 1907 had revealed. Following the failure of the Knickerbocker Trust Company, the rest of the banking system almost collapsed. The elderly J. P. Morgan and other senior Wall Street figures agreed to support the establishment of a public lender of last resort that would be able to supply funds to troubled financial firms when no private institution would do it.

For almost two decades, Greenspan had headed an institution that was designed to save financial capitalism from itself. For him to claim that the market economy is innately stable wasn't merely contentious; it was an absurdity. If he had seriously believed what he wrote, he would surely have followed the lead of his fellow Randians and argued for the abolition of the Fed and the reestablishment of the principle that struggling financial institutions should be allowed to fail. This he never did. Instead, he helped make it easier for financiers to take on extra leverage and risk while pursuing a monetary policy that often seemed designed to protect them from their mistakes.

The combination of a Fed that can print money, deposit insurance, and a Congress that can authorize bailouts provides an extensive safety net for big financial firms. In such an environment, pursuing a policy of easy money plus deregulation doesn't amount to free market economics; it is a form of crony capitalism. The gains of financial innovation and speculation are privatized, with the bulk of them going to a small group of wealthy people who sit at the apex of the system. Much of the losses are socialized. Such a policy framework isn't merely inequitable; it is also destabilizing. Once the Fed abdicates its responsibility of preventing excessive risk-taking, rational irrationality will eventually ensure that the system moves toward what Minsky referred to as Ponzi finance. By June 2003, this process was well advanced. In the two and a half years that remained before Greenspan's retirement, it would become irreversible.

18. THE LURE OF REAL ESTATE

he American fascination with real estate began with the arrival of the *Mayflower*, or shortly thereafter. For much of the pre-Revolutionary era, land was so plentiful that the colonial authorities often gave it away to farmers and local notables. In the mid-eighteenth century, as the population increased, speculators started subdividing sections of Virginia, New England, New York, Pennsylvania, and Ohio. Many of the great figures of the Revolutionary era, including George Washington, Benjamin Franklin, and Patrick Henry, were active land dealers. After the English had been driven out, Thomas Jefferson wanted to give small farmers the right to acquire land for nothing, or next to nothing; Hamilton said speculators should be allowed to accumulate sizeable tracts and develop them. His view won out, and in the years following the Revolutionary War, the United States witnessed its first property boom. Speculators vied over land confiscated from Tory landowners; developers drew up ambitious plans for new settlements and towns. Values appreciated sharply, and quick fortunes were made before the boom turned to bust.

During the subsequent two centuries, the same pattern was repeated at regular intervals. During the 1830s, a mad land rush began in what was then the Northwest Territories, much of it financed by newly formed "wildcat" banks, which issued handsome notes but had little in the way of real capital. "In 1836 every ship arriving at Detroit was packed with immigrants and speculators, with hundreds of passengers often arriving on a single vessel," Willis F. Dunbar and George S. May described in their 1995 history of the Wolverine state. "Land offices at Detroit and Kalamazoo were swamped with business. Long lines formed before their doors, and purchasers sometimes paid fancy prices for a place further up in the line. In Kalamazoo a sea of tents and makeshift shacks sheltered the men who sought to buy land."

In the 1880s, following the arrival of the Southern Pacific and Sante Fe railroads, Southern California played host to another real estate frenzy, during which much of Los Angeles was built. Forty years later, the action was in southern Florida, which savvy developers such as Carl Fisher, who created Miami Beach, and George Merrick, who built Coral Gables, were promoting as a semitropical nirvana. ("It's June in Miami," read a sign that Fisher erected in Times Square.) At the market's peak, in 1925 and early 1926, condominiums in choice areas of Miami were changing hands at astronomical prices. "The whole city had become one frenzied real-estate exchange," Frederick Lewis Allen wrote in *Only Yesterday*, his classic account of the 1920s. "There were said to be 2,000 real-estate offices and 25,000 agents marketing house-lots or acreage . . . Motor-busses roared down Flagler Street, carrying 'prospects' on free trips to watch dredges and steam-shovels converting the outlying mangrove swamps and the sandbars of the Bay of Biscayne into gorgeous Venetian cities for the American homemakers and pleasure-seekers of the future."

What was new about the real estate boom that ended in 2006 was its geographic spread. In earlier eras, bubbles had been confined to particular localities: this time, the speculative mania spread from coast to coast. Although some depressed cities, such as New Orleans and Cleveland, missed out on it, most big centers of population experienced enormous run-ups in home prices. From Miami to San Francisco, and from San Diego to Boston, real estate replaced the stock market as the main topic of financial conversation, and the major venue for get-rich-quick schemes.

Contrary to some accounts, the boom didn't begin in 2003 or 2004. Robert Shiller has put together a chart that shows inflation-adjusted U.S. home prices going back to 1890. (See Figure 18.1.) It clearly demonstrates that prices started to appreciate at an unprecedented rate in the mid-1990s. In many individual cities, the increases were even more dramatic than Shiller's chart suggests. In the four-year period between December 1998 and December 2002 alone, house prices jumped by almost 70 percent in San Francisco and Boston, and by about 50 per-

FIGURE 18.1: HOUSE PRICES

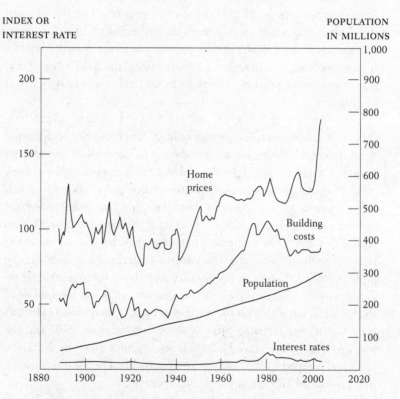

1890–2008, along with Building Costs, Population, and Long-Term Government Bond Interest Rates, annual 1890–2008

cent in Los Angeles, Miami, and Washington, D.C. (These figures and those that follow are not adjusted for inflation. They come from the S&P/Case-Shiller Home Price Indices, which the same Robert Shiller helped to develop.)

Overall, between the fourth quarter of 1996 and the fourth quarter of 2006, average house prices nationwide rose by 129 percent. Figures from the Fed confirm that the housing boom was a lengthy phenomenon. Between 1997 and 2002, the total value of real estate owned by American households went from $8.8 trillion to $14.5 trillion. In the ensuing four years, it rose to $21.9 trillion. The $13.1 trillion increase in real estate wealth over the nine-year period from 1997 to 2006 was roughly equivalent to $125,000 for every household in the country. (Of course, the actual gains weren't divided equally.) In dollar terms, the housing bubble wasn't merely comparable to the dot-com bubble; it was much bigger. (Between 1996 and 1999, the total value of corporate equities owned by American households increased by about $5 trillion.)

Among economists, there is still some debate about when precisely the real estate boom turned into a bubble. Since there is no accepted definition of a bubble, this dispute cannot be definitively resolved. As I pointed out in chapter 1, by the end of 2002 home prices had already moved beyond their historical ranges relative to incomes and rents. But it was beginning in 2003, at about the same time that the Fed was cutting interest rates to historic lows, that they really departed from reality. A standard measure of whether homes are overvalued is the ratio of median home prices to median household incomes. (If the prices of all the homes in the country were lined up in ascending order, the median home price would be the one smack in the middle of the line. The same goes for the median income.) Figures from Harvard's Joint Center for Housing Studies show that between 1980 and the late 1990s, this ratio stayed pretty steady, at about three. By 2002, the ratio had jumped to 3.6, and by 2006 it had reached 4.6, indicating that prices had become seriously unaffordable.

In some real estate hotspots, such as Los Angeles–Long Beach, and San Francisco–Oakland, house prices have long been expensive relative to incomes, but during the bubble years the degree of unaffordability moved to unprecedented extremes. In 1996, the ratio of median home prices to median household incomes was already 4 in

Los Angeles–Long Beach, and it was 4.5 in San Francisco–Oakland. By 2002, the ratios had jumped to 5.6 and 6.8 respectively, and by 2006 they had reached 10 and 9.8. These figures bear inspecting. At the peak of the boom, families in these cities who were earning $50,000 a year were buying $500,000 homes, and families who were earning $100,000 a year were buying $1 million homes. In order to acquire a reasonably spacious house in a half-decent area, middle-class families were being forced to pay prices that, even a decade before, would have been considered the preserve of the ultrarich.

On the East Coast, the level of overvaluation was less excessive, but the relative price jumps were comparable. In 1996, typical homes in the New York area were selling for 3.7 times household incomes; ten years later, the price-to-income ratio had risen to 7.1. In greater Miami over the same period, the ratio went from 3.3 to 7.2, and in Washington, D.C.–Northern Virginia it went from 2.9 to 5.7.

I should stress, again, that these statistics apply to apartments and houses that were nothing special: they were just standard middle-class accommodation. Further up the income and house price curves, in the snootier parts of town and in exclusive suburbs, the bubble was even more pronounced. With all the money that financial firms were generating, Manhattan and other money centers were particularly affected. In 1998, the median price of a Manhattan condominium apartment was $345,000, according to figures compiled by the Corcoran Group. By 2002, the price had risen to $687,000, and by 2007 a typical 900-square-foot Manhattan condo was selling for $1.1 million. The cost of larger apartments had become even more prohibitive. According to Corcoran, by 2007 the price of a typical three-bedroom condo had reached $2.7 million. And if you had won the lottery and decided to buy a town house on the East Side, a typical one would have cost you $9.3 million.

Every bubble is different, but almost all of them share three common features: policymakers beholden to the illusion of stability; financial innovations that make speculating easier; and New Era thinking typified by overconfidence and disaster myopia.

In real estate bubbles, particularly, monetary policy is key. Low interest rates provide the helium that inflates the bubble. Once house prices start rising, the mortgage rate effectively sets their upper limit, and the relationship is pretty much one to one. If the interest rate on thirty-year fixed mortgages is 10 percent, somebody with enough income to make a monthly payment of $2,500 can take out a loan of $285,000. Adding a down payment of 20 percent, the upper limit on the house price he (or she) can afford is $342,000. If the mortgage rate falls to 5 percent, the same person can buy a home costing $564,000, assuming he can afford the bigger down payment.

The Fed couldn't have done much more to bring down mortgage rates. In January 2001, the federal funds rate stood at 6 percent, and the average rate on thirty-year fixed mortgages was 7.03 percent. Two years later, the funds rate had been slashed to 1.25 percent, and the thirty-year rate had fallen to 5.92 percent. In January 2005, the funds rate was still at 2.5 percent, and the long-term mortgage rate was 5.71 percent. By that stage of the bubble, however, only fuddy-duddies were taking out thirty-year fixed-rate loans: between 2001 and 2006, the proportion of mortgages issued that were traditional fixed-rate products fell from three fifths to a third. With Greenspan's encouragement, the majority of home buyers were taking out adjustable-rate mortgages, which offered even lower fixed rates for a specified period—usually one, five, or eight years. "The traditional fixed-rate mortgage may be an expensive way of owning a home," the Fed chairman said in 2004. "Recent research within the Federal Reserve suggests that many homeowners might have saved tens of thousands of dollars had they held adjustable-rate mortgages rather than fixed-rate mortgages during the past decade."

Greenspan's stubborn refusal to acknowledge the real estate bubble has already been noted. He was perfectly aware of the link between monetary policy and home prices, but in April 2002, appearing before the Joint Economic Committee of Congress, he put forward two reasons why the real estate market wasn't susceptible to a dot-com-style bubble. First, homes are much more difficult to trade than stocks: they are less liquid. Second, "A home in Portland, Oregon, is not a close substitute for a home in Portland, Maine, and the 'national' housing market is better understood as a collection of small, local housing markets. Even if a bubble were to develop in a local market, it would not necessarily have implications for the nation as a whole."

Greenspan's first point was accurate: buying or selling a home is costly and time-consuming. But liquidity is only one aspect of specu-lation. Access to financing is just as important, and it is easier to raise money in the real estate market than in any other. If you are lucky, your stockbroker might allow you to open a margin account that dou-bles the amount of money you can invest in stocks and bonds. In the housing market, banks routinely allow mortgagers to borrow four times the amount they put down, and between 2002 and 2006 leverage ratios were often much higher.

The power of leverage and the availability of modestly priced fi-nancing means that housing markets, far from being unsuitable ven-ues for speculation, are chronically susceptible to it. (In recent years, housing bubbles have occurred as far afield as Ireland, Spain, South Africa, and Australia.) Once real estate prices start to go up, potential home buyers come to expect further increases, and this makes them willing to pay more for any given property. Meanwhile, as Minsky noted, banks readily issue bigger mortgages, because the value of the collateral that underpins these loans is going up. Rising prices create more demand, which leads to higher prices.

It is this phenomenon that distinguishes stable markets from un-stable ones. In the market for cars or airline tickets, a rise in prices leads to a fall in demand, and prices fall back. But in markets that contain a speculative element, such as real estate, higher prices can generate higher demand. To be sure, rising prices will also generate an increase in supply, in the form of a construction boom, but in the time it takes for all the new houses to be built and marketed, prices on existing homes can go up enormously. During a speculative bubble, the laws of supply and demand don't get repealed, but they do get suspended—something that Greenspan and other utopian economists ignored.

To be fair to him, the Fed chairman wasn't the only senior policy-maker who was talking up the housing market. In 1993, Henry G. Cisneros, the secretary of housing and urban development in the Clinton administration, launched the National Homeownership Strat-egy, which was aimed particularly at increasing home ownership rates among minority groups. Throughout the 1990s, Cisneros and other officials pressed banks and mortgage lenders to expand their lending in poor and minority areas, partly by aggressively enforcing the Com-munity Reinvestment Act of 1977, which had instructed the Fed and other regulators to force banks "to help meet the credit needs of the local communities in which they are chartered." (The banks had largely brought this legislation on their own heads by "redlining" entire neighborhoods and refusing to lend there.) The policy of leaning on the banks had some success: between 1990 and 2000, the overall percentage of households who owned their own homes rose from 64.2 to 66.2, and the increase was particularly noticeable among African Americans and Hispanics.

President George W. Bush, when he came to office in 2001, took up the Clinton administration's agenda, promoting an "ownership society." In 2002, he called on mortgage lenders to help create an additional 5.5 million minority homeowners by the end of the decade. A year later, he signed the American Dream Downpayment Act, which offered up to $10,000 to low-income households that were struggling to make a down payment on a new home. In early 2004, the home ownership rate hit an all-time high of more than 69 percent, and the rate among minorities for the first time approached 50 percent. Later in the year, Bush made home ownership a big plank of his reelection campaign. "America is a stronger country every single time a family moves into a home," he said in October 2004.

The Clinton and Bush administrations both pressed Fannie Mae and Freddie Mac, the two government-sponsored mortgage giants, to increase their funding of home loans to middle-class and low-income lenders. Neither firm issues mortgages directly. They buy home loans from banks and other lenders, some of which they keep on their books and some of which they convert into mortgage-backed securities, which they sell to investors. By 2008, Fannie and Freddie together owned about $1.5 trillion in home loans and mortgage-backed securities, and they had issued mortgage guarantees worth roughly another $3.5 trillion. Although these activities were confined to the lower and middle reaches of the real estate market, their sheer scale helped to support the entire industry. The very existence of Fannie and Freddie made the mortgage securities market more liquid, freed up money for mortgage originators to make new loans, and helped to keep mortgage rates down. (The firms also enriched their own senior executives, but that is another story.)

Financial innovation, the second integral element of speculative bubbles, comes in many forms. During the 1990s, the development of online trading made buying and selling stocks a lot cheaper, and the rise of websites and chat rooms devoted to investing helped to create a culture supportive of stock market speculation. More recently, the rapid growth of hedge funds and other investment funds devoted to the energy sector contributed to the rise of speculation in the oil market.

For decades, the business of buying and selling homes was a fairly simple one, consisting largely of Realtors, savings and loans, banks, and home buyers. During the 1990s, home financing became a lot more complicated, and a lot more competitive. New types of mortgages proliferated, and so did new entrants to the industry. As the bubble developed, the pace of innovation accelerated. Banks and mortgage companies began to offer, in addition to regular fixed-rate and adjustable-rate mortgages, interest-only loans, stated-income loans ("liar loans"), and option ARMs. These exotic mortgages varied in a number of ways, but they shared a common attribute: by taking out one of them, a borrower could purchase a more expensive property than he (or she) would have been able to afford on the basis of a more conventional loan.

Interest-only (IO) loans are an example of what Minsky termed speculative finance. Condo flippers and other home buyers who had no interest in keeping hold of the properties they purchased for extended periods found them particularly attractive. For an initial period—often it was five years—the borrower didn't have to pay down any of the principal, which meant his monthly payments would be much lower. In May 2005, the monthly payment on a $500,000 house financed with an interest-only loan was roughly $2,100, compared with a monthly payment of about $3,000 on a fully amortizing, thirty-year fixed-rate loan. According to LoanPerformance, a mortgage industry research firm, the share of interest-only loans in new originations went from close to zero in 2003 to about 20 percent in the second half of 2005. In some bubble markets, deferring principal payments became the new norm. Research carried out for the *San Francisco Chronicle* showed that in the first two months of 2005, interest-only loans accounted for almost 70 percent of the mortgages originated in Marin, San Francisco, and San Mateo counties.

Many interest-only mortgages were also stated-income loans. In the early stages of the real estate boom, most mortgage applicants still had to verify their income by presenting their W-2 forms or tax returns from the previous two or three years. For those who wanted to buy a home but who couldn't afford to take out a big enough loan, this posed something of a problem, but not one that proved insurmountable. Many banks, rather than investigating borrowers' incomes, began to rely heavily on their credit ratings. In the FICO ratings scale, which the Fair Isaac Corporation originally developed, credit scores range from 300 (dismal) to 850 (perfect). (The typical person scores about 725.) As long as a loan applicant could show a certain credit rating—620 on the FICO scale was a common cutoff—many lenders deemed him (or her) eligible for a "stated-income verified-assets" loan or a "stated-income stated-assets" loan. In the first case, the lending institution would check that the person hadn't exaggerated his net worth but wouldn't check his income; in the second case, the lender wouldn't try to verify the applicant's income or assets.

Stated-income loans were originally designed for the self-employed and others who had trouble verifying their incomes. By 2004 and 2005, borrowers of all types were applying for them and being approved. Some estimates suggest that more than a third of all the mortgages issued in these years were stated-income loans—and the figure was significantly higher than that in places such as Arizona, California, and Florida. The full scope of the deception associated with these products still hasn't fully emerged, but they undoubtedly earned their nickname: liar loans. In 2006, an organization called the Mortgage Asset Research Institute examined a hundred stated-income loans and compared them to IRS records: in almost 60 percent of the cases, they discovered, the borrowers had exaggerated their income by more than 50 percent.

Deliberately lying to a lender about your income is a federal crime. In this instance, though, the supposed victim was often a co-conspirator. Loan officers at banks and mortgage lending companies were paid on commission. At many such firms, the loan application process had been automated. As long as the right figures were entered into the computer, the underwriting software, which was supplied by third-party lenders, approved the loan. "Bank employees—i.e., underwriters and bank processors—return applications back to mortgage brokers with instructions to send back an application with a higher stated income," Steven Krystofiak, president of an organization called the Mortgage Brokers Association for Responsible Lending, told a Fed hearing in

2006. "The systems allow mortgage brokers to 'play' with different incomes more than fifteen times until they get the results they want."

Option ARMs, which were often marketed as "pick-a-payment loans," amounted to Ponzi finance, pure and simple. For the first year or more of the loan, borrowers could choose from a variety of monthly payments, with the minimum one set at a level that didn't even cover the interest on the loan. If a home buyer elected this payment option, as many did, the interest she hadn't paid was added to the principal, meaning that the amount she owed increased every month!

Even now it is hard to get data on exactly how many option ARMs were taken out, but it was a large number. According to one industry estimate, during the first five months of 2006 about one in eight of the home loans issued nationwide were option ARMs. In the Bay Area, according to the *San Francisco Chronicle*'s Kathleen Pender, 29 percent of mortgages issued in 2005 were option ARMs.

The primary driver of this deterioration in credit standards was the buoyant mortgage securitization market. IO loans, option ARMs, and other "exotic" mortgages started out as fringe products offered by upstart companies, such as New Century and Ameriquest. But Wall Street firms quickly seized upon them to create new types of mortgage bonds, known as "Alt-A" bonds, which were backed by mortgages that fell somewhere between prime and subprime. Between 2001 and 2006, Alt-A originations rose from $60 billion to $400 billion, an increase of more than 550 percent.

The ability to shunt newly issued stated-income loans and option ARMs onto Wall Street firms, often within days of their origination, provided banks and other mortgage lenders with a form of insurance. As long as there was sufficient demand for Alt-A mortgage securities, the lenders didn't have to worry about the true costs of their actions, because they wouldn't be the ones incurring them: if mortgage defaults turned out to be higher than expected, the investors who purchased the mortgage securities would suffer the loss. This was a case of market-induced moral hazard. Rather than encouraging lenders to allocate capital wisely, the market was sending signals that greatly distorted their behavior. If mortgage lenders had been forced to keep some of the loans they originated on their books, they would have been a lot more careful, but there was no such requirement. Like a vacationer driving a fully insured rental car, mortgage lenders could be as reckless as they wished.

Understandably enough, customers flocked to loans that involved less-stringent income requirements and lower monthly payments. This presented established lenders, such as Chase Home Finance, Countrywide, and Washington Mutual with a dilemma—a prisoner's dilemma, actually. Individually, the senior managers of these firms would have preferred to stick with more traditional loans, which were safer and had a longer track record. But in the frenzied atmosphere of a bubble, companies that stick to the old ways of doing things lose market share, their stock prices suffer, and their top managers get criticized. In the language of game theory, going with the crowd is a dominant strategy: it is the rationally irrational thing to do.

The experience of Angelo Mozilo, the chairman and chief executive of Countrywide, which in 2006 was the country's biggest mortgage originator, is illustrative. Since its foundation in 1969, Countrywide had portrayed itself as a conservative issuer of prime loans, but it had also adopted a "matching strategy," which committed it to offering its customers any deal that its rivals were offering. When other firms introduced new types of loans, Countrywide did the same; when they shaved points off a particular product, so did Countrywide.

Looked at in terms of the prisoner's dilemma, Countrywide was playing "tit for tat" in the game against its competitors. For a firm determined to become the leading home lender in the country, this was a logical strategy, but between 2004 and 2007 it led Countrywide to issue a vast number of nontraditional mortgages, including many interest-only loans and option ARMs. Behind the scenes, Mozilo got concerned, fearing that the firm could have difficulty selling some of its option ARMs to Wall Street firms for securitization. "We have no way, with any reasonable certainty, to assess the real risk of holding these loans on our balance sheet," he warned in an internal e-mail sent on September 25, 2006. The next day, in another e-mail, Mozilo said that Countrywide should move quickly to sell its option ARMs, noting that "pay options are currently mispriced in the secondary market."

Mozilo could have ordered his underlings not to issue any more option ARMs, but he didn't. He appears to have been reluctant to do anything that could have led to a short-term fall in Countrywide's profits and stock price: between 2005 and 2007, he reaped about $140 million in profits by exercising options and selling stock. In public, Mozilo stuck to the line that Countrywide was a responsible lender, which, relative to some of its competitors, it was. But when the subprime crisis began, and the market for mortgages froze up, the firm's holdings of dubious home loans, nearly all of which were waiting to be securitized, brought it to the brink of collapse. Mozilo's fears turned out to be well founded, but trapped as he was in the logic of rational irrationality, he hadn't done anything about them.

The third ever-present factor in speculative bubbles is crowd psychology. From Tulipmania to Florida in the 1920s to the dot-com mania, overconfidence, disaster myopia, and copycat behavior were perhaps the defining attributes of what transpired. Each of these things was also strongly in evidence during the later stages of the housing boom, when a remarkable consensus emerged that American home prices could move in only one direction: up.

Direct evidence of what people are thinking is often hard to find, but in 2005 Bob Shiller and Karl Case, of Wellesley College, conducted a survey of home buyers in San Francisco and asked them how they thought prices would move in the ensuing ten years. The average expected price increase was 14 percent a year, which, over a decade, would have translated into another doubling of home values from an already very elevated level. (At the time of the survey, the median sales price for homes in San Francisco was about $750,000.) This was the average opinion. "About a third of the respondents reported truly extravagant expectations—occasionally over 50% a year," Shiller reported in his 2008 book, *The Subprime Solution*.

This looks to have been a classic case of people assuming that recent trends are typical and extrapolating from them: the representativeness heuristic. Between January 1995 and January 2005, home prices in San Francisco had risen about 180 percent, according to the S&P Case-Shiller indices. Sometimes it is reasonable to expect the future to resemble the past. In this case, though, home buyers had failed to think through the full implications of their forecasts. At 14 percent a year, the average expected rise in prices implied that by 2025 the median sale price would be $3 million. Even for a city located next to the technology capital of the world, that seems a bit excessive.

Apparently, residents of the Bay Area, and many other Americans, had forgotten the experience of the early 1990s, when for a number of years real estate prices dropped in some areas that previously had seen big jumps. Between April 1990 and April 1996, San Francisco home prices fell by 11 percent. This figure doesn't account for inflation, which erodes the value of things. If inflation is taken into account, Bay Area home values fell by about a third over this six-year period, which is a major slump.

One of the characteristics of bubbles is that they erase prior history from the minds of the participants—thus the phrase "disaster myopia." Shiller has compared the spread of optimistic thinking to the progress of a virulently contagious disease, and he is surely onto something. In May 2005, *Fortune* ran a cover story entitled "Real Estate Gold Rush," which detailed the increasingly crowded world of property investing, condo flipping, and buying on spec. One of the ordinary Americans featured on the magazine's cover was Zareh Tahmassebian, a goateed twenty-two-year-old from Las Vegas who owned or part-owned more than a dozen houses in and around Phoenix. Tahmassebian, the son of Armenian immigrants, drove the reporter who wrote the story to a new housing development near Tempe, Arizona, where he owned several semibuilt homes. "This wood made money for me," Tahmassebian said, gesturing at an unfinished frame. "I don't own it—but I own the rights. I put a ten percent deposit down. I haven't even made a mortgage payment yet, and it's already gone up $45,000. What a country!"

This vignette could easily have come from Detroit in 1835, Los Angeles in 1885, or Miami in 1925. At the peak of a bubble, stories of ordinary people getting rich circulate widely, exerting great psychological pressure on others to join the herd. Like the participants in Solomon Asch's visual experiments in the 1950s, many people who don't share the consensus view of the market start to feel left out. Eventually, it reaches the stage where it appears that the really crazy people are those *not* in the market—a point often missed by economists who claim that stupidity and irrationality lie at the heart of bubbles.

After the bust, it can sometimes seem like the investors who lost money must have known that they were acting recklessly and heading for trouble. During the bubble, though, the dangers aren't obvious at all. Between 2002 and 2006, real estate financing was cheap and readily available, and most real estate experts were ruling out the possibility of the market plummeting. "I don't foresee any national decline in home price values," Frank Nothaft, the chief economist at Freddie Mac, told *BusinessWeek* in June 2005. "Freddie Mac's analysis of single-family houses over the last half century hasn't shown a single year when the national average housing price has gone down." (This was the same Nothaft who in 2002 had made similar statements to me.) As late as early 2006, Harvard's prestigious and supposedly independent Joint Center for Housing was reassuring people that rapid immigration and population growth would continue to underpin the demand for residential real estate. "House price appreciation should remain positive in most markets," the Joint Center said in its annual report on the nation's housing market. And it went on: "Over the longer term, the outlook for housing markets is favorable." In such circumstances, even in the most overheated markets, buying real estate just didn't seem very risky to many ordinary people. The bigger risk appeared to be getting left out of the market. Among first-time buyers, a common attitude was: if we don't buy now, prices will just keep going up and we'll never be able to afford it.

If rationality is defined in the extreme sense of Robert Lucas—having a mathematically correct model of the entire economy in your head and acting upon it—the participants in the housing bubble were irrational. But if rationality is making the best judgment you can on the basis of limited information, most home buyers acted rationally. It is easy to say that they should have known better, but many of them were trapped in something akin to an information cascade. With modest ranch houses selling for more than $1 million in parts of Northern California, and poky two-bedrooms fetching similar sums in Manhattan, there was probably hardly anybody in the country who didn't suspect, in their heart of hearts, that real estate was overvalued: this information was their "private signal." But people also had to take account of the "public signal" that the market was sending to them: properties were being sold at these values every day, and prices were still going up.

In such circumstances, it takes a brave and self-confident person to back his personal judgment against the judgment of the market, and the information it conveys. As in the story of the two rival restaurants that open next to each other, people tend to assume that other people know more than they do. Whenever this happens, the most likely outcome is that everybody ends up following the public signal and doing the same thing. In this case, that meant buying real estate. The information that homes are overvalued didn't get reflected in the market, and prices kept appreciating—for a while, anyway.

Even more sophisticated buyers, including many of the condo flippers and buy-on-spec investors, sensed little danger of getting caught by a sudden slump. "It's a risk," said Debbie Smith, one of the mom-and-pop property speculators featured in *Fortune*. "But I really feel it's a lot less risky than the stock market. Even if it does crash, it's not like it's worth nothing—like a stock, where the value can go all the way to zero." Added Zareh Tahmassebian, "You just hold on 'til it comes right back up." Looking back, comments like these sound flip and irresponsible. At the time they were made, though—the spring of 2005—why should Smith and Tahmassebian have thought any differently? In September 2005, the Federal Reserve Bank of New York published an examination of the housing market by three respected real estate economists: Charles Himmelberg, of the New York Fed; Christopher Mayer, of Columbia; and Todd Sinai, of Wharton. "[O]ur analysis reveals little evidence of a housing bubble," it concluded. "In high-appreciation markets like San Francisco, Boston, and New York, current housing prices are not cheap, but our calculations do not reveal large price increases in excess of fundamentals."

19. THE SUBPRIME CHAIN

ntil the early 1990s, the practice of extending loans to people with poor credit histories, folks regular banks didn't want anything to do with, was known as "hard money lending" or "B&C lending." In many poor and minority neighborhoods, the main source of this type of credit was individual pawnbrokers, who demanded objects of value as collateral for the loans, and loan sharks, who relied on the threat of violence to ensure repayment. There were also more organized consumer lending companies, such as Beneficial Finance, a company founded in Elizabeth, New Jersey, in 1914, whose salesmen went door to door offering loans for the purchase of household goods, which were repaid in fixed installments. Most of the loans issued by Beneficial and its rivals were small ones: in the early 1960s, a few hundred dollars was the typical amount.

Things began to change when the consumer lenders started to issue second mortgages—the phrase "home equity loan" hadn't been invented—to people whose primary lenders wouldn't give them another loan. They found plenty of homeowners willing to pay an interest rate of 5 or 6 percent above the ordinary mortgage rate to get their hands on an extra $10,000 or $20,000. By 1979, Beneficial had issued more than $4 billion in second mortgages, and it was making profits of $100 million a year.

Most banks and thrifts had nothing to do with hard lending, which was seen as déclassé. The hefty interest rates that the consumer finance companies levied—as high as 15 or 20 percent—and the aggressive tactics they used to deal with tardy debtors, such as employing "repo men," prompted many critics to accuse them of predatory behavior. "We were lepers, scum of the earth," a former executive at Beneficial told the financial journalists Paul Muolo and Mathew Padilla. "That's how we were viewed."

Even if banks had wanted to engage in hard lending, they couldn't have done so: state usury laws placed limits on the interest rates they were allowed to charge. The birth of the modern subprime industry can be dated to the 1980 passage of the Depository Institutions Deregulation and Monetary Control Act, which allowed banks and thrifts to charge borrowers whatever rates they wanted. The Alternative Mortgage Transaction Parity Act of 1982 further loosened restrictions on lenders, allowing them to charge variable interest rates and demand balloon payments when a loan matured. And the home loan industry got another boost in the Tax Reform Act of 1986, which eliminated the tax deduction for interest on consumer and auto loans but kept the deduction on mortgage payments.

Despite these pieces of legislation, during the 1980s and '90s most firms that issued mortgages to people with poor credit histories still tended to be scrappy consumer finance companies rather than banks. Some of them, such as Beneficial, Household Finance, and Associates First Capital, of Texas, had been around for years. Others, such as Long Beach Mortgage, Aames Capital, ContiMortgage, and First Plus, were more recent creations. None of these firms had any depositors. Some of them financed their lending by borrowing from banks and other financial institutions; others tapped wealthy individuals, such as doctors and lawyers, for loans. In the early 1990s, a cheaper and more reliable source of financing arrived, in the form of "warehouse loans" from Wall Street banks that were entering the business of cobbling together subprime mortgages and transforming them into residential mortgage-backed securities (RMBSs) and collateralized debt obligations (CDOs).

The securitizing of prime mortgages, which Lewis Ranieri and Salomon Brothers had pioneered back in the 1970s, was already a big business. Wall Street traders were on the lookout for other cash streams to securitize, and subprime mortgages, which are generally regarded as loans issued to borrowers with a FICO rating below 640, offered an attractive opportunity. The high interest rates these loans carried would translate into high-yielding bonds, which would be irresistible to investors.

That was the theory, anyway, and when firms such as Prudential Securities, Lehman Brothers, and Bear Stearns tried it out, it worked. The investment banks lent money at a rate of 6 or 7 percent to mortgage companies such as ContiMortgage and Long Beach Mortgage, which passed on the money to subprime borrowers, charging them a substantially higher rate—10 percent, or even more. Once the loan agreements had been signed, the mortgage company sold the loans to a Wall Street firm, often the same one that had extended it credit in the first place, for securitization. As the Wall Street traders had predicted, hedge funds and other investors proved eager to buy the new subprime mortgage bonds, which were known as "private label" mortgage-backed securities, to distinguish them from "public label" mortgage bonds that had the backing of Fannie and Freddie.

For a time, the new model of securitization-driven subprime lending appeared to work to the advantage of everybody involved. Many cash-strapped American families who had previously been turned away by banks and thrifts got the opportunity to buy a home; mortgage brokers and mortgage lenders reaped hefty fees and commissions; Wall Street discovered a lucrative new business; bond market investors received higher yields. In 1995, according to the trade magazine *Inside B&C Lending*, $65 billion worth of subprime loans were issued in the United States, of which about $18.5 billion worth were converted into securities. By 1997, subprime originations had almost doubled, to $124.5 billion, of which about $66 billion worth were securitized.

Policymakers and economists from both parties welcomed this development. For years, local politicians and community activists had been calling for financial institutions to extend more loans in poor and minority areas, and to people with checkered credit histories: the subprime lenders were doing just that. (According to a study by the Federal Reserve Bank of New York, the typical subprime borrower in 2006 had a FICO score of 623.) "The main thing that innovations in the mortgage market have done over the past 30 years is to let in the excluded: the young, the discriminated against, the people without a lot of money in the bank to use for a down payment," Harvey Rosen, a Princeton economist who during the Bush administration served briefly as chairman of the White House Council of Economic Advisers, said in 2007. Rosen's statement was contained in an article defending the subprime industry written by Austan Goolsbee, an economist at the University of Chicago, who now holds a senior post in the Obama administration, and published in *The New York Times*.

The reason banks had been so reluctant to lend to the poor and underprivileged goes back to George Akerlof's work on "lemons" in the secondhand car market. When the owner of a used car puts it up for sale, he signals to potential buyers that there might well be something wrong with it. Similarly, when somebody applies for a high-interest loan, he sends the lender a signal that he badly needs the money and that he couldn't get a regular loan, probably because of previous credit problems. In both of these cases, key information is hidden: the car buyer doesn't know the true state of the vehicle, and the lender doesn't know whether the loan applicant has the capacity or discipline to repay on time. Historically, the way banks had dealt with this problem, known to economists as "adverse selection," was by instituting a system of rationing. Unless a borrower satisfied a bank's minimum credit standards, he couldn't get a loan, and that was that.

Subprime lenders were more flexible. They offered mortgages carrying many different interest rates depending on a person's credit history and how much money he could put down. A loan applicant with a FICO rating of just 600 and a down payment of 10 percent, say, would be charged a higher rate than somebody with a FICO rating of 630 and a 20 percent down payment, but he wouldn't necessarily be denied a loan. "[L]enders have taken advantage of credit-scoring models and other techniques for efficiently extending credit to a broader spectrum of consumers," Alan Greenspan said in April 2005. "The widespread adoption of these models has reduced the costs of evaluating the creditworthiness of borrowers, and in competitive markets cost reductions tend to be passed through to borrowers. Where once more-marginal applicants would simply have been denied credit, lenders are now able to quite efficiently judge the risk posed by individual applicants and to price that risk appropriately."

To economists who thought like Greenspan, the rapid growth of subprime lending seemed to represent the invisible hand in action. Purely for reasons of self-interest, some of the most highly paid people in the country—Wall Street traders, hedge fund managers, and other institutional investors—were providing the funding for millions of struggling Americans to buy a home. Many, perhaps most, of these rich people had never been to any of the neighborhoods where the money they lent to subprime mortgage lenders and invested in subprime securities ended up, but that didn't matter. Through the workings of the market, their selfish pursuit of profit was being transmuted into a socially desirable outcome, and resources were being allocated efficiently.

The first blow to this view came in 1997 and 1998, when it emerged that subprime borrowers were defaulting and refinancing at higher levels than had been anticipated, leaving their lenders with big losses. The investors who had been buying subprime mortgage securities cut back their purchases. In the fall of 1998, when the Russian financial crisis roiled many financial markets, the demand for subprime mortgage securities evaporated, leaving many mortgage lenders without any financing. Six of the top ten firms, including ContiMortgage, AMRESCO, and First Plus, filed for bankruptcy, shut down, or were sold.

What should have been a warning to the financial establishment about the perils of risky lending turned into an opportunity to enter the business on the cheap. The senior executives of America's biggest banks and thrifts may have looked down òn the subprime lenders, but they envied their rapid growth. Between 1998 and 2002, Citigroup bought Associated First Capital; Washington Mutual bought Long Beach Mortgage; First Union, which later merged with Wachovia, bought the Money Store; JPMorgan Chase bought Advanta; and HSBC bought Household Financial. (Angelo Mozilo's Countrywide built up its own subprime division; eventually, it became the biggest subprime issuer of all.) Subprime lending was no longer something suspect and shady; it had entered the mainstream. In 2001 and 2002, when the Fed slashed interest rates, the market for subprime mortgage securities, which were still sporting high yields, revived strongly, prompting Wall Street firms to go in search of more loans to securitize. The subprime lenders were glad to help them out. In 2001, the total value of sub-prime originations jumped by a quarter, to $173.3 billion, according to *Inside B&C Lending*. In 2002, the figure was $213 billion; in 2003 it was $332 billion. And the housing market was just warming up.

Between 2004 and 2006, lenders originated more than $1.7 trillion in subprime mortgages, with the peak of $625 billion coming in 2005. During the same three-year period, Wall Street issued more than $1.3 trillion in subprime mortgage securities, which means that roughly three quarters of all subprime loans were securitized. By this stage, nontraditional mortgage lending was rivaling traditional lending. If sub-prime and Alt-A originations are classed together, as they should be, they came to $1 trillion in 2006, which meant that they comprised about 40 percent of the mortgage loans issued in that year. The num-ber of subprime mortgages issued went from 624,000 in 2001 to 3.44 million in 2005, an increase of more than 450 percent.

In the old days, hard-money lending had been a simple but labor-intensive business, based on a direct, long-term relationship between the borrower and lender. The consumer finance companies kept the loans they issued on their books, which gave them an incentive to be careful. Beneficial insisted that the combined value of the first and second mortgages on a property didn't exceed 80 percent of the property's value. Subprime lending, as it evolved in the 1990s, was a sprawling, fee-driven business in which the borrowers and ultimate lenders—the purchasers of subprime mortgage bonds—had virtually no interaction at all. Between them, there was a long chain of interme-diaries: mortgage brokers, mortgage lenders, Wall Street traders, rating agencies, and investment management firms, each of which was look-ing to make a quick score. Figure 19.1 shows how the various bits of the mortgage chain fitted together, and the financial flows between them.

The notion that the self-interested machinations of all the players in the subprime business would work out for the best turned out to be an illusion—the illusion of harmony. Far from solving the hidden-information problems that Akerlof had indentified, the industry had

FIGURE 19.1: THE MORTGAGE CHAIN

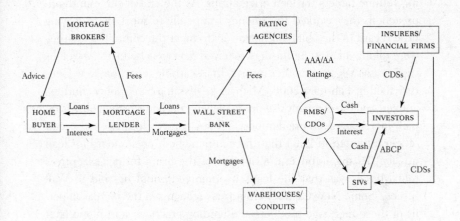

simply ignored them. Nowhere in the lengthy mortgage chain did anybody play the role of an old-fashioned bank loan officer, screening borrowers to ensure they could afford the loans they had applied for, and then monitoring their behavior. Wall Street banks sometimes hired third parties to examine the subprime loans they were purchasing; for the most part, though, they relied on the representations of the mortgage lenders. The buyers of subprime securities at the end of the mortgage chain didn't do much analysis of their own, either; they relied on the credit rating agencies, which classed the vast majority of subprime RMBSs and CDOs as investment-grade.

Between 2005 and 2007, according to the Center for Public Integrity, the five biggest issuers of subprime loans were Countrywide: $97.2 billion; Ameriquest: $80.7 billion; New Century: $76 billion; First Franklin, which Merrill Lynch purchased in 2007: $68 billion; and Long Beach Mortgage, which was part of Washington Mutual: $65.2 billion. The mortgage lenders depended heavily on automated prequalification software, and their underwriting and compliance departments rarely objected to loans that met its requirements.

At the fastest-growing mortgage lending companies, such as Ameriquest and New Century, both of which were based in Orange County, California, the internal culture was more akin to a Wall Street boiler room than a traditional bank. Account executives had to meet demanding volume targets for loan originations. As the end of the month approached, they worked the phones frantically to meet them, paying little regard to the ability of borrowers to meet the commitments they were taking on. Top performers received generous bonuses as well as trips to Las Vegas and other resorts. In a scathing report on New Century filed in February 2008, Michael J. Missal, a bankruptcy court examiner, said the company's senior management "had a brazen obsession with increasing loan originations." New Century's former chief credit officer admitted in 2004 that the company had "no standard for loan quality." Its main concern, a number of the firm's former executives told Missal, was that the loans it originated could be sold to Wall Street. "Some New Century employees recognized the increased perils of these mortgage products and lending practices starting no later than 2004, and recommended changes to manage and minimize risk," Missal noted. "These recommendations, however, were either largely rejected or ignored by Senior Management."

As the housing bubble progressed, the typical subprime loan got bigger and riskier. In 2001, the average value of a subprime mortgage was $151,000; four years later, it was $259,000. In 1999, almost half of all subprime mortgages had a fixed interest rate, and practically none of them was interest-only. Six years later, more than 80 percent of subprime loans had an adjustable rate, and more than a quarter of them were interest-only.

At the peak of the boom, in 2005 and 2006, more than two-thirds of subprime borrowers were taking out "2/28 hybrid ARMs." To describe one of these creatures as a mortgage is something of a stretch. They were really just leveraged bets on the direction of house prices. For the first two years, the borrower was guaranteed a fixed rate—6 or 7 percent, say. After that, the rate would float up to a much higher level—somewhere between 10 and 15 percent was typical—where it would remain for twenty-eight years. Following the rise in the interest rate, 2/28 borrowers would typically see their monthly payments increase by between 50 and 100 percent. Clearly, many of them couldn't have afforded such a big jump. Some knew what they were doing— gambling that home prices would continue to appreciate, in which case they could refinance before the two years were up. Others didn't realize the risks they were taking; they were victims of predatory lending.

Subprime mortgages are complicated products, with many different features, including interest rates that vary, fees of various descriptions, and prepayment penalties. Many subprime borrowers were financially unsophisticated, and all too many mortgage lenders exploited the information advantage they had over their customers. The Center for Responsible Lending, which is based in North Carolina, has put together some egregious examples of predatory lending, of which the following is one:

> Ira and Hazel purchased their home in 1983, shortly after getting married, financing their purchase with a loan from the Veterans' Administration. By 2002, they had nearly paid off their first mortgage. The elderly couple got a call from a lender, urging them to consolidate all of their debt into a single mortgage. The lender assured the husband, who had excellent credit, that the couple would receive an interest rate between 5–6%, which would reduce their monthly payments. However, according to the couple, when the lender came to their house to have them sign the paperwork for their new mortgage, the lender failed to mention that the loan did not contain the low interest rate which they had been promised. Instead, it contained an interest rate of 9.9% and an annual percentage rate of 11.8%. Moreover, the loan contained 10 "discount points" ($15,289) which were financed into the loan, inflating the loan amount and stripping away the couple's equity. Under the new loan, the monthly mortgage payments increased to $1,655.00, amounting to roughly 57% of the couple's monthly income. Moreover, the loan contained a substantial prepayment penalty, forcing them to pay $7,500 to escape this predatory loan.

Most Wall Street firms didn't get involved in this type of lending directly, but they helped to facilitate it. As the demand for subprime securities exploded, banks and investment banks were so eager to get their hands on home loans that they often bought them off lenders for more than their face value. Take a typical $200,000 loan issued in 2005. Lehman Brothers, or Morgan Stanley, or one of their rivals, would offer to buy it for, say, $206,000—a premium of three percentage points. The Wall Street banks could afford to be profligate: they were charging hefty commissions and fees to the purchasers of sub-prime bonds. For every $100 million of ordinary subprime mortgage securities a Wall Street firm sold, it pocketed somewhere between $500,000 and $1 million. On more complex products, such as collateralized debt obligations, the commissions were even more generous.

The five biggest issuers of subprime mortgage securities in 2005 and 2006, according to *Inside Mortgage Finance*, were Lehman Brothers: $106 billion; RBS Greenwich Capital: $99.3 billion; Countrywide Securities, a division of Countrywide Financial: $74.5 billion; Morgan Stanley: $74.3 billion; and Credit Suisse First Boston: $73.4 billion. Some of these mortgage bonds ended up being diced and sliced into CDOs. Accurate figures for CDO issuance are hard to come by, but according to Bloomberg News, the five biggest underwriters in the first eight months of 2005 were Merrill Lynch, Citigroup, Wachovia, Goldman Sachs, and Lehman Brothers.

For all their supposed complexity, RMBSs and CDOs were, at root, fairly simple products. If each mortgage is thought of as an individual stock, an RMBS can be thought of as a mutual fund that pools the cash flows from a large number of stocks (loans) and pays them out to investors in the fund. Subprime CDOs were analogous to funds of funds. Their managers combined pieces from many different RMBSs, sometimes along with some whole loans, to create a new portfolio of interest-bearing assets.

A typical RMBS comprised several thousand home loans, and it carried the name or initials of its Wall Street issuer. For example, Goldman Sachs launched GSAMP TRUST 2006-NC2 in August 2006; it consisted of 3,949 mortgages that New Century had issued in the second quarter of 2006. For that vintage of securitizations, it was fairly typical. The average value of the loans was about $223,000, and nearly 90 percent of them were 2/28 ARMs. Two fifths had been taken out to buy properties; the rest had been issued for "cash out" refinancing of existing mortgages. About half the homes were in California and Florida, and the borrowers had an average FICO rating of 626.

Now, lending more than $200,000 to any given individual home-owner in this pool would clearly have been a hazardous enterprise. Almost a third of them had FICO scores below 600, indicating serious problems in their credit history. The basic rationale for investing in an RMBS (or a CDO) was that financing loans to several thousand questionable borrowers was much safer than lending to any individual. Why would that be? Wall Street had three answers: diversification, subordination, and the building up of reserves.

The argument for diversification was the same one that applies to salting away your retirement savings in mutual funds rather than investing in individual stocks. If you put all of your money in one company and it goes bankrupt, you lose everything; if you invest in five hundred companies, through an index fund, say, and one of them goes out of business, it shouldn't have much impact on the value of the fund. A bit more formally, the Nobel-winning financial theorist Harry Markowitz demonstrated back in the 1950s that diversification allows investors to minimize the impact of particular damaging events, or what is often referred to as "idiosyncratic risk." If the oil price plummets, the oil stocks in your retirement fund will probably go down, but cheaper gas frees up cash that gets spent on other things, and the stock in the sectors that benefit, such as retailers and restaurants, should go up. Losses in one part of the portfolio are made up in another.

With mortgage bonds, diversification is based on geography. When home prices are falling in Illinois or Ohio, they might well be going up in New Mexico and Arizona. By pulling together home loans from all across the country, the Wall Street issuers of mortgage securities were inoculating investors against the possibility of a particular housing market falling: that was what they claimed to be doing, anyway. Even if some homeowners defaulted, the vast majority would carry on making their monthly payments, and the bondholders would continue to receive their interest payments.

The second layer of protection came in the form of seniority. Extending the mutual fund analogy, most RMBSs issued four different classes of stock: super senior, senior, mezzanine, and junior (or equity). If any of the nearly four thousand mortgages in GSAMP TRUST defaulted, the owners of junior securities were first in line to bear any losses. The mezzanine investors wouldn't be affected until the equity investors had been wiped out; the senior investors wouldn't be affected until the mezzanine investors had been hit; and so on. (To compensate for the extra risk they were bearing, the junior and mezzanine investors received higher interest rates.) Finally, the typical RMBS was designed so that, initially, the total monthly payments from mortgage holders exceeded the interest payments the RMBS made to investors. This "excess spread" was used to build up a reserve fund that could be used to offset any later losses.

Super senior and senior mortgage securities typically carried AAA, AA, or A credit ratings: the mezzanine tranches were usually rated BB or above; and the equity tranche, which was exposed to the first losses on loan defaults, typically wasn't rated. The key to the investor appeal of mortgage securities was that they carried higher yields than corporate bonds with the same rating: if an AAA bond issued by IBM was yielding 5.5 percent, say, an AAA subprime mortgage security issued by Goldman Sachs or Lehman Brothers might be yielding 5.75 or 6 percent. Since both securities carried the same imprimatur from the rating agencies, mortgage bonds looked like a bargain.

As long as house prices were going up, the only checks on the growth of subprime lending were the rating agencies and the government regulators, both of which are supposed to prevent market failures. Rating agencies are a private-sector solution to the problem of hidden information: by delving into the companies and products they cover, and assigning grades based on what they find, they perform an essential screening task. Suppliers of capital, rather than being forced to figure out whether every specific company or bond is a sound bet, can rely on the educated opinion of a rating agency.

This assumes, of course, that the rating agencies' ratings are wholly objective and reasonably accurate. When it came to subprime mortgage securities, they were neither. Under the "issuer pays" model of credit ratings, Wall Street firms, such as Goldman Sachs and Morgan Stanley, paid the three big rating agencies—Moody's, Standard & Poor's, and Fitch—generous fees to rate their products. This payment system was also used in the corporate bond market, but the complexity and opaqueness of mortgage securities accentuated the conflict of interest that it inevitably involved.

Originally, rating agencies had charged investors to see their ratings, but in the 1970s they started assessing fees on the issuers—corporations, municipalities, and Wall Street firms. Partly because the rating agencies were viewed as quasi-public entities, the incentive problems associated with this payment system were for decades ignored. In the 1980s and '90s governments in the United States and other countries ordered banks to vary their capital reserves according to the credit ratings of the securities they held, thereby formally incorporating the rating agencies into the financial regulatory system. Under this system of risk-weighted capital requirements, Fitch, Moody's, and Standard & Poor's replaced government officials as the primary monitors of bank balance sheets. If they deemed a certain class of assets as risky, banks that owned some of them were obliged to hold more capital.

With the rise of securitization, the rating business received another boost. Since asset-backed securities, such as mortgage bonds, are more complicated than ordinary bonds, the agencies were able to charge high fees for rating them: the price of rating a $100 million RMBS was three or four times the price of rating a $100 million municipal bond—about $30,000–$40,000 versus about $10,000. As the market in mortgage securities mushroomed, structured finance became the rating agencies' main source of revenues. (In 2005, according to *The New York Times*, it accounted for more than 40 percent of Moody's revenues.) For decades, the agencies had operated as divisions of big publishing companies: Moody's was part of Dun and Bradstreet; S&P was (and is) part of McGraw-Hill. With their revenues growing rapidly, their corporate owners increasingly viewed them as valuable profit centers in their own right. In 2000, Moody's was split off from Dun and Bradstreet. It issued stock and endowed its senior executives with the customary "incentive" packages. "In my view, the focus of Moody's shifted from protecting investors to being a market-driven organization," Jerome S. Fons, a former managing director at Moody's, told a congressional hearing in October 2008. "[M]anagement's focus increasingly turned to maximizing revenues. Stock options and other incentives raised the possibility of large payoffs."

Rather than adopting an arm's-length approach and establishing a set of standards for issuers of RMBSs and CDOs to meet, the agencies worked closely with Wall Street banks, instructing them on how to structure their offerings to achieve the investment-grade ratings investors demanded. As the subprime boom continued, the investment bankers routinely played the rating firms off one another, shopping around for a favorable rating. If the analysts at Moody's weren't looking benignly upon a particular securitization, the banker in charge of the offering would call up their rivals at S&P or Fitch and invite them to have a look. Comparisons have been made to the corporate scandals earlier in the decade, when auditing firms such as Arthur Andersen compromised their independence by entering into lucrative consulting agreements with firms such as Enron and WorldCom.

Fitch, Moody's, and S&P have vociferously contested this analogy. "We will never tell an arranger what it should or should not do," S&P said in a commentary it published in August 2007. "We merely react to the proposals made by the arrangers and in each case only to the extent of telling them the likely impact of these proposals on the rating outcome. To call upon the agencies to cease to do so would be a major step away from the openness, transparency, and dialogue that has been urged on them by the international regulatory community." Still, the historical record is clear. In 2005 and 2006, Wall Street firms issued more than $1 trillion worth of subprime RMBSs and CDOs, the great majority of which Fitch, Moody's, and S&P rated as AAA or AA. Since the summer of 2007, almost all these issues have been savagely downgraded; many of them have stopped trading.

So, were the rating agencies corrupt or merely incompetent? As one of the Moody's executives in charge of monitoring credit quality, Jerome S. Fons, a former staff economist at the Fed who spent seventeen years at Moody's, was in as good a position as anybody to answer this question. "My view is that a large part of the blame can be placed on the inherent conflicts of interest found in the issuer-pays business model and rating shopping by issuers of structured securities," he told Congress.

A drive to maintain or expand market share made the rating agencies willing participants in this shopping spree. It was also relatively easy for the major banks to play the agencies off one another because of the opacity of the structured transactions and the high potential fees earned by the winning agency. Originators of structured securities typically chose the agency with the lowest standards, engendering a race to the bottom in terms of rating quality. While the methods used to rate structured securities have rightly come under fire, in my opinion, the business model prevented analysts from putting investor interests first.

While all this was happening, the nation's top financial cop, the chairman of the Fed, was averting his eyes. In a September 2007 interview with the CBS show *60 Minutes*, Greenspan conceded that while he had been aware of widespread abuses in the subprime market, "I had no notion of how significant they had become until very late. I didn't really get it until very late in 2005 and 2006." Unlike Greenspan, most federal regulators actually believed in regulation, but a weak and balkanized system of oversight frustrated their efforts.

At the start of the mortgage chain, there was no federal supervision of mortgage brokers, who had been multiplying like fruit flies. By 2004, according to one study, there were more than fifty thousand mortgage broker firms in the United States, employing more than four hundred thousand people. Many states made local brokers obtain licenses, which typically involved proving they had reached a certain educational level and posting a surety bond, but only a few states imposed a fiduciary duty on them to act in the best interests of their clients. Even in California and other places where such laws were on the books, they were rarely enforced. Aggrieved individuals were free to sue their brokers for negligence or fraud, but this was a forbidding undertaking.

The regulation of subprime lenders was (and is) a horrible muddle, with a variety of federal agencies supervising different parts of the industry and, in some cases, different parts of the same firm. At the top of the pile, the Fed was responsible for regulating the big bank holding companies, such as Citigroup, JPMorgan Chase, and Wachovia, which owned some of the biggest lenders. The Office of the Comptroller of the Currency, an independent division of the Treasury Department, regulated nationally chartered banks, such as Citibank and Wells Fargo Bank; the Federal Deposit Insurance Corporation supervised somewhat smaller banks that weren't part of the Federal Reserve system; and the Office of Thrift Supervision regulated S&Ls, such as Countrywide and Washington Mutual. In an ideal system, these regulators would have come together and imposed a set of uniform standards on the subprime lenders. Instead, they engaged in turf wars, which allowed the big financial institutions to play one off against another, much as they manipulated the rating agencies.

Even if the federal regulators had done a better job, they didn't supervise many mortgage lenders, which were incorporated at the state level. To the extent that these firms issued securities to investors, the SEC had some oversight, but the main onus for regulating them fell on state officials, who were often swamped. According to Mark Zandi, the cofounder of the Moody's website Economy.com, thirty examiners at the California Department of Corporations shared responsibility for regulating nearly five thousand consumer finance companies, including ones as big as Ameriquest and New Century. "The massive workload effectively reduced examiners to bookkeepers who could only check to make sure that companies had adequate reserves and were not overcharging borrowers," Zandi wrote in his 2008 book, *Financial Shock*, an informative account of the subprime crisis. "Mortgage companies could expect an examination from state regulators about once every four years."

What was needed was for somebody at the national level to raise the alarm about lending standards and confront Greenspan's policy of laissez-faire, but practically nobody did this. The person who came closest was one of the Fed chairman's own colleagues, the late Edward Gramlich, who served as a Fed governor from 1997 to 2005. A moderate Democrat, Gramlich had previously taught at the University of Michigan and worked for the Congressional Budget Office. Over a number of years, he called for the Fed and other agencies to take tougher action against predatory lending, which, he said in December 2000, "destroys people and communities and is a clear blight." But Gramlich was no critic of subprime lending per se; to the contrary, he repeatedly praised its role in creating millions of new homeowners. In 2004, he pointed to rising subprime delinquencies as a worrying sign, but concluded that, on balance, the social value of the industry was "probably a strong positive." As late as 2007, shortly before his death, Gramlich wrote, "The subprime market, for all its warts, is a promising development, permitting low-income and minority borrowers to participate in credit markets."

Lacking in Gramlich's analysis, and that of his fellow policymakers, was any appreciation of what the deterioration in lending standards portended for the economy as a whole. Convinced that the financial system was innately stable, they regarded problems in the subprime market as strictly a microeconomic issue, and their main concern was that credit would continue to flow to low- and middle-income families. The mortgage lenders, with even their critics praising their role in the economy, didn't have to worry about anybody in Washington interfering with their business. In the best nineteenth-century tradition, the housing bubble and subprime craze would be allowed to run their course.

20. IN THE ALPHABET SOUP

o anybody familiar with Minsky's financial instability hypothesis, the deterioration of credit standards looked worryingly familiar. The U.S. economy was experiencing a credit boom of the sort usually associated with poorly run economies in Latin America and parts of Eastern Europe: an overly lax monetary policy had unleashed a self-sustaining property bubble and a wassail of irresponsible lending. For the moment, however, the continuing rise in house prices disguised the rot. It is a safe bet that most of the top policymakers at the Fed and in the Bush administration had never heard of Minsky, or, if they had, had dismissed him as an alarmist—not that this would have surprised him. "As a previous financial crisis recedes in time, it is quite natural for central bankers, government officials, bankers, businessmen, and even economists to believe that a new era has arrived," Minsky wrote. "Cassandra-like warnings that nothing basic has changed, that there is a financial breaking point that will lead to a deep depression, are naturally ignored in these circumstances."

The widespread complacency about the economy wasn't just a matter of disaster myopia, although that certainly played a role. Among policymakers, Wall Street executives, and economists, there was also a conviction that advances in financial technology had enabled banks and other lenders to manage the hazards of their business more effectively than they had in the past. By securitizing loans rather than keeping them on their balance sheets, they could distribute credit risks to investors; through the application of new mathematical tools, they could gauge precisely what risk remained on their books; and by buying and selling newfangled derivatives, they could use the market to hedge their exposures.

In June 2006, five months after he replaced Alan Greenspan, Ben Bernanke noted that in the past a bank's lending decisions had relied mainly on the personal judgments of loan officers. "Today, retail lending has become more routinized as banks have become increasingly adept at predicting default risk by applying statistical models to data, such as credit scores," Bernanke went on. "Other tools include proprietary internal debt-rating models and third-party programs that use market data to analyze the risk of exposures to corporate borrowers that issue stock." While challenges remained, Bernanke concluded, "banking organizations of all sizes have made substantial strides over the past two decades in their ability to measure and manage risks."

Nobody could quibble with Bernanke's point that Wall Street was becoming more quantitative: the research and risk departments of big financial firms were teeming with physicists, applied mathematicians, and statisticians. But the proper role of statistical models is as a useful adjunct to an overall strategy of controlling risk, not as a substitute for one. At many banks and investment banks, quantitative techniques were being used to rationalize a reckless increase in leverage. By tweaking the models as was required, it was possible to present virtually any increase in lending as "safe."

The very existence of the models also gave senior bankers and policymakers a false sense of security. Risk management, long an imprecise and intuitive discipline, appeared to have been converted into a hard science. A fog of acronyms and mathematical symbols obscured what should have been obvious—too many financial institutions were lending heavily to an overheated property market. Like pilots on a modern airliner, the regulators and Wall Street CEOs had come to rely on the computers to tell them if anything was amiss. However, the risk-management systems that had been put in place at firms such as Citigroup, UBS, and Merrill Lynch had a much shorter record than the autopilots installed on Boeings and Airbuses, and they turned out to be far less reliable. When severe turbulence hit, many of them stopped working.

A realistic assessment of the risks facing the U.S. financial system would have begun with a closer look at some of the securitizations Wall Street was churning out. The Wall Street firms and the rating agencies had both failed to probe the underlying logic of combining pools of subprime loans. In any group of assets, be it a stock, a mutual fund, or an RMBS, the benefits of diversification depend on the assets being truly diverse; in a statistical sense, they need to have a low degree of correlation. The subprime loans that were used in mortgage securitizations weren't diverse at all. Most of them were situated in bubble areas, such as California, Nevada, and Florida, and the borrowers who had taken them out all had low credit ratings.

Combining a hundred 2/28 mortgages from Fort Lauderdale with a hundred 2/28 loans from Las Vegas and another hundred from Orange County didn't provide any real diversification of risk; it simply joined like with like. "The best way I can put it is this way," the head of one Wall Street investment firm said to me shortly after the subprime crisis began. "You take hundreds of drunks staggering down the street, and you make them put their arms under each other's shoulders and lock hands. Then you rely on the fact that they are all falling in different directions to keep the entire group upright. Oh, and you call it a Triple A security."

A more formal way of making the same point is to say that RMBSs and CDOs carried an enormous amount of "systematic" risk. With corporate bonds, the main systematic risk factor is the state of the economy: if it falls into recession, most companies see their revenues fall. With mortgage bonds, the big systematic risk factor is the state of the housing market. Combining subprime mortgages magnified rather than diminished the exposure to this risk. Most subprime borrowers were hoping to refinance their loans within a couple of years, but their ability to do this depended on home prices continuing to increase at a healthy clip. If prices stopped going up, or—Lord forbid—started to fall back, the borrowers wouldn't build up any equity before their loans reset, and for many of them, the costs of refinancing would be prohibitive. With millions of homeowners facing a big spike in their monthly payments, a rash of defaults and foreclosures would be inevitable.

In such a scenario, even the holders of senior and super senior paper would be far from safe, because the subordinate tranches were too thin to provide them with much protection. In a typical RMBS securitization, the equity and mezzanine layers together represented less than 10 percent of the principal balance of the outstanding mortgages; more than 90 percent of the securities in the deal were classed as super senior or senior. This structure was designed to insulate the senior paper from minor shocks—not a major reversal in the housing market. If defaults started to mount up, the holders of mezzanine and junior tranches would quickly get wiped out, leaving the rest of the investors, who thought they were holding high-grade debt, to bear the bulk of the losses.

None of this was hidden knowledge. With each mortgage securitization, the Wall Street firm behind the deal issued a lengthy prospectus detailing the subordination structure of the securities being issued, the nature of the underlying loans, and other risk factors involved in investing. For example, the prospectus Goldman Sachs filed for GSAMP TRUST 2006-NC2 said it was issuing $882 million in mortgage-backed securities, of which about $700 million S&P and Moody's had rated "AAA/Aaa." There was another $124 million in securities that the rating agencies had assigned AA or A ratings, and $30 million that had been rated between "BBB+/Baa" and "BBB−/Baa." Another $27 billion was rated below BBB−. In this particular offering, the mezzanine and equity ranches amounted to less than 7 percent of the total offering, making them an extremely slim layer of protection.

Rather than listing the individual homeowners or properties in a given pool of subprime mortgages, the prospectuses provided summary details. Ninety percent of the almost four thousand mortgages in the GSAMP TRUST were adjustable-rate loans, more than 50 percent of them had balloon payments attached to them, and about 38 percent of them had loan-to-value ratios in excess of 80 percent—all indications of questionable credit quality.

Most investors relied on the rating agencies and didn't concern themselves with details. Hedge funds were eager buyers of the most junior tranches of subprime RMBSs and CDOs, which sported juicy yields. Mutual funds, university endowments, and many foreign investors snapped up the more senior paper, which carried the same rating as bonds issued by Exxon Mobil and Johnson and Johnson. In many cases, the most difficult parts of the securitizations to market were the intermediate ("mezzanine") securities, which didn't have a sterling credit rating or a particularly high yield. To solve this problem, Wall Street came up with the ingenious concept of "mezzanine CDOs"— CDOs composed of the junior claims of other mortgage securities. By judiciously including slices of many different RMBSs, and by building in a big enough excess spread, the investment firms were able to convince the rating agencies to assign an AAA rating to many of these CDOs. Even by Wall Street standards, that was a neat trick.

If all this sounds like alchemy, so it was. But unlike what had taken place during the dot-com bubble, it wasn't exclusively a matter of cynical investment bankers foisting worthless securities onto gullible investors. As the securitization boom continued into 2006 and early 2007, some of the biggest holders of subprime RMBSs and CDOs ended up being the very banks and investment banks that had created them.

They didn't intend this to happen, of course. Some of it came about through the shadow banking system. The off-balance-sheet special-purpose vehicles and SIVs, which firms such as Citigroup had set up, acted like mini banks. They issued short-term debt to investors and used the cash they raised to buy long-term assets from their parent companies, such as mortgage securities, corporate loans, and securitized car loans. The numbers involved were large: in August 2007, SIVs linked to big financial institutions had more than $300 billion in assets, according to Moody's Investors Service. The SIVs associated with Citigroup alone had assets of almost $100 billion.

Legally, these shell companies were independent entities. Economically, they were still attached to their parents, like well-to-do college students. In order to give investors some reassurance about buying the short-term paper that the SIVs issued, their sponsor firms had provided them with guaranteed credit lines, which they could draw on as needed. The SIVs' assets and liabilities remained part of their families' overall finances—even if their parents refused to admit it. (Apart from the odd footnote, the public accounts of Citigroup, Bank of

America, and other big banks made no reference to the SIVs and other off-balance-sheet vehicles they had created.)

The growth of the shadow banking system helped to disguise the exposures that many big banks had to mortgage securities and other asset-backed paper, but it wasn't the only means by which Wall Street kidded the public (and itself) about its true state. As the securitization boom continued, many big Wall Street firms, such as Merrill Lynch and UBS, also took direct ownership of many RMBSs and CDOs that their own trading desks had created. They ate their own cooking, and got poisoned.

The process worked like this. As the supply of subprime paper increased, the interest-rate premiums on subprime bonds decreased. Between 2001 and 2003, the yield on subprime RMBSs was two to three percentage points (two hundred to three hundred basis points) higher than the rate on prime RMBSs: in 2004–2006, the gap fell to one to two percentage points (one hundred to two hundred basis points). In the credit markets, every basis point counts. With spreads diminishing, investors started to balk at buying so much subprime paper, particularly the super senior tranches, which carried the lowest interest rates. Wall Street firms, rather than cutting back on the number of subprime securitizations they were doing, which would have meant forgoing hefty underwriting fees and bonuses, continued to market RMBSs and CDOs in great quantities. To get the deals done, however, some of them were forced to retain the super senior paper they couldn't sell to other investors.

Between February 2006 and September 2007, UBS's CDO desk, which had previously sold all of the securities it issued, accumulated $50 billion in mortgage assets. Citigroup's investment bank, which had greatly expanded its CDO business, accumulated more than $50 billion in super senior tranches. Merrill Lynch, which was the leading issuer of CDOs, built up a stockpile of more than $40 billion in mortgages and mortgage securities. Other Wall Street firms, such as Morgan Stanley and Lehman, took on smaller but still very significant mortgage exposures.

By late 2006, house prices were falling in many parts of the country. Still, firms such as Citigroup, Merrill, and UBS refused to scale back their mortgage businesses. Some of them even ramped them up further. In April 2007, UBS's CDO desk presented a pessimistic view of the subprime market to the firm's management, but shortly after that it requested permission to increase its holdings of super senior securities. During the first half of 2007, Merrill created about $30 billion in CDOs, which kept it at first place in the Wall Street rankings. But the firm didn't make clear publicly that it had resorted to bailing out some of its own deals, and neither did any of the other firms that were doing the same thing. On June 17, 2007, Merrill reported quarterly profits of $2.1 billion, an increase of 31 percent compared to the same period in 2006. In a memo to Merrill's employees, CEO Stan O'Neal referred to the fact that conditions in the CDO market had become more difficult and expressed confidence in the firm's ability to weather them. "More than anything else the quarter reflected the benefits of a simple but critical fact: we go about managing risk and market activity every day at this company," O'Neal said. "It's what our clients pay us to do, and as you all know, we're pretty good at it."

The risk-management techniques that Merrill and many other big financial firms had adopted depended heavily on value-at-risk (VAR) models, which dated back to the 1990s, when they were promoted as a means of avoiding a repeat of previous financial blowups, such as the collapse of Barings Bank and the bankruptcy of Orange County. The keys to the appeal of the VAR (or "VaR") methodology were its simplicity and its apparent precision. By following a fairly straightforward series of steps, the market-risk department of a bank could provide senior management with an exact dollar estimate of the firm's losses under a worst-case scenario. In its 1994 annual report, for example, J.P. Morgan, one of the pioneers of the VAR methodology, revealed that the daily VAR of its trading book was $15 million at the 95 percent confidence level, which meant that the probability of its losing more than $15 million in any given trading session was less than one in twenty.

In addition to offering an instant snapshot of the dangers a firm such as Morgan faced, VAR modeling provided a way for it to monitor changes in risk. For example, when a bank sells some Treasury bonds and buys some volatile technology stocks, its VAR rises by a certain amount, say $10 million, giving its management a precise read on how much extra risk it has taken on. "In contrast with traditional risk measures, VaR provides an aggregate view of a portfolio's risk that accounts for leverage, correlations, and current positions," Philippe Jorion, a professor of finance at the University of California, Irvine, wrote in his 1996 book, *Value at Risk: The New Benchmark for Controlling Market Risk*, which helped to popularize the methodology. "As a result, it is truly a forward looking risk measure."

According to Wall Street folklore, the concept of value-at-risk originated in the late 1980s, when, following the stock market crash of 1987, the late Sir Dennis Weatherstone, J.P. Morgan's British-born chairman, asked his division heads to put together a one-page briefing that answered the question "How much can we lose on our trading portfolio by tomorrow's close?" Morgan's quantitative analysts came up with a statistical way of providing Sir Dennis with the information he wanted, and the firm began using it in a daily "4:15 report." During the early 1990s, J.P. Morgan started marketing the method, which it called RiskMetrics, to other financial firms. In 1995, it published a technical guide on the Internet that established RiskMetrics as the industry standard for VAR modeling. Other big banks, such as Citigroup and Bankers Trust, which was later taken over by Deutsche Bank, developed similar risk models around the same time as Morgan did, or even earlier, but it was J.P. Morgan's VAR methodology that took off.

Even the regulators endorsed it. In 1996, the Basel-based Bank for International Settlements, which helps set global accounting standards, said that banks should be allowed to use their own VAR models to calculate how much capital they needed to hold in reserve. Under the old system, governments had simply ordered banks to maintain a certain level of capital. Now the regulators allowed firms to carry less capital if their VAR models suggested they weren't carrying a lot of risk. This system of "risk-based" capital requirements was incorporated in the 2004 "Basel II" banking accord, which the governments of most advanced countries, including the United States, agreed to use as the basis for their own regulatory systems.

VAR modeling did (and does) provide some valuable information. "It helps you understand what you should expect to happen on a daily basis in an environment that is roughly the same," David Viniar, Goldman Sachs's chief financial officer, told *The New York Times*. Unfortunately, VAR was ill suited to the task its promoters had appropriated for it: preventing financial calamities. The problem is largely conceptual, and it relates to the illusion of predictability. If risk is defined as the chance of something disastrous happening between now and a certain date, it is impossible to quantify accurately, because, as Keynes and others pointed out, the future is inherently unpredictable. There are innumerable ways that bad things can happen, some of which are currently unknown or unappreciated. No statistical model, however sophisticated, can hope to capture more than a few of the possibilities.

The defenders of VAR sidestepped this problem by redefining risk as volatility and assuming that the future would resemble recent history. In the simplest version of VAR, which involves a portfolio consisting of a single asset class, the risk modeler calls up some data and looks at how much the portfolio has jumped around in the past, perhaps by calculating its standard deviation. The next step involves invoking the ghost of Louis Bachelier—this is where the illusion of predictability comes in—and assuming that daily movements in financial prices follow the bell curve, or normal distribution, which places exact numbers on the likelihood of unlikely events. (For example, in any given trading session the probability of a stock rising or falling by more than three times its standard deviation is about 0.003, less than one in three hundred.) Now the analyst is virtually done: a bit more fiddling with the computer, and the final dollar VAR figure will pop up on his screen.

Most portfolios consist of more than one asset, which complicates the arithmetic. Another complication is the existence of "fat tails." By the turn of the century, most economists had come to accept Benoit Mandelbrot's argument that big movements in financial markets are more frequent than the bell curve predicts. To deal with this problem, some VAR modelers used different probability distributions, which fit the data more closely than the normal distribution, or so they claimed; others sought to avoid using any probability distributions at all, relying on historical simulations. The RiskMetrics estimate of volatility was based on a technique called exponential smoothing. Some VAR modelers relied on a complicated statistical method known as GARCH (generalized autoregressive conditional heteroskedasticity). Yet others used Monte Carlo simulation, a random sampling technique that was developed by nuclear physicists working at Los Alamos in the 1940s.

Playing around with VAR models kept Wall Street quantitative analysts occupied. It didn't solve the basic problem that historical data are of limited use in predicting future moves in the markets, especially extreme ones. Almost all statistical models are basically extrapolative; they take past data and project forward from it. Under some circumstances, this can work; under others, it can prove disastrous. During a period such as 2002–2006, when the markets were unusually tranquil, virtually any model would have understated the "tail risk" of a big move in one direction or another. There simply wasn't enough variation in the data to generate anything but relatively benign forecasts.

VAR models also tend to exaggerate the benefits of diversification. Typically, a big bank such as Citigroup or Wells Fargo has a wide variety of assets on its books: consumer loans, corporate loans, Treasury bonds, high-grade corporate bonds, junk bonds, mortgage bonds, stocks, currencies, commodities, and all manner of derivatives. In regular circumstances, the prices of some of these assets will move in opposite directions: if investors move out of junk bonds, higher-grade corporate bonds may benefit, whereas mortgage bonds might not be affected at all. In statistical terms, this means that some of the assets are negatively correlated, and others are hardly correlated at all. VAR models take account of these offsetting effects. In estimating the worst-case losses of entire portfolios, or balance sheets, the models reward those that are widely diversified and punish those that are heavily invested in one or two assets.

Unfortunately, during periods of great stress, the relationships between different asset classes tend to change dramatically. As the big hedge fund Long-Term Capital Management discovered to its cost during the international financial crisis of 1998, many assets that seem to have little or nothing in common suddenly move in the same direction. Prior to the blowup, for example, the correlation coefficient between certain bonds issued by the governments of the Philippines and Bulgaria was just 0.04: as the crisis unfolded, their correlation coefficient rose to 0.84. (A correlation coefficient of zero means two assets have no relationship; a coefficient of one means they move in perfect unison.) During a period of market upheaval, as a Wall Street saying has it, "all correlations go to one." Investors panic and sell many different types of assets at the same time. When this happens, even a bank or financial institution that appears to be well diversified can suffer losses much bigger than a VAR model would have predicted, especially if it is highly leveraged (as Long-Term Capital was). Thus, the ultimate irony about VAR-based risk management: when it is needed most is precisely when it performs most poorly.

The use of VAR models also contributes to rising leverage levels. As the stock and bond markets entered a period of unusual tranquillity, market-based VAR estimates fell sharply, encouraging banks to run down their capital. A hypothetical (and simplified) example should make this clear: Bank X has $500 billion worth of assets, and its VAR is $25 billion. If banks aim to keep enough reserves on hand to cover twice their VAR, Bank X's capital requirement is $50 billion, which means its leverage ratio—total assets/total capital—is ten, a fairly conservative number. Now assume that Bank X's risk department reports that its VAR has halved, to $12.5 billion. The bank now has surplus capital of $25 billion, which it can use to invest in risky assets. Once it does this, it will have assets of $500 billion and capital of $25 billion; its leverage ratio will have doubled, to twenty. With higher gearing, Bank X's return on equity (ROE) and return on assets (ROA), two measures of profitability, will rise, and so, quite probably, will its stock price. But if something unexpected happens, such as a collapse in the bond market, it will be much more vulnerable.

As with the slumping quality of mortgage credit, the potential problems with relying on VAR to manage risk weren't exactly hidden. RiskMetrics, the pioneer of the technique, said in a 1997 introduction to its popular CreditMetrics product: "We remind our readers that no amount of sophisticated analytics will replace experience and professional judgment in managing risks." In a textbook on risk management published in 2004, the economists Linda Allen, Jacob Boudoukh, and Anthony Saunders wrote, "The relative prevalence of extreme market moves, even after adjusting for current conditions, is the reason we need additional tools over and above the standard VaR risk measurement tool." Even Philippe Jorion warned that VAR worked only "under normal market conditions."

Those comments came from defenders of VAR. Its critics, such as the author and former options trader Nassim Nicholas Taleb, had for years been describing it as charlatanism. "I believe that the VAR is the alibi bankers will give shareholders (and the bailing-out taxpayer) to show documented due diligence and will express that their blow-up came from truly unforeseeable circumstances and events with low probability—not from taking large risks they did not understand," Taleb wrote in 1997, during an exchange with Jorion. "I maintain that the due diligence VAR tool encourages untrained people to take misdirected risk with the shareholders', and ultimately the taxpayer's money."

Taleb's skepticism proved well founded. Many firms used VAR models to justify raising their bets. At UBS, for example, "business planning relied on VAR, which appears as the key risk parameter in the planning process," the firm subsequently revealed in a report to stockholders. "When the market dislocation unfolded, it became apparent that this risk measure methodology had not appropriately captured the risk inherent in the business having subprime exposures." The VAR models used by UBS's risk department incorporated just five years of data, which meant they didn't take account of any prior periods of market upheaval. Moreover, the risk department failed to supplement its VAR calculations with any fundamental analysis of what was happening in the outside world. It relied on VAR estimates "even though delinquency rates were increasing and origination standards were falling in the U.S. mortgage market. It continued to do so throughout the build-up of significant positions in subprime assets that were only partially hedged . . . No warnings were given to Group Senior Management about the limitations of the presented numbers or the need to look at the broader contextual framework . . ."

UBS should be complimented for being so open about its internal failures: no American bank has published such a mea culpa. To a greater or lesser extent, however, they all made the same errors, taking on more risk, levering up their balance sheets, and greatly increasing the fragility of the financial system. The risk models the banks used can't be held directly responsible for their recklessness, but they certainly acted as enablers, providing their senior executives with ready-made alibis, just as Taleb had predicted. In addition to placing their trust in rating agencies and risk models, the men who ran the big Wall Street firms took comfort from the fact that at least some of the dubious assets on their balance sheets were insured. Which brings us to the final ingredient of the subprime alphabet soup.

J.P. Morgan has much to answer for—the firm, not the man. As well as unleashing VAR models on an unsuspecting public, it played a key role in developing credit insurance in the form of credit default swaps

(CDSs). The word "swaps" is used in the derivatives business, and it has caused a lot of unnecessary confusion. Credit default swaps aren't really swaps at all; they should be called credit insurance contracts. As with VAR, Morgan didn't invent the concept of credit insurance—the late Bankers Trust also has claims to that honor—but it turned it into a major industry. In 1997, a group of math whizzes in Morgan's derivatives department took $9.7 billion in loans that it had issued to about three hundred corporations, placed them in a special-purpose vehicle, and distributed tranches of the SPV to investors. This sounds like a routine securitization, but it came with a twist. The investors—insurance companies and other banks, mainly—didn't get to own the loans, which remained on Morgan's books; they merely agreed to take on the risk of Morgan's borrowers defaulting. In return, Morgan agreed to pay them what were effectively insurance premiums. As long as the borrowers kept making their interest and principal payments, the investors would receive a steady stream of income—some $700 million a year in total. But if some of the borrowers defaulted, the owners of the SPV stood to make up the full value of the loans. These mutual obligations were defined in legal agreements, which were called credit default swaps.

The 1997 deal accomplished several things: it removed $9.7 billion in credit risks from Morgan's balance sheet, freeing up capital the firm could use elsewhere; it transferred these risks to other financial institutions that had more of an appetite for them; and it created securities that could be traded, thus allowing investors to get exposure to an asset class—bank loans—that they had previously been excluded from. To a traditional banker, the idea of separating risk from lending seemed revolutionary. In her informative account of the recent development of the credit markets, *Fool's Gold*, Gillian Tett, a reporter at the *Financial Times*, describes the thinking of Blythe Masters, one of the members of the Morgan team. Separating lending and risk "would overturn one of the fundamental rules of banking: that default risk is an inevitable liability of the business . . . For the first time in history, banks would be able to make loans without carrying all, or perhaps even any, of the risk involved themselves."

Masters's ingenuousness, as reported by Tett, is almost charming. To anybody familiar with financial history, the very idea of banks being able to extend credit without worrying about the consequences should have set off alarm bells. Once Morgan had demonstrated how to do this with bank loans, the obvious next step was to apply the same technique to different types of credit products, such as mortgage-backed securities. This didn't prove too difficult, and between 1998 and 2004, the issuance of credit default swaps increased exponentially. The two most popular products were "single-name CDSs," which provided their holders with protection against the default of a particular loan or bond, and "basket CDSs," which insured a basket of loans or bonds.

Since credit default swaps weren't regulated, there was plenty of scope for creativity. An important development was the creation of CDSs that didn't have anything to do with the issuer of the underlying debts. For example, Citigroup could agree to provide protection to Goldman Sachs on some mortgage bonds issued by Merrill Lynch: in this case, Goldman would pay premiums to Citigroup, and if the Merrill bonds got downgraded, say, Citigroup would pay Goldman an agreed sum of money. There was also nothing to prevent the issuance of two or more CDSs on the same bond or loan: if Bank A had some loans it wanted to insure, it could buy protection from Bank B, which could lay off some of the risk on Bank C, which could buy protection from Hedge Fund Z, and so on.

Buying or selling default protection in the form of a CDS allowed Wall Street firms and investors to express a view on the future creditworthiness of a particular borrower, or group of borrowers. This, and the fact that they didn't involve laying out much money up front, made CDSs perfect vehicles for speculation and hedging. By 2004, according to the Bank for International Settlements, about $4.5 trillion in credit derivatives had been issued. (The figure refers to the face value of the debt insured.) Between 2004 and 2006, with the rapid increase in subprime mortgage securitization, the CDS business got another enormous boost.

As explained earlier, many Wall Street firms that issued RMBSs and CDOs ended up keeping slices of these deals on their own books, which they were keen to hedge. On the other side of the market, many hedge funds and institutional investors were eager to take a long or short position in subprime. To help out both sides, financial engineers created new variants of credit default swaps: some were linked to particular securitizations, others to broad subprime credit indexes, such as the ABX index. By the end of 2005, virtually every big firm on Wall

Street was heavily involved in the credit insurance market. So were big commercial banks, such as Citigroup and Bank of America, and some top insurance companies, particularly AIG. In June 2007, the notional value of outstanding CDSs had reached an astonishing $42.6 trillion, according to the Bank for International Settlements. (Some estimates put the figure even higher.)

To free market economists, this all seemed like healthy innovation: risks were being chopped up and apportioned to institutions that wanted to bear them. Others weren't so convinced. In February 2003, in his annual letter to shareholders of his company, Berkshire Hathaway, Warren Buffett warned that "large amounts of risk, particularly credit risk, have become concentrated in the hands of relatively few derivatives dealers, who in addition trade extensively with one another. The troubles of one could quickly infect the others . . . Linkage, when it suddenly surfaces, can trigger serious systemic problems." Referring to his partner, Charles Munger, Buffett went on: "Central banks and governments have so far found no effective way to control, or even monitor, the risks posed by these contracts . . . In our view, however, derivatives are financial weapons of mass destruction, carrying dangers that, while now latent, are potentially lethal."

As the credit insurance market continued to expand, none of the issues that Buffett highlighted got resolved. The providers of credit insurance were effectively taking on the same default risks that banks did when they lent money, but unlike banks, they didn't set aside any capital to cover possible losses. Most CDSs were "unfunded," meaning the provider of protection didn't put up collateral. If and when a default occurred, the provider had to pay out. Until then, however, it simply collected the premiums. For any financial firm, the promise of receiving cash without locking up capital is extremely attractive: with the economy humming, and credit defaults at historic lows, it proved irresistible.

In increasing financial firms' (contingent) liabilities without bolstering their capital reserves, the growth of the CDS market effectively added even more leverage to the system. Since many firms had laid off some of the risks they took on, net exposures were smaller than gross exposures: how much smaller, it was tough to tell. Most CDSs traded privately, and there was no central repository of trades. From the outside, it was impossible to determine who owed what to whom. Even from the inside, key information was often hidden. Given the chainlink structure of many CDS transactions, issuers and buyers were indirectly exposed to problems at firms several links down the chain, creating an additional layer of "network risk" that couldn't be quantified or hedged. As Buffett had noted, this spillover created systemic risk issues. In the event of a crisis, firms would be justifiably suspicious of each other, and liquidity could quickly dry up, which is what happened in 1998. And, in fact, this occurred again, on a more minor scale, in the spring of 2005, when the rating agencies unexpectedly revised downward their outlook for the debt of General Motors. With investors in shock, the spreads (premiums) on CDSs of all kinds shot up dramatically, and many Wall Street banks and hedge funds suffered big losses. On this occasion, the markets stabilized, and in May 2005 Alan Greenspan sang the praises of credit derivatives, saying their development "has contributed to the stability of the banking system by allowing banks, especially the largest, systemically important banks, to measure and manage their credit risks more effectively."

Greenspan acknowledged some concerns about the CDS market—including the possibility that losses suffered by nonbanks, such as hedge funds, could cause them to liquidate their positions simultaneously, causing a 1998-style downward spiral—only to dismiss them with his by-now standard argument about counterparty monitoring. "In essence, prudential regulation is supplied by the market through counterparty evaluation and monitoring rather than by authorities," Greenspan said. "We regulators are often perceived as constraining excessive risk-taking more effectively than is demonstrably possible in practice . . . [P]rivate regulation generally has proved far better at constraining excessive risk-taking than has government regulation."

In some areas, Greenspan's free market beliefs made him an outlier. In the case of derivatives such as CDSs, Greenspan was merely stating the official view of the Fed and other international banking regulators. After he retired in January 2006, his successor, Ben Bernanke, made no effort to reverse the Fed's hands-off stance. The idea that CDSs facilitated the spreading and management of risk had attained the status of official dogma, and so had faith in VAR-based risk management. Unless something disastrous happened, none of the regulatory authorities would seriously question the Wall Street line. Congress, meanwhile, was busy trying to further lighten the legal burdens that financial firms faced. In October 2006, President Bush signed the Financial Services Regulatory Relief Act of 2006, which allowed banks to keep even less capital in reserve. The House of Representatives approved the bill by 417 votes to 15. The Senate passed it by unanimous consent.

21. A MATTER OF INCENTIVES

conomics, when you strip away the guff and the mathematical sophistry, is largely about incentives. Communism collapsed because it failed to encourage innovation, enterprise, and hard work; capitalism has thrived, broadly speaking, because it rewarded these things, while punishing conservatism and dawdling. The market system is heartless and unforgiving, but, as even Marx and Engels pointed out, it is uniquely productive. During its short existence, the German leftists noted in 1848, it had "accomplished wonders far surpassing Egyptian pyramids, Roman aqueducts, and Gothic cathedrals: it has conducted expeditions that put in the shade all former exoduses of nations and crusades."

In the 1970s, the resurrection of free market economics was based largely on the argument that high taxes and excessive regulation were stifling the economy. "By taxation, by inflation, by the remorseless flood of regulations and legislation, by controls and by the constant and arbitrary interventions of authority, successive governments since the war have cumulatively taken away both the pleasure and the rewards that once made risk-taking worthwhile," Sir Keith Joseph, the primary intellectual architect of Thatcherism, said in 1976. "By this attitude we have driven out some wealth-creators; discouraged others; shrivelled the impulse to expand and throttled enterprise." Margaret Thatcher and Ronald Reagan both got elected on promises to restore incentives to work and invest. They were viewed as economic radicals, but some of what they said was common sense. Beyond a certain level—what it is can be debated—taxes discourage effort and encourage evasion. Excessive regulations, such as the ones that used to govern the airline industry, stifle competition and preserve high prices.

In seeking to restore market incentives to some parts of the economy, the original deregulators—the most important of whom, Alfred E. Kahn, was a liberal Democrat appointed by Jimmy Carter—had economic logic on their side: well-meaning government interventions can prove counterproductive. But as often happens during revolutions, the second- and third-generation insurgents went too far, forgetting, or ignoring, the equally well established truth that markets, too, can create damaging incentives.

In February 2005, Alan Greenspan visited Kirkcaldy, Scotland, the birthplace of Adam Smith, where he hailed "Smith's demonstration of the inherent stability and growth of what we now term free-market capitalism," noting that "[t]he vast majority of economic decisions today fit those earlier presumptions of individuals acting more or less in their rational self-interest." As Greenspan was paying homage to the invisible hand, the U.S. economy was hurtling ahead, propelled by a set of distorted market incentives that his own policies had helped to create. In one sense, Greenspan had it right: nearly all the participants in the boom were acting "in their rational self-interest." The hard-working Latino immigrant in Riverside County looking to buy a first home; his mortgage broker searching the Internet and trying to find him an interest-only loan with an especially low teaser rate; the Las Vegas condo flipper starting to look farther afield, to Texas or Arizona; the Orange County mortgage lender sitting in his gleaming office building near John Wayne Airport and sending out for a sushi lunch; the Wall Street banker rushing to put together a new CDO; the rating agency analyst staring at a pile of junky loans and pronouncing them as safe as T-bills; the Connecticut hedge fund manager reaching for the higher yield that subprime securities offered; the German regional banks diversifying out of Treasury bonds; the Florida newspaper publisher rushing out another glossy real estate supplement; yea, even the Fountainhead

himself jetting over to Fife at the behest of a Labor prime minister—
all of these individuals were aping Adam Smith's butchers and bakers
and pursuing their own ends.

Unfortunately, this was an outbreak of rational irrationality. With
mortgage rates low and real estate values still rising, the invisible hand
was doing a highly effective job of coordinating people's actions through
the price system. But the outcome it had picked out was a ruinous
housing and credit bubble. In Table 21.1, I have put together some of
the biggest market distortions, and the results they generated.

TABLE 21.1: INCENTIVES AND THE HOUSING BOOM

DECISION-MAKER	DISTORTED INCENTIVE	RESULTS
Homeowners/Real Estate Speculators	Rapidly rising house prices. Unusually low mortgage rates.	Borrowers take on too much debt.
Mortgage Lenders	Rapidly rising house prices. Growth of mortgage securitization market.	Decline in lending standards. Creation of "exotic" mortgages, such as 2/28 subprime loans.
Banks/Investment Banks	Investors seeking "yield." Low interest rates. Development of credit insurance. Risk-based regulation plus VAR models.	Issuance of $1.5 trillion in subprime mortgage securities, 2003–2006. Banks put many subprime securities on their books. Banks hold less capital and lever up their balance sheets.
Credit Rating Agencies	Paid by issuers. Generous fees.	Most subprime securities rated "AAA" or "AA."
Hedge Funds/Sovereign Wealth Funds/Mutual Funds	Ultralow interest rates. Investment-grade ratings for subprime securities.	Search for "yield." Heavy demand for subprime securities.
Regulators/Policymakers	"The Great Moderation." Low inflation. Illusion of harmony/Illusion of stability.	Disaster myopia. Interest rates too low. Deregulation pressed too far.

What the table doesn't show is how the various incentive problems aggravated and reinforced one another. At any one point in time, incentives can get distorted in a particular market. But the memory of past busts, together with financial regulations and restrictive social conventions, usually preserve a modicum of stability. During the Greenspan era, however, lax monetary policy, deregulation, and financial innovation shocked the economy out of its stable configuration, placing it on the bubble path. No single one of these factors can be held solely responsible; it was the combination that did the damage.

Take, for example, the triptych of securitization, credit insurance, and risk-based capital requirements. This enabled a bank to issue questionable loans or buy questionable assets, shunt them off into an SIV, and then protect itself against the risk of default by purchasing some credit default swaps. Even before the development of alphabet soup finance, the presence of deposit insurance and implicit government guarantees meant that banks, especially the biggest ones, were apt to take too many risks—this is the issue of moral hazard. But the combination of securitization, credit insurance, and reforms to the regulatory structure greatly accentuated this problem. "[T]here is an immutable law of insurance that says that, while hedging can reduce the risk to an individual party taking out the insurance, it increases the risk for the system as a whole because of moral hazard," John Plender, a veteran commentator for the *Financial Times*, noted in October 2006. "That is, the mere existence of insurance means people become less risk averse. And that, complete with the marked decline in risk premiums and lending standards, is the story of the credit markets this decade."

Actually, there was another factor that played an important contributory role: the enormous "incentive packages" that many traders and senior executives on Wall Street received. This ultragenerous compensation structure didn't create the subprime industry and larger credit boom, but it helps to explain how they progressed to such extremes. Once the credit bubble got started, the men who ran the biggest financial institutions in the country were determined to surf it, regardless of the risks involved. From where they sat, and given the financial incentives they faced, pursuing any other strategy would have been irrational.

In 2006, James E. Cayne, the CEO of Bear Stearns, was paid $33.85 million, including a $17.1 million cash bonus, $14.8 million in restricted stock, and $1.7 million in options. At the end of the year, Cayne owned about 7 million shares in Bear and about 800,000 options; his overall stake in the company was worth about $1.1 billion.

In 2006, Richard S. Fuld, Jr., the CEO of Lehman Brothers, was paid $40.5 million, including a cash bonus of $6.25 million, $10.9 million in restricted stock, and $10.1 million in options. At the end of the year, Fuld owned 10.52 million shares in Lehman and 3.3 million options; his overall stake in the company was worth about $930 million.

In 2006, Lloyd C. Blankfein, the CEO of Goldman Sachs, was paid $54.72 million, including a cash bonus of $27.2 million, $15.7 million in restricted stock, and $10.5 million in options. At the end of the year, Blankfein owned 2.6 million shares in Goldman and 837,000 options; his overall stake in the company was worth about $581 million.

In 2006, Stanley O'Neal, the CEO of Merrill Lynch, was paid $48 million, including a cash bonus of $18.5 million and a stock grant of $26.8 million. At the end of the year, O'Neal owned 1.36 million shares in Merrill and 1.88 million options; his overall stake in the company was worth about $270 million.

In 2006, John J. Mack, the CEO of Morgan Stanley, was paid $41.41 million, including $36.2 million in restricted stock and $4 million in options. At the end of the year, Mack owned 2.75 million shares in Morgan and 1.2 million options; his overall stake in the company was worth about $245 million.

In 2006, Charles ("Chuck") Prince, the CEO of Citigroup, earned $25.98 million, including a cash bonus of $13.2 million and a stock award of $10.6 million. At the end of the year, he owned 1.6 million shares in Citi and about 1 million stock options; his overall stake in the company was worth about $140 million.

In 2006, Kenneth Lewis, the CEO of Bank of America, was paid $27.87 million, including a bonus of $6.5 million, $11.7 million in restricted stock, and $5 million in options. (In addition, Lewis exercised existing options worth $77 million.) At the end of the year, Lewis owned 3.9 million shares in Bank of America and 1.925 million options; his overall stake in the company was worth about $230 million.

The problem of excessive pay isn't peculiar to Wall Street: its effects just happen to be more pernicious there. When a highly paid rogue CEO such as Enron's Kenneth Lay or WorldCom's Bernie Ebbers creates or condones a culture of deception in a misguided effort to boost his firm's stock price, the consequences for the employees and stockholders of the company can be severe. When a Wall Street CEO such as Cayne or Fuld levers up his firm's equity capital thirty or forty to one in search of extra profits, his actions can bring down the entire economy. Wall Street remuneration schemes take no account of this externality. When the markets are rising, and deals are getting done, traders, investment bankers, and their bosses are paid magnificently; when things go wrong, the shareholders of the firms, and in extreme circumstances the taxpayers, suffer the bulk of the losses.

The market failure begins on the trading floor, where, as is now widely recognized, individuals have an incentive to take excessive risks with the firm's capital. Although traders are usually full-time employees, a useful way to think about them is as entrepreneurs who enter profit-sharing agreements to rent out part of their firms' balance sheets. Without access to cheap funding, even the smartest traders are helpless. But with the backing of a mighty Citigroup or Goldman, they can make enormous bonuses. Some banks give their traders up to half of the profits they generate above a certain target. But the traders' losses are capped. If their trades generate large losses, they might lose their jobs, but they don't have to write the firm a check. Incentive schemes of this type are equivalent to the bank giving traders nonrecourse loans to finance their bets: if the trades turn out badly, the firm has no recourse to their personal assets or the bonuses they earned in previous years.

Another way to characterize such arrangements is as a "trader's option," because they give the employee a free option on the upside to his trades. Some banks try to mitigate this problem by charging their trading desks a rental fee on the firm's money they trade with. If the desk invests in risky areas, such as commodities, the rental fee is higher than if it invests in Treasury bonds, say. When these schemes work, traders get rewarded only if they create positive risk-adjusted returns, commonly known as "alpha." This type of reward structure can mitigate incentive problems, but it doesn't eliminate them. Clever traders will try to game the system by taking risks that aren't reflected in the benchmark they are judged against. Take the practice of writing credit default swaps. In exchange for receiving a positive return most of the time, the providers of credit protection bear the hidden "tail risk" of a low probability of a very bad outcome. "These strategies have the appearance of producing very high alphas [high return for low risk], so managers have an incentive to load up on them," says Raghuram Rajan, the economist whose 2005 warnings I detailed in the introduction. "Every once in a while, however, they will blow up." But the disaster can take a long time to materialize. In the meantime, traders, who are paid on an annual basis, will be more than willing to take the gamble.

The top executives of financial firms have the responsibility of managing the risks that their institutions take on. In many ways, however, they face a similar set of incentives to the ones facing traders. If things go well, the firm's shares go up, and so does the value of their stock options; if things go badly, they have extremely generous "retirement" packages to fall back on. In fact, the "CEO's option" turns out to be an even bigger problem than the "trader's option." Even the most gung-ho trading desks face some trading limits; Wall Street CEOs can, and have, put entire firms on the line.

The development of elephantine compensation packages for Wall Street CEOs followed the pattern of other industries. During the 1960s and '70s, many commentators and investors expressed concern that CEOs were more interested in building up personal fiefdoms, complete with lavish headquarters, plush corporate resorts, and private jets, than in acting in the interests of shareholders. In an extremely influential paper published in 1976, Michael Jensen, now of Harvard, and the late William Meckling depicted the relationship of CEOs and stockholders as a "principal-agent" problem, a dilemma that arises, to some extent, whenever one party (the principal) employs another (the agent) to do a job. As anybody who has hired a contractor knows, it can be difficult to monitor an agent's behavior: the contractor may say he is working diligently, but is he telling the truth? Often, that information is hidden. Two common but partial solutions to this problem are to pay the agent after the completion of the job, or to offer him a success fee.

With public companies, the shareholders are the principals and the CEO is their agent. Since corporations are big and complicated, it is hard to tell from the outside whether a CEO is doing a good job. One way to align the interests of stockholders and CEO that is obvious in retrospect is to remunerate the latter with large numbers of shares, or stock options. If that were done, Jensen and others argued, CEOs would come to view themselves as owners instead of hired employees, and the result would be much better management. "On average, corporate America pays its most important leaders like bureaucrats," Jensen and Kevin Murphy, an economist who is now at the University of Southern California, argued in a 1990 article. "Is it any wonder that so many CEOs act like bureaucrats rather than the value-maximizing entrepreneurs companies need to enhance their standing in world markets?"

Corporate America sat up and listened. As recently as 1980, fewer than one in three chief executives had been granted stock options; by 1994, the proportion had risen to seven in ten. In the ensuing years, enormous options grants became the norm, enabling prominent CEOs such as Jack Welch, of General Electric, and Michael Eisner, of Disney, to build up fortunes worth hundreds of millions of dollars. The Jensen doctrine quickly spread to Wall Street, where executives such as Sanford "Sandy" Weill, of Citigroup, and Maurice "Hank" Greenberg, of AIG, accumulated dynastic wealth. Some free market economists credited the changes in remuneration structure with reinvigorating corporate America. Even Jensen eventually conceded that it also created serious problems, many of which came to light during the great accounting scandals of 2001–2002.

During the technology stock bubble, firms such as Lucent Technologies and America Online used auditing tricks to exaggerate their earnings; others, such as Enron, WorldCom, and Adelphia, engaged in outright fraud, creating false revenues and hiding losses. "I was a defender of the move toward stock options and more liberal rewards for CEOs," Jensen told me in 2002. "But I'm now a critic of where we got to." It was no coincidence that the accounting scandals emerged after the bursting of the bubble. Many firms' stock prices had become wildly overvalued, and their managers, pockets bulging with stock options, were struggling to create profits that would justify them. "For a long time now, we've had a situation in which the stock prices of many firms had been too high," Jensen went on. "That is to managers what heroin is to a drug addict."

The accounting scandals demonstrated how poorly designed incentive schemes and an asset price bubble can combine to devastating effect. Tyco's Dennis Kozlowski, WorldCom's Bernie Ebbers, and Adelphia's John Rigas were pilloried and jailed for their mendacity, but individual failings were only part of the story. "It is important to recognize that this doesn't come about as a result of crooks," Jensen said to me. "It wasn't as if the Mafia had taken over corporate America. We are too quick to say—and the media feeds this—that if a bad thing happens it's because a bad person did it, and that person had evil intentions. It is much more likely that there were some bad systems in place."

In banking, the CEO incentive problem is even more severe than in other industries. This is partly because the existence of deposit insurance, securitization, and the widespread assumption that some institutions are "too big to fail" induce moral hazard, but the speculative nature of finance also plays a role. On Wall Street, many decisions, such as whether to enter a certain business or underwrite a certain deal, can be thought of as risky gambles. In certain states of the world, they will pay off; in others, they won't. It is a fundamental principle of corporate finance that firms should carry out projects that are expected to generate economic profits and should forgo projects that are expected to result in a loss. For example, consider a bank thinking of participating in a deal that has a two-thirds chance of producing a $60 million profit and a one-third chance of generating a $60 million loss. A bit of simple arithmetic suggests the net expected profit of this deal is $20 million ($[\frac{2}{3} \times \$60$ million$] - [\frac{1}{3} \times \$60$ million$] = \$20$ million$). The bank should go ahead with it.

Now consider another, bigger prospect. This one has $\frac{99}{100}$ chance of generating a profit of $100 million, and a $\frac{1}{100}$ chance of generating a loss of $10 billion. (The deal might involve entering a new business line, such as investing in mortgage securities.) In this case, the venture's expected value is a loss of $1 million ($[\frac{99}{100} \times \$100{,}000{,}000] - [\frac{1}{100} \times \$10{,}000{,}000{,}000] = -\$1$ million$), and the bank should turn it down. But will its CEO do that? Let's assume he is paid $2 million a year plus a bonus equal to 2 percent of the firm's profits. If he accepts the deal, there's a 99 percent chance it will pay off; he will earn $4 million (his salary plus a bonus of $2 million). If he accepts the deal and the unlikely occurs, the bank will have to write off $10 billion, but he will still earn $2 million.

The example shows that Wall Street CEOs can have an incentive to accept risky bets that aren't in the long-term interest of their firms. (In the long run, unlikely things happen). The high leverage that Wall Street firms employ only accentuates the problem. At a business such as Microsoft or Exxon Mobil, the term "enhancing shareholder value" really means something. Since these firms have very little debt, acting in the shareholders' interest is equivalent to maximizing the value of the firm. But Wall Street banks employ enormous leverage. At the end of 2006, Lehman Brothers had $19.2 billion in shareholders' equity and $484 billion in liabilities; Bear Stearns had $12.1 billion of equity and $338 billion in liabilities; Merrill Lynch had $39 billion in equity and $802 billion in liabilities. In thinly capitalized businesses like these, the debt holders' investments represent a great deal of the company's value, whereas the shareholders' equity is a mere sliver. Incentivizing a CEO to focus exclusively on shareholder value creates a potential conflict of interest.

Finally, some economists are recognizing these problems. In a 2009 paper, Lucian Bebchuk and Holger Spamann, of Harvard Law School, pointed out that giving a Wall Street CEO a big package of restricted stock or stock options amounts to giving him a heavily levered and asymmetric bet on the value of the firm's assets. If the bank's investments do well, the stockholders, including the CEO, get to pocket virtually all the gains. But if the firm suffers a catastrophic loss, the equity holders quickly get wiped out, leaving the bondholders and other creditors to shoulder the bulk of the burden. "These highly levered structures gave executives powerful incentives to take excessive risks," Bebchuk and Spamann note. Indeed, under certain circumstances, a rational Wall Street CEO "will be willing to literally bet the bank."

A superficially compelling but ultimately unconvincing counter to this argument is that CEOs such as Jimmy Cayne and Dick Fuld had built up such large stakes in their companies that they had every incentive to be cautious, rather than reckless, lest their vast fortunes be endangered. The fault in this reasoning is that it starts at the end of the story rather than at the beginning. By January 2007, to be sure, most Wall Street CEOs were enormously rich, at least on paper. But much of this wealth was the result of their firms' having exploited the property bubble and credit boom, risky strategies that, until then, had paid off. (Between 1998 and 2006, the profits of the U.S. financial sector went from $165 billion to $427 billion. As a share of the total profits produced by all domestic industries, the profits of the financial sector jumped from 23 percent to 32 percent.) Nobody is suggesting that Cayne and Fuld and O'Neal knowingly embraced opportunities that they expected would bring down their companies. Rather, they encouraged their underlings to take gambles that appeared likely to pay off, but which also involved the possibility of the firm making enormous losses. At the time, this possibility seemed distant, which is why the CEOs took the chance. In the words of Bebchuk and Spamann, "The mere fact that a risky strategy turned out to produce losses ex post does not mean it was not rational to follow it ex ante." If things had turned out differently, the Wall Street CEOs would have been lionized as financial geniuses. Until August 2007, many of them *were* lionized.

O'Neal, for example, was the first African American to head a big Wall Street firm. On becoming Merrill's president and chief operating officer in 2001, he spent much of his time cutting staff, slashing expenses, and cutting back marginal business lines, a strategy that earned him a reputation as an unimaginative number cruncher. But after taking the CEO title in late 2002, he instigated a rapid expansion in Merrill's mortgage business, which saw it purchase a big mortgage lender, First Franklin, and become the number one issuer of CDOs. Merrill's profits soared, and so did its stock price. Changing tack, the financial media treated O'Neal as a visionary. In April 2004, *Fortune* described him as "a turnaround genius." In July 2006, *Euromoney* put him on its cover and proclaimed, "Look at his track record; listen to what he says."

In the midst of a credit bubble, sitting on the sidelines simply isn't a realistic option for somebody running a big, publicly owned financial institution. The main reason Wall Street CEOs receive such big pay packages is to encourage them to deliver extraordinary growth. Controlling costs and maintaining product quality are two of their tasks, but it is rapid expansion in market share that fires up a firm's stock price and raises the boss's standing, Even if the Wall Street chiefs privately harbored reservations about moving into risky areas, such as subprime lending, once their rivals had entered the field, and were making money, the peculiar but compelling logic of the prisoner's dilemma took over.

The experience of Chuck Prince provides an illuminating case study. By the end of 2004, Citigroup's investment banking arm was widely perceived to be falling behind its rivals. Prince, who had taken over as CEO in 2003, came under pressure to rev it up. A corporate lawyer by profession, he had risen to the top of the sprawling Citi conglomerate as the legal adviser to its creator, Sandy Weill, who had resigned after getting caught up in Eliot Spitzer's investigation of Wall Street analysts. At the start of 2005, according to *The New York Times*, Citi's board asked Prince and his colleagues to develop a growth strategy for the bank's bond business. One of the most senior board members, Robert Rubin, the former Treasury secretary, who also served as the chairman of the board's executive committee, advised Prince to raise Citi's tolerance for risk and expand its activities in rapidly growing areas, provided the firm also upgraded its oversight of them. "We could afford to seek more opportunities through intelligent risk taking," Rubin later told *The New York Times*. "The key word is 'intelligent.'"

Theoretically, Prince could have refused to act on Rubin's advice and told the board that he didn't think it was a good idea for a bank of Citi's stature to take on more risk, however intelligently it was done. But Citi's stock price hadn't gone anywhere in five years, and its rivals, such as Wachovia, UBS, and Merrill Lynch, were already heavily involved in mortgage bonds and CDOs. Being cautious would have involved forgoing a significant growth opportunity, something Prince, whose authority was already being questioned, couldn't afford to do. He authorized a rapid expansion of Citi's securitization businesses, especially those dealing with subprime mortgages and loans from private equity (leveraged buyout) companies. In the language of game theory, going with the crowd was a "dominant" strategy; given what everybody else was doing, it was the rational thing to do.

This was the context for Prince's famous interview with the *Financial Times*, in July 2007, in which he said, "[A]s long as the music is playing you've got to get up and dance." In the first half of 2007, according to data that the Securities Industry and Financial Markets

Association collated, banks operating in the United States originated about $260 billion worth of CDOs. By summer, though, the problems that had been building up in the subprime market could no longer be ignored. House prices peaked in the summer of 2006, and delinquencies and foreclosures spiked up. In December 2006, the rating agency Fitch warned that "the large number of borrowers facing scheduled payment increases in 2007 should continue to put negative pressure on the sector," and on December 28, 2006, Ownit Mortgage Solutions, an aggressive Californian subprime lender, filed for bankruptcy, starting a trend. In February 2007, HSBC, the big British bank, announced a $10.5 billion write-off, due mostly to losses at its American subprime subsidiary, the former Household Finance Corp., which it had bought in 2003. A few weeks later, New Century's shares were suspended amid fears the firm would have to file for bankruptcy, which, on April 2, it duly did.

In June 2007, just a few weeks before Prince's *Financial Times* interview, Bear Stearns was forced to inject $3.2 billion into two hedge funds it managed, which had suffered big losses on their holdings of subprime securities. But the private equity business was still thriving, and Blackstone, one of the biggest buyout firms, had just issued stock on the New York Stock Exchange. Prince conceded that a full-scale blowup in subprime could cause liquidity to dry up in other asset-backed securities markets, leaving Citi and other banks saddled with numerous loans of questionable value that they couldn't sell. (Liquidity is the ability to sell in bulk.) Still, he insisted, Citi had no intention of pulling back. "The depth of the pools of liquidity is so much larger than it used to be that a disruptive event now needs to be much more disruptive than it used to be," Prince said. "At some point, the disruptive event will be so significant that instead of liquidity filling in, liquidity will go the other way. I don't think we're at that point."

Prince's reference to dancing and the game of Musical Chairs was a remarkably candid description of the situation in which he found himself. Some Wall Street CEOs, such as O'Neal and Cayne, at times appeared blissfully unaware of the risks their firms were taking. But Prince was here openly acknowledging the possibility of a catastrophe and saying that despite it all, he and Citi would continue to surf the bubble, hoping to get out before they came a cropper. The logic of rational irrationality has rarely been spelled out more clearly.

Whether he knew it or not, Prince was channeling Keynes, who, in chapter 12 of *The General Theory*, pointed to the inconvenient fact that "there is no such thing as liquidity of investment for the community as a whole." Whatever the asset class may be—stocks, bonds, real estate, or anything else—if everybody tries to sell it at the same time, prices will collapse and the market will seize up. Given this possibility, Keynes said, financiers were forced to keep a close eye on the "mass psychology of the market," which could change at any moment.

This is the inevitable result of investment markets organised with a view to so-called 'liquidity . . . For it is, so to speak, a game of Snap, of Old Maid, of Musical Chairs—a pastime in which he is victor who says *Snap* neither too soon nor too late, who passes the Old Maid to his neighbour before the game is over, who secures a chair for himself when the music stops. These games can be played with zest and enjoyment, though all the players know that it is the Old Maid which is circulating, or that when the music stops some of the players will find themselves unseated.

22. LONDON BRIDGE IS FALLING DOWN

I n 1996, the London Borough of Southwark and the Royal Institute of British Architects, together with the *Financial Times* newspaper, held a competition to design a new footbridge across the Thames, from the proposed Tate Modern art gallery to St. Paul's Cathedral. A team that included the architect Sir Norman Foster, the sculptor Sir Anthony Caro, and the engineering firm of Ove Arup submitted the winning entry: a spectacular "lateral suspension" bridge with steel balustrades projecting out at obtuse angles from a narrow aluminum roadway. The design looked like something out of a science fiction movie; its originators insisted it would support five thousand pedestrians. The British government, which was looking to commemorate the upcoming millennium, agreed to help finance the project, which became known as the Millennium Bridge.

On June 10, 2000, Queen Elizabeth opened the bridge, and thousands of people set off across it. Within minutes, the footway started to tilt and sway alarmingly, forcing some pedestrians to cling to the side rails. Several of them reported feeling "seasick." The authorities promptly shut the bridge, claiming that too many people were using it; when they reopened it, the shaking began again. On Monday, June 12,

2000, amid great embarrassment, the bridge was closed down for an indefinite period. Initially, the source of the swaying was a mystery: some people suspected the bridge's foundations, others an unusual air pattern. The engineers from Ove Arup concluded that the real problem was the pedestrians on the footway. The bridge had been designed to swing gently to and fro in the breeze, but its designers hadn't taken adequate account of how the people walking across the bridge would exaggerate its movements.

When any of us walks, lifting and dropping each foot in turn, we produce a slight sideways force. If hundreds of people are walking in a confined space, and some happen to walk in step, they can generate enough lateral momentum to move a footbridge. Once the footway starts swaying, more pedestrians adjust their gait to get comfortable, stepping to and fro in sync with the bridge. If everybody does this at the same time, the sideways forces can increase dramatically, and the bridge can start to lurch violently. In other words, the wobble can feed on itself. The engineers concluded that this is what had happened on the Millennium Bridge, and they even devised a mathematical formula to describe the self-reinforcing process, which they termed "synchronous lateral excitation." To prevent the problem from recurring, they installed dozens of shock absorbers under the bridge, around its supporting piers, and at one of its ends. In February 2002, the bridge was reopened, minus its disturbing lurches; since then there haven't been any problems.

What does all this have to do with financial markets? As the economist Hyun Song Shin pointed out in a prescient 2005 paper, the answer is: quite a lot. Most of the time financial markets are relatively calm, trading is orderly, and participants can buy and sell in large quantities. But whenever a crisis hits, many of the biggest players—banks, investment banks, hedge funds—rush to reduce their exposures, causing liquidity to dry up. Where previously there was heterogeneity and diversity of opinion, now there is unanimity: everybody wants to get out. "Financial markets are the supreme example of an environment where individuals react to what's happening around them, and where individuals' actions affect the outcomes themselves," wrote Shin, who grew up in Korea and taught at Oxford and London School of Economics before moving to his current post at Princeton. "The pedestrians on the bridge are like banks adjusting their stance and the movements of the bridge are like price changes. You want diversity, but the market price is a lightning rod that imposes uniformity. There have been many instances of failure of liquidity of this type."

The Ove Arup engineers discovered that there was a critical threshold for the amount of pedestrian traffic using the Millennium Bridge. With fewer than one hundred and sixty people on it, there was no danger; with any more than that number, the dreaded wobble was likely to develop. Today's financial markets operate in much the same way, Shin suggested. As long as liquidity remains above a certain level, markets enable people to spread risks and invest in long-term assets, such as real estate, with confidence. But if liquidity falls below a certain threshold, "all the elements that formed a virtuous circle to promote stability now will conspire to undermine it," Shin noted. The financial markets can become highly unstable, and in a worst-case scenario, they can cease to operate at all. "What we don't know is where the threshold is," Shin concluded.

On the morning of Thursday, August 9, 2007, BNP Paribas, one of France's biggest banks, announced that it was suspending redemptions from three of its investment funds that had substantial holdings of American mortgage securities. Citing "evaporation of liquidity in certain segments of the U.S. securitization market," BNP said it was "impossible to value certain assets fairly regardless of their quality or credit rating." A month earlier, Standard & Poor's and Moody's had unnerved subprime investors by announcing they were reviewing the credit ratings on almost $18 billion worth of mortgage bonds. Since then, the subprime markets had been in turmoil, with prices falling and some issues ceasing to trade at all. The three BNP funds were small: taken together, the combined value of their assets before the suspension was just €1.6 billion ($2.2 billion), a fraction of the €600 billion that BNP had under management. Relative to the trillions of dollars that are traded on the world's financial markets every day, a couple of billion dollars is a rounding error. But BNP's announcement sent stocks tumbling. Most European markets closed down about 2 or 3 percent; on Wall Street, the Dow fell 387 points, almost 3 percent.

This sell-off was mild compared with the reaction in the global credit markets. Investors rushed for the safety of government bonds, sending their yields down sharply. In the interbank lending market, where banks extend credit to one another on a daily basis, lending activity largely dried up—something that hadn't been seen since the global financial crisis of September 1998. Banks rely on the interbank market to fund their day-to-day operations; if this funding is withdrawn, they can get into serious trouble very quickly. To head off this danger, the European Central Bank announced that it would make €95 billion in emergency credits available for institutions that couldn't obtain loans elsewhere. In the United States, the Federal Reserve also pumped more cash into the system. Brian Sack, senior economist at Macroeconomic Advisers, a leading U.S. economics consultancy, told a reporter that the day's events "had a feel of liquidity problems similar to some of the past episodes like 1998. I am not saying it is as intense as 1998, but it certainly looked like that."

The next day, Friday, August 10, things got worse, prompting the European Central Bank to inject another €61 billion into the system and the Fed to assure the markets that it would supply big banks with as much short-term credit as they needed. The market was facing an acute case of hidden information. With trading in many mortgage securities halted, banks, investment banks, hedge funds, mutual funds, university endowments, pension funds, and other financial institutions were holding countless pieces of paper that previously had been immensely valuable but that were now of indeterminate worth. There simply weren't any buyers.

This shock to the system caused all sorts of problems. Some highly leveraged investors faced demands for more collateral and were forced to reduce their positions. Margin calls and forced selling is the classic recipe for a market blow-up, but this wasn't a 1987-style crash. Instead of spiraling down, the mortgage securities market had simply frozen up. Banks and other lenders had no way to estimate how exposed to it other financial institutions might be. Rather than extending credit to a rival firm that could turn out to be insolvent, they had opted to hoard their capital, forcing the European Central Bank and the Fed to step in as the lenders of last resort.

The information problem was so bad that many financial institutions didn't know what their own subprime holdings were worth. Because of the opaqueness of the mortgage securitization chain, there was no way for them to work backward and figure out valuations based on the worth of the underlying mortgages. As far as the owners of the mortgage securities were concerned, this sort of granular information simply didn't exist. Previously, they had relied on the market to value the various tranches of each securitization. Now, however, the pricing system, on which all free market economies rely, had broken down. Hayek's telecommunications system was no longer emitting any price signals; the market had failed, and the great credit crunch of 2007–2009 had begun.

Most liquidity crises are short-lived. The market shuts down for a few days while investors garner enough information to establish new prices, then trading starts up again. This time, the market for subprime securities failed to reopen. So did the market for many other asset-backed securities, such as those based on credit card receivables, student loans, and auto loans. Many other credit markets operated at substantially reduced capacity, causing severe problems for financial institutions that relied heavily on short-term financing.

The first institutions to be hit were the SIVs, conduits, and other off-balance-sheet entities that made up the shadow banking system. These shell companies had financed their investments in mortgage securities and other long-term assets by issuing short-term bonds called asset-backed commercial paper (ABCP) to banks, investment funds, and other financial firms. Practically overnight, the market for paper issued by SIVs disappeared. In August and September, the amount of outstanding ABCP fell by about $370 billion.

Many more-visible financial institutions also struggled to find financing. In late August, Countrywide Financial secured a $2 billion capital injection from Bank of America. Northern Rock, Britain's fifth-biggest mortgage lender, wasn't so lucky. The bank, which was based in Newcastle, a city in the northeast of England, didn't have any direct connection to the U.S. subprime market, but its practice of raising large amounts of money from other financial institutions had prompted questions about its viability. In the middle of September, many of Northern Rock's depositors started queuing up to withdraw their savings. The British government, fearing the depositors' panic would spread, agreed to rescue the bank.

Because of their quarterly reporting season, it wasn't until October and November that the big American banks started to report some of the subprime losses that had been festering on their books since the summer. During October, Merrill, Citigroup, and UBS announced write-downs of $7.9 billion, $6.5 billion, and $3.4 billion, respectively. In those days, $5 billion meant something. By the end of the month, Merrill's board had forced Stan O'Neal to resign; a week later, Citigroup's Chuck Prince was a goner, too. Some of the articles devoted to O'Neal's departure noted his achievement in emerging from rural Alabama to the summit of American finance; more of them focused on his $160 million retirement package. Prince, who had also risen from humble beginnings, received even shorter shrift. Rather than subjecting himself to questions about why his skills at Musical Chairs had failed him, he issued a statement saying resignation was "the only honorable course for me to take."

In the ensuing months, almost all of Prince's peers announced that their firms had suffered heavy losses, but none resigned. Several borrowed a trick from Morgan Stanley's John Mack, who, just before Christmas, twinned the announcement of $9.4 billion in write-offs with news of a $5 billion equity injection on the part of a Chinese sovereign wealth fund. Even if Wall Street had gotten itself into a mess, Morgan's announcement seemed to signal that there were plenty of rich (and not necessarily very smart) foreigners ready to bail it out. The subprime crisis was front-page news, but there was still surprisingly little public recognition of the damage it might do. On December 31, 2007, the Dow closed out the year at 13,264.82, slightly above the level it had been at on August 1.

Policymakers, too, underestimated the calamity that was unfolding. In March 2007, on Capitol Hill, Ben Bernanke said the problem in the subprime market "seems likely to be contained"—a message he stuck to throughout the summer, despite cries of outrage from, among others, Jim Cramer, the CNBC *Mad Money* host. "Bernanke is being an academic. He has no idea how bad it is out there," Cramer shouted on August 3. "[H]e's nuts! They're nuts! They know nothing." The Fed had more knowledge than Cramer suggested, but its analysis was faulty. When the securitization markets seized up, Bernanke and his colleagues assumed it was a temporary liquidity crisis that would fairly quickly resolve itself. In the interim, the Fed would play its traditional role during stressful times, as a lender of last resort, providing loans to banks that needed them. On August 17, it cut the rate of interest at which it extends credit to banks—the discount rate—by half a percentage point, to 5.75 percent, and extended the terms of the loans it provided, but it didn't alter the federal funds rate. Between September and early December, with the turmoil in the credit markets persisting, the Fed cut both the discount rate and the funds rate by a total of 1 percentage point. This was a significant policy shift, but it hardly amounted to the drastic action that Cramer and some of his Wall Street buddies were demanding. "I and others were mistaken early on in saying that the subprime crisis would be contained," Bernanke said to me in a 2008 interview. "The causal relationship between the housing problem and the broad financial system was very complex and difficult to predict."

On one level, it is easy to sympathize with Bernanke. Some years ago, Paul Samuelson, who was one of the Fed chairman's former teachers at MIT, suggested that economics wasn't much help in understanding speculative busts. A more useful discipline to study, he said wryly, was the physics of avalanches. The Grand Old Man of economics was making a serious point: most of the regularities in the data that economists have identified are "equilibrium" relationships, meaning they hold when the economy is operating more or less normally. During a serious economic dislocation, many established connections break down and new ones emerge, rendering analysis and prediction doubly difficult.

Avalanches, on the other hand, have some fairly predictable dynamics. As a pile of snow tumbles down a mountain, it displaces more snow in its path, which adds to its weight and force. The case against Bernanke is that, until the economy was snowed under, he failed even to acknowledge the gathering deluge. As late as October 2007, at a meeting of central bankers, executives, and economists, someone asked him how a central bank should handle the policy risks posed by a housing bubble, to which he replied that he had no way of knowing whether there had been such a bubble. By this stage, home prices were falling steadily nationwide, something the Fed simply hadn't prepared for. "You could think about Texas in the 1980s, when oil went down, or California in the 1990s, when the peace dividend hit the defense industry, but those were regional things," a Fed policymaker told me during a round of interviews in 2008. "A national decline in house prices hadn't occurred since the 1930s."

Bernanke's failure to countenance a housing bubble reflected a failure of imagination. It also reflected the Fed's institutional view that its proper role was not to go around bursting bubbles but to let them burst of their own accord. This argument was, in turn, tied to a belief that the economy was fundamentally a well-grounded entity, with strong self-equilibrating tendencies: the illusion of stability. Bernanke, despite his reputation as an expert on the Great Depression, shared this benign view of modern capitalism. The period from 1929 to 1933 he saw as a historic anomaly, during which the monetary authorities had made the disastrous error of allowing the money supply to fall sharply and the banking system to collapse, thereby converting a recession into a cataclysm. As long as the Fed didn't repeat that error, Bernanke believed, the economic fallout from the subprime crisis would be, well, *contained*.

The Fed chairman and his colleagues took solace from the fact that, despite its rapid growth, the subprime market remained relatively small. All told, there was roughly $12 trillion worth of U.S. home mortgages outstanding, of which the subprime market accounted for just $1 trillion, or thereabouts. At the beginning of 2007, the U.S. stock market was worth about $18 trillion. Even if half of the value of subprime mortgages got wiped out—an extreme assumption, it seemed to many at the Fed—the resultant loss in wealth would be equivalent to about a 3 percent move in the stock market, which is a regular occurrence. Bernanke and his colleagues also believed that the great bulk of any subprime losses would be concentrated outside of the banking system, which itself had roughly $14 trillion in assets. After all, the spreading of risk was purported to be the great benefit of securitization; it was the very reason Alan Greenspan had supported the concept in the first place.

In the final months of 2007 and the first part of 2008, each of these reassuring arguments unraveled, beginning with the revelation that big banks remained financially responsible for many billions of dollars' worth of subprime securities and other troubled assets that they had shifted to SIVs and other shell companies. With the collapse of the asset-backed commercial paper market, the only way many of these creations could finance themselves was by calling on the credit lines that their parent companies had established. Far from distributing the risks associated with subprime, securitization and the construction of the shadow banking system had helped to concentrate it at the heart of the financial world, in giant global banks such as Citigroup, JPMorgan Chase, and HSBC. When this fact emerged, it caused great consternation at the Fed and the Treasury Department. "We knew that the banks were creating conduits and SIVs, which issued commercial paper," a senior American policymaker told me in 2008. "I don't think we recognized to what extent it could come back on the balance sheet when confidence eroded."

Treasury Secretary Henry "Hank" Paulson briefly promoted the farfetched idea of some of the biggest banks establishing an $80 billion "super SIV" to bail out their own individual SIVs, but the question immediately arose: Who would provide financing for such a super SIV? Unless the federal government agreed to do it—an option that, at this stage, Paulson was unwilling to countenance—the plan was a nonstarter. In November, HSBC accepted reality and announced a plan to incorporate two SIVs with $45 billion in assets onto its own balance sheet. A month later, Citigroup, which had established the first SIV back in 1988, reversed a previous statement and said it would move $49 billion in assets onto its books from no fewer than seven SIVs. These toxic assets—the phrase was already being bandied about—were separate from the roughly $55 billion in subprime securities that Citigroup had accumulated on its own account, and they dwarfed the $7.5 billion that the firm had gone out and raised from an Abu Dhabi investment fund.

The implosion of the shadow banking system was just one of several factors that amplified the subprime bust, elevating it into the worst financial breakdown since the 1930s. Arguably, the most important was "synchronous lateral excitation." With the market for securitized products frozen, banks and other financial institutions were forced to sell many other types of financial assets, causing their prices to fall and the crisis to intensify. In a manner analogous to what happened to the Millennium Bridge, the initial disturbance fed on itself, getting bigger and bigger. Unfortunately, there was no way to shut down the credit markets and clear them of overexcited people.

As Hyun Song Shin had suggested might happen, market prices played a key role in coordinating this self-defeating behavior. The other key factors were leverage and a set of accounting rules that obliged financial firms to recognize losses quickly. For decades, banks valued many of the assets they held at the cost they bought them for. Beginning in the 1990s, however, the regulatory authorities had encouraged owners of financial assets to substitute market prices wherever possible, and in September 2006 this policy was formalized in Financial Accounting Standards Board Rule 157. To many people, the shift to "mark-to-market" accounting seemed like an advance for accuracy, timeliness, and transparency, but as Gary Gorton, an economist at Yale, pointed out in a 2008 paper, it also involved a commitment to Chicago School economics. "The logic follows from the idea that if markets are efficient, that is, if prices aggregate the information and beliefs of market participants, then this is the best estimate of 'value,'" Gorton wrote.

In a world where financial markets are subject to bubbles and crashes, forcing banks to use volatile daily prices as a basis of long-term valuation can greatly accentuate the cyclicality of the entire financial system: indeed, combined with a laissez-faire attitude to banks' leverage, it can practically guarantee the emergence of booms and busts. The following example, which I have adapted from a set of lectures that Shin delivered in 2008, will, hopefully, serve to illustrate the problem.

TABLE 22.1: THE LOSS SPIRAL

Panel A		Panel B		Panel C	
ASSETS	LIABILITIES	ASSETS	LIABILITIES	ASSETS	LIABILITIES
200	190 Debt	198	190 Debt	160	152 Debt
	10 Equity		8 Equity		8 Equity
Leverage Ratio: 200/10 = 20		Leverage Ratio: 198/8 = 24.75		Leverage Ratio: 160/8 = 20	

(Figures in $bn)

(Adapted from H. S. Shin's Clarendon Lectures in Finance, Oxford University, June 2–4, 2008)

The leverage ratio of a Wall Street firm is equal to the value of its total assets divided by the value of its equity capital. Let's say a particular Wall Street firm has a target leverage ratio of 20—a quite conservative figure by the standards of the early 2000s. And let's further assume it has $200 billion in assets, which it funds with $10 billion in equity and $190 billion in debt. (Its balance sheet is shown in Panel A of Table 22.1.) Now let's assume that the market value of the bank's assets fall by 1 percent, or $2 billion, perhaps because of a slump in its portfolio of subprime securities. Under mark-to-market accounting, the bank has to recognize these losses straightaway, which does a surprising amount of damage to its balance sheet. After making the change, its assets are worth $198 billion. Since it still has debts of $190 billion, its equity is reduced to $8 billion, a drop of 20 percent.

Such a fall demonstrates how leverage can magnify small losses; but that isn't the end of it. The bank's leverage ratio is now too high: with assets of $198 billion and equity of $8, it has risen to 24.75. (The revised balance sheet is shown in Panel B of Table 22.1.) In order to restore its leverage target of 20, the bank has to sell $38 billion in assets and pay down $38 billion in debt. After this is done, it has assets of $160 billion, debts of $152 billion, and equity of $8 billion. (This balance sheet is shown in Panel C of Table 22.1.) As these numbers make clear, restoring the bank's target leverage ratio involves shrinking its balance sheet considerably, and engaging in substantial asset sales. If instead of simply restoring its target leverage ratio, the bank decides to reduce it—a common reaction to losses—it will be forced to sell even more assets.

This is just one institution. In a period of market turmoil, all big financial institutions face similar pressures to deleverage. This is where the parallel with the Millennium Bridge becomes particularly tight. "Mark-to-market accounting ensures that any price change shows up immediately on the balance sheet," Shin wrote. "So, when the bridge moves, banks adjust their stance more than they used to, and marking to market ensures that they all do so *at the same time*."

The result is another glaring example of rational irrationality. As banks try to shrink their balance sheets simultaneously, the prices of the assets they are selling will fall, causing them to incur further losses and frustrating their efforts to reduce their leverage. Unless something interferes with this process, it can lead to a disastrous "loss spiral," in which tumbling prices generate more losses and selling, which leads to further falls in prices. Figure 22.2, which is also adapted from Shin's lectures, illustrates this self-reinforcing process and compares it to the one that shut down the Millennium Bridge.

The vicious circle of falling prices and losses is the logical complement of the virtuous circle that operates during the up stage of the economic cycle. During good times, rising asset values give a boost to banks' equity capital, prompting them to make more loans and accumulate more assets. Since they all do this together, the rising demand for financial assets keeps prices rising, In both the vicious and virtuous circles, it is worth noting, the demand curve for financial assets is upward sloping: rising prices generate more demand; falling prices generate less demand. As in the housing market, it is this suspension of the normal laws of supply and demand that makes the situation unstable. Whenever demand curves have the wrong shape, the reassuring nostrums of Economics 101 don't apply. Prices might settle into a narrow band, but they can also cycle around wildly, or they can gain a momentum of their own and explode in one direction. Appealing to the "efficiency" of the market to resolve this problem is no help. It is the speculative element present in all financial markets that gives the demand curve its positive incline.

By late 2007, many financial firms were trapped in a loss spiral of a sort similar to the one in Figure 22.2. From the outside, this was fairly difficult to detect. Banks and investment banks don't announce

FIGURE 22.2: THE VICIOUS CIRCLE

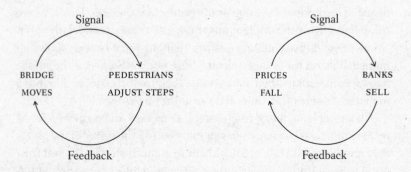

(Adapted from H. S. Shin's Clarendon Lectures in Finance, Oxford University, June 2–4, 2008)

when they have decided to reduce their leverage ratios and shrink their balance sheets; they just go ahead and do it. But an inspection of their public accounts reveals what was happening. In the summer of 2007, when the subprime crisis began, Merrill Lynch had more than $1 trillion in assets. A year later, in September 2008, its balance sheet had been trimmed to about $875 billion, a reduction of an eighth. In November 2007, Morgan Stanley also had about $1 trillion in assets; a year later, it had about $660 billion, a reduction of a third. In December 2007, Citigroup's balance sheet totaled almost $2.2 trillion; a year later it had shrunk to slightly above $1.9 trillion, a fall of more than a tenth. In November 2007, Goldman Sachs had $1.1 trillion in assets; a year later, the total was $885 billion, a drop of about a fifth. To each of these firms, slimming down and reducing leverage was a sensible and necessary strategy. From a system-wide perspective, it only added to the downward momentum and the potential for further blowups.

The loss spiral in the financial sector was but one of several separate but linked vicious circles buffeting the economy. In the slumping housing market, foreclosures were rising sharply, causing a glut of forced sales and adding to the pressure on prices. Between the third quarter of 2007 and the third quarter of 2008, average home prices across the country dropped 17 percent, according to the S&P/Case-Shiller index. In Phoenix, for example, between September 2007 and September 2008, average house prices fell 32 percent. In Miami during the same period, the average price decrease was 28 percent; in San Diego, it was 26 percent. To a nation that had grown accustomed to the value of its homes rising every year, these were alarming figures.

In the subprime industry, where mortgages had been designed on the assumption that prices would keep rising forever, the falling housing market had a shattering impact. Many borrowers who had taken out 2/28 subprime loans in 2005 and 2006 hadn't built up enough equity to cover the fees associated with a refinancing, and they were facing an extremely costly reset in their monthly payments. The turmoil in the credit markets was adding to this problem. With a 2/28 loan, typically the interest rate after two years is tied to the London interbank offered rate (LIBOR), which, since the summer of 2007, had climbed sharply. Rather than looking at a rise of $200 or $300 in their monthly payments, borrowers were facing hikes of $500, $600, or even more. By February 2008, roughly one in four subprime lenders was at least one month behind on his payment, according to the financial information firm Equifax.

For many homeowners, missing a monthly payment was the first step toward being evicted. In May 2008 alone, according to Realty Trac, another financial information company, lenders served foreclosure filings—default notices, auction sale notices, and bank repossessions—on 261,255 properties across the United States. The highest rates were recorded in Nevada (where one in every ninety-six Las Vegas householders received a foreclosure filing), California, Arizona, and Florida. Some of these financial disputes were settled without going to a final foreclosure. Banks were increasingly amenable to short sales, in which a home was sold for less than the mortgage, with the lender swallowing the loss. In some circumstances, they also agreed to modify loans by, for example, extending their terms. When these options failed, though, eviction was usually the result. Between August 2007 and October 2008, according to Realty Trac, 936,439 homes were foreclosed on.

An undetermined but significant number of mortgage holders left their homes willingly. Rather than continuing to make payments on loans that were now bigger than the properties' values, they chose to hand over the keys. By the spring of 2008, according to Mark Zandi, of the Moody's website Economy.com, about 8.5 million homeowners, or about one in seven mortgage holders, had "negative equity" in their homes, giving them an economic incentive to pack their bags and leave. Every time a homeowner did this, another property was left vacant, and the stock of unsold homes expanded, putting more pressure on sellers to reduce their prices. "The housing market was trapped in a self-reinforcing negative cycle," Zandi noted. "This had occurred, briefly, in California and New England in the early 1990s but never in so many parts of the country. There was no obvious way out of the cycle, and no guarantee that house prices would stop falling soon."

The slump in the housing market was doing serious damage to the rest of the economy, especially to the construction industry, which previously had been a major source of economic growth. In the first half of 2007, builders were breaking ground on about 1.5 million homes a year; by the summer of 2008, the number of monthly starts had virtually halved. The slump in residential investment, which includes renovation and remodeling, was one of the main reasons why the economy stalled in the final three months of 2007 and the first quarter of 2008. Having expanded at an annual rate of more than 3 percent between April and September of 2007, inflation-adjusted GDP barely grew at all between October 2007 and March 2008. Joblessness started to pick up. In December 2007, the unemployment rate jumped from 4.7 percent to 5 percent, as manufacturers and construction firms slashed their payrolls. With home prices falling and foreclosures rising, there was little hope of stabilizing the economy, or the financial system.

As the months passed, attention focused on some of the Wall Street firms that were most closely associated with the mortgage securitization industry: Merrill, Bear Stearns, and Lehman Brothers. Of these three, Merrill had taken the strongest steps to bolster its position, hiring as its new CEO John Thain, the former head of the New York Stock Exchange, and raising $6.6 billion from a group of investors that included Kuwaiti and Korean sovereign wealth funds. Bear and Lehman, which were known as savvy and aggressive trading houses, remained under the control of the executives who had led them to this pass. Both insisted they had adequate capital—in October 2007, Bear had raised $1 billion from a Chinese investment firm.

Actually, their finances were precarious. Unlike commercial banks, such as Citigroup, they didn't have access to the Fed's lending facilities, which were steadily expanded in the winter of 2007–2008. Like all Wall Street firms, they depended on the ready availability of credit from private-sector sources, and they needed lots of it. By 2006 and 2007, all of the big investment banks had turned into hedge funds in disguise. Taking advantage of the credit bubble, they had raised enormous sums of money on a short-term basis and used it to finance long-term investments, such as mortgage securities, arbitrage trades, and derivatives of various kinds. At the end of 2007, Bear and Lehman both had leverage ratios of more than thirty to one. With this sort of leverage, a mere 4 percent drop in the value of a firm's assets can wipe out its entire capital base.

Bear was the smallest of the top Wall Street banks, and its leading figures—such as its chairman, Jimmy Cayne, a championship bridge player, and its former CEO Alan "Ace" Greenberg, who at the age of eighty still came to work every day—had reputations as mavericks. In 1998, with Long-Term Capital Management on the brink of collapse, Bear had been the only Wall Street firm that refused to participate in the rescue. (As LTCM's prime broker, it argued that it already had a big exposure to the firm.) In the period since 2000, Bear had established itself in the fast-growing hedge fund business, acting as the prime broker to dozens of funds, including some of the biggest. At the end of 2007, it had more than $60 billion in hedge fund deposits on its books, which it used to help pay for its own operations.

When the subprime crisis began, this success turned out to be double-edged. Bear's creditors, including its hedge fund clients, were in a position similar to depositors in a commercial bank facing financial challenges before the advent of deposit insurance. They had their money in a bank with lots of illiquid investments; if forced to repay them all at short notice, the bank would struggle to come up with the cash. Such a situation places the depositors in a prisoner's dilemma. In principle, they would all benefit from leaving their money in the bank and preventing a panic. On an individual basis, however, each has a strong incentive to close out his account before everybody else. Since this incentive structure is common knowledge, withdrawing money immediately is a dominant strategy. The inevitable result, fans of Jimmy Stewart and the 1946 Frank Capra film *It's a Wonderful Life* won't need reminding, is a run on the bank.

During early March, rumors about Bear's financial health began to circulate. Many Bear employees suspected that short sellers were spreading malicious stories to drive down the firm's stock. The worst thing about bank runs is that they can be self-fulfilling: once the logic of the prisoner's dilemma takes over, even an economically sound institution can be felled. To this day, Bear's senior executives insist the firm was in this category. Its mortgage exposures, although considerable, were smaller than those of many of its rivals. (It had $2 billion in subprime securities, $15 billion in prime and Alt-A securities, and $16 billion in commercial mortgage bonds.) On Monday, March 10, it had about $17 billion in cash.

That same day, Bear issued a statement saying, "There is absolutely no truth to the rumors of liquidity problems that circulated today in the market." Rather than ending the gossip about Bear's position, the statement only drew attention to it. The next day, with Bear's stock trading below $70—a year earlier, it had been above $150—and the cost of insuring its debt rising sharply, a number of financial institutions signaled a reluctance to do business with the firm. ING, the Dutch financial services conglomerate, informed Bear it wouldn't renew about $500 million in loans. Nervous hedge funds were calling other Wall Street firms and asking them to take over their derivatives trades with Bear in return for a fee, but on Tuesday, Goldman Sachs sent an e-mail to hedge funds warning them it would no longer agree to do this. Rumors circulated that Credit Suisse had done the same thing.

To the hedge fund community, it appeared that the rest of the Street was giving up on Bear. Many big funds, including Renaissance Technologies and D.E. Shaw, started pulling money out of Bear, as did some of Bear's individual clients. The firm was also having difficulty raising funding in the repo market, an obscure but immensely important place, where financial firms borrow money on an overnight basis by selling some of their assets to other firms and agreeing to repurchase them the following day. ("Repo" is short for "repurchase.") Repo lending is fully secured: the lender takes possession of the borrower's assets as collateral, sometimes with a third party acting as a custodian; it is widely regarded as ultrasafe. In normal times, contracts are rolled over routinely, often for months on end, and many firms rely on repos to finance a big part of their balance sheet. Of the $395 billion in assets that Bear had on its books at the end of 2007, more than $100 billion was being funded in the repo market. But now some of Bear's repo counterparties were refusing to roll over existing repo agreements or enter into new ones.

From the perspective of individual investors, hedge funds, and rival investment banks, pulling away from Bear seemed like a prudent shedding of risk. The view from Bear's gleaming octagonal headquarters on Madison Avenue and Forty-sixth Street was rather different. "As the week progressed, unfounded rumors grew into fear, and our liquidity cushion dropped precipitously on Thursday, as customers withdrew cash and repo counterparties increasingly refused to lend against even high-quality collateral," Alan Schwartz, Bear's chief executive, said on Capitol Hill a few weeks later. "There was, simply put, a run on the bank."

By the afternoon of Thursday, March 13, Bear's cash reserves had been reduced to just $2 billion, which meant it didn't have enough money to meet its obligations the following morning. The firm had two options: raise more money or file for bankruptcy. On Thursday evening, officials from the New York Federal Reserve arrived at 383 Madison, and so did a team of investment bankers from JPMorgan Chase, which was Bear's clearing bank. The next morning, the Fed announced it would provide temporary financing to Bear, with JPMorgan Chase acting as the conduit. On Sunday, March 16, JPMorgan Chase purchased Bear for two dollars a share, a price that many people, when they first saw it, assumed to be a misprint. (Amid outrage from Bear's shareholders, the price was subsequently raised to ten dollars.) The subprime crisis, already more than seven months old, was entering its epic and, for taxpayers, costliest stage.

23. SOCIALISM IN OUR TIME

ome years ago, the Bank of England and the Financial Services Authority, the UK's main financial regulator, held a series of meetings with big firms operating in the City of London to discuss their risk-management systems. The officials were particularly interested in what sort of "stress testing" the firms had done to examine how they would hold up in a crisis. Such exercises involve simulating financial disruptions on a computer. Major banks and investment banks carried them out routinely, but the regulators were concerned that the testing wasn't rigorous enough. Generally speaking, firms simulated only minor shocks. The public officials asked the bankers why their firms had failed to explore the possibility of a real blowup. Was it a result of disaster myopia, or a failure to appreciate the dangers of contagion? No, one of the attendees replied. It was nothing like that. The problem was that risk departments didn't have any incentive to simulate genuine disasters. If such an awful eventuality materialized, the simulators would likely lose their bonuses and possibly their jobs. And, in any case, the authorities would step in and rescue the bank.

"All of the other bankers assembled began subjecting their shoes to intense scrutiny," Andrew Haldane, the executive director for financial stability at the Bank of England, recalled in a speech he gave in February 2009. "The unspoken words had been spoken. The officials in the room were aghast. Did banks not understand that the official sector would not underwrite banks mismanaging their risks? Yet history now tells us that the unnamed banker was spot-on . . . When the big one came, his bonus went and the government duly rode to the rescue."

On the evening of Thursday, March 13, 2008, Ben Bernanke, Timothy Geithner, the head of the New York Fed, and other top officials held a conference call to discuss what to do about Bear Stearns, which was on the brink. Their first instinct was to let market forces take their course: rescuing Bear would send a signal to other firms that the government would bail out firms that had taken on too much risk. When Geithner went to bed later that night, he still believed Bear should be allowed to file for bankruptcy. During his brief sleep, however, members of his staff, working at Bear's headquarters, discovered a morass of trades, pledges, and other commitments. Bear reportedly had some hundred and fifty million trades on its books, with more than five thousand different counterparties. The Fed was particularly worried about its derivatives positions, including but not confined to sales and purchases of CDSs, and its mortgage portfolio, much of which it had used as collateral for loans in the repo market. "It became clear that Bear's involvement in the complex and intricate web of relationships that characterize our financial system, at a point in time when markets were especially vulnerable, was such that a sudden failure would likely lead to a chaotic unwinding of positions in already damaged markets," Geithner subsequently said to Congress. "Moreover, a failure by Bear to meet its obligations would have cast a cloud of doubt on the financial position of other institutions whose business models bore some superficial similarity to Bear's, without due regard for the fundamental soundness of those firms."

Bernanke, Geithner, et al. were learning something Minsky and other critics of the utopian model had been saying for decades: the institutional details of the financial system matter not just for the firms concerned, but for the economy as a whole. When big banks collapse, there are enormous spillovers that policymakers have to take into account, even if they'd much prefer not to. "The problem wasn't the size of Bear Stearns—it wasn't the fact that some creditors would have borne losses," a senior official at the Fed told me later in 2008. "The problem was—people use the phrase 'too interconnected to fail.' That's not totally accurate, but it's close enough." In the repo market, for example, Bear had raised a lot of funding from money market mutual funds. "If Bear had failed," the senior official went on, "all these money market mutual funds, instead of getting their money back on Monday morning, would have found themselves with all kinds of illiquid collateral, including CDOs and God knows what else. It would have caused a run on that entire market. That, in turn, would have made it impossible for other investment banks to fund themselves."

Rather than risking such a calamity, government officials explored ways of propping up Bear, at least temporarily. Having the Fed lend it money directly was problematic. Precisely to prevent Wall Street investment banks from relying on the government to rescue them in the event of losses, the Fed's discount window, through which it lent to commercial banks such as JPMorgan Chase and Bank of America, wasn't open to them. Under Section 13.3 of the Federal Reserve Act, the Fed did have the right, under "unusual and exigent circumstances," to lend to any "individual, partnership, or corporation" as it deemed necessary, but it hadn't used this authority since the 1930s.

Now was the time. On the morning of Friday, March 14, the Fed's governors formally invoked Section 13.3 and extended $13 billion to Bear via JPMorgan Chase. Forty-eight hours later, the Fed took two more important steps, both of which also relied on its powers under Section 13.3. To facilitate JPMorgan Chase's takeover of Bear, it agreed to shoulder the risk of losses on $30 billion of Bear's toxic mortgage assets that Morgan didn't want anything to do with. (The figure was later reduced to $29 billion.) And it announced it would open the discount window to other Wall Street firms that needed cash, accepting as collateral a wide range of assets, including mortgage securities. The latter move was deemed necessary to prevent a creditors' run on other investment banks, such as Lehman Brothers and Morgan Stanley, when the market opened on Monday, March 17. (Privately, Geithner referred to the move as "foaming the runways.")

Taken together, the Fed's actions represented a historic enlargement of its role and the first acknowledgment that, ultimately, some of the losses from the subprime debacle would have to be socialized. Although operationally independent, the Fed is really just another branch of the federal government. When it makes a financial commitment, it does so, ultimately, on behalf of the U.S. taxpayer. In extending the lender-of-last-resort facility to Wall Street firms, accepting mortgage securities as collateral, and agreeing to shoulder the losses on Bear's $30 billion mortgage portfolio, the U.S. government appeared to be saying it would use the taxpayers' resources to prevent further financial collapses and also to put a floor under the mortgage market. When I interviewed Bernanke later in 2008, he was perfectly open about this policy. "I think we did the right thing to try to preserve financial stability," he said of the Bear intervention. "That's our job. Yes, it's moral hazard-inducing, but the right way to address this question is not to let institutions fail and have a financial meltdown."

If, immediately following the Bear rescue, Bernanke and Treasury Secretary Henry "Hank" Paulson had come out and stated categorically that no systemically important financial institution would be allowed to fail, their words would have had a salutary effect. But they equivocated. In their appearances on Capitol Hill and elsewhere, they stressed the unique circumstances of Bear's sale to JPMorgan Chase. Paulson in particular inveighed against the dangers of moral hazard, letting it be known that it was he who had insisted on the two-dollar-a-share purchase price.

This rowing back partly reflected political pressures. In the weeks after the sale of Bear to JPMorgan Chase, right-wing critics accused Bernanke and Paulson of rewarding reckless behavior and doing Wall Street's bidding. *The Wall Street Journal* published an editorial entitled "Pushovers at the Fed." This criticism ignored the fact that some of Bear's senior executives and investors had lost hundreds of millions of dollars in the forced sale. However, in protecting Bear's creditors from any losses, the authorities had undoubtedly prevented other Wall Street firms, and their shareholders, from incurring big losses.

Arguably, this government intervention was perfectly justifiable. With the credit markets having been locked up for more than half a year, it was silly to go on pretending that this was simply a liquidity crisis. It had evolved into a full-blown banking crisis. The collapse in the value of subprime securities and other asset-backed securities had permanently wiped out hundreds of billions of dollars of bank capital. There was a growing suspicion that some major financial institutions were insolvent, or close to insolvent. History demonstrates that in such circumstances the only way for policymakers to get ahead of the problem is to acknowledge its scale, excise some of the bad debts, and recapitalize the banks deemed able to survive.

In Japan during the 1990s, this didn't happen, and the country endured a decade of economic stagnation following the bursting of a stock and real estate bubble. At about the same time, in Scandinavia, by contrast, governments took quick and effective action to resolve a large-scale banking crisis. In Finland, the government combined more than forty savings banks into one state-owned savings bank; in Norway, the government nationalized the country's three biggest banks, wiping out their shareholders; in Sweden, the government seized control of the two largest banks and shunted their toxic assets into a state-owned company. In a March 2008 column, I quoted a speech by Stefan Ingves, a senior official at the International Monetary Fund, who, as an official in the Swedish government, had helped to devise its policies. The main lesson learned, Ingves said, was that "you cannot rely on the private sector or markets alone to solve systemic banking problems."

Rather than publicly acknowledging this fact, Paulson and Bernanke continued to act in the hope that, given time, the financial system would fix itself. The Fed's policy of gradually expanding its lending programs to provide bigger loans for longer periods to more and more financial institutions was based entirely on this proposition. Within the central bank, it was known as the "finger in the dike" strategy. The Fed's lending tactics were innovative and well executed, but they didn't resolve the underlying problem: the mountain of bad debts sitting on banks' balance sheets.

Events gradually pushed the Bush administration in a more radical direction. Hitherto, its response to the financial crisis had been distinctly modest. In the housing market, it encouraged borrowers and lenders to come together in a "Hope Now Alliance," which was designed to prevent avoidable foreclosures. Early in 2008, it introduced a $168 billion stimulus program, largely made up of income tax rebates. Behind the scenes, however, some officials were starting to plan for the worst. At the Treasury Department, officials put together a memo discussing a series of "break-the-glass" actions that the federal government could take in another emergency. These included buying toxic assets from the banks; leaving the assets in the banks but insuring them; buying equity stakes in the banks; and launching a massive, publicly financed mortgage-refinancing plan, which would stabilize the financial system from the ground up. "These actions would move the focus of financial markets policy back from the Fed to the Treasury, which would be appropriate in what was a problem reflecting inadequate capital rather than insufficient liquidity," Phillip Swagel, a Harvard-trained economist who was the assistant secretary for economic policy at the Treasury Department, later recalled in a firsthand account of the credit crisis. "But these options all required Congressional approval, and there was no prospect of getting approval for any of this."

Swagel's strictures are well noted. The American political system was designed to prevent effective government action rather than to facilitate it, and many senior congressmen remained wedded to the nostrums of Milton Friedman. This became clear as the slump in the housing market caused a sharp deterioration in the finances of Fannie Mae and Freddie Mac, the two big government-sponsored mortgage companies. Rising delinquencies were hitting their insurance divisions, which had guaranteed millions of prime mortgages, and the collapse in the subprime market was causing big problems for their investment arms, which had accumulated more than a trillion dollars' worth of mortgages and mortgage securities.

In the summer of 2008, the stock prices of Fannie and Freddie fell sharply, reflecting worries about their ability to service their heavy debts. For the Bush administration, allowing the mortgage companies to default wasn't even an option. America's foreign debtors, such as China, were heavy holders of their bonds, which they regarded as government-guaranteed. If Fannie and Freddie had defaulted, the creditworthiness of the United States would have been called into question, and the dollar might well have collapsed. Also, Fannie and Freddie, despite their financial troubles, were still crucial props for the housing market. If they weren't there to buy and insure mortgages, the cost of home loans would go up, which was the last thing the economy needed.

On Sunday, July 13, Paulson stood on the front steps of the Treasury Building and asked Congress for the power to raise the federal government's lines of credit to Fannie and Freddie; to inject capital into them by purchasing their stock and bonds; and, if necessary, to place them in a government-run "conservatorship"—whatever that meant. (Paulson referred to this option as a "bazooka," which would be handy to have in reserve.) Congress agreed to the request, but only under duress. "When I picked up my newspaper yesterday, I thought I woke up in France," Senator Jim Bunning, a Republican from Kentucky, said at a hearing. "But no, it turns out socialism is alive and well in America."

From the perspective of Bunning and those who thought like him, worse was to come—a lot worse. Immediately after Labor Day, Paulson and Bernanke called in the CEOs of Fannie and Freddie to inform them that they were toast. On Sunday, September 7, Paulson fired his bazooka, announcing that Fannie and Freddie would enter a conservatorship, which turned out to mean backdoor nationalization. The U.S. government took an 80 percent ownership stake in each of the companies, appointed new managements, and agreed to provide them with as much as $100 billion each in fresh capital. Although Fannie and Freddie would remain nominally independent, the Treasury Department would effectively control them.

Despite some ritual denunciations from the right, there was surprisingly little opposition to Paulson's move. (Even the editorial page of *The Wall Street Journal* gave it grudging support.) Ultimately, despite cries about socialism in America, the prospect of Fannie and Freddie defaulting on their debts was too awful to contemplate. Even the most recalcitrant Republican congressman didn't want to be held responsible for a collapse in the United States' ability to finance its massive debts, or for a deep recession. Until now, the economy at large had held up surprisingly well during the financial crisis, but consumers were cutting back their spending, and many firms were discharging workers. A Keynesian vicious circle of weakening demand begetting more layoffs and further falls in demand was becoming visible. In August, the unemployment rate had reached 6.1 percent.

Still, nobody, not even New York University's Nouriel Roubini, whose gloomy prognostications had earned him the nickname Dr. Doom, expected the scale of the financial collapse that was to come. On Tuesday, September 9, just two days after the government takeover of Fannie and Freddie, stock in Lehman Brothers fell almost 45 percent after reports that it had failed to secure a multibillion-dollar investment from a Korean bank. In the ensuing days, Lehman suffered the same fate Bear Stearns had endured in March. Despite protests that its finances were sound, money drained out of the firm, and by the end of the week it was almost out of cash.

This time, however, there would be no government-engineered rescue. On the evening of Friday, September 12, Paulson and Geithner summoned some of Wall Street's top executives to the New York Fed and told them they wanted an "industry solution" to Lehman's problems. The investment bank had approached Bank of America and Barclays, a big British bank, about being taken over, and talks continued over the weekend. By Sunday afternoon, however, both suitors had dropped out, and Lehman prepared a bankruptcy petition. Paulson, Bernanke, and Geithner allowed it to go right ahead, and in the early hours of Monday, September 13, Lehman, which had been founded in 1850, filed for Chapter 11.

The hands-off approach that the Treasury Department and the Fed adopted toward Lehman represented a stunning and inexplicable reversal of the policy of not allowing big, interconnected financial firms to collapse. Even now, it hasn't been fully explained. Bernanke subsequently insisted to the Economic Club of New York that Lehman didn't have enough collateral for the Fed to lend to it. When I interviewed him, he said that the option of saving Lehman never even came up. "With Bear Stearns, with all the others, there was a point when someone said, 'Mr. Chairman, are we going to do this or not?' With Lehman, we were never anywhere near that point. There wasn't a decision to be made."

This explanation, which Paulson seconded, has the sound and feel of a post hoc rationalization. Although Bank of America quickly dropped out of the bidding for Lehman and turned its attention to Merrill Lynch, which it ended up buying, Barclays remained interested. As late as Sunday morning, the British firm thought it had a potential deal to buy Lehman, possibly with a Bear-style guarantee from the Fed for some of its mortgage portfolio. Talks reportedly broke down over the Treasury Department's insistence that Barclays make a public pledge to meet all of Lehman's commitments before the markets opened in Asia that evening. Barclays said it couldn't do that without first obtaining shareholder approval. If the American government had been determined to save Lehman at any cost, the Fed, despite Bernanke's protestations, could certainly have kept it afloat for a few days until Barclays did the necessary paperwork.

Many people suspect Paulson and Bernanke let Lehman go bankrupt to reestablish the principle that irresponsible behavior would be punished. For months, the Treasury Department had been urging Lehman to raise more capital; Paulson had called Lehman's CEO, Richard Fuld, Jr., and personally prevailed upon him to do it. Fuld had procrastinated, infuriating Paulson. In his frank account of the crisis, Phillip Swagel writes, "The feeling at Treasury . . . was that Lehman's management had been given abundant warning that no federal assistance was in the offing, and market participants were aware of this and had time to prepare. It was almost as if Lehman management was in a game of chicken and determined not to swerve." Monday, September 15, Swagel goes on, "felt like a good day at Treasury in that the market was allowed to work (and it was too soon to know the full adverse ramifications)."

The authorities' renewed commitment to laissez-faire lasted less than forty-eight hours. (Congressman Barney Frank, of Massachusetts, subsequently quipped that Monday, September 15, should be declared "Free Market Day.") On the evening of Tuesday, September 16, the Fed rescued AIG, the big insurance company, which over the previous week had revealed to the government that it, too, was fast running out of cash. Between January 2, 2008, and Labor Day, AIG's stock price had fallen by two-thirds, but few outsiders had realized it was on the verge of collapse. On Monday, September 15, as news of its dire state became public, its stock tumbled another 60 percent.

The source of AIG's problems turned out to be the roughly $400 billion in credit protection it had provided to banks and other financial institutions, much of it in the form of credit default swaps on subprime mortgage bonds. With the prices of these securities falling, its counterparties were demanding that it put up more collateral, and the rating agencies were threatening a downgrade. If this downward spiral had been allowed to continue for even a few more days, AIG would have been forced to file for bankruptcy. With the strong encouragement of the Treasury, the Fed invoked Section 13.3 of the Federal Reserve Act and promised to lend AIG up to $85 billion. As collateral for this huge loan, it demanded AIG's entire assets, including its profitable life and property insurance divisions. The Fed also obtained warrants entitling it to a 79.9 percent equity stake in AIG. In addition to the two biggest mortgage companies in the country, the U.S. taxpayer now owned the country's largest insurance company.

The reasons for the government's policy U-turn have invited endless speculation. Some traders and commentators have speculated that in saving AIG, the Fed and the Treasury acted to protect the interests of Goldman Sachs, Paulson's former firm. Shortly after the bailout, *The New York Times* reported that Goldman had purchased $20 billion in CDSs from AIG and was the firm's biggest trading partner. Goldman said most of its positions with AIG were hedged, and described its overall exposure as "immaterial." It later turned out, however, that one of the things AIG did with the money it got from the Fed was pay Goldman $13 billion. It also emerged that a day before rescuing AIG, Paulson and Geithner had met with Lloyd Blankfein, Goldman's chief executive, and several other senior Goldman executives, as well as some representatives of other Wall Street firms, to discuss the insurance company's' plight.

The whispered accusations against Paulson and Bernanke remain just that. Following the bailout, AIG paid similar sums to other financial firms that were its counterparties on credit default swaps, including Deutsche Bank and Société Générale. There is no need for a Goldman conspiracy theory to explain the government's actions. Paulson and Bernanke rescued AIG because they feared the company's sudden collapse would have sparked a financial panic that could have brought down any number of financial firms, not just Goldman. As Bernanke explained to Congress, "The Federal Reserve took this action because it judged that, in light of the prevailing market conditions and the size and composition of AIG's obligations, a disorderly failure of AIG would have severely threatened global financial stability." Or, as Swagel notes:

"Saving AIG was not what anyone wanted, but at the time it seemed like the only possible course of action."

AIG's balance sheet was much bigger than Lehman's, and so were its off-balance-sheet commitments. If AIG had been allowed to go out of business, it may well have been possible to fence in its property and casualty insurance operations, which had been operated conventionally, but the firm's now infamous financial products division, which was based in London, was a black hole. AIG was also a big player in the repo markets, where, seeking to earn extra money, it had lent out many of the securities it owned. It had insured the returns of many money market mutual funds. What impact its sudden demise would have had on those markets is impossible to say.

Paulson and Bernanke were guilty; their crimes were inconsistency and self-deception. In rescuing Bear, they had acknowledged the reality that, in a world of highly leveraged, massively interconnected financial capitalism, firms at the hub of the system can't be allowed suddenly to implode; the collateral damage is just too great. But during the ensuing months, as the markets calmed down somewhat, Paulson and Bernanke had allowed themselves to imagine they were back in a simpler, more just world, one in which the financially irresponsible were held accountable. How else to explain the quixotic decision to let Lehman, a bigger and more interconnected firm than Bear, come crashing down in a single weekend?

Even before the AIG rescue, the folly of that determination was becoming evident. On Tuesday, September 16, the Reserve Primary Fund, a big money market mutual fund that had bought more than $700 million in short-term debt issued by Lehman, which was now worthless, announced that its customers would no longer be allowed to withdraw cash from their accounts because it didn't have enough to pay them all: its net asset value had fallen below a dollar a share. Since the founding of the first money market fund in 1970, only one other fund had "broken the buck." Fearing that other firms would find themselves in a similar position to the Reserve Primary Fund, private and institutional investors began pulling their money out of money market funds, raising the possibility of a full-scale run on the industry. In just a few days, almost $150 billion was withdrawn.

This was a truly alarming development, and not just for the mutual fund industry. With about $3.5 trillion in assets, money market funds are major players in the financial system. Through investing in commercial paper and other short-term debts, they provide day-to-day funding for many financial and nonfinancial firms. Now, faced with growing redemptions, many of the funds began to hoard their cash, causing the commercial paper and repo markets to sputter badly. Money was simply drying up. By comparison, the credit freeze of August 2007 had been minor.

Synchronous lateral excitation was again at work. With their own access to funds disappearing, many banks reduced their credit lines to hedge funds and other clients, and demanded more collateral. The stage appeared set for a ruinous round of panic selling, more margin calls, and more selling. Goldman and Morgan Stanley, the only two remaining big independent investment banks, began to experience the same pressures that had brought down Lehman and Bear. Rumors circulated, which may well have been true, that the two firms were having trouble raising money. On Wednesday, September 17, Goldman's stock, which the previous week had been trading above $150, dipped below $100. "Both Goldman and Morgan were having a run on the bank," a top Wall Street executive subsequently told me. "People started withdrawing their balances. Counterparties started insisting that they post more collateral."

The dreaded "meltdown" that Bernanke and others had feared appeared to be occurring. Fed officials discussed creating a "lifeline" that would give Goldman and Morgan more access to the central bank's funds. Bernanke, though, had seen enough. After agreeing just the previous day to extend $85 billion to AIG, he had little appetite for lending more Fed money to Goldman and Morgan, and he wasn't even sure it would work. On Wednesday evening, in a conference call with other officials, he asked Paulson to accompany him to Capitol Hill to make the case for a federal bailout of the entire banking industry. "We can't keep doing this," Bernanke said. "Both because we at the Fed don't have the necessary resources, and for reasons of democratic legitimacy, it's important that the Congress come in and take control of the situation." Paulson agreed. The next day, after briefing the president, the two men went up to the Hill.

Following the example of Caesar's army in 49 B.C., the American government had crossed the Rubicon. On October 3, 2008, on Congress's second try, it granted the Treasury Department the authority to spend up to $700 billion—about 5 percent of GDP—on buying up toxic bank assets. In its small print, the bailout bill allowed the Treasury secretary to use the money in other ways. After Treasury officials realized that purchasing assets at low prices would force banks to recognize even more losses, Paulson sensibly shelved the original plan and switched to recapitalizing the banks directly through the purchase of preference shares.

There is no need to dwell on the machinations and recriminations that accompanied the progress of the Troubled Asset Relief Program, such as the row over executive compensation at banks that received capital injections, and the decision to lend TARP money to Chrysler and General Motors. The important point is the principle the program established. After more than a year, the U.S. government had explicitly taken responsibility for resolving the financial crisis. The talk of leaving it to the market, of relying on the economy's recuperative properties, of finding a private-sector solution—this had all been jettisoned. Having allowed global capitalism to move to the cliff's edge, terrifying their electors, the politicians finally had pledged to do whatever was necessary to prevent it from toppling over. This alone was enough to restore a semblance of order.

Similar events played out in other advanced countries. The financial stabilization programs that were adopted in the United States and elsewhere involved three elements: a pledge not to let systemically important institutions collapse; a commitment to use taxpayers' money to socialize some of the losses that had been incurred; and an endorsement of unorthodox central bank policies aimed at kick-starting the credit markets. All of these policies were based on the belated recognition that if private decision-makers were left to react to market incentives on an individual basis, they would pursue collectively self-defeating actions, such as withdrawing their money from financial firms and refusing to lend. Only the government could overcome the threat of rational irrationality and get people to coordinate on a more favorable outcome.

In the United States, the policy involved the Treasury Department, the Federal Deposit Insurance Corporation, and the Federal Reserve

Bank. Although the Treasury's capital injections received most of the publicity, the other elements of the package were at least equally important.

In November 2008, the FDIC agreed to guarantee debts issued by big financial institutions, thereby transferring the credit risks involved in lending to these companies from investors to the taxpayer. By January 2009, most of the big banks in the country, including Citigroup, Wells Fargo, JPMorgan Chase, Goldman Sachs, and Bank of America, had taken advantage of this "Temporary Liquidity Guarantee Program" to raise money from investors, and so had some nonbank financial companies, such as GE Capital.

The federal government also agreed to shoulder much of the risk of further losses on a $306 billion pool of toxic assets owned by the troubled Citigroup and a $118 billion pool owned by the supposedly healthy Bank of America. An ostensible rationale for the latter deal was that some of the insured assets emanated from Merrill Lynch, which Bank of America had purchased with official encouragement. In actuality, both insurance schemes provided a politically expedient way of ring-fencing some of the crud on the firms' balance sheets without setting up a government-run "bad bank," as the Swedes did in the early 1990s, and the Japanese did a decade later. Paulson and his colleagues didn't need to go to Congress for approval for this plan. They simply made an agreement with Citi that the firm would bear the first $29 billion in losses on the asset pool, the Treasury and the FDIC would take the next $15 billion, and the Fed would eat 90 percent of the rest. (The deal with Bank of America was similar.) The price the government exacted from Citi for this deal—$7 billion in preferred stock—was artificially low. Columbia's Glenn Hubbard, Harvard's Hal Scott, and Chicago's Luigi Zingales calculated that the potential cost to taxpayers of the insurance scheme was about $60 billion. Since Citigroup's entire market capitalization at the end of 2008 was less than $40 billion, it might have been cheaper to nationalize the entire firm than insure its toxic assets, but explicit public ownership was precisely the outcome the Treasury Department and the White House were seeking to avoid.

As far as financial stabilization policy was concerned, the accession to the White House of Barack Obama changed little. Geithner moved from the New York Fed to the Treasury Department and picked up the policies he had helped Paulson and Bernanke to design. Rather than considering outright nationalization of troubled banks, as some commentators were calling for, the new administration stuck with the more indirect approach of the TARP, the insurance schemes, and the various Fed/Treasury financing programs. It supplemented these inherited policies with another stimulus package; a series of bank stress tests, which many independent experts regarded as a charade; and a renewed effort to purchase toxic assets, which struggled to get off the ground.

Through it all, the Fed's role remained key. Even seasoned central bank watchers had had difficulty keeping up with all its new loan facilities and asset-purchase programs. The true measure of them was the expansion in the Fed's balance sheet, which saw it go from roughly $900 trillion in August 2007 to $2.1 trillion in May 2009. In September 2008, the Fed started lending to money market mutual funds that faced redemptions; in the following couple of months, it said it would help finance the purchase of commercial paper, provide loans to buyers of asset-backed securities, and purchase mortgage securities issued by Fannie and Freddie. In January 2009, it announced it would start buying Treasuries, and in March it said it would extend its asset-backed securities lending program, an attempt to revive the securitization markets, to up to $1 trillion. None of these schemes was an overt giveaway, but many of them involved allowing financial firms to raise money on assets that other lenders wouldn't accept as collateral, with the Fed taking most of the downside risk. Having the central bank provide credit to troubled companies and financing to frozen markets is another way of quietly providing subsidies to the financial sector.

John Kenneth Galbraith once quipped that in America the only respectable socialism is socialism for the rich. Actually, Galbraith was wrong: socialistic schemes designed to help Wall Street have to be disguised. When they are carried out in the open, as was the case with the TARP, they create uproar. Evidently, many people would rather see financial collapses than bank bailouts. The attraction of loan guarantees and complicated insurance and financing arrangements is that while Wall Street investors understand the fiscal commitments they involve, most congressmen and editorial writers do not. These opaque schemes allow the government to use the power of the public purse to stabilize the markets without disturbing the populace: hence their proliferation.

In April 2009, the International Monetary Fund put a price tag on the efforts Western governments had taken to shore up their financial systems: roughly $10 trillion, of which about half was in the form of direct commitments and half was in insurance schemes and other guarantees. Had this money been well spent? It came too late to prevent the sharpest economic downturn since the 1930s. The dramatic *journées* of September and October 2008 hit U.S. consumers and businesses like an electric shock, prompting them to slash their expenditures. During the last three months of the year, consumer spending on durable goods, such as autos and boats, fell 22 percent on an annualized basis; total private investment fell 23 percent; and exports fell 24 percent. In some ways, the first quarter of 2009 was worse. Investment fell at an annual rate of 49 percent; exports fell at an annual rate of 31 percent. Overall GDP fell at an annualized rate of more than 6 percent. As demand for goods and services plummeted, firms laid off workers. Between September 2008 and June 2009, more than 5 million jobs were eliminated, and the unemployment rate jumped from 6.2 percent to 9.5 percent.

The recession was global. From Ireland to Germany to Japan, spending and output slumped. Between April 2008 and March 2009, world industrial production fell by almost 15 percent, prompting the economic historians Barry Eichengreen and Kevin O'Rourke to comment, in April 2009, "World industrial production, trade, and stock markets are diving faster now than during 1929–30."

The worldwide slump demonstrated that Minsky and Sweezy had been right when they said the fortunes of the economy at large couldn't be divorced from what happened on Wall Street. In a financially driven economy, interruptions in credit flows and problems at major financial institutions will eventually have an impact on the spending decisions, and employment prospects, of many people who don't have any direct link to the financial markets. Wall Street and Main Street, for all their mutual suspicion, are locked in a symbiotic embrace.

Despite the global recession, though, the government interventions did succeed in preventing a wholesale collapse of the financial system, despite bank losses and write-offs that, by the end of 2008, had reached $1 trillion. ("[A]s Hank Paulson said publicly, 'You don't get much credit for averting a disaster,'" Bernanke remarked to me.) By the summer of 2009 there was evidence, finally, that the lending crunch had eased. In many credit markets the cost of borrowing had fallen considerably and loan volumes had increased. The number of financial firms relying on the Fed for financing had come down sharply. Even some securitization markets, such as those based on credit card receivables and auto loans, had revived, albeit with the Fed's help. Global stock markets had rebounded sharply, with the Dow moving back above 9,500.

In early June, the Treasury Department announced that ten big banks, including JPMorgan Chase, Goldman Sachs, and Morgan Stanley, would be allowed to repay $68 billion in loans they had obtained through the TARP program, indicating that the government no longer considered these firms vulnerable to another financial shock. In mid-July, Goldman Sachs, which ten months earlier had been on the verge of collapse, announced record quarterly earnings of $3.44 billion, setting the stage for the return of eight-figure bonuses. "There is a very good chance for seeing the U.S. economy and the world economy get back to the point when it is growing again over the next few quarters," Geithner remarked during a trip to Europe.

There was evidence to back up Geithner's optimism. In the second quarter of 2009, U.S. GDP declined at an annual rate of just 1 percent, or thereabouts. With auto sales and other forms of spending rebounding in many areas of the country, economic forecasters were predicting growth would turn positive in the third quarter. Even in the depressed real estate market, there was good news. During June, according to the closely watched Case-Shiller indices, home prices rose in eighteen out of twenty big cities. "When I saw these numbers, I danced a jig," Karl E. Case, the Wellesley economist who helped develop the indices, told *The New York Times*. "It appears that the housing market is stabilizing quicker than people thought it would." On August 12, 2009, almost two years to the day after the beginning of the subprime crisis, the Fed's Open Market Committee issued a statement predicting a "gradual resumption of sustainable economic growth." Thirteen days later, President Obama said he intended to appoint Ben Bernanke to a second term as Fed chairman.

If the financial crisis and recession were coming to an end, Americans and countless other people around the world had a much-derided force to thank: active government intervention. Amid the encouraging economic news, hardly anybody stopped to consider what would have happened if policymakers had adhered to the laissez-faire shibboleths they had parroted before the onset of the crisis—if instead of flooding the financial system with cheap loans, injecting taxpayers' money into banks, and making a commitment not to allow a repeat of the Lehman collapse, they had stood back and allowed the invisible hand free reign. Perhaps the reason so few considered this counterfactual is that it is patently absurd. During an economic crisis, when markets have failed, even many conservative economists are relieved to see the government step in: practically nobody is willing to risk creating another Great Depression by relying on free enterprise. But that, surely, raises the question of why anybody believed in utopian economics to begin with. Like VAR-based risk modeling, the miraculous self-stabilizing power of the market fails just when it is most needed. "Thanks to a strong economic policy effort an even darker scenario seems to have been avoided," the Organisation for Economic Co-operation and Development, an international economic research organization based in Paris, commented. "But this is no reason for complacency; the need for determined policy action remains across a wide field of policies."

CONCLUSION

O ur extended tour of market failure is almost over. If the reader feels like he or she has read two books, or, possibly, three, I beg indulgence and say, with a hat tip to Flaubert, that while brevity is a virtue, God is in the details—something utopian economics failed to recognize. At the end of a book largely devoted to economic theories, it may be laboring the point to say that ideas matter, but the point is far from universally accepted.

In the philosophy of history, four names loom large: Macaulay, Marx, Keynes, and Rudge. To the Macaulay school, individual initiative is the primary driver of history: great men create great events, and it is only through their actions that ideas influence reality. Marx didn't overlook the role that individuals and ideas play. However, he viewed them as secondary to the vast impersonal forces that drive historical change, the most important of which is materialism, or class warfare. Keynes, as I noted in the introduction, claimed that ideas promulgated by economists and political philosophers have primary importance, writing, "Indeed the world is ruled by little else." As for Rudge, one of the characters in Alan Bennett's play *The History Boys*, his was the nihilistic voice of post-postmodernism. When one of his teachers asked him how he defined history, he replied, "Well, it's just one fucking thing after another." (The industrialist Henry Ford is reputed to have said something similar.)

There is something in each of these theories. If Ronald Reagan, instead of appointing Alan Greenspan to the Fed in 1987, had talked Paul Volcker into staying on for another four or eight years, things would have turned out differently. Volcker's successor as Fed chairman, rather than being a former disciple of Ayn Rand, would probably have been another (small *c*) conservative banker. Such a figure surely wouldn't have allowed two speculative bubbles to inflate in less than a decade, and he certainly wouldn't have taken quite so cavalier an approach to financial regulation. When historians come to write about the "Greenspan Bubbles," they will do so with good cause: more than any other individual, the former Fed chairman was responsible for letting the hogs run wild.

Even if Greenspan hadn't been at the Fed, however, history would have proceeded in the same general direction: the free market counter-revolution would have continued, and so would the rapid growth of the financial sector. Both of these phenomena reflected the playing out of some of Marx's deep forces. By the early 1970s, under the on-slaught of rising government spending, globalization, and growing demand for natural resources, the social contract between workers and corporations that underpinned the postwar boom was fraying badly, and so were other features of the Keynesian settlement, such as modest inflation and the Bretton Woods monetary system. Free market economics offered an intellectual alternative to the Kennedy-Johnson-Nixon consensus, which was known in the United Kingdom as "Butskellism." Financialization and the rise of the stock market provided an alternative means of mobilizing and disciplining the economy. If corporate managers and government officials couldn't restructure declining industries, control the budget deficit, and boost languishing profit rates, perhaps financial markets could do the job. Circumstance had turned in Wall Street's favor.

The Rudge/Ford view of the world must also be accorded some respect. For all the efforts of economists and journalists, such as myself, to rationalize credit crunches, financial collapses, and other extreme events, there is inevitably an element of randomness and capriciousness to individual occurrences. If Jimmy Cayne had spent less time playing bridge and more time analyzing the subprime market; if Dick Fuld's efforts to persuade Korean investors to buy a stake in Lehman Brothers hadn't fallen through; if AIG's finances hadn't deteriorated sharply the very same weekend that Lehman was collapsing . . . Playing the counterfactual game is fun, and it can be illuminating. By the summer of 2008, however, a financial collapse was virtually inevitable. Following the forced marriage of Bear Stearns and JPMorgan Chase, hopes of a revival in the credit market gradually dissipated. Much of Wall Street was running out of money and confidence. The only question was whether the government would step in before or after another calamity.

While Keynes, characteristically, overstated his case, there can be no argument that, in this instance, the application of misguided ideas was largely responsible for setting the U.S. economy on its disastrous trajectory. Individual homeowners, mortgage lenders, and bankers reacted to the immediate financial incentives they faced, but the macroeconomic and regulatory framework in which they were operating reflected more than twenty years of free market idolatry. Between the collapse of communism and the outbreak of the subprime crisis, an understandable and justified respect for market forces mutated into a rigid and unquestioning devotion to a particular, and blatantly unrealistic, adaptation of Adam Smith's invisible hand.

Milton Friedman, who died in 2006, said the test of an economic theory is that it should explain a lot with a little. But the modern theory of the invisible hand that Friedman and others promoted explains too much with too little. At its core, it says simply: self-interest plus competition equals nirvana. There is no mention in this equation of the institutions of modern capitalism, such as multinational corporations, derivatives markets, universal banks, and mutual funds. Information asymmetries, uncertainty, copycat behavior, network effects, and disaster myopia—the invisible hand metaphor abstracts from all of these awkward features of reality, too. Don't worry, its defenders say, the market will take care of things. Just make sure that competition reigns, prevent the emergence of monopolies, and a good outcome is guaranteed.

Actually, some free market economists aren't saying this anymore. Alan Greenspan has blamed the subprime collapse on the misleading risk models that private-sector enterprises relied on. Richard Posner has castigated the misguided actions of bankers and other financiers, entitling his recent book *A Failure of Capitalism*. Although some conservatives are still blaming everything on Fannie Mae/Freddie Mac, or the Bush-Clinton vision of an "Ownership Society," this antigovernment posturing is hard to take seriously. As happened in the 1930s, the unfettered free market has disgraced itself in full public view. "Our system failed in basic fundamental ways," Treasury Secretary Timothy Geithner said in March 2009. "To address this will require comprehensive reform. Not modest repairs at the margin, but new rules of the game."

Geithner's statement was commendably bold, but an entirely new system of economic supervision and regulation cannot be constructed out of thin air. Vested interests have to be confronted; conflicting aims have to be reconciled. Above all, a new way of thinking about the economy has to be articulated as a replacement for utopian economics—an economic philosophy that acknowledges the usefulness of markets but also their limitations, that recognizes the existence of Hayek's telecommunications system but also its tendency to break down. Reality-based economics provides just such a philosophy. Drawing on both theory and experience, it affords the concept of market failure a central position, recognizing the roles that human interdependence and rational irrationality play in creating it. If further calamities are to be avoided, policymakers need to make a big mental shift and embrace this eminently practical philosophy.

So far, there is little sign of this happening. While the economic downturn has generated popular support for economic reforms of various kinds, much of the political class—on both sides of the Atlantic—remains trapped in an antiquated rhetorical tug-of-war. In Washington in particular, the debates on health care and financial reform may lead you to believe the only choice is between liberty and socialism: either you are for free markets or you are a rabid government interventionist. That is absurd. If this book hasn't succeeded in anything else, I hope it has demonstrated that the idealized free market is a fiction, an invention: it has never existed, and it never will exist.

In its place, we have a hybrid of private and public enterprise, of decentralized activity and central supervision. Such a mixed system isn't easy to reduce to intellectual slogans and sound bites. However, it has passed what economists refer to as the market test. In every advanced country, the private sector supplies most of the goods and services that people want to buy, but government-financed institutions also play a significant role, both in providing things that the market can't, or won't, supply and in laying down rules and regulations. Some of these laws, such as those defining extensive agricultural subsidies in the United States and the European Union, promote specific economic interests. Others, such as health and safety guidelines, are designed to protect the public interest.

Effective government is a matter of getting the balance right between autonomy and coordination. Too much supervision, and healthy innovation will be stifled. Too little oversight, and the economy can veer off in the direction of boom and bust, and it can also generate all sorts of negative externalities, such as pollution and urban blight. Fortunately, the concept of rational irrationality provides a way for policymakers to think about this trade-off. In many cases of government action, the problem is one of remedying private incentive structures that give rise to socially damaging activities. The free market economists were perfectly right when they said that incentives are important; but getting them right involves much more than blind reliance on the free market. In all too many cases, that is the source of the problem.

In the pragmatic spirit of reality-based economics, let us address Lenin's question: "What is to be done?" Beginning with the housing market, there is nothing wrong with the general principle of securitization. In the prime mortgage area, where "conforming" loans that meet the underwriting standards of Fannie Mae and Freddie Mac are bundled together into bonds, it has worked pretty well for more than twenty-five years. When some bright sparks on Wall Street extended the idea to subprime mortgages, underwriting standards quickly decayed, and the outcome was disastrous. Rather than spreading risk, securitization ended up disguising and concentrating it, thereby creating an enormous negative spillover, which almost brought down the financial system.

To prevent a recurrence, banks that create and distribute mortgage securities should be forced to keep some of them on their books, perhaps as much as a fifth. This would make them monitor the types of loans they purchased, which, in turn, would discipline mortgage lenders. Second, mortgage brokers and mortgage lenders should be regulated at the federal level. Mortgages are relatively simple and highly useful inventions that lenders, by varying the borrowing terms and adding in semihidden fees, can quickly transform into baffling and dangerous products. Understaffed state regulatory agencies cannot be relied on to deal with this problem. The federal government should toughen up the predatory lending laws, imposing draconian penalties for issuing loans that borrowers can't reasonably afford to repay.

Adopting an idea of Elizabeth Warren, of Harvard Law School, the Obama administration and Democrats in Congress have proposed a new government agency to regulate financial products marketed to consumers—a Consumer Financial Protection Agency. This seems sensible. The government prevents companies from selling harmful drugs and children's toys that catch fire, but mortgage lenders have been free to peddle subprime option ARMs that were designed to explode after a few years, forcing the borrower into costly refinancing. Utopian economics is based on the idea that people know their own best interests, but this assumes they have all the information they need, and can understand it. In the case of mortgages and other financial products, the relevant information is often hidden or complicated: invariably, the seller knows more than the buyer. "Why are the most risky products sold to the least sophisticated borrowers?" Edward Gramlich, the late economist and Fed governor, asked in a 2007 paper. "The question answers itself. The least sophisticated borrowers are probably duped into taking these products."

But lenders weren't the only ones who acted deceitfully. Many home buyers took out loans they knew they weren't qualified for, fibbing about their ability to repay them. The government should outlaw stated-income loans and enforce the existing fraud laws for mortgage applicants, which make it a crime to misrepresent your personal finances. The evidence demonstrates that applicants who lie about their incomes are far more likely to default on their loans. And the effects of mortgage defaults, as we have all seen, quickly spill over into the rest of the economy.

Perhaps the biggest lesson we have learned is one Hyman Minsky taught as far back as the 1980s: Wall Street needs taming. On an individual level, banks, investment banks, and other financial companies provide essential services. Taken together, however, their self-interested actions have created and amplified economic disturbances, largely through the use of leverage and the excessive accumulation of risk. The proper role of the financial sector is to support innovation and enterprise elsewhere in the economy. But during the past twenty years or so, it has grown into Frankenstein's monster, lumbering around and causing chaos.

The new regulatory system will have to reflect the government safety net that now exists for the likes of Citigroup, Goldman Sachs, and even GE Capital, which has been allowed to issue government-guaranteed debt. Firms that can rely on Uncle Sam to bail them out have a big incentive to take risky gambles. If these gambles work out well, their employees and stockholders reap the rewards; if things go wrong, the taxpayers foot some of the bill. To offset these perverse incentives, regulators should impose maximum leverage ratios on banks and other financial firms, and they should also oblige them to hold more than adequate levels of liquidity and capital in reserve. In addition, banks must be prevented from hiding liabilities and risks in SIVs and other shell companies. From the fringe banking crisis of the 1970s to the collapse of the shadow banking system in 2007, recent history demonstrates that opacity is a recipe for trouble. The big financial institutions will squawk about these restrictions, which will reduce their profitability. Let them. In choosing to shelter under the government safety net, they have abrogated their right to behave like hedge funds.

On the subject of hedge funds and other nonbanks, we now know that the labels attached to financial institutions are often misleading. AIG is an insurance company; Fannie Mae is a mortgage company; GE Capital is an industrial-financing company. Effectively, however, these firms were all big financial intermediaries: that is, banks. The collapse of any of them would have caused chaos throughout the financial system. In recognition of this reality, any business that deals in money and is large and interconnected enough that its failure would seriously endanger many other financial firms must be subjected to the same capital, liquidity, and reporting requirements as big banks.

The more systemic risk an institution poses, the more tightly it should be controlled. Under the balkanized system of regulation that existed prior to 2009, many firms that created systemic risk were allowed to operate as they pleased. "AIG exploited a huge gap in the regulatory system," the Fed chairman, Bernanke, said to Congress in

March 2009. "There was no oversight of the financial-products division. This was a hedge fund, basically, that was attached to a large and stable insurance company, made huge numbers of irresponsible bets, took huge losses." And, Bernanke could have added, ended up taking $180 billion from the taxpayer, in cash and credit lines.

The same principles that govern financial institutions should be applied to derivatives and other complex financial products: if they pose a potential threat to the stability of the system, they should be regulated. It is shocking that the $60 trillion credit default swap industry could have grown up with no oversight. Greenspan's argument that self-interest would drive Wall Street counterparties to regulate one another ignored the problem of hidden information. Firms such as Morgan Stanley and Bank of America are exposed not merely to their own counterparties, but also to potential problems at their counterparties' counterparties, their counterparties' counterparties' counterparties, and so on. When a problem arises somewhere in the financial network, nobody knows where the losses are located, or where they might ultimately end up. Hoarding cash is a privately rational action. Credit dries up.

Despite Geithner's radical statement of intent, the Obama administration's proposed regulatory overhaul doesn't fully deal with the problem of rational irrationality: it amounts to tinkering with the existing system rather than fundamentally reforming it. Under the proposed reforms, the administration would oblige banks to keep some of the mortgage securities they distribute on their own books, but just 5 percent. Unlike in the 1930s, no thought has been given to splitting up the essential utility aspects of the financial system—customer deposits, check clearing, and other payment systems—and the casino aspects, such as investment banking and proprietary trading. There will be no return to the Glass-Steagall Act, which means "too big to fail" financial supermarkets, such as Bank of America and JPMorgan Chase, will continue to dominate the financial system.

The administration has said new mandatory capital requirements will be extended to any financial firm "whose combination of size, leverage and interconnectedness could pose a threat to financial stability if it failed," but none of these terms has been defined, and it isn't clear how far the new rules will be applied to big hedge funds, private equity firms, and the finance arms of industrial companies. If there is any wiggle room, excessive risk-taking and other damaging behavior will simply migrate to the unregulated sector. Imposing restrictions on the biggest hedge funds and private equity firms could well lead to a drastic shrinkage in these industries, which would be no great loss. Much of the activity that such firms engage in amounts to a zero-sum game. It doesn't yield any economic gains for society at large.

The proposed central clearinghouse for derivatives transactions is a good idea that doesn't go far enough. By imposing leverage limits on traders, and demanding adequate collateral for exposed positions, the clearinghouse could eliminate a lot of counterparty credit risk. Unfortunately, the administration's proposal applies only to "standardized" derivatives. Firms such as Goldman Sachs and Morgan Stanley would still be allowed to trade "customized" derivatives without public disclosure or central clearing. Given the creativity of the Wall Street financial engineers, it wouldn't take them long to exploit this loophole.

In another sop to Wall Street, the remit of the Consumer Financial Protection Agency won't extend to complex securities that financial firms trade among themselves. Evidently, the White House has swallowed the Wall Street line that precertification of derivatives and other financial products would stifle innovation. But that is exactly the point. "The goal is not to have the most advanced financial system, but a financial system that is reasonably advanced but robust," Viral V. Acharya and Matthew Richardson, two economists at NYU's Stern School of Business, wrote in a recent paper. "That's no different from what we seek in other areas of human activity. We don't use the most advanced aircraft to move millions of people around the world. We use reasonably advanced aircrafts whose designs have proved to be reliable."

Executive pay is yet another issue that remains to be tackled in any meaningful way. Even some top bankers have conceded that current Wall Street remuneration schemes lead to myopic behavior and excessive risk-taking. Lloyd Blankfein, the chief executive of Goldman Sachs, has suggested that traders and senior executives should receive most of their bonuses in deferred payments. Firms such as Morgan Stanley and UBS have already introduced claw-back schemes that allow the firm to rescind some or all of traders' bonuses if their investments turn sour.

These seem like encouraging signs. Without explicit government involvement, however, efforts to reform Wall Street compensation won't survive the next market upturn. The problem is our old friend the prisoner's dilemma. While it is in the interest of Wall Street as a whole to control rampant short-termism and irresponsible risk-taking, each individual firm has an incentive to pay star traders what they want when they want it. As soon as business picks up, some struggling banks will go out and hire disaffected traders from firms that have introduced pay limits, and the compensation reforms will break down. In this case, as in many others, the only way to coordinate on the socially desirable outcome is to enforce compliance, and the only body that can do that is the government.

This doesn't mean that government regulators would be setting the pay of individual traders and executives. It does mean that the Fed, as the agency primarily responsible for ensuring financial stability, would issue a set of rules for Wall Street compensation that all firms would have to follow. They might be obliged to hold some, or all, of their traders' bonuses in escrow accounts for a lengthy period, or to pay bonuses to their senior executives in the form of restricted stock that doesn't vest for five or ten years. (This was one of Blankfein's suggestions.) Once again, the aim must be to prevent the emergence of rationally irrational behavior. Unless some restrictions are placed on people's actions, they will inevitably revert to it.

The Great Crunch wasn't just an indictment of Wall Street: it was a failure of monetary policy and economic analysis. From the late 1990s onward, the Fed stubbornly refused to recognize the dangers that speculative bubbles present, adopting a hands-off stance that it still hasn't publicly repudiated. The Fed's refusal to prick the stock market and credit bubbles was partly a matter of political cowardice: it didn't want to be attacked for bringing on an economic downturn. But the Greenspan approach also reflected an underlying belief that the American economy was a wondrous, self-correcting mechanism—the illusion of stability—and that it would quickly bounce back from any speculative bust.

A formal renunciation of the Greenspan doctrine is long overdue. In an ideal world, Ben Bernanke would give a speech acknowledging the Fed's failures and blunders in which he was complicit, and pledge to return the Fed to its traditional role, which a former Fed chairman, William McChesney Martin, famously defined as "taking away the punch bowl just when the party gets going." This is unlikely to happen, and change may have to be imposed on the Fed policymakers. At the moment, their so-called dual mandate is to ensure "maximum sustainable employment and price stability." Morgan Stanley's Stephen Roach has suggested that Congress alter the Fed's mandate to include the preservation of financial stability. The addition of a third mandate would mesh with the Fed's new regulatory role as the primary monitor of systemic risk, and it also would force the central bank's governors and staff to think more critically about the financial system and its role in the broader economy.

It is a pity that economists outside the Fed can't be legally obliged to acknowledge their errors and reconsider their views. To their credit, a few of them have voluntarily begun the truth-and-reconciliation process. In a blog post entitled "The Unfortunate Uselessness of Most 'State of the Art' Academic Monetary Economics," Willem Buiter, a professor at London School of Economics who has also served on the Bank of England's Monetary Policy Committee, wrote: "[T]he typical graduate macroeconomics and monetary economics training received at Anglo-American universities during the past 30 years or so, may have set back by decades serious investigations of aggregate economic behaviour and economic policy-relevant understanding. It was a privately and socially costly waste of time and resources."

As Buiter pointed out, the issue was partly a methodological one. Under the influence of Robert Lucas and other mathematically inclined theorists, research "tended to be motivated by the internal logic, intellectual sunk capital and esthetic puzzles of established research programmes rather than by a powerful desire to understand how the economy works—let alone how the economy works during times of stress and financial instability. So the economics profession was caught unprepared when the crisis struck." In creating this state of unreadiness, the role of free market ideology cannot be ignored. Even today, all too many economists see their primary role as defending the market system against possible encroachments. Privately, they are often willing to acknowledge that a particular industry is wracked by market failure and needs reforming. Somehow, though, these individual flaws don't add up to an overall critique.

In the back (or front) of their minds, many centrist economists who have no association with the Chicago School still have a vision of the invisible hand satisfying wants, equating costs with benefits, and otherwise working its magic. Take Harvard's Greg Mankiw, the author of two popular textbooks and the founder of the Pigou Club, which supports higher carbon taxes. In a May 2009 column in *The New York Times*, Mankiw conceded that teachers of freshman economics would now have to mention some issues previously relegated to more advanced courses, such as the role of financial institutions, the dangers of leverage, and the perils of economic forecasting. And yet, Mankiw stated: "Despite the enormity of recent events, the principles of economics are largely unchanged. Students still need to learn about the gains from trade, supply and demand, the efficiency properties of market outcomes, and so on. These topics will remain the bread-and-butter of introductory courses."

Note the phrase "the efficiency properties of market outcomes"! What do you suppose that refers to? Builders constructing homes for which there is no demand? Mortgage lenders foisting costly subprime loans on little old ladies of limited education? Wall Street banks levering up their equity capital by thirty or forty to one? The global economy entering its steepest downturn since the 1930s? Of course not. What Mankiw was referring to was the textbook economics that he and others have been teaching for decades: the economics of Adam Smith, Leon Walras, and Milton Friedman. In the world of utopian economics, the latest crisis of capitalism is always a blip.

As memories of September 2008 fade, revisionism and disaster myopia will become increasingly common. Many will say the Great Crunch wasn't so bad, after all, downplaying the massive government intervention that prevented a much, much worse outcome. Incentives for excessive risk-taking will revive, and so will the lobbying power of banks and other financial firms. If these special interests succeed in blocking meaningful reform, we could well end up with the worst of all worlds: a financial system dominated by a handful of firms that are "too big to fail," but that can take on as much risk as they please, secure in the knowledge that if things go wrong the taxpayer will be there to bail them out. Such an arrangement would amount to crony capitalism writ large, and it would make a mockery of the democratic ideals that both major parties claim to represent. Before the political will for reform dissipates, it is essential to put Wall Street in its place and to confront utopian economics with reality-based economics. Hopefully, this book can play a small part in that effort.

AFTERWORD: THE GREAT DISCONNECT

During the first three months of 2010, realtors in the Hamptons— the upscale summer retreat on the eastern end of Long Island— noticed an encouraging development. Properties that had been on the market for many months, or years, were starting to sell, particularly the most expensive houses and estates. Twenty-eight such properties changed hands for at least $5 million each, compared to seven in the same quarter of 2009. "It's as active in the Hamptons as I've ever seen," Alan Schnurman, a local real estate investor, told the Associated Press. What motivated this burst of activity? January and February is bonus season on Wall Street, which had just enjoyed the most profitable year in its history. The New York–based securities industry, after posting total losses of $42.6 billion in 2008, generated $55 billion in profits in 2009, smashing the previous record, and it paid out $20.3 billion in bonuses. As winter gave way to spring, the Wall Street gusher continued to spew money. Between January and March 2010, Citigroup's investment banking division made more than $2.5 billion in profits. Goldman Sachs's traders enjoyed their best quarter ever, generating an astonishing $7.4 billion in net revenues.

Barely a year and a half after the collapse of Lehman Brothers, Wall

Street was once again doing well for itself—obscenely well, it seemed to many people who weren't attending open houses in Southampton and East Hampton. "[F]or most Americans these huge bonuses are a bitter pill and hard to comprehend," noted Thomas P. DiNapoli, the comptroller of New York State, whose office tracks Wall Street profits. "Taxpayers bailed them out, and now they're back making money while many New York families are struggling to make ends meet." In other parts of the country, Americans weren't merely resentful; they were practically ready to lynch the Wall Street bonus recipients, and the politicians who had rescued them. "Hank, Americans don't like bailouts," Sarah Palin, John McCain's running mate, had warned Treasury Secretary Henry Paulson in October 2008. By the summer of 2010, riding a populist revolt, the former governor of Alaska had emerged as the front-runner for the G.O.P. presidential nomination in 2012.

And yet, judged purely in economic terms, the Bush-Obama rescue program had proved fairly successful. Beginning in July 2009, U.S. GDP had expanded for four consecutive quarters, confirming the predictions of recovery that Timothy Geithner and Ben Bernanke had made. The rate of growth was modest rather than spectacular—about 3 percent on an annualized basis—but it belied the doomsters' prognostications. The Great Recession, as it was now known, had ended more quickly than expected. In May 2010, the Organization for Economic Co-operation and Development, an economic research body based in Paris, said the world economy would grow by 4.6 percent for 2010 and 4.5 percent for 2011. Despite widespread fears of a "double dip" recession, the global recovery appeared to be continuing.

Aside from allowing Lehman to collapse, policymakers had avoided the mistakes of the 1930s. By injecting taxpayers' money into struggling financial institutions and guaranteeing their debts, they had arrested the vicious cycle of falling asset prices, panic selling, and further falls in prices. By reducing short-term interest rates virtually to zero, they had halted a similar downward spiral in the real estate market. (With the cost of mortgage loans at historic lows, bargain seekers entered the market, putting something of a floor under prices.) And by introducing tax cuts and additional public spending programs, governments had counteracted the economy-wide vicious cycle in which tumbling demand for goods and services prompted firms to reduce their work forces, unemployment rose, and demand slipped further.

The authorities in Washington and elsewhere had demonstrated that Keynes had been right: economies suffering from a speculative bust didn't have to be left to nature's cure or, more accurately, to the markets' cure, which Andrew Mellon, Herbert Hoover's Treasury Secretary, famously described as "liquidate, liquidate, liquidate." But while the aggressive use of fiscal and monetary policy could be labeled "Keynesian," other elements of the rescue program didn't fit neatly into any paradigm. The Fed's innovative liquidity programs harked back to Walter Bagehot's edict that central banks should lend freely in a crisis, while its resort to buying up Treasury bonds and mortgage securities—so-called quantitative easing—was akin to the "helicopter drop" of cash that Milton Friedman had advocated as a cure for deflation. The bank bailouts and other less-visible subsidies to the financial sector weren't associated with any particular economic creed: they were emergency measures that had been adopted reluctantly. Rather than relying on a particular theory of the crisis or a single policy tool, policymakers had adopted a flexible and pragmatic approach, trying a number of things together and adjusting the mix as they went along. "You can't point to one thing alone: there were three or four things," Nariman Behravesh, chief economist at IHS Global Insight, a leading economics consulting firm, said to me early in 2010. "Look, U.S. policymakers pulled out all the stops, and it worked."

Only on Wall Street was the recovery palpable, however. Elsewhere, there was a stark contrast between public sentiment and the optimistic statements of policymakers and economists. In July 2010, 9.5 percent of the U.S. workforce was still out of work, and that didn't include more than eleven million people who had stopped looking for jobs or who had been forced to accept part-time employment. Taking account of these folks, the March 2010 rate of "underemployment" was 16.5 percent—about one in six. Even for those fortunate enough to be in work, worries remained. Many households were saddled with mortgages bigger than the value of their homes. In Miami, real estate prices were about 50 percent below their 2006 peak; in Las Vegas, they were down 55 percent; nationwide, the decline was about 30 percent. Rather than going out and spending, many households and firms were hoarding cash and rebuilding their savings. In the second quarter of 2010, the annualized growth rate of U.S. GDP fell back to 1.6 percent, raising more fears of a return to recession.

Across the Atlantic, meanwhile, the financial crisis had never really gone away. In the fifteen-country Euro bloc, GDP fell 4.2 percent in 2009, compared to a decline of 2.4 percent in the United States. Modest growth returned during the first quarter of 2010, but another blowup in the markets quickly overshadowed it. As the recession had deepened, many countries, the United States included, had run up huge budget deficits, which were starting to spook investors in government bonds. In early May, the European Union, together with the International Monetary Fund, finalized a Euros 110 billion (about $140 billion) lending package for Greece, where government spending exceeded tax revenues by about 13 percent of GDP. Far from calming the markets, the Greek bailout created fears of similar problems emerging in Spain, Portugal, and other heavily indebted European countries. With speculators continuing to short the Euro, the EU hastily created a Euro 750 billion stabilization fund, which could be used to aid other member governments that ran into difficulties funding their operations.

If this was a recovery, it was a fragile and embittered one. While the authorities' response to the crisis had prevented a wholesale economic collapse, it had failed the political test of winning popular support—something Timothy Geithner freely admitted. "My basic view is that we did a pretty successful job of putting out a severe financial crisis and avoiding a Great Depression or Great Deflation type of thing," the Treasury Secretary told me in early 2010. "We saved the economy, but we kind of lost the public doing it."

Given the nature of the policies that the Bush and Obama administrations had adopted, public anger was inevitable. By the end of 2009, almost all the big banks had repaid their TARP bailouts, but they continued to be the recipients of official largesse. With the Fed holding short-term interest rates at virtually zero, firms like Citigroup and Goldman Sachs could borrow money from one arm of the government (the Fed) or from investors (by issuing short-term commercial paper) for next to nothing and lend it to another arm of government (the Treasury) at an interest rate of 3 or 4 percent. By playing "the spread," any moderately competent Wall Street trader could generate large returns for his desk and a big bonus for himself without actually doing what banks are supposed to do: furnishing money to firms and funding capital investments. While bank profits were soaring, many businesses and individuals were still finding loans hard to come by.

The other losers in this game were those who had cash stashed in a savings account or money market mutual fund. "What we have right now is a situation where every saver in the country is, essentially, paying a huge tax to bail out the banking system," noted Raghuram Rajan, the University of Chicago economist, who, back in 2005, had issued a fateful warning about the dangers of a financial blowup. "We are all getting screwed on our money market accounts—getting 0.25 percent—and the banks are making a huge spread on nearly every asset they hold, because they are financing them at pretty close to zero rates."

The Obama administration didn't come out and say so, but enabling the banks to make big profits was one of its policy objectives. Rather than seizing control of sickly institutions, such as Citi and Bank of America, it had settled on a policy of allowing them to earn their way back to sound health, while also encouraging them to raise money from private investors. This was the rationale behind the controversial "stress tests," which the Treasury Department and the Fed carried out in the spring of 2009, and which were meant to find out how much new capital the banks needed to survive a deep recession. In May 2009, when Geithner announced that the nineteen biggest U.S. banks needed to raise just $75 billion, many economists had accused him of understating the banks' remaining exposure to toxic assets. In fact, the official loss estimates were similar to those produced by independent analysts. But the government stress testers were assuming that other parts of the banks' businesses, particularly their trading operations, would record greatly enlarged profits in 2009 and 2010, which would help them withstand big losses in real estate and commercial lending. Buried in the Treasury's official report on the stress tests was the prediction that Citigroup's net revenues in 2009 and 2010 would exceed its loan-loss provisions by $49 billion. For Bank of America, the projected profit figure was $75.5 billion. For Wells Fargo, it was $60 billion.

When these enormous profits duly materialized and the banks distributed some of them to their employees, the public was outraged. Critics accused the Obama administration of overlooking less offensive options for stabilizing the financial system. One idea, widely canvassed in early 2009, would have been to seize control of troubled firms, move their tarnished assets into a state-run "bad bank," and eventually refloat them on the stock market as smaller, healthier institutions. Twenty years previously, during the savings and loans crisis, this approach had been adopted successfully. Theoretically, it would have enabled the government to fire reckless bank managers, wipe out bank shareholders, and impose a "haircut" on bank creditors, thereby punishing the guilty rather than rewarding them with a bailout. "While the Obama administration had avoided the conservatorship route, what it did was far worse than nationalization: it is ersatz capitalism, the privatizing of gains and the socializing of losses," the Nobel-winning economist Joseph Stiglitz wrote in his 2010 book, *Freefall: America, Free Markets, and the Sinking of the World Economy.*

Members of the administration countered that its critics had greatly underestimated the practical difficulty of pursuing the nationalization option. If the government had seized Citi, one senior Treasury official told me, it could well have created creditor "runs" at other banks suspected of being on the government target list. The only way to prevent this from happening, the official said, would have been to spend $3 trillion and take over all the big banks. That figure may be an exaggeration, but the fear of sparking another financial crisis was a real one, and so were the political concerns of the White House and the Treasury Department. Neither President Obama nor Geithner had any appetite for a policy option that smacked of radicalism and big government.

In economic terms, the most serious problem with the rescue programs was not that they further enriched the loathed bankers but that they exacerbated some serious incentive problems at the heart of the financial system. By extending trillions of dollars in loans, capital injections, and debt guarantees to troubled firms, the U.S. government and its counterparts overseas had greatly extended the public safety net for banks and other financial entities. Left unchecked, this expansion will surely lead to more blowups, followed by even bigger bailouts.

The problem is one of rational irrationality. Once people in the financial sector come to believe the government will cap their losses, they have an incentive to step up their risk-taking. Simply announcing that there won't be any more bailouts won't solve the problem—a point noted by two Bank of England economists in an important paper published in November 2009. "Ex ante, they"—policymakers—"may well say 'never again'" wrote Andrew Haldane and Piergiorgio Allesandri,

"But the ex post facto cost of a crisis means such a statement lacks credibility. Knowing this, the rational response by market participants is to double their bets. This adds to the cost of future crises. And the larger these costs, the lower the credibility of 'never again' announcements. This is a doom loop."

The Dodd-Frank Wall Street Reform and Consumer Protection Act, which President Obama signed in July 2010, while containing many worthwhile individual measures, didn't really get to grips with this problem. I stand with the judgment of the previous chapter that, taken overall, the reform effort amounts to "tinkering with the existing system rather than fundamentally reforming it." Any comparison with FDR's regulatory response to the Great Depression is specious. By the end of Roosevelt's first term, the financial system had been transformed. The House of Morgan and other big banks had been split up into their investment banking and commercial banking components; through the newly founded SEC, the government was exercising close supervision of Wall Street; through the Reconstruction Finance Corporation, which had acquired and kept equity stakes in many big financial firms, it was forcing reluctant bankers to extend credit; and through the Justice Department, it was prosecuting a number of prominent financiers. At the end of 2010, there are fewer independent Wall Street firms than there were a few years ago, and the survivors have a bit less freedom to maneuver than they used to have. Overall, though, the financial system looks pretty much the same as it did in 2007.

Overseas, the same is true. For all their attacks on American free market dogmatism, European and Asian governments have shown little inclination to clean up their own financial systems. The big European countries, in particular, which have a lot of big universal banks, lobbied strenuously against any attempt to break them up. On the torturous issue of bank capital requirements something similar happened. Under the auspices of the Bank for International Settlements, in Basel, Switzerland, negotiators from dozens of countries spent many months discussing a new set of international banking regulations. When the talks began, there was talk of forcing banks to build up excess reserves of capital during periods of prosperity and of imposing a surcharge on the very biggest ones. But in September 2010, when the new capital standards were announced, they were so modest that many big banks, having replenished their coffers, already satisfied them.

Here in the United States, after all the mergers that the government had orchestrated during the crisis, six huge firms—Bank of America, Citigroup, Goldman Sachs, JPMorgan Chase, Morgan Stanley, and Wells Fargo—now dominate the financial industry, wielding enormous market power and political influence. (Together, their assets come to about 60 percent of GDP.) The ratings agencies remain unreformed, and so do the myopic compensation packages for Wall Street traders and CEOs that helped bring on the crisis. The one really innovative idea that the administration put forward—imposing a hefty "pollution tax" on the risk-taking of financial institutions—didn't feature in the Dodd-Frank reform bill and has faded from view.

After all that had happened, forcing financial institutions to maintain more capital, shifting derivatives trading onto exchanges, and setting up a new agency to protect consumers from predatory lenders were the least that could have been done. And even in those areas, the Dodd-Frank bill contained a number of sops to the financial lobby. The big U.S. banks still don't face any hard caps on leverage; neither do their international competitors, such as Barclays, Deutsche, and UBS. A significant but undetermined amount of derivatives trading is exempt from the new regulations, and the issuance and trading of naked credit default swaps—bets that a certain company or country will go bankrupt—remains perfectly legal. The new consumer protection bureau, rather than operating as a stand-alone body, in the manner of the Food and Drug Administration and the Environmental Protection Agency, is housed inside the Fed, an institution that failed abjectly in overseeing the mortgage market. (Confirming the old adage that nothing succeeds like failure, the Fed was also given new power to act as a "systemic risk regulator," overseeing the activities of the biggest banks.)

During the debate on Capitol Hill, it is true, some steps were taken to toughen up the reform bill, notably the inclusion of the so-called Volcker Rule, which prohibits banks from proprietary trading and places limits on how much money they can invest in hedge funds and private equity funds. When this directive is enforced, it may prompt Goldman and Morgan Stanley to give up the commercial banking licenses they acquired in 2008 and revert to being investment banks. Bank of America, Citi, JPMorgan, and Wells, which are much more invested in commercial lending, will have to scale back their proprietary trading desks. (Citi has already done so.)

But former Fed chairman Paul Volcker's laudable idea, which the White House adopted at the start of 2010, was that non-depository institutions shouldn't be allowed to shelter under the government safety net, and, legally, at least, they won't be able to. The U.S. government now has the legal power, during a crisis, to take them over and close them down. (In the cases of Bear Stearns and Lehman Brothers, this authority was lacking.) However, it is one thing to empower the Treasury and the Federal Deposit Insurance Corporation to fire senior bankers, wipe out stockholders, and impose losses on creditors. It is quite another thing for the authorities to exercise these powers. If Goldman, say, was to run into serious trouble shortly after giving up its banking license, it is hard to believe that the Treasury and Fed would shut it down and let the dominoes fall where they may. With the markets plummeting, and with creditors, depositors, and other counterparties rushing to liquidate their positions, the authorities would come under enormous pressure to prop up the firm, or find a healthier rival to take it over. Then we would be back to September 2008.

Despite the best intentions of Volcker and others, the big six banks and an undetermined number of other financial firms are almost certainly still too big to fail. Taxpayer rescues of systemically important institutions can't be legislated away: the real issue is what can be done to reduce their likelihood. Apart from regulating individual lines of business that involve big risks, a tricky enterprise at the best of times, the options are greatly reducing the leverage that banks can take on or breaking them up, so the failure of any one of them would no longer pose an insurmountable risk to the system. Neither of these ideas is exactly revolutionary. Practically everybody agrees that excessive leverage played a key role in the crisis, and the idea of splitting up the largest banks has won the support not just of progressive economists but of the British Conservative Party, which formed a coalition government in May 2010, of Mervyn King, the governor of the Bank of England, and even of Alan Greenspan, the former Fed chairman. "If the banks are too big to fail, they are too big," Greenspan said in October 2009, and he went on to say, "In 1911, we broke up Standard Oil. So what happened? The individual parts became more valuable than the whole. Maybe that's what we need."

But far from insisting on smaller banks and drastic reductions in leverage and smaller banks, the Obama administration connived against measures designed to bring these things about. Senator Susan Collins, of Maine, and Senator Blanche Lincoln, of Arkansas, both proposed amendments that would have forced the biggest banks to hold substantially more capital—and real capital, not hybrid securities that are more like subordinated debt. After the Senate passed the Collins and Lincoln amendments, the White House and Treasury pushed Congress to drop them from the final legislation. A move to break up the biggest banks, such as Wells Fargo and Bank of America, which was sponsored by Senator Ted Kaufman, of Delaware, and Senator Sherrod Brown, of Ohio, didn't even get that far. The Democratic leadership in the Senate joined with Republicans to kill the amendment, which was voted down 61–33. "If we'd been for it, it probably would have passed," a senior Treasury official told *New York* magazine. "But we weren't, so it didn't."

The doom loop cannot be wished away, and neither, despite the best efforts of some Chicago stalwarts, can the failures of utopian economics. When, toward the end of 2009, I was reporting a story for *The New Yorker* about the Chicago School's reaction to the economic crisis, Robert Lucas, the proponent of the rational expectations hypothesis, refused to be interviewed. ("Bob looks like a refugee from Verdun," one of his colleagues said.) Eugene Fama, the expounder of the efficient markets hypothesis, told me that his pet theory "did quite well in this episode." Contesting the standard account that the financial markets spun out of control bringing the rest of the economy down with them, Fama argued that the markets were casualties of the recession rather than its instigator. He said the economic slowdown predated the collapse of the U.S. mortgage market. As job and income growth slowed, some homeowners couldn't make their monthly payments, especially subprime borrowers. The credit markets, acting as a rational discounting mechanism, repriced subprime mortgage securities at lower levels, and banks that had invested heavily in them suffered big losses, which prompted them to cut back their lending. "As a consequence, we had a so-called credit crisis," Fama said. "It wasn't really a credit crisis: it was an economic crisis." But if the subprime blowup didn't cause the recession, what did? "That's where economics has always broken down," Fama said with a chuckle. "We don't know what causes recessions. Now, I'm not a macroeconomist, and I don't feel badly about that."

Ingenuity and denial often go hand in hand. Appearing at the annual meeting of the American Economic Association, Ben Bernanke defended the Fed's reluctance to raise interest rates during the housing boom, saying that financial innovation and lax supervision rather than cheap money was responsible for creating the bubble. This sounded suspiciously like a rationalization of Greenspan's argument that policymakers ought to leave the financial markets to their own devices (except, of course, after a crash, when the policymakers should slash interest rates). However, Bernanke did add that policymakers must remain open to raising interest rates to head off future bubbles—a clear departure from Greenspan and another sign that pragmatism had replaced wishful thinking as the ruling ideology in Foggy Bottom.

At the International Monetary Fund, another bastion of economic orthodoxy, things were changing too. In a paper entitled "Rethinking Macroeconomic Policy," Olivier Blanchard, the IMF's chief economist, and two of his colleagues, conceded that policymakers had put too much emphasis on low inflation and not enough on financial stability, arguing that the latter should be made an explicit policy goal. Furthermore, central banks should consider raising their inflation targets—from 2 to 4 percent, say—so they would have more room to cut interest rates in a recession. As doubts persisted about the global economic recovery, the IMF also backed away from its traditional insistence on balanced budgets. In early 2010, its director general, Dominique Strauss-Kahn, argued that, for the time being, governments should maintain their Keynesian stimulus programs rather than trying to spend and raise taxes.

Even in the academic world, where, as Paul Samuelson famously quipped, progress normally proceeds funeral by funeral, there was a brief outbreak of self-analysis. At the same meeting of economists where Bernanke spoke, a panel of eminent scholars addressed the question "How Should the Financial Crisis Change How We Teach Economics?" Harvard's Benjamin Friedman implicitly took issue with his colleague Greg Mankiw's view that economists should continue to emphasize the pre-crisis orthodoxy, noting, "[M]any in our profession seem to like to write and teach, not about the world in which we live, but about the world in which they wish that we lived." During my visit to Chicago, Gary Becker, the most eminent living member of the Chicago School, conceded to me that financial markets weren't fully efficient and that certain ideas associated with Chicago, particularly the rational expectations hypothesis, hadn't fared well. Judge Richard Posner, the conservative jurist, explained why he had recently converted to Keynesian thinking, saying more recent macro doctrines couldn't explain the financial crisis or what needed to be done about it. "I think the challenge is to the economics profession as a whole, but to Chicago most of all," Posner said. Even Eugene Fama conceded that the banking system needed tighter supervision to prevent future blowups and bailouts.

Utopian economics is on the defensive, just like it was in the 1930s, but it is too early to hail the triumph of reality-based economics. For one thing, the political environment is very different from the one that Roosevelt and Keynes operated in. During the Great Depression, many of the unemployed went hungry, and there was real desperation: it was widely accepted that free market dogma had failed and that the authorities should step in to put things right. Despite its global scope, the Great Recession doesn't really compare with the Great Depression, and many ordinary people remain suspicious of government interventions to correct market failures. "I think you are not going to see a huge increase in the role of government in the economy: I'm more and more confident of that," Gary Becker said. "Economists will be struggling to understand how this crisis happened and what you can do to head off another one in the future, but it will be nothing like the revolution in the role of government and in the thinking that dominated the economics profession for decades after the Great Depression."

As if to confirm Becker's point, the summer of 2010 saw a powerful reaction against Keynesian deficit spending. On both sides of the Atlantic, there were calls for an end to stimulus programs; in Germany and Britain, the center-right coalition governments of Angela Merkel and the newly elected David Cameron moved to cut public spending and raise taxes. Partly a reaction to the Greek debt crisis, this policy turnaround also reflected a revival of the "Treasury view" of the late 1920s and early 1930s, which saw the main threat to economic recovery not as a shortage of overall demand but as a dearth of confidence in the public finances on the part of businessmen and investors. With the triumph of the "General Theory," this argument had seemingly been consigned to history, but here it was again, modified hardly at all, on the lips of conservatively minded economists, commentators, and policymakers. "Germany has never agreed to an austerity package to this extent, but these cuts have to be made in order for the country to establish a stable economic future," Chancellor Merkel said in announcing the German budget cuts.

To be sure, budget deficits equal to ten percent of GDP or more, which some countries, such as the United States and Britain were running, couldn't be sustained indefinitely. (Germany's deficit was much smaller: less than five percent of GDP.) But the best way to bring down deficits is to get the economy going again, which leads to higher tax revenues and lower spending on unemployment benefits. Shifting to retrenchment during the early stages of a recovery smacked of the mistake that the second Roosevelt administration made in 1936–37, when, giving in to Wall Street orthodoxy, it slashed spending and raised taxes to balance the budget, only to see the U.S. economy plunge back into recession. The economists advising President Obama, fortunately, had no intention of repeating this policy error. In an article in the *Financial Times*, Lawrence Summers, the head of the National Economic Council, pointed out that reviving growth and reducing the deficit were complementary rather than competing objectives. "Reducing the spectre of prospective deficits will enhance near-term growth," Summers wrote. "And ensuring adequate growth in the near term will reduce long-term deficits." In September 2010, the U.S. administration proposed another round of tax cuts and infrastructure spending.

Without the original $787 billion stimulus program, the public finances and the overall economy would almost certainly have been even weaker. Persuading the public to take account of a counterfactual is far from easy, however, and opinion polls showed that most Americans agreed with conservative economists who said the stimulus program had failed. The economic arguments put forward against the stimulus, such as the claim that increases in government spending generate offsetting falls in private spending, were largely specious, but they jibed with the ordinary American's feeling that many, if not most, tax dollars are wasted.

In the United States, at least, efforts to correct market failures often run into an entrenched skepticism about the efficacy of government actions. Another challenge facing reality-based economics more generally is that, unlike utopian economics, it isn't a fully formed ideology. (Ben Friedman again: "Few ideas offer more appeal than a model that is simple, elegant, and wrong.") Rather than supplying a single, all-encompassing way of thinking about the world, reality-based economics basically says that things are complicated, and no one theory can explain everything. Competitive markets sometimes work well; in other cases they send the wrong price signals. Financial-incentive schemes can elicit hard work and innovation; they can also encourage myopic, destructive behavior. Some economic events can be predicted with precision; others are impossible to forecast. Typically, various outcomes are possible and which one is selected depends on all sorts of things, including the past behavior of the system and participants' (biased) expectations of the future. (This is the problem of "multiple equilibria.")

In the language of chaos theory, the economy is a complex adaptive system. Of course, acknowledging the complexity of the economy only gets you so far; as economists, we want to know how the chaos gets resolved. Fortunately, reality-based economics provides some analytical concepts that have great explanatory power, such as negative externalities (Pigou), rational irrationality (Keynes), disaster myopia (Minsky), and the representative heuristic (Kahneman and Tversky). The challenge today is to develop these ideas, supplement them with new ones, and apply them to particular policy problems. As I hope I have made clear, some progress has already been made in this direction, and, as you read this book, economists unhappy with the ruling orthodoxy are busy applying game theory, principal-agents models, the mathematics of chaos, and new statistical techniques to deepen the insights of Keynes, Pigou, and Minsky.

Some of this research is taking place within established economics departments. Wealthy benefactors unhappy with the state of economics are also supporting some of it. Paul Woolley, a veteran English fund manager who now teaches at the London School of Economics, has endowed a Centre for the Study of Capital Market Dysfunctionality, which is already producing high-level theoretical work that challenges the efficient markets hypothesis. George Soros has endowed an Institute for New Economic Thinking, which in April 2010 held its inaugural conference at King's College, Cambridge, the home of Keynes. One of the guest speakers was Lord Adair Turner, an economist and businessman who chairs the Financial Services Authority, which oversees the British financial system. In a wide-ranging talk entitled "Economics, Conventional Wisdom, and Public Policy," Turner explored many of the same themes that this book has raised, stating: "The proposition is that we need a fundamental challenge to recent conventional wisdom. I strongly endorse that proposition."

The fact that somebody of Turner's views could be appointed as the top regulator in what is, by many measures, the world's largest financial market demonstrates that progress is possible, and it is only fitting, I think, to end with something else Turner said in Cambridge. After raising the question of whether economists should pursue rational-irrationality type models with rational actors, or behavioral models that incorporate emotional and instinctive behavior, Turner said the answer is we need pursue both of these approaches, and others too:

> We need to recognize, as Adam Smith did in his *Theory of Moral Sentiments*, that humans are part rational and part instinctive. We need to accept that the economist must, as Keynes said, be "mathematician, historian, statesman, and philosopher in some degree." And we need to understand, as Mervyn King and others have put it in a recent paper, that because beliefs and behaviors adapt over time in response to changes in the economic and social environment, that "there are probably few genuinely 'deep' (and therefore stable) parameters or relationships in economics" as distinct from in the physical sciences, where the laws of gravity are as good an approximation to reality one day as the next. Which, I'm afraid, is going to make doing and communicating new economic thinking rather hard. Because one of the key messages we need to get across is that while good economics can help address specific problems and avoid specific risks, and can help us think through appropriate responses to continually changing problems, good economics is never going to provide the apparently certain, simple, and complete answers which the pre-crisis conventional wisdom appeared to. But that message is itself valuable, because it will guard against the danger that in the future, as in the recent past, we sweep aside commonsense worries about emerging risks with assurances that a theory proves that everything is okay.

In the economy, as in other areas of human endeavor, everything is seldom okay. And the very thought that it might be—disaster myopia—often generates patterns of behavior that ensures it isn't. Such is the beauty and challenge of economics.

NOTES

PREFACE TO THE 2021 EDITION

viii Goldman Sachs and Morgan Stanley: See John Cassidy, "The Great Corona-virus Divide: Wall Street Profits Surge as Poverty Rises," *New Yorker*, October 16, 2020, available at https://www.newyorker.com/news/our-columnists/the-great -coronavirus-divide-wall-street-profits-surge-as-poverty-rises.

ix median household income: See the median wage chart from a databank maintained by the St Louis Federal Reserve Bank, "Real Median Household Income in the United States," available at https://fred.stlouisfed.org/series /MEHOINUSA672N.

ix just 45 percent of Americans: This figure is taken from a Gallup poll published August 13, 2018, Frank Newport, "Democrats More Positive about Socialism than Capitalism," available at https://news.gallup.com/poll/240725/democrats -positive-socialism-capitalism.aspx.

x "The textbook model is definitely broken": See Wendy Carlin, "How a New Economics Syllabus Is Preparing Students from the Real-World Economy," *Prospect*, May 3, 2018, available at https://www.prospectmagazine.co.uk/economics -and-finance/new-economics-model-teaching-syllabus.

x the CORE website is a good place to start: https://www.core-econ.org/.

x "Too much energy has been and still is . . .": Thomas Piketty, *Capital in the Twenty-First Century*, trans. Arthur Goldhammer (Cambridge, Mass.: Belknap Press, 2014), 574.

xi "provide an overall vision for economic policy . . .": See Suresh Naidu, Dani Rodrik, and Gabriel Zucman, "Economics after Neoliberalism," *Boston Review*, February 15, 2019, available at http://bostonreview.net/forum/suresh-naidu -dani-rodrik-gabriel-zucman-economics-after-neoliberalism.

xiii Congress allotted $454 billion to the Fed: See Jeanna Smialek, "How the Fed's Magic Money Machine Will Turn $454 Billion into $4 Trillion," *New York Times*, March 26, 2020, available at https://www.nytimes.com/2020/03/26/business/ economy/fed-coronavirus-stimulus.html.

xiii the Fed went from being a lender of last resort: This paraphrase is from Michael Feroli, chief U.S. economist, J.P. Morgan, "Fallout from COVID-19: Global Reces- sion, Zero Interest Rates and Emergency Policy Actions," J.P. Morgan, March 27, 2020, available at https://www.jpmorgan.com/global/research/fallout-from-covid19.

xiv "the greatest market failure the world has ever seen": Nicholas Stern, "Summary of Conclusions," in *The Stern Review: The Economics of Climate Change* (Lon- don: HM Treasury, 2006), viii.

xiv "Bangladesh would be completely underwater": Quoted in Peter Dizikes, "Cli- mate Expert Emphasizes the Fierce Urgency of Now," *MIT News*, April 11, 2019, available at https://news.mit.edu/2019/economist-nicholas-stern-warns -renewable%20energy-0411.

xv changing weather patterns could displace: Jon Henley, "Climate Crisis Could Displace 1.2bn People by 2050, Report Warns," *Guardian*, September 9, 2020, available at https://www.theguardian.com/environment/2020/sep/09/climate -crisis-could-displace-12bn-people-by-2050-report-warns.

xv "It has seemingly become impossible . . .": Richard Schmalensee and Robert N. Stavins, "Policy Evolution under the Clean Air Act," *Journal of Economic Per- spectives* 33, no. 4 (Fall 2019): 45.

xv In 1985, corporate profits: Carl Shapiro, "Protecting Competition in the Ameri- can Economy: Merger Control, Tech Titans, Labor Markets," *Journal of Economic Perspectives* 33, no. 3 (Summer 2019): 70.

xvi "Google, Amazon, and Facebook are conglomerates . . .": Matt Stoller, *Goliath: The 100-Year War Between Monopoly Power and Democracy* (New York: Simon & Schuster, 2019), 448.

xvii the net worth of Amazon's founder: Andy Kiersz and Taylor Nicole Rogers, "Jeff Bezos Is the First Person in History to Be Worth More Than $200 Billion. Here's How the World's Richest Man Makes and Spends His Fortune," *Business In- sider*, August 26, 2020, available at https://www.businessinsider.com/jeff-bezos -net-worth-life-spending-2018-8.

xvii "COVID-19 has been tragic for the many . . .": Quoted in Oxfam International, "Pandemic Profits for Companies Soar by Billions as Poorest Pay Price," Sep- tember 9, 2020, available at https://www.oxfam.org/en/press-releases/pandemic -profits-companies-soar-billions-more-poorest-pay-price.

INTRODUCTION: THE GREAT FINANCIAL CRISIS

4 Greenspan and Waxman's exchange: See transcript of remarks of "The Financial Crisis and the Role of Federal Regulators," House Committee on Oversight and Government Reform, Washington, D.C., October 23, 2008, available at http://oversight.house.gov/documents/20081024163819.pdf.

11 "The crisis is primarily . . .": Richard Posner, "Financial Crisis: A Business Failure to a Government Failure?" lecture before the Columbia University chapter of the Federalist Society, New York, November 24, 2008.

12 "When the music stops . . .": Quoted in Michiyo Nakamoto and David Wighton, "Citigroup Chief Stays Bullish on Buy-outs," *Financial Times*, July 9, 2007.

13 124 systemic banking crises . . . : See Luc Laeven and Fabian Valencia, "Systemic Banking Crises: A New Database," International Monetary Fund Working Paper, November 2008, available at www.imf.org/external/pubs/ft/wp/2008/wp08224.pdf.

14 "Practical men, who believe . . .": John Maynard Keynes, *The General Theory of Employment, Interest, and Money* (New York: Harvest/BJ, 1964), 383.

1. RAGHURAM RAJAN'S PRESCIENT WARNING

18 Levittown and home price inflation: See John Cassidy, "The Next Crash," *New Yorker*, November 11, 2002, 123.

19 Increases in home prices 2003 to 2006: Robert J. Shiller, *Irrational Exuberance*, 2nd ed. (Princeton, N.J.: Princeton University Press, 2005), 12–13.

19 "the biggest bubble in history . . .": "The Global Housing Boom," *Economist*, June 16, 2005.

19 "The home-price bubble feels . . .": Quoted in Jonathan R. Laing, "The Bubble's New Home," *Barron's*, June 20, 2005.

19 "We are not going to see . . .": Quoted in Cassidy, "The Next Crash," 123.

19 "upon sale of a house . . .": Alan Greenspan, "The Mortgage Market and Consumer Debt," remarks at America's Community Bankers Annual Convention, Washington, D.C., October 19, 2004, available at www.federalreserve.gov/BoardDocs/Speeches/2004/20041019/default.htm.

20 Greenspan's remarks at Reagan Presidential Library: See Andrew Bridges, "Federal Reserve Chairman Says Postwar Economy Resilient," Associated Press, April 10, 2003.

20 "Did the housing bubble . . .": See transcript of press briefing by director of National Economic Council, Al Hubbard, and chairman of Council of Economic Advisers, Ben Bernanke, Crawford, Texas, August 9, 2005, available at http://georgewbush-whitehouse.archives.gov/news/releases/2005/08/20050809-7.html.

20 The Jackson Hole symposium: See "The Greenspan Era: Lessons for the Future," Jackson Hole, Wyoming, August 25–27, 2005, available at www.kc.frb.org/publicat/sympos/2005/sym05prg.htm.

21 "There is no doubt . . .": Alan S. Blinder and Ricardo Reis, "Understanding the Greenspan Standard," paper presented at the Federal Reserve Bank of Kansas City Economic Symposium, Jackson Hole, Wyoming, August 25–27, 2005, available at www.kc.frb.org/publicat/sympos/2005/PDF/Blinder-Reis2005.pdf.

21 "While the system now exploits . . .": Raghuram G. Rajan, "Has Financial Development Made the World Riskier?" paper presented at the Federal Reserve Bank of Kansas City Economic Symposium, Jackson Hole, Wyoming, August 25–27, 2005, available at www.kc.frb.org/publicat/sympos/2005/PDF/Rajan2005.pdf.

22 "By allowing institutions to . . .": Don Kohn, "Commentary: Has Financial Development Made the World Riskier?" response to Raghuram G. Rajan presented at the Federal Reserve Bank of Kansas City Economic Symposium, Jackson Hole, Wyoming, August 25–27, 2005, available at www.kc.frb.org/publicat/sympos/2005/PDF/Kohn2005.pdf.

23 "the basic, slightly lead-eyed . . .": Quoted in Malcolm D. Knight, "General Comment: Has Financial Development Made the World Riskier?" remarks at the Federal Reserve Bank of Kansas City Economic Symposium, Jackson Hole, Wyoming, August 25–27, 2005, available at www.kc.frb.org/publicat/sympos/2005/PDF/GD5_2005.pdf.

23 "The conventional wisdom . . .": John Kenneth Galbraith, *The Affluent Society* (Boston: Mariner Books, 1998), 9.

2. ADAM SMITH'S INVISIBLE HAND

27 "It is striking to me . . .": Alan Greenspan, *The Age of Turbulence* (New York: Penguin Press, 2007), 260.

27 "One man draws out . . .": Adam Smith, *The Wealth of Nations*, Books 1–3 (New York: Penguin Books, 1997), 109–10.

28 In China between 1981 . . . : *Poverty Data: A Supplement to World Development Indicators 2008*, World Bank, December 2008.

28 "The shepherd, the sorter . . .": Smith, *Wealth of Nations*, Books 1–3, 116–17.

29 iPod's manufacturing chain: See Greg Linden, Kenneth L. Kraemer, and Jason Dedrick, "Who Captures Value in a Global Innovation System? The Case of Apple's iPod," Personal Computing Industry Center, June 2007, available at http://pcic.merage.uci.edu/papers/2008/WhoCapturesValue.pdf.

29 Investigation into iPod manufacturing standards: "The Stark Reality of iPod's Chinese Factories," *Mail on Sunday*, August 18, 2006.

30 "intends only his own gain . . .": Smith, *Wealth of Nations*, Books 4–5, 32.

31 "Every man, as long as . . .": Ibid., 273–74.

31 Little "else is required . . .": Quoted in Ian Simpson Ross, *The Life of Adam Smith* (Oxford: Clarendon Press, 1995), 108.

32 "People of the same trade . . .": Smith, *Wealth of Nations*, Books 1–3, 232.

32 "It is not from the benevolence . . .": Ibid., 119.

32 "Adam Smith's flash of genius . . .": Milton and Rose Friedman, *Free to Choose* (New York: Avon Books, 1980), 5.

33 "Laissez-faire, in short . . .": Quoted in M. Blaug, *Economic Theory in Retrospect* (Homewood, Ill.: Richard D. Irwin, 1962), 201.

34 "[T]he sole end for which . . .": John Stuart Mill, *On Liberty* (Millis, Mass.: Agora Publications, 2003), 11.

34 "erecting and maintaining certain . . .": Smith, *Wealth of Nations*, Books 4–5, 274.

34 "The principle of laissez-faire . . .": Quoted in D. P. O'Brien, *The Classical Economists* (London: Morrison and Gibb, 1978), 272.

35 "[T]he admitted functions of government . . .": John Stuart Mill, *Principles of Political Economy with Some of Their Applications to Social Philosophy* (New York: Longmans, Green and Co., 1909), 800.

35 "The bank, no doubt . . .": Smith, *Wealth of Nations*, Books 1–3, 414.

35 "Such regulations may . . .": Ibid., 423–24.

36 Mackay on speculative manias: Charles Mackay, *Memoirs of Extraordinary Popular Delusions and the Madness of Crowds*, available at www.gutenberg.org/dirs/etext96/ppdel10.txt.

3. FRIEDRICH HAYEK'S TELECOMMUNICATIONS SYSTEM

37 "regard for [Smith's] theories . . .": Greenspan, *Age of Turbulence*, 265.

38 "Chastened at home . . .": John Patrick Diggins, *Proud Decades: America in War and Peace, 1941–1960* (New York: W. W. Norton, 1989), 312.

38 Background on Friedrich Hayek: See John Cassidy, "The Price Prophet," *New Yorker*, February 7, 2000.

39 "more unsatisfactory the more . . .": F. A. Hayek, in Stephen Kresge and Leif Wenar, eds., *Hayek on Hayek* (Chicago: University of Chicago Press, 1994), 49.

41 "To assume that all . . .": F. A. Hayek, "Socialist Calculation," collected in *Individualism and Economic Order* (Chicago: University of Chicago Press), 202.

41 "an immensely complicated mechanism . . .": W. W. Bartley III and Stephen Kresge, eds., *The Collected Works of F. A. Hayek, Volume III: The Trend of Economic Thinking—Essays on Political Economists and Economic History* (Chicago: University of Chicago Press, 1991), 26.

41 "the really central problem . . .": F. A. Hayek, "Economics and Knowledge," collected in *Individualism and Economic Order*, 50.

42 "how to secure the best . . .": F. A. Hayek, "The Use of Knowledge in Society," collected in *Individualism and Economic Order*, 71–78.

42 "We must look . . .": Ibid., 86–87.

43 "The most significant fact . . .": Ibid.

43 "State purchases increased . . .": Nikolai Shmelev and Vladimir Popov, *The Turning Point: Revitalizing the Soviet Economy* (London: I. B. Tauris, 1990), 170.

Quoted in Thomas Sowell, *Basic Economics: A Citizen's Guide to the Economy*, 3rd ed. (New York: Basic Books, 2007), 17.

45 "In the end . . .": F. A. Hayek, *The Road to Serfdom* (Chicago: University of Chicago Press, 1994), 82.

45 "[P]lanning leads to dictatorship . . .": Ibid., 78.

45 "We are rapidly abandoning . . .": Ibid., 17.

45 "few people, if anybody . . .": Ibid., 202.

46 "The hall holds three thousand . . .": Recounted in *Hayek on Hayek*, 105.

47 "We used to talk . . .": Quoted in Cassidy, "The Price Prophet," 50.

4. MARKETS AND WELFARE: WALRAS AND PARETO

50 "is the most direct way of illustrating . . .": Robert S. Pindyck and Daniel Rubinfeld, *Microeconomics*, 4th ed. (Upper Saddle River, N.J.: Prentice Hall, 2005), 591.

51 "the greatest of all economists . . .": Joseph Schumpeter, *History of Economic Analysis* (New York: Oxford University Press, 1954), 827.

55 "even when some people are . . .": Amartya Sen, *Collective Choice and Social Welfare* (San Francisco: Holden-Day, 1970), 22.

57 "The Ministry of Production in the Collectivist State . . .": See Blaug, *Economic Theory in Retrospect*, 539.

58 "avoid much of the social waste . . .": Oskar Lange and Fred M. Tyler, *On the Economic Theory of Socialism* (New York: McGraw-Hill, 1964), 104.

59 "Competition forces entrepreneurs . . .": Ibid., 98.

60 "By all reports . . .": Milton and Rose Friedman, *Two Lucky People* (Chicago: University of Chicago Press, 1998), 55.

5. ARROW AND DEBREU'S FAMOUS PROOF

64 "optimal point can be achieved . . .": Kenneth J. Arrow, "An Extension of the Basic Theorems of Classical Welfare Economics," Cowles Foundation Paper 54, reprinted from Proceedings of the Second Berkeley Symposium on Mathematical Statistics and Probability, University of California Press, 1951, available at http://cowles.econ.yale.edu/P/cp/p00b/p0054.pdf.

65 "the single most important . . .": E. Roy Weintraub, "On the Existence of a Competitive Equilibrium: 1930–1954," *Journal of Economic Literature* 21, no. 1 (March 1983): 13.

66 "You know . . .": Quoted in Weintraub, "On the Existence," 21.

66 Von Neumann's paper: John Von Neumann, "A Model of General Economic Equilibrium," *Review of Economic Studies* 13, no. 1 (1945–1946): 1–9.

67 "He felt the field was . . .": Quoted in Weintraub, "On the Existence," 29.

67 Arrow and Debreu's paper: Kenneth J. Arrow and Gérard Debreu, "Existence of an Equilibrium for a Competitive Economy," Cowles Foundation Paper 87, re-

printed from *Econometrica* 22, no. 3 (July 1934), available at http://cowles.econ
.yale.edu/P/cp/p00b/p0087.pdf.

68 "What is this idealized . . .": William D. Nordhaus, "The Ecology of Markets,"
Proceedings of the National Academy of Sciences of the United States of America
89, no. 3 (February 1, 1992): 846.

69 Arrow's 1953 paper: Kenneth J. Arrow, "The Role of Securities in the Optimal
Allocation of Risk-Bearing," *Review of Economic Studies* 31 (1964): 91–96.

70 "breaks down completely . . .": Roy Radner, "Competitive Equilibrium under
Uncertainty," *Econometrica* 36, no. 1 (January 1968): 35.

70 Counterexamples to the Debreu-Arrow model: G. Debreu, "Excess Demand
Functions," *Journal of Mathematical Economics* 1 (1974): 15–21; R. Mantel,
"On the Characterization of Aggregate Excess Demand," *Journal of Economic
Theory* 7 (1974): 348–53; H. Sonnenschein, "Do Walras' Identity and Continu-
ity Characterize the Class of Community Excess Demand Functions?" *Journal
of Economic Theory* 6 (1973): 345–54.

70 "In the aggregate . . .": Kenneth Arrow, "Rationality of Self and Others in an
Economic System," available in R. M. Hogarth and M. W. Reder, eds., *Rational
Choice* (Chicago: University of Chicago Press, 1987), 204.

71 "Anything goes: The Sonnenschein-Mantel-Debreu Theorem": Andreu Mas-
Colell, Michael D. Whinston, and Jerry R. Green, *Microeconomic Theory* (New
York: Oxford University Press, 1995), 598.

71 "Economics so effortlessly . . .": Quoted in Fred Ackerman, "Still Dead After All
These Years: Interpreting the Failure of General Equilibrium Theory," Global Development and Environment Institute, Working Paper no. 00–01, November 1999, 15.

6. THE MARKET EVANGELIST: MILTON FRIEDMAN

72 "I regard him as . . .": Paul Krugman, "Who Was Milton Friedman?" *New York
Review of Books*, February 15, 2007.

73 "Put yourself in 1932 . . .": Quoted in Lanny Ebenstein, *Milton Friedman: A
Biography* (New York: Palgrave, 2007), 18.

73 "In later years . . .": Milton and Rose Friedman, *Two Lucky People*, 58.

74 Friedman and Stigler pamphlet: Ebenstein, *Milton Friedman*, 50.

74 "It was not reviewed . . .": Quoted in ibid., 137.

74 "Fundamentally, there are only . . .": Milton Friedman, *Capitalism and Freedom*
(Chicago: Chicago University Press, 1962), 13.

75 "Our minds tell us . . .": Ibid., 2.

75 "The list is far . . .": Ibid., 35.

75 "If the public wants . . .": Ibid., 31.

75 "The great advances . . .": Ibid., 3

76 "On the one hand . . .": Ibid., 8.

76 "Historical evidence speaks . . .": Ibid., 9.

77 "The Great Depression, like most . . .": Ebenstein, *Milton Friedman*, 118.

77 "I would like to say . . .": Ben S. Bernanke, remarks at the Conference to Honor Milton Friedman, University of Chicago, Chicago, Illinois, November 8, 2002, available at http://federalreserve.gov/boarddocs/speeches/2002/20021108/default.htm.

77 "will put pressure . . .": Friedman, *Capitalism and Freedom*, 47.

79 "There is always a temporary . . .": Milton Friedman, "The Role of Monetary Policy," *American Economic Review* 58, no. 1 (March 1968): 11; from a presidential address delivered at the American Economic Association, Washington, D.C., December 29, 1967.

79 "a Keynesian in economics": See, for example, David R. Francis, "Supply Siders Take Some Lumps," *Christian Science Monitor*, October 1, 2007.

79 "Friedman and Phelps . . .": Quoted in Friedman, *Two Lucky People*, 231–32.

80 "By now considerable evidence . . .": Milton and Rose Friedman, *Free to Choose* (New York: Avon Books, 1971), 195.

80 "If one storekeeper . . .": Ibid., 212.

80 "The consumer is protected . . .": Ibid., 215.

81 "if we continue to grant . . .": Ibid., xx.

81 "The two ideas . . .": Ibid., 297.

81 "Reagan was especially . . .": Martin Anderson, *Revolution* (San Diego: Harcourt, 1988), 172.

82 "due almost entirely . . .": Naomi Klein, *The Shock Doctrine: The Rise of Disaster Capitalism* (New York: Metropolitan Books, 2007), 591.

83 "From 1973 to 1995 . . .": Friedman, *Two Lucky People*, 408.

83 "What's the single most important . . .": Quoted in Daniel Yergin amd Joseph Stanislaw, *Commanding Heights* (New York: Simon & Schuster, 1998), 150–51.

7. EUGENE FAMA AND THE EFFICIENT MARKETS HYPOTHESIS

88 Bachelier's theory of speculation: See Peter L. Bernstein, *Capital Ideas: The Improbable Origins of Modern Wall Street* (New York: Free Press, 1993), 17–18.

88 "[t]he mathematical expectation . . .": Quoted in ibid., 21.

88 "Suppose you see . . .": Benoit Mandelbrot and Richard Hudson, *The (Mis)behavior of Markets: A Fractal View of Risk, Ruin, and Reward* (New York: Basic Books, 2006), 52.

89 "even if his powers . . .": Quoted in Bernstein, *Capital Ideas*, 134.

90 Fama's follow-up paper: Eugene Fama, "Efficient Capital Markets: A Review of Theory and Empirical Work," *Journal of Finance* 25, no. 2 (1970): 383–417; summarized in Bernstein, *Capital Ideas*, 137–38.

90 "The past history of stock prices . . .": Burton Gordon Malkiel, *A Random Walk Down Wall Street: The Best and Latest Investment Advice Money Can Buy*, 6th ed. (New York: W. W. Norton, 1996), 161.

94 "If the cotton-price changes fit . . .": Mandelbrot and Hudson, *(Mis)behavior of Markets*, 168.

94 "In fact, the bell curve . . .": Ibid., 13.
95 "[L]arge changes tend to . . .": Ibid., 248.
96 "Modern finance was the . . .": Ibid., 167.

8. THE TRIUMPH OF UTOPIAN ECONOMICS

97 "One cannot find . . .": Quoted in John Cassidy, "The Decline of Economics," *New Yorker*, December 2, 1996, 54.
98 "I loved the *Foundations* . . .": Kenneth Arrow, in William Breit and Barry T. Hirsch, eds., *Lives of the Laureates*, 4th ed. (Boston: MIT Press, 2004), 279.
100 "[T]he relevant question . . .": Milton Friedman, "The Methodology of Positive Economics," in *Essays in Positive Economics* (Chicago: University of Chicago Press, 1953), 15.
102 "I write down a bunch of equations . . .": Interview with the author, October 1996; quoted in John Cassidy, "The Decline of Economics," *New Yorker*, December 2, 1996, 55.
103 "Monetary shocks just . . .": Quoted in ibid.
104 "We insist on at least . . .": Quoted in ibid., 51.
104 "Academic economics has . . .": Quoted in ibid.
104 "It's very clear that . . .": Quoted in ibid.
105 "The assumption of 'rational expectations' . . .": Michael Woodford, "Revolution and Evolution in Twentieth-Century Macroeconomics," Princeton University mimeo, 1999, 23.
105 "In the wake of the October . . .": Richard Clarida, Jordi Gali, and Mark Gertler, "The Science of Monetary Policy: A New Keynesian Perspective," *Journal of Economic Literature* 37, no. 4 (December 1999): 1661–707.
107 "Macroeconomics was born . . .": Robert Lucas, "Macroeconomic Priorities," *American Economic Review* 93, no. 1 (2003): 1703. The appearance was somewhat misleading. To achieve it, Lucas assumed that all individuals have identical preferences and share the same (accurate) expectations about the future. Introducing heterogeneity to a rational expectations model causes all sorts of difficulties.

9. CLIMATE CHANGE, SPILLOVERS, AND PROFESSOR PIGOU

112 "We speculate that . . .": Charles Monnett and Jeffrey S. Gleason, "Observations of Mortality Associated with Extended Open-Water Swimming by Polar Bears in the Alaskan Beaufort Sea," *Polar Biology* 29 (2006): 681.
112 "It's a moral issue . . .": Some observers claimed Gore and others had exaggerated the threat that climate change posed to the polar bear. However, in 2008, the Bush administration listed it as a threatened species, citing evidence that warming seas were destroying its natural habitat.

112 "major disruption to economic . . .": The Stern Review Report on the Economics of Climate Change, ii, available at www.hm-treasury.gov.uk/stern_review_report.htm.

112 "threatens the basic elements . . .": Ibid., vi.

113 "Climate change presents . . .": Ibid., i.

113 Description of climate change mechanism: I am, here, relying on the consensus view of scientists, as expressed, for example, in "Climate Change 2007," a report by the Intergovernmental Panel on Climate Change. Although most experts subscribe to this consensus, some eminent dissidents question the evidence that global warming is a genuine phenomenon and/or that it is the product of human economic activity. For an interesting account of their views, see Lawrence Solomon, The Deniers (Minneapolis, Minn.: Richard Vigilante Books, 2008).

113 the ten warmest years: "Climate of 2007 Annual Report," National Climatic Data Center, January 15, 2008, available at www.ncdc.noaa.gov/oa/climate/research/2007/ann/global.html#gtemp.

113 "In common with many other . . .": Stern Review Report, 24.

114 Economists' criticism of Stern Report: See, for example, William Nordhaus, "The Stern Review on the Economics of Climate Change," May 3, 2007, available at http://nordhaus.econ.yale.edu/stern_050307.pdf.

115 Study of British civil servants: See M. G. Marmot and Richard G. Wilkinson, Social Determinants of Health (New York: Oxford University Press, 2006), 19.

115 "Tall and handsome . . .": Quoted in Robert Skidelsky, John Maynard Keynes (London: Macmillan, 1983), 210.

115 "Pigou carried himself . . .": Ibid.

116 "machinery or method of thinking . . .": A. C. Pigou, The Economics of Welfare, 4th ed. (London: Macmillan, 1962), 5.

116 "[E]ven in the most advanced . . .": Ibid., 129.

116 "The study of these . . .": Ibid., 129–30.

116 "Industrialists are interested . . .": Ibid., 172.

117 "costs are thrown upon . . .": Ibid., 134.

117 "extraordinary restraints": Ibid., 192.

118 "no-one can continue to believe . . .": Blaug, Economic Theory in Retrospect, 551.

119 "is not capable of telling us . . .": Keynes, The General Theory, 275.

119 "Einstein actually did for Physics . . .": Arthur Cecil Pigou, "Mr. J. M. Keynes' General Theory of Employment, Interest and Money," Economica (New Series) 3, no. 10 (May 1936): 115.

119 Coase's paper: Ronald H. Coase, "The Problem of Social Cost," Journal of Law and Economics 3, no. 1 (October 1960): 1–44.

120 Coase's case for public goods: "The Lighthouse in Economics," Journal of Law and Economics 17, no. 2 (1974): 357–76.

120 "We should expunge the cost . . .": Terry L. Anderson, "Donning Coase-coloured Glasses: A Property Rights View of Natural Resource Economics," Australian Journal of Agricultural and Resource Economics 48, no. 3 (September 2004): 460.

121 "I tend to regard . . .": Robert Coase, Nobel lecture, December 9, 1991, available at http://nobelprize.org/nobel_prizes/economics/laureates/1991/coase-lecture.html.

121 "inter-relations of the various . . .": Pigou, *Economics of Welfare*, 194.

122 Greg Mankiw's Pigou Club: "Pigovian Questions," Greg Mankiw's blog, December 9, 2006, available at http://gregmankiw.blogspot.com/2006/12/pigovian-questions.html.

10. FRANCIS BATOR'S TAXONOMY OF MARKET FAILURES

126 "to sustain 'desirable' . . .": Francis M. Bator, "The Anatomy of Market Failure," *Quarterly Journal of Economics* LXXII, no. 3 (August 1958): 351.

126 "imperfect information, inertia . . .": Ibid., 352.

129 "The successful competitor . . .": US v. Aluminum Co. of America, 148 F.2d 416, 430 (2d Cir. 1945).

129 "[W]e have an economic . . .": John Kenneth Galbraith, *The New Industrial State* (Boston: Houghton Mifflin, 1967), 6.

130 "If you are right . . .": Quoted in John Cassidy, "The Force of an Idea," *New Yorker*, January 12, 1998, 32.

131 "I was saying all this . . .": Ibid., 33.

132 "cut off Netscape's air supply . . .": From Department of Justice documents, available at www.usdoj.gov/atr/cases/f2600/v-a.pdf.

133 "In these kinds of markets . . .": Ibid., 34.

134 "[T]here are large ready-made . . .": Galbraith, *Affluent Society*, 223.

134 "[T]o a far greater degree . . .": Ibid., 224.

134 "We need not pursue . . .": Francis Bator, *The Question of Government Spending* (New York: Harper and Brothers, 1960), 98.

135 "After the transistor . . .": Paul M. Romer, "Economic Growth," available at www.econlib.org/library/Enc/EconomicGrowth.html. For more on Romer, see Paul M. Romer, "Endogenous Technological Change," Part 2: "The Problem of Development: A Conference of the Institute for the Study of Free Enterprise Systems," *Journal of Political Economy* 98, no. 5 (October 1990): S71–S102.

136 "That knowledge is both . . .": David Miles and Andrew Scott, *Macroeconomics: Understanding the Wealth of Nations* (New York: John Wiley and Sons, 2002), 123.

11. THE PRISONER'S DILEMMA AND RATIONAL IRRATIONALITY

143 Flood's babysitting experiment: See William Poundstone, *The Prisoner's Dilemma: John Von Neumann, Game Theory, and the Puzzle of the Bomb* (New York: Doubleday, 1992), 103.

143 Non-cooperative pair experiment: Ibid., 106–107.

145 "Both Flood and Dresher . . .": Ibid., 122.
147 90 percent of the players choose: Ken Binmore, *Game Theory: A Very Short Introduction* (New York: Oxford University Press, 2007), 21.
149 "Adding together the component . . .": Garrett Hardin, "The Tragedy of the Commons," *Science* 162 (1968): 1244.
150 "Game theorists get . . .": Binmore, *Game Theory*, 67.

12. GEORGE AKERLOF'S MARKET FOR LEMONS

151 "I belonged to . . .": From George Akerlof's Nobel autobiography, available at http://nobelprize.org/nobel_prizes/economics/laureates/2001/akerlof-autobio .html.
152 "a major reason as to why . . .": George Akerlof, "Writing 'The Market for Lemons': A Personal and Interpretive Essay," available at http://nobelprize.org/ nobel_prizes/economics/articles/akerlof/index.html.
153 "[M]ost cars traded . . .": George Akerlof, "The Market for 'Lemons': Quality Uncertainty and the Market Mechanism," *Quarterly Journal of Economics* 84 (1970): 489.
154 "was potentially an issue . . .": Akerlof, "Writing 'The Market for Lemons.'"
155 "marginally attached": Bureau of Labor Statistics, *Issues in Labor Statistics*, Summary 90–04 (April 2009): 1.
156 "it is quite possible . . .": Akerlof, "The Market for 'Lemons,'" 494.
157 2006 health care spending: "National Health Spending in 2006: A Year of Change for Prescription Drugs," *Health Affairs* 27, no. 1 (2008): 14.
158 "The most obvious . . .": Kenneth J. Arrow, "Uncertainty and the Welfare Economics of Medical Care," *American Economic Review* 53, no. 5 (December 1963): 948.
158 "the cost of medical care . . .": Ibid., 961.
158 "Insurance removes the incentive . . .": Ibid., 962.
159 "really comes down to . . .": Juan Dubra, "Interview with Kenneth Arrow," Munich Personal Research Papers in Economics Archive, March 2005, 17, available at http://mpra.ub.uni-muenchen.de/967/1/MPRA_paper_967.pdf.
161 Insurable deposit limits: In October 2008, during the turmoil on Wall Street, the Federal Deposit Insurance Corporation temporarily raised the limit from $100,000 to $250,000. On January 1, 2010, the limit is supposed to revert to $100,000, but many observers expect the higher figure to be made permanent.
161 Moral hazard of deposit insurance: See Asli Demirgüç-Kunt and Harry P. Huizinga, "Market Discipline and Deposit Insurance," *Journal of Monetary Economics* 51, no. 2 (March 2004); and James R. Barth, Gerard Caprio, Jr., and Ross Levine, *Rethinking Banking Regulation: Till Angels Govern* (Cambridge: Cambridge University Press, 2005).
161 "Banks can offer . . .": Asli Demirguc-Kunt and Edward J. Kane, "Deposit Insurance Around the Globe: Where Does It Work?" *Journal of Economic Perspectives* 16, no. 2 (Spring 2002): 176.

162 Cost of savings-and-loan crisis: See Timothy Curry and Lynn Shibut, "The Cost of the Savings and Loan Crisis: Truth and Consequences," *FDIC Banking Review*, available at www.fdic.gov/bank/analytical/banking/2000dec/brv13n2_2.pdf.

163 "As Adam Smith recognized . . .": William Seidman, "Lessons of the Eighties: What Does the Evidence Show?" presentation at NIKKIN, Seventh Special Seminar on International Finance, Tokyo, September 18, 1996, 57.

163 "In effect, the Arrow-Debreu . . .": Joseph E. Stiglitz, "Information and the Change in the Paradigm in Economics," Nobel Prize lecture, December 8, 2001, 506, available at http://nobelprize.org/nobel_prizes/economics/laureates/2001/stiglitz-lecture.html.

164 "The older market failures . . .": Joseph E. Stiglitz, *Whither Socialism?* (Cambridge, Mass.: MIT Press, 1994), 42–43.

165 "remove the widespread . . .": Ibid., 32.

13. KEYNES'S BEAUTY CONTEST THEORY OF INVESTING

167 "Above the block-trading desk . . .": John Cassidy, "Wall Street Bedlam as Bulls Turn Tail," *Sunday Times* (London), October 18, 1987.

168 "Thus it appears that . . .": Shiller, *Irrational Exuberance*, 99–100.

169 "The outstanding fact is . . .": Keynes, *The General Theory*, 149–50.

169 "A conventional valuation . . .": Ibid., 154.

170 "our existing knowledge . . .": Ibid., 152.

170 "foreseeing changes in the conventional . . .": Ibid., 154–55.

171 "to outwit the crowd . . .": Ibid., 155.

171 "the competitors have to pick . . .": Ibid., 156.

172 "is so difficult to-day . . .": Ibid., 157.

172 "For it is the essence . . .": Ibid., 157–58.

172 "For it is not sensible . . .": Ibid., 155.

173 "[W]hile adulteration . . .": Quoted in Peter V. Mini, "Keynes on Markets: A Survey of Heretical Views," *Journal of Economics and Sociology* 55, no. 1 (January 1996): 100.

174 "The idea that supply . . .": R. F. Harrod, *The Life of John Maynard Keynes* (London: Macmillan, 1963), 465.

175 "spontaneous urge to action . . .": Ibid., 161.

176 "We should not conclude . . .": Ibid., 162–63.

14. HERD BEHAVIOR AND THE DOT-COM BUBBLE

177 "Worldly wisdom teaches . . .": David S. Scharfstein and Jeremy C. Stein, "Herd Behavior and Investment," *American Economic Review* 80, no. 3 (June 1990): 465–79.

177 "The underlying idea is that . . .": Jeremy Stein, interview with the author, summer 1998.

178   Fund manager performance: Judith Chevalier and Glenn Ellison, "Career Concerns of Mutual Fund Managers," National Bureau of Economic Research Working Paper 6394, 1998.

178   "being bold and good . . .": Harrison Hong, Jeffrey D. Kubik, and Amit Solomon, "Security Analysts' Career Concerns and Herding of Earnings Forecasts," *RAND Journal of Economics* 31, no. 1 (Spring 2003): 123.

179   "It sent a message . . .": Quoted in John Cassidy, *Dot.con: The Greatest Story Ever Sold* (New York: HarperPerennial, 2002), 122–23.

179   "[I]f they want to beat their . . .": Quoted in "Valuing Those Internet Stocks," *BusinessWeek*, February 8, 1999.

179   "I simply can't analyze . . .": Quoted in *Fidelity Magellan Annual Report*, March 31, 1999, available at www.secinfo.com/d1RUq.6c.htm.

179   "Time has come . . .": "Fidelity Magellan Fund-FMAGX-Rated 'Aggressive Buy' and Vanguard 500 Index Fund-VFINX-Rated 'Buy' by FidelityAdviser.com," *Business Wire*, April 1, 1999.

180   "Is the stock market in a speculative bubble?": Lauren R. Rublin, "Party On! America's Portfolio Managers Grow More Bullish on Stocks and Interest Rates," *Barron's*, May 3, 1999, 31–38.

181   Pension fund investment in the Internet bubble: Eli Ofek and Matthew Richardson, "DotCom Mania: The Rise and Fall of Internet Stock Prices," *Journal of Finance* 57, no. 3 (June 2003): 1122.

181   "From an efficient markets perspective . . .": Markus K. Brunnermeier and Stefan Nagel, "Hedge Funds and the Technology Bubble," *Journal of Finance* 59, no. 5 (October 2004): 2013–40.

182   "follow the advice of financial . . .": Andrei Shleifer, *Inefficient Markets: An Introduction to Behavioral Finance* (New York: Oxford University Press, 2000), 10.

183   "[R]ational arbitrage can . . .": Ibid., 174.

184   "This risk comes from . . .": Ibid., 14–15.

184   "We were too early in calling . . .": Mitchell Pacelle, "Soros to Appoint a CEO After Firm's Chaotic Year," *Wall Street Journal*, August 10, 1999, C1.

185   Fama update on the efficient market hypothesis: Eugene G. Fama and Kenneth R. French, "The Cross-Section of Expected Stock Returns," *Journal of Finance* 47, no. 2 (June 1992): 427–65.

185   Jegadeesh and Titman model: Narasimhan Jegadeesh and Sheridan Titman, "Momentum," Working Paper, October 23, 2001, available at http://papers.ssrn.com/sol3/Delivery.cfm/SSRN_ID299107_code020205500.pdf?abstractid=299107&mirid=1.

185   "The strategy of chasing the winners . . .": Sheridan Titman, interview with the author, summer 1998.

186   "[P]ricing irregularities . . .": Burton G. Malkiel, "The Efficient Market Hypothesis and Its Critics," *Journal of Economic Perspectives* 17, no. 1 (Winter 2003): 59–82.

187   "Upon him we have brought . . .": Solomon Asch, "Opinions and Social Pressure," *Scientific American* 193, no. 5 (November 1955): 32.

187   "Even when the difference . . .": Ibid., 34.

188   "[C]onsensus, to be productive . . .": Ibid., 35.

188 Berns's confirmation of Asch: Gregory S. Berns et al., "Neurobiological Correlates of Social Conformity and Independence During Mental Rotation," *Journal of Biological Psychology* 58 (2005): 245–53.

189 "It is not surprising . . .": Morton Deutsch and Harold Gerard, "A Study of Normative and Informational Social Influences upon Individual Judgment," *Journal of Abnormal and Social Psychology* 51 (1955): 635.

190 "public information stops . . .": Sushil Bikhchandani, David Hirshleifer, and Ivo Welch, "Learning from the Behavior of Others: Conformity, Fads, and Informational Cascades," *Journal of Economic Perspectives* 12, no. 3 (Summer 1998): 155.

15. PSYCHOLOGY AND ECONOMICS: KAHNEMAN AND TVERSKY

192 "There are some situations . . .": Adam Smith, *Theory of Moral Sentiments* (London: Henry G. Bohn, 1853), 22.

193 "The pleasure which . . .": Smith, *Theory of Moral Sentiments*, 273.

193 "overweening conceit which . . .": Smith, *Wealth of Nations*, Books 1–3, 209–10.

193 "[t]aking the whole kingdom on average . . .": Ibid., 211.

193 "our telescopic faculty is defective . . .": Pigou, *The Economics of Welfare*, 25.

194 "We spent hours each day . . .": Daniel Kahneman, Nobel Prize autobiography, available at http://nobelprize.org/nobel_prizes/economics/laureates/2002/kahneman-autobio.html.

195 "put too much faith . . .": Amos Tversky and Daniel Kahneman, "Judgement under Uncertainty: Heuristics and Biases," *Science* 185, no. 4157 (1974): 1126.

195 "Steve is very shy . . .": Ibid., 1124.

196 Hot hand theory: Thomas Gilovich, Robert Vallone, and Amos Tversky, "The Hot Hand in Basketball: On the Misperception of Random Sequences," *Cognitive Psychology* 17 (1985): 295–314.

196 "with little or no regard . . .": Tversky and Kahneman, "Judgement under Uncertainty," 1126.

197 Likelihood of getting killed in a terrorist attack: See N. Wilson and G. Thomson, "Deaths from International Terrorism Compared with Road Crash Deaths in OECD Countries," *Injury Prevention* 11 (2005): 332–33.

197 "Payoffs for accuracy . . .": Tversky and Kahneman, "Judgment under Uncertainty," 1128.

198 Thaler's mental shortcuts: See Richard H. Thaler, *Winner's Curse: Paradoxes and Anomalies of Economic Life* (Princeton, N.J.: Princeton University Press, 1992).

198 "inspired a new generation . . .": Nobel Prize press release, October 9, 2002, available at http://nobelprize.org/nobel_prizes/economics/laureates/2002/press.html.

199 "[T]he average individual bidder/manager . . .": Richard Roll, "The Hubris Hypothesis of Corporate Takeovers," part 1, *Journal of Business* 59, no. 2 (1986): 199–200.

199 "Disaster Myopia in International Banking": Described in James M. Guttentag, "Subprime Crisis, Part II: The Lender Role," available at http://finance.yahoo .com/expert/article/mortgage/33783.

200 "For these employees . . .": David Laibson, "Impatience and Savings," NBER Reporter: Research Summary (Fall 2005), available at www.nber.org/reporter/ fall05/laibson.html.

200 "[T]his pattern of investment . . .": Ibid.

201 "There are some thoughts . . .": Daniel Kahneman interview with Michael Schrage, *strategy + business* (winter 2003), 123.

203 "The brain doesn't like . . .": Quoted in John Cassidy, "Mind Games," *New Yorker*, September 18, 2006, 32.

203 Gift certificate study: Samuel M. McClure, David Laibson, George Loewenstein, and Jonathan D. Cohen, "Separate Neural Systems Value Immediate and Delayed Monetary Rewards," *Science* 306 (October 15, 2004).

203 "Why would anyone . . .": Quoted in Cassidy, "Mind Games," 34.

204 "It isn't a wholesale . . .": Quoted in ibid., 37.

16. HYMAN MINSKY AND PONZI FINANCE

205 "The recent market turmoil . . .": Justin Lahart, "In Time of Tumult, Obscure Economist Gains Currency," *Wall Street Journal*, August 18, 2007.

206 "To businessmen . . .": Quoted in "Hyman P. Minsky," in Philip Arestis and Malcolm C. Sawyer, eds., *A Biographical Dictionary of Dissenting Economists* (Cheltenham, UK: Edward Elgar Publishing, 2001), 412. Author's note: Minsky wrote his own biographical entry.

207 "[T]he Wall Streets of the world . . .": Hyman Minsky, *Stabilizing an Unstable Economy* (New York: McGraw-Hill, 2008), 4.

208 "leads to an expansion . . .": Ibid., 199.

209 "Such loans impart . . .": Ibid., 261.

209 "a spiral of declining investment . . .": Ibid., 239.

209 "The first theorem . . .": Hyman Minsky, "The Financial Instability Hypothesis," Working Paper no. 74, Jerome Levy Economics Institute of Bard College, May 1992, 7–8.

210 "In a world with capitalist . . .": Minsky, *Stabilizing an Unstable Economy*, 280.

212 "was part of the process that . . .": Ibid., 265.

212 "Like all entrepreneurs . . .": Minsky, "Financial Instability Hypothesis," 6.

214 "The downside aspect . . .": Paul Davidson, *Financial Markets, Money and the Real World* (Cheltenham, UK: Edward Elgar, 2002), 115–16.

215 "For a new era . . .": Minsky, *Stabilizing an Unstable Economy*, 6.

216 Sweezy's introduction to Marxist economics: Paul M. Sweezy, *The Theory of Capitalist Development: Principles of Marxian Political Economy* (New York: Oxford University Press, 1942; reprint, New York: Monthly Review Press, 1956).

216 "Is the casino society . . .": Harry Magdoff and Paul M. Sweezy, *Stagnation and the Financial Explosion* (New York: Monthly Review Press, 1987), 149.

217 "[T]he Federal Reserve must broaden . . .": Minsky, *Stablizing an Unstable Economy*, 349.

17. ALAN GREENSPAN SHRUGS

222 "a very small probability event": Transcript of meeting of the Federal Reserve's Open Market Committee, June 24, 2003.

226 "In the field of economics . . .": Interview with the author, October 2008.

226 "brought down numerous . . .": Alan Greenspan, "Economic Flexibility," speech before the HM Treasury Enterprise Conference, London, England, January 26, 2004, available at http://federalreserve.gov/boarddocs/speeches/2004/20040126/default.htm.

228 "It turned out that he was . . .": Quoted in John Cassidy, "The Fountainhead," *New Yorker*, April 24, 2000, 172.

228 "She did things in . . .": Quoted in ibid., 168.

229 "nothing more than . . .": Alan Greenspan, "Antitrust" and "Gold and Economic Freedom," in Ayn Rand, *Capitalism: The Unknown Ideal* (New York: Signet Books, 1967), 100.

229 "As Fed chairman . . .": Greenspan, *Age of Turbulence*, 373.

229 "could undermine the competitiveness . . .": Alan Greenspan, "Need for Financial Modernization," testimony before the Committee on Banking, Housing, and Urban Affairs, U.S. Senate, February 23, 1999, available at http://federalreserve.gov/boarddocs/testimony/1999/19990223.htm.

230 "Risks in financial markets . . .": Alan Greenspan, "Impact of Derivatives on Financial Markets," testimony before the Telecommunications and Finance Subcommittee, House Energy and Commerce Committee, May 25, 1994.

230 "a major failure of counterparty . . .": Greenspan, *Age of Turbulence*, 371.

231 "Recognizing the dangers . . .": Rick Schmitt, "Prophet and Loss," *Stanford Magazine*, March/April 2009, available at www.stanfordalumni.org/news/magazine/2009/marapr/features/born.html.

231 "Greenspan told Brooksley . . .": Quoted in Peter S. Goodman, "Taking a Hard New Look at a Greenspan Legacy," *New York Times*, October 9, 2008.

231 "I certainly am not . . .": Quoted in Schmitt, "Prophet and Loss."

232 "to mitigate the fallout . . .": Alan Greenspan, testimony before the Committee on Banking and Financial Services, U.S. Congress, July 22, 1999, available at http://federalreserve.gov/boarddocs/hh/1999/july/testimony.htm.

232 "There appears to be enough evidence . . .": Alan Greenspan: "Risk and Uncertainty in Monetary Policy," remarks to the annual meeting of the American Economic Association, San Diego, January 3, 2004, available at www.federalreserve.gov/boarddocs/speeches/2004/20040103/default.htm#f8.

233 "caused it by deviating . . .": John B. Taylor: "The Financial Crisis and the Policy Responses: An Empirical Analysis of What Went Wrong," paper presented at a conference organized by the Bank of Canada, Ottawa, November 14, 2008, available at www.stanford.edu/~johntayl/FCPR.pdf.

233 "was held lower than . . .": Richard W. Fisher, "Confessions of a Data Dependent," remarks before the New York Association for Business Economics, New York, November 2, 2006, available at www.dallasfed.org/news/speeches/fisher/2006/fs061102.cfm.

233 "In many respects . . .": Greenspan, *Age of Turbulence*, 368.

18. THE LURE OF REAL ESTATE

235 History of land speculation: Donald G. Holtgrieve, "Land Speculation and Other Processes in American Historical Geography," *Journal of Geography* 75, no. 1 (January 1976).

236 "In 1836 every ship . . .": Willis F. Dunbar and George S. May, *Michigan: A History of the Wolverine State* (Grand Rapids, Mich.: Wm. B. Eerdmans Publishing Company; 3rd rev. sub. ed., 1995), 224.

236 "The whole city had become . . .": Frederick Lewis Allen, *Only Yesterday: An Informal History of the 1920s* (New York: HarperPerennial Modern Classics, 2000), 235.

238 S&P/Case-Shiller Home Price Indices: www2.standardandpoors.com/portal/site/sp/en/us/page.topic/indices_csmahp/2,3,4,0,0,0,0,0,0,0,0,0,0,0,0,0.html.

238 In the ensuing four years . . . : Table B.100, Federal Reserve Flow of Fund Accounts, available at www.federalreserve.gov/releases/z1/Current/annuals/a2005-2008.pdf.

238 Figures from Harvard's . . . : See the Metro Affordability Index in "The State of the Nation's Housing 2007," Joint Center for Housing Studies, Harvard University, available at www.jchs.harvard.edu/publications/markets/son2007/index.htm.

239 In 1998, the median . . . : The Corcoran Report 2008, Corcoran Group, available at www.corcoran.com/guides/pdf/CorcoranReport-2008.pdf.

240 "Recent research within . . .": Alan Greenspan, "Understanding Household Debt Obligations," remarks at the Credit Union National Association 2004 Governmental Affairs Conference, Washington, D.C., February 23, 2004.

240 "A home in Portland, Oregon . . .": Alan Greenspan, "Monetary Policy and the Economic Outlook," Joint Economic Committee, U.S. Congress, April 17, 2002.

242 "America is a stronger country . . .": Quoted in Zachary Karabell, "End of the 'Ownership Society,'" *Newsweek*, October 11, 2008.

243 According to LoanPerformance . . . : See "The State of the Nation's Housing 2006," Joint Center for Housing Studies; available at www.jchs.harvard.edu/publications/markets/son2006/index.htm, Harvard University, 17.

243 Research carried out for . . . : Kelly Zito, "High Interest in Interest-only Home Loans," *San Francisco Chronicle*, May 20, 2005.

244 in almost 60 percent . . . : Mark Sharick, et al., "Eighth Periodic Mortgage Fraud Case Report to Mortgage Bankers Association," Mortgage Asset Research Insti-

tute, Inc., April 2006, available at www.marisolutions.com/pdfs/mba/MBA8th-CaseRpt.pdf.

244 "Bank employees . . .": Steven Krystofiak, written testimony to the Federal Reserve, August 2006.

245 According to one industry . . . : See "Nightmare Mortgages," *BusinessWeek*, September 11, 2006.

245 In the Bay Area . . . : Kathleen Pender, "Mortgage Options Explode," *San Francisco Chronicle*, April 13, 2006.

245 Alt-A originations rose . . . : See Ronald Temple, "Clarifying the U.S. Mortgage Crisis: Context and Consequences," Lazard Asset Management, available at www.lazardnet.com/lam/us/tpd/pdfs/Inv_Research_Mortgage_Crisis.pdf.

246 "We have no way . . .": "Excerpts of E-mails from Angel Mozilo," U.S. Securities Exchange Commission, available at http://sec.gov/news/press/2009/2009-129-email.htm.

247 conducted a survey of home buyers . . . : Robert Shiller, *The Subprime Solution* (Princeton, N.J.: Princeton University Press, 2008), 45.

248 "This wood made money . . .": Grainger David, "Riding the Boom," *Fortune*, June 27, 2005, 58.

249 "I don't foresee . . .": "Housing Bubble—or Bunk?" available at www.businessweek.com/bwdaily/dnflash/jun2005/nf20050622_9404_db008.htm.

249 "House price appreciation . . .": "The State of the Nation's Housing 2006," 9.

250 "Our analysis reveals . . .": "Assessing High House Prices: Bubbles, Fundamentals, and Misperceptions," Federal Reserve Bank of New York, Staff Report No. 218, September 2005.

19. THE SUBPRIME CHAIN

252 "We were lepers . . .": Quoted in Paul Muolo and Matthew Padilla, *Chain of Blame: How Wall Street Caused the Mortgage and Credit Crisis* (Hoboken, N.J.: John Wiley and Sons, 2008). My account of the history of subprime lending relies heavily on this excellent book, which was written by two journalists who have covered the story as closely as anybody. Muolo is executive editor of *National Mortgage New*; Padilla is a reporter at *The Orange County Register*.

253 65 billion worth of . . . : See Souphala Chomsisengphet and Anthony Pennington-Cross, "The Evolution of the Subprime Mortgage Market," *Federal Reserve Bank of St. Louis Review* (January/February 2006): 37–38, tables 3 and 4.

254 According to a study . . . : Adam B. Ashcraft and Til Schuermann, "Understanding the Securitization of Subprime Mortgage Credit," Federal Reserve Bank of New York, Staff Reports No. 318, March 2008, 15.

254 "The main thing that . . .": Quoted in Austan Goolsbee, "'Irresponsible' Mortgages Have Opened Doors to Many of the Excluded," *New York Times*, March 29, 2007.

254 "[L]enders have taken . . .": Alan Greenspan, remarks at the Federal Reserve System's Fourth Annual Community Affairs Research Conference, Washington,

D.C., April 8, 2005, available at http://federalreserve.gov/boarddocs/speeches/2005/20050408/default.htm.

256 In 2002, the figure . . . : Ashcraft and Schuermann, "Understanding the Securitization."

256 The number of subprime mortgages . . . : Peter L. Swan, "The Political Economy of the Subprime Crisis: Why Subprime Was So Attractive to Its Creators," Working Paper, January 23, 2009, available at http://papers.ssrn.com/sol3/papers.cfm?abstract_id=1320783.

257 Between 2005 and 2007 . . . : "The Subprime 25," Center for Public Integrity, available at www.publicintegrity.org/investigations/economic_meltdown/the_subprime_25/.

258 "Some New Century . . .": Final Report of Michael J. Missal, Bankruptcy Court Examiner, New Century Trs Holdings, Inc., United States Bankruptcy Court for the District of Delaware, February 29, 2008.

259 "Ira and Hazel . . .": Quoted in Ashcraft and Schuermann, "Understanding the Securitization," 70.

260 The five biggest issuers . . . : See "The Subprime 25."

260 according to Bloomberg News . . . : Gregory Cresci, "Merrill, Citigroup Record CDO Fees Earned in Top Growth Market," Bloomberg News, August 30, 2005.

260 Goldman Sachs launched GSAMP . . . : More information in Ashcraft and Schuermann, "Understanding the Securitization," 13.

263 In 2005, according to . . . : Gretchen Morgenson, "Debt Watchdogs: Tamed or Caught Napping?" New York Times, December 7, 2008.

263 "In my view . . .": Testimony of Jerome S. Fons, Committee on Oversight and Government Reform, United States House of Representatives, October 22, 2008.

264 "We will never tell an arranger . . .": "Structured Finance: Commentary," Standard & Poor's, August 23, 2007.

264 "My view is that . . .": Fons testimony.

265 "I had no notion . . .": Alan Greenspan interview with 60 Minutes, September 16, 2007.

265 By 2004, according to one . . . : Figures from Wholesale Access, reported in Jeff Bailey, "With Mortgages, Instant Wealth for Middlemen," New York Times, October 8, 2005.

266 "The massive workload . . .": Mark Zandi, Financial Shock: A 360° Look at the Subprime Mortgage Implosion and How to Avoid the Next Financial Crisis (Upper Saddle River, N.J.: Pearson Education, 2009), 154–55.

266 "destroys people and communities . . .": Remarks by Governor Edward M. Gramlich, made at the Federal Reserve Bank of Philadelphia, Community and Consumer Affairs Department Conference on Predatory Lending, Philadelphia, Pennsylvania, December 6, 2000.

266 "probably a strong positive . . .": Remarks by Governor Edward M. Gramlich, made at the Financial Services Roundtable Annual Housing Policy Meeting, Chicago, Illinois, May 21, 2004.

266 "The subprime market . . .": Edward Gramlich, "Booms and Busts: The Case of
  Subprime Mortgages," paper for Subprime Mortgages: America's Latest Boom
  and Bust Economic Symposium, Federal Reserve Bank of Kansas City, Jackson
  Hole, Wyoming, August 30–September 1, 2007.

20. IN THE ALPHABET SOUP

268 "As a previous financial . . .": Minsky, *Stabilizing an Unstable Economy*, 233.
269 relied mainly on the . . . : Ben Bernanke, "Modern Risk Management and Banking Supervision," remarks at the Stonier Graduate School of Banking, Washington, D.C., June 12, 2006.
271 In a typical RMBS securitization . . . : Ashcraft and Schuermann, "Understanding the Securitization," 30.
273 UBS's CDO desk . . . : See "Shareholder Report on UBS Write-Downs," UBS,
  April 18, 2008.
273 Citigroup's investment bank . . . : Citigroup Earnings Release, 4th quarter 2007,
  January 15, 2008.
273 Merrill Lynch, which was . . . : Susan Pulliam, Serena Ng, and Randall Smith,
  "Merrill Upped Ante as Boom in Mortgage Bonds Fizzled," *Wall Street Journal*,
  April 16, 2008, A1.
274 "More than anything . . .": Quoted in Jenny Anderson, "Merrill Painfully Learns
  the Risks of Managing Risk," *New York Times*, October 12, 2007.
274 In its 1994 . . . : Philippe Jorion, *Value at Risk: The New Benchmark for Managing Financial Risk*, 2nd ed. (New York: McGraw-Hill, 2000), 107.
274 "In contrast with traditional . . .": Ibid., xxii.
275 "It helps you understand . . .": Quoted in Joe Nocera, "Risk Mismanagement,"
  New York Times Magazine, January 2, 2009.
277 the correlation coefficient . . . : Linda Allen, Jacob Boudoukh, and Anthony
  Saunders, *Understanding Market, Credit, and Operational Risk: The Value at
  Risk Approach* (Hoboken, N.J.: Wiley-Blackwell, 2004), 103.
278 "We remind our readers . . .": "CreditMetrics Technical Document," RiskMetrics, April 1997, available at www.riskmetrics.com/publications/techdocs/cmt
  dovv.html.
278 "The relative prevalence of . . .": Allen et al., *Understanding Market*, 35.
278 "I believe that . . .": "Against Value at Risk: Nassim Taleb Replies to Philippe
  Jorion," 1997, available at www.fooledbyrandomness.com/jorion.html.
279 "business planning relied on . . .": UBS, "Shareholder Report on UBS's Write-
  Downs," 34.
279 "even though delinquency . . .": Ibid., 38–39.
280 "would overturn . . .": Gillian Tett, *Fool's Gold: How the Bold Dream of a Small
  Tribe at J.P. Morgan Was Corrupted by Wall Street Greed and Unleashed a Catastrophe* (New York: Free Press, 2009), 44–45.

281 an astonishing $4.5 trillion . . . : "Triennial Central Bank Survey of Foreign Ex-
     change and Derivatives Market Activity in 2007—Final Results," Bank for In-
     ternational Settlements, December 2007, 21.
282 "[l]arge amounts of risk . . .": Warren Buffett, Berkshire Hathaway letter to
     shareholders, February 21, 2003. Buffett's annual missives are available at
     www.berkshirehathaway.com/letters/letters.htmlWarren Buffett.
283 "has contributed to the stability . . .": "Risk Transfer and Financial Stability,"
     remarks by Chairman Alan Greenspan to the Federal Reserve Bank of Chicago's
     Forty-first Annual Conference on Bank Structure, Chicago, Illinois, May 5, 2005,
     available at www.federalreserve.gov/boarddocs/speeches/2005/20050505/default
     .htm.

21. A MATTER OF INCENTIVES

285 "accomplished wonders far surpassing . . .": Karl Marx and Frederick Engels,
     The Communist Manifesto (London: Verso, 1998), 38.
285 "By taxation, by inflation . . .": Sir Keith Joseph, "Monetarism Is Not Enough,"
     The Stockton Lecture, 1976, Centre for Policy Studies, London, available at
     www.margaretthatcher.org/commentary/displaydocument.asp?docid=110796.
286 "Smith's demonstration of . . .": Alan Greenspan, "Adam Smith," Adam Smith
     Memorial Lecture, Kirkcaldy, Scotland, February 6, 2005, available at www
     .federalreserve.gov/boarddocs/speeches/2005/20050206/default.htm.
288 "[T]here is an immutable . . .": John Plender, "The Credit Business Is More Per-
     ilous Than Ever," *Financial Times*, October 13, 2006.
289 CEO compensation: All figures taken from 2007 proxy statements.
291 "These strategies have the appearance . . .": Rajan, "Has Financial Development
     Made the World Riskier?"
291 In an extremely influential . . . : Michael C. Jensen and William H. Meckling,
     "Theory of the Firm: Managerial Behavior, Agency Costs and Ownership Struc-
     ture," *Journal of Financial Economics* 3, no. 4 (1976): 305–60.
292 "On average, corporate . . .": Michael C. Jensen and Kevin J. Murphy, "CEO
     Incentives—It's Not How Much You Pay, But How," *Harvard Business Review*,
     no. 3 (May–June 1990): 138–53.
292 "I was a defender . . .": Quoted in John Cassidy, "The Greed Cycle: How the
     Financial System Encouraged Corporations to Go Crazy," *New Yorker*, Septem-
     ber 23, 2002, 75.
293 "It is important . . .": Quoted in ibid., 76.
294 "These highly levered . . .": Lucian A. Bebchuk and Holger Spamann, "Regulat-
     ing Bankers' Pay," Harvard John M. Olin Discussion Paper No. 641, 1, available
     at http://papers.ssrn.com/sol3/papers.cfm?abstract_id=1410072.
294 "will be willing to . . .": Ibid., 15.
295 Between 1998 and 2006 . . . : Figures extracted from Table 6.16D, National
     Income and Product Accounts, Bureau of Economic Analysis, U.S. Depart-

ment of Commerce, July 31, 2009, available at www.bea.gov/national/nipaweb/
TableView.asp?SelectedTable=239&Freq=Qtr&FirstYear=2007&LastYear=
2009.

295 "The mere fact . . .": Bebchuk and Spamann, "Regulating Bankers," 23.

295 described him as "a turnaround genius": Quoted in John Cassidy, "Subprime
Suspect," *New Yorker*, March 31, 2008.

296 "We could afford to . . .": Quoted in Nelson D. Schwartz and Eric Dash, "Where
Was the Wise Man?" *New York Times*, Sunday Business, April 27, 2008, 1.

296 In the first half . . . : "Global CDO Market Issuance Data," Securities Industry
and Financial Markets Association, available at www.sifma.org/research/pdf/
SIFMA_CDOIssuanceData2008.pdf.

297 "The depth of the pools . . .": Quoted in Nakamoto and Wighton, "Citigroup
Chief Stays Bullish."

298 "there is no such thing . . .": Keynes, *The General Theory*, 155–56.

22. LONDON BRIDGE IS FALLING DOWN

300 "The pedestrians on the bridge . . .": Hyun Song Shin, "Commentary: Has
Financial Development Made the World Riskier?" presentation to the Federal
Reserve Bank of Kansas City Economic Symposium, Jackson Hole, Wyoming,
August 2005, 383, available at www.kc.frb.org/publicat/SYMPOS/2005/PDF/
Shin2005.pdf.

301 "all the elements that formed . . .": Ibid., 385.

301 "evaporation of liquidity . . .": "BNP Paribas Investment Partners Temporarily
Suspends the Calculation of the Net Asset Value of the Following Funds, Parvest
Dynamic ABS, BNP Paribas ABS EURIBOR and BNP Paribas ABS EONIA,"
BNP Paribas press release, August 9, 2007.

302 "had a feel of liquidity . . .": "ECB injects E95bn to aid markets," *Financial
Times*, August 10, 2007, 1.

304 "seems likely to be . . .": Ben S. Bernanke, "The Economic Outlook," testimony
before the Joint Economic Committee, U.S. Congress, March 28, 2007.

304 "Bernanke is being an academic . . .": Quoted in John Cassidy, "Anatomy of a
Meltdown," *New Yorker*, December 1, 2008, 55.

305 "I and others . . .": Ben Bernanke, interview with the author, quoted in ibid., 55.

305 A more useful discipline to study . . . : Paul Samuelson, interview with the author, 1998.

305 "You could think about Texas . . .": Cassidy, "Anatomy of a Meltdown," 56.

307 "We knew that the banks . . .": Interview with the author, September 2008.

308 "The logic follows . . .": Gary Gorton, "The Panic of 2007," paper presented at
the Federal Reserve Bank of Kansas City Economic Symposium, Jackson Hole,
Wyoming, August 2008.

308 a set of lectures . . . : See, for example, Hyun Song Shin, "Endogenous Risk,"
Clarendon Lectures in Finance, Oxford University, June 2–4, 2008.

309 "Mark-to-market accounting . . .": Shin, "Commentary: Has Financial Development Made the Word Riskier?" 384.

311 Between the third quarter . . . : Case-Shiller Home Price Indices.

312 In May 2008 alone . . . : "Foreclosure Activity Increases 6 Percent in May," RealtyTrac press release, June 13, 2008, available at www.flippingfrenzy.com/2008/06/14/may-2008-foreclosure-statistics.

312 Between August 2007 and October . . . : Cited in "85,000 Homes Lost in October," CNNMoney.com, November 13, 2008, available at http://money.cnn.com/2008/11/13/real_estate/foreclosures_october/index.htm?postversion=2008111303.

312 "The housing market was trapped . . .": Zandi, *Financial Shock*, 172.

314 "There is absolutely no truth . . .": For these and other details of Bear's demise, see, for example, Kate Kelly, "Fear, Rumors Touched Off Fatal Run on Bear Stearns," *Wall Street Journal*, May 28, 2008; and Roddy Boyd, "The Last Days of Bear Stearns," *Fortune*, March 31, 2008.

315 "As the week progressed . . .": Alan Schwartz, testimony before the U.S. Senate Banking Committee, April 3, 2008, available at http://banking.senate.gov/public/_files/SchwartzStmt4308.pdf.

23. SOCIALISM IN OUR TIME

317 "All of the other bankers . . .": Andrew G. Haldane, "Why Banks Failed the Stress Test," speech given at the Marcus-Evans Conference on Stress-Testing, February 9–10, 2009.

318 "It became clear . . .": Timothy F. Geithner, testimony before the U.S. Senate Committee on Banking, Housing and Urban Affairs, Washington, D.C., April 3, 2008.

318 "The problem wasn't . . .": Quoted in Cassidy, "Anatomy of a Meltdown," 59.

320 "I think we did . . .": Ibid., 60.

321 "you cannot rely . . .": John Cassidy, "The Economy of Fear," *Condé Nast Portfolio*, April 2008.

322 "These actions would move . . .": Phillip Swagel, "The Financial Crisis: An Inside View," paper presented to the Brookings Panel of Economic Activity, March 2009, 25.

323 "When I picked up . . .": Jim Bunning, statement before the Senate Banking Committee on the Federal Reserve Monetary Policy Report, July 15, 2008.

324 "With Bear Stearns . . .": Quoted in Cassidy, "Anatomy of a Meltdown," 62.

325 "The feeling at Treasury . . .": Swagel, "The Financial Crisis," 24.

325 "felt like a good . . .": Ibid., 32.

326 Goldman had purchased . . . : Gretchen Morgenson, "Behind Insurer's Crisis, Blind Eye to a Web of Risk," *New York Times*, September 27, 2008.

326 It also emerged that . . . : Joe Hagan, "Tenacious G.," *New York*, July 26, 2009.

326 "The Federal Reserve took this . . .": Ben Bernanke, testimony before the Senate Committee on Banking, Housing and Urban Affairs, Washington, D.C., September 23, 2008.

327 "Saving AIG was . . .": Swagel, "The Financial Crisis," 32.

328 "Both Goldman and Morgan . . .": Quoted in Cassidy, "Anatomy of a Meltdown," 49.

328 "We can't keep doing this . . .": Quoted in ibid.

330 Columbia's Glenn Hubbard . . . : Glenn Hubbard, Hal Scott, and Luigi Zingales, "From Awful to Bad: Reviewing the Bank Rescue Options," *Wall Street Journal*, February 7, 2009, A11.

332 In April 2009 . . . : IMF Global Financial Stability Report, April 2009, available at www.imf.org/external/pubs/ft/GFSR/index.htm.

332 "World industrial production . . .": Barry Eichengreen and Kevin H. O'Rourke, "A Tale of Two Depressions," Centre for Economic and Policy Research, June 4, 2009, available at www.voxeu.org/index.php?q=node/3421.

332 "[A]s Hank Paulson . . .": Cassidy, "Anatomy of a Meltdown," 63.

333 "There is a very good . . .": Quoted in Chris Giles, "Geithner Sees Signs of US and Global Recovery," *Financial Times*, July 14, 2009, 1.

333 "When I saw . . .": David Streitfeld, "Index Shows an Improvement in Home Prices," *New York Times*, August 25, 2009, available at www.nytimes.com/2009/08/26/business/economy/26econ.html?_r=1&em.

333 "gradual resumption of sustainable . . .": Federal Reserve press release, August 12, 2009, available at www.federalreserve.gov/newsevents/press/monetary/20090812a.html.

334 "Thanks to a strong . . .": Organization for Economic Cooperation and Development, *Economic Outlook*, no. 85 (June 2009): 5.

CONCLUSION

338 "Our system failed . . .": Timothy F. Geithner, testimony before the Committee on Financial Services, U.S. Congress, Washington, D.C., March 26, 2009.

340 "Why are the most risky . . .": Edward M. Gramlich, "Booms and Busts: The Case of Subprime Mortgages," paper presented to the Federal Reserve Bank of Kansas City Economic Symposium, Jackson Hole, Wyoming, August 31, 2007.

341 "AIG exploited a huge gap . . .": Ben S. Bernanke, testimony before the Committee on Budget, U.S. Senate, Washington, D.C., March 3, 2009.

342 "a hedge fund, basically . . .": Ibid.

343 "The goal is not . . .": Viral V. Acharya and Matthew Richardson, "Repairing a Failed System: An Introduction," White Paper, from the series "Restoring Financial Stability: Policy Recommendations from NYU Stern," 2008, available at http://whitepapers.stern.nyu.edu/summaries/intro.html.

345 "[T]he typical graduate . . .": Willem Buiter, "The Unfortunate Uselessness of Most 'State of the Art' Academic Monetary Economics," *Financial Times*, March 3, 2009, available at www.ft.com/maverecon.

346 "Despite the enormity . . .": N. Gregory Mankiw, "That Freshman Course Won't Be Quite the Same," *New York Times*, May 23, 2009.

AFTERWORD: THE GREAT DISCONNECT

347 Twenty-eight such properties . . . : Prudential report.

347 "It's as active in the Hamptons . . .": Quoted in "Hamptons Home Sales Have Huge Rebound," *The Huffington Post*, April 22, 2010 (Originally published in Associated Press), available at http://www.huffingtonpost.com/2010/04/22/hamptons-home-sales-have_n_547596.html.

347 The New York–based security . . . : "DiNapoli: Wall Street Bonuses Rose Sharply in 2009," press release, Office of the New York State Comptroller, available at http://www.osc.state.ny.us/press/releases/feb10/022310.htm.

347 Goldman Sachs's traders . . . : The Goldman Sachs Group, Inc. Q1 2010 Earnings Call Transcript, April 20, 2010.

348 "[F]or most Americans . . .": "DiNapoli: Wall Street Bonuses."

348 "Hank, Americans don't . . .": Quoted in Henry M. Paulson, *On the Brink* (New York: Business Plus, 2010), 226.

348 Beginning in July . . . : Figures extracted from Table 1.1.1, "Percent Change From Preceding Period in Real Gross Domestic Product, National Income and Product Account Tables," Bureau of Economic Analysis, available at http://www.bea.gov/national/nipaweb/SelectTable.asp?Selected=y.

348 In May 2010 . . . : Brian Love, "OECD raises global growth forecast due to Asia," Reuters, May 26, 2010.

349 "You can't point . . .": Interview with the author, February 2010.

349 Close to 10 percent . . . : Employment Situation News Release, Bureau of Labor Statistics, April 2, 2010, available at http://www.bls.gov/news.release/archives/empsit_04022010.htm.

349 In Miami, real estate . . . : Case-Shiller Home Price Indices.

350 "My basic view is . . .": Quoted in John Cassidy, "No Credit," *New Yorker*, March 15, 2010.

351 "What we have right . . .": Interview with the author, January 15, 2010, available at http://www.newyorker.com/online/blogs/johncassidy/2010/01/interview-with-raghuram-rajan.html.

351 Buried in the Treasury's . . . : "The Supervisory Capital Assessment Program: Overview of Results," Board of Governors of the Federal Reserve, May 7, 2009, 21, 24, and 37, available at http://www.financialstability.gov/docs/SCAPresults.pdf.

352 "While the Obama . . .": Joseph Stiglitz, *Freefall: America, Free Markets, and the Sinking of the World Economy* (New York: W. W. Norton, 2010), 135.

352 "Ex ante, they . . .": Piergiorgio Alessandri and Andrew G. Haldane, "Bank on the State," Bank of England, November 2009, 11, available at http://www.bankofengland.co.uk/publications/speeches/2009/speech409.pdf.

355 "If the banks . . .": Quoted in Michael McKee and Scott Lanman, "Greenspan Says U.S. Should Consider Breaking Up Large Banks," *Bloomberg News*, October 15, 2009.

356 "If we'd been . . .": Quoted in John Heilemann, "Obama Is From Mars, Wall Street Is From Venus," *New York*, May 22, 2010, available at http://nymag.com/news/politics/66188/.

356 "did quite well . . .": Interview with the author, January 13, 2010, available at http://www.newyorker.com/online/blogs/johncassidy/2010/01/interview-with-eugene-fama.html.

357 Appearing at the annual . . . : Ben S. Bernanke, remarks at the Annual Meeting of the American Economic Association, Atlanta, Georgia, January 3, 2010, available at http://www.federalreserve.gov/newsevents/speech/bernanke20100103a.htm.

357 In a paper . . . : Olivier Blanchard, et al. "Rethinking Macroeconomic Policy," International Monetary Fund, February 12, 2010, available at http://www.imf.org/external/pubs/ft/spn/2010/spn1003.pdf.

357 "[M]any in our profession . . .": 2010 American Economic Association Annual Meeting, video available at http://www.aeaweb.org/webcasts/assa2010.php.

358 "I think the challenge . . .": Interview with the author, January 13, 2010, available at http://www.newyorker.com/online/blogs/johncassidy/2010/01/interview-with-richard-posner.html.

358 "I think you are . . .": Interview with the author, January 14, 2010, available at http://www.newyorker.com/online/blogs/johncassidy/2010/01/interview-with-gary-becker.html.

359 "Germany has never . . .": Darren Mara and Andrew Bowen, "German Government Unveils Unprecedented Austerity Plan," Reuters, July 6, 2010, available at http://www.dw-world.de/dw/article/0,,5658604,00.html.

359 "Reducing the spectre . . .": Lawrence Summers, "America's Sensible Stance on Recovery," *Financial Times*, July 18, 2010, available at http://www.ft.com/cms/s/0/966e25b8-9295-11df-9142-00144feab49a.html.

361 "The proposition is that . . .": Adair Turner, "Economics, Conventional Wisdom, and Public Policy," remarks at Institute for New Economic Thinking, Cambridge, England, April 2010, available at http://ineteconomics.org/sites/inet.civicactions.net/files/INET%20Turner%20%20Cambridge%2020100409.pdf.

ACKNOWLEDGMENTS

his book was conceived in 2007, reconceived in 2008, and written in 2009, but its genesis goes back a lot farther. I have been writing about finance since 1986 and thinking about economics since 1984, when, during my college entrance interview, Nick Crafts and David Soskice, two former fellows of University College, Oxford, introduced me to the prisoner's dilemma. I didn't get it then, but they let me in anyway, and I've been hooked on economics ever since. Thanks to them.

At Farrar, Straus and Giroux, I would like to thank Eric Chinski for acquiring the book, supporting it all along, and providing invaluable editorial guidance. At *The New Yorker*, I would like to thank David Remnick for giving me time off to write, and Pam McCarthy for arranging the details. Over the years, my editors Emily Eakin, Cressida Leyshon, John Bennet, Henry Finder, and Dorothy Wickenden have all been extremely helpful. At the late *Condé Nast Portfolio*, Joanne Lipman and Kyle Pope encouraged me to think and write about many of the issues raised in the book. Scott Moyers, my agent at the Wylie Agency, has provided wise counsel and encouragement throughout.

A book as broad-ranging as this one is inevitably a work of synthesis: much of the thinking and analysis are my own, but the details are from all over. I have relied extensively on my own reporting, for *The New Yorker* mainly, and also on other published accounts. Wherever possible, I have tried to acknowledge the source of theories, figures, and quotes. Genevieve Smith checked facts, compiled the notes, and corrected my arithmetic. Without all the hard work she did, under great time pressure, I would not have completed the book.

Thanks, finally, to my family for putting up with my crankiness and frequent disappearances into my study during the last year. The book is dedicated to them.

INDEX

Aames Capital Corporation, 252
Abrechnungsamt, 39
Abu Dhabi, 307
ABX index, 281
Acharya, Viral V., 343
Addams, Jane, 75
Adelphia Communications Corporation, 292, 293
adjustable-rate mortgages (ARMs), 240, 243, 245, 246, 258, 260, 271, 340
Advanced Research Projects Agency (ARPA), 137
Advanta Bank Corporation, 255
Affluent Society, The (Galbraith), 23, 134
Afghanistan War, 232
African Americans, 242, 295
Age of Turbulence, The, (Greenspan), 27, 229
Air Force, U.S., 133
Akerlof, George, 151–54, 163, 165, 175, 254, 256
Albert-Ludwigs-Universität, 47

Alchian, Armen, 143
Alcoa, Inc., 6, 228
Allen, Frederick Lewis, 236
Allen, Linda, 278
Allende, Salvador, 82
Allesandri, Piergiorgio, 352–53
Alphabet, xv–xvi; *see also* Google
Al Qaeda, 17
Alt-A bonds, 245, 256
Alternative Mortgage Transaction Parity Act (1982), 252
Amazon, viii, xv, xvi, xvii, 25, 182, 183
"ambiguity aversion," 202
American Airlines, 133
American Dream Downpayment Act (2003), 242
American Economic Association, 78, 105, 107, 232, 357
American Economic Review, The, 74, 125, 153, 158, 177
American General Finance, Inc., 225

American International Group (AIG), 4, 282, 292, 325–27, 337, 341

America Online (AOL), 171, 179, 181, 292

Ameriquest Mortgage Company, 245, 257, 266

Amherst College, 163

AMRESCO, 255

Amtrak, 52

"Anatomy of Market Failure, The" (Bator), 126

Anderson, Martin, 72, 81–82

anti-Semitism, 73

antitrust laws, xvi, 80, 128, 131–33, 140

Apostles, 168–69

Apple, xv, xvi, 29, 131

Army, U.S., 206; Air Corps, 62; Corps of Engineers, 17

ARPANET, 137

Arrow, Kenneth, xii, 8, 62–64, 67–71, 101, 102, 125, 126, 158, 159, 163

Arthur, W. Brian, 130–31

Arthur Andersen, 264

Asch, Solomon, 187–89, 248

asset-backed securities (ABSs), 213, 227, 263, 273, 297, 303, 306, 321, 331

Associates First Capital, 252, 255

asymmetric information, 206, 337

AT&T, 104, 135

Atomic Energy Commission, U.S., 65

Attlee, Clement, 45

austerity policies, ix, 359

Australia, 241

Axelrod, Robert, 146

Aylwin, Patricio, 83

Bachelier, Louis, 87–89, 91, 93, 276

Bagehot, Walter, 106, 349

Baker, James, 227

Bank of America, 199, 212, 213, 225, 273, 282, 289, 303, 319, 324, 330, 342, 351, 354

Bank of England, 34, 317–18, 352, 355; Monetary Policy Committee, 345

Bankers' Panic (1907), 234

Bankers Trust, 212, 275, 280

Bank for International Settlements, 226, 275, 281, 282, 353

Baran, Paul, 137

Barclays Bank, 324, 354

Barings Bank, 230, 274

Barone, Enrico, 57, 58

Barro, Robert, 100

Barron's, 19, 180

Bartlett, Bruce, 21

Bator, Francis, 125–27, 134, 137–38, 164

Baumol, William, 129

Bayh-Dole Act (1984), 136

B&C lending, 251

Bear Stearns, 253, 289, 294, 297, 313–16, 318–20, 327, 328, 337, 355

Beatles, 151

Beauty Contest theory, 171–72, 177, 179, 181, 182, 186

Bebchuk, Lucian, 294, 295

Becker, Gary, 122, 357, 358

behavioral economics, 10, 198–201, 203

Behravesh, Nariman, 349

Bell Laboratories, 135

Beneficial Finance, 251–52, 256

Bennett, Alan, 335

Bentham, Jeremy, 53

Berkshire Hathaway Inc., 282

Berlin Wall, fall of, 48

Bernanke, Ben, 7, 11, 20, 232, 269, 283, 323, 331, 333, 344, 348, 357; Friedman lauded by, 77; response to market meltdown of, 4, 318, 320, 323–28, 341–42; subprime crisis underestimated by, 20, 304–306

Beveridge, William, 44

Bezos, Jeff, xvii

Biden, Joseph, xv

Biggs, Barton, 179

Bikhchandani, Sushil, 190–91

Bill and Melinda Gates Foundation, 55*n*

Binmore, Ken, 150

Black, Fischer, 91, 93

Black Monday crash of 1987, 105–106, 166–68, 177, 227

Black Panther Party, 151

Black-Scholes option pricing formula, 91, 93, 95

Blackstone Group, 297

Blair, Tony, 7

Blanchard, Olivier, 357

Blankfein, Lloyd C., 289, 343, 344

Blaug, Mark, 118

Blinder, Alan, 20

bliss point, 64, 68

Bloomberg News, 260

BNP Paribas Bank, 301

Boeing, 137

Bohr, Niels, 75

Bolsheviks, 57

Book-of-the-Month Club, 46

Born, Brooksley E., 230, 231

Boudoukh, Jacob, 278

Bourbaki, Nicolas, 67

Bowles, Sam, x

Brazil, 86

Bretton Woods monetary system, 336

Bright, John, 45

Britain, *see* United Kingdom

Broadcom Corporation, 29

Brookings Institution, 215

Brown University, 73, 190

Brown, Sherrod, 356

Brunnermeier, Markus, 180–82

bubbles, 8–10, 36, 86, 102, 105, 124, 186, 189, 191, 207, 221, 308; credit, 219, 225, 287, 288, 293, 313, 334; dot.com, 171, 178–81, 184, 186, 238, 347, 270; efficient market hypothesis violated by, 198; Greenspan and, 8–9, 11, 19, 227, 231–33, 240–41, 288, 336, 344; real estate, see housing bubble; South Sea, 36, 180;

technology, 8, 181–82, 200–201, 292–93; trend following and, xii

Buccleuch, Duke of, 26

Buffett, Warren, 231, 282, 283

Buiter, Willem, 345

Bulgaria, 277

Bunning, Jim, 323

Burns, Arthur, 72

Bush, George H. W., 21, 227

Bush, George W., xiii, 4, 20, 254, 268, 371*n*; antitrust policy of, 129, 132; deregulation efforts of, 284; home ownership promoted by, 242, 338; stimulus packages of, 174; tax cuts of, 222, 232

BusinessWeek, 179, 249

Butskellism, 336

California, University of: Berkeley, 50, 63, 98, 132, 151, 194, 198; Irvine, 71, 190, 275; Los Angeles (UCLA), 143, 190, 198

California Department of Corporations, 266

California Institute of Technology (Caltech), 198

California Public Employees' Retirement System, 180

Callaghan, James, 79

Cambridge University, 39, 40, 66, 115, 168–69, 175

Camerer, Colin, 198, 202

Canada, 33, 157

Capital in the Twenty-First Century (Piketty), x–xi

Capitalism and Freedom (Friedman), 72, 74–77

Capitalism, Socialism, and Democracy (Schumpeter), 44

Capra, Frank, 314

Carlin, Wendy, x, xii

Carlyle, Thomas, xi

Carnap, Rudolf, 65

Carnegie, Andrew, 128
Carnegie Mellon University, 100, 198
Caro, Anthony, 299
Carter, Jimmy, 7, 286
Case, Karl E., 19, 247, 333
Caterpillar Corporation, 224
Cayne, James E., 289, 290, 294, 295, 297, 314, 336–37
Center for Public Integrity, 257
Center for Responsible Lending, 259
Central Intelligence Agency (CIA), 17, 65; World Factbook, 157
Chamberlin, Edward, xii
Champernowne, David, 66
Chase Home Finance, 246
Chase Manhattan Bank, 216; see also JPMorgan Chase
Cheney, Dick, 227
Chevalier, Judith, 178
Chevron Corporation, 102
Chicago, University of, 70, 79, 88, 100, 103, 119, 122, 163, 254, 330; Booth School of Business, 20, 89, 198; Chilean economists at, 82; Committee on Social Thought, 46; Economics Department, 62; efficient market hypothesis developed at, 86, 89, 91; Friedman at, 38, 46, 73, 74; Hayek at, 38, 46–47; Lange at, 57, 59, 206; Lucas at, 97–98, 136; Law School, 120
Chicago Board Options Exchange, 93
Chicago School, xi, xii, 8, 38, 106, 126, 129, 152, 170, 174, 182, 308, 345, 356, 357
Chicago Tribune, 74
Chile, 82–83, 129
China, 28, 29, 45, 286, 304, 313, 322
Christianity, 45
Chrysler Corporation, 130, 130, 329
Churchill, Winston, 45, 115, 221
Cicero, 45
Cisco Systems, Inc., 184
Cisneros, Henry G., 241

Citigroup, 4, 12, 88, 102, 214, 277, 290, 296–97, 304, 347, 350, 351–52, 354; Associated First Capital purchased by, 255; compensation of CEOs of, 289, 292; credit default swaps of, 281, 282; deregulation and, 229; disaster myopia of, 199; Federal Reserve and, 265, 313; government safety net for, 330, 341; reduction in assets of, 311; risk-management system at, 269–70, 275; shadow banking system and, 225–26, 307; suprime mortgage securities issued by, 260, 272–73
Citron, Bob, 230
City College, 62
classical economics, 33–34, 118–19, 127, 134; new, 103, 104
Clayton Antitrust Act (1914), xvi, 128
climate change, xi, xiv–xv, 9–10, 112–14, 122, 123
Clinton, Bill, 7, 23, 131, 132, 228, 229, 242, 338
CLSA Emerging Markets, 18–19
CNBC television network, 304
Coase, Ronald, 119–21
Coase theorem, 121–23
Cobden, Richard, 45
Coca-Cola Corporation, 155
Cohen, Jonathan, 203
collateralized debt obligations (CDOs), 13, 21, 139, 252, 257, 260, 263, 264, 270–74, 281, 286, 296–97, 307, 319
collateralized mortgage obligations (CMOs), 213, 214
Collins, Susan, 356
Columbia Broadcasting System (CBS), 265
Columbia University, 62, 67, 73, 74, 79, 93, 104, 163, 250, 330; Earth Institute, 83
Columbine massacre, 197
Columbus, Christopher, 75
Commerce Department, U.S., 215

Commodity Futures Trading Commission (CFTC), 231

communism, 38, 43, 45, 59–60; collapse of, 7, 44, 48, 285, 337

Community Reinvestment Act (1977), 241

Comptroller of the Currency, Office of, 265

Congress, U.S., 14, 78, 264, 318, 322, 323, 326, 330, 340–42, 345; bailouts authorized by, 4, 234, 328–29; deregulation efforts in, 7, 215, 217, 229, 231, 284; health care reform in, 157; Joint Economic Committee, 240; and savings and loan industry collapse, 13, 162; tax legislation in, 167, 222

Congressional Budget Office, 266

Conservative Party, British, 47

Constitution of Liberty, The (Hayek), 47

Consumer Financial Protection Agency, 340, 343

Consumer Product Safety Commission, 80

Contimortgage Corporation, 252, 253, 255

Continental Illinois Bank, 215

conventional wisdom, 23, 178, 231

Corcoran Group, 239

CORE Project, x–xi, xii

Corn Laws, 33–34

Coronavirus Aid, Relief, and Economic Security Act (CARES Act), xiii

Corrigan, E. Gerald, 227

Countrywide Financial Corporation, 246–47, 255, 257, 260, 265, 303

Cournot, Antoine Augustin, 50

Court of Appeals, U.S., D.C. Circuit, 132

COVID-19 pandemic, vii–x, xiii–xiv, xvii

Cowles, Alfred, 61

Cowles Commission, 61–63, 66–67

Craigslist, 160

Cramer, Jim, 304–305

credit bubble, 219, 225, 287, 288, 293, 313, 334

credit default swaps (CDSs), xiii, 13, 22, 231, 279–83, 288, 291, 318, 325–26, 342

CreditMetrics, 278

Credit Suisse First Boston, 260, 315

Dadd, Mark, 104

Dallow, Richard, 18

Dartmouth College, 185

Das Kapital (Marx), xii

Davidson, Paul, 214–15

Debreu, Gérard, 67, 69–71, 101, 102, 125, 126, 163

Debs, Eugene, ix–x

Declaration of Independence, 26, 81

Defense Department, U.S., 133, 137, 142

Democratic Party, 3, 24, 123, 164, 228, 266, 286, 340

Democratic Socialists, Chilean, 82

Depository Institutions Deregulation and Monetary Control Act (1980), 252

deregulation, ix, 4, 7, 20–23, 162, 165, 229–30, 233, 234, 252, 288

D.E. Shaw Group, 315

Deutsch, Morton, 189

Deutsche Bank, 275, 326, 354

Dickens, Charles, 36

Diggins, John Patrick, 38

Dimensional Fund Advisors, 91

DiNapoli, Thomas P., 348

Dion, Donald, Jr., 179–80

disaster myopia, xii, 9–10, 199, 206, 226, 239, 247–48, 268, 317, 337, 346, 360

"Disaster Myopia in International Banking" (Guttentag and Herring), 199

Disney Corporation, 292

division of labor, 28–29

Dodd-Frank Wall Street Reform and Consumer Protection Act, xiii, 353, 354

Dole, Bob, 227
dot.com bubble, 171, 178–81, 184, 186, 238, 347, 270
Dow Jones Industrial Average, 87, 95, 166–68, 301, 304, 333
Dresher, Melvin, 142–43, 145
Druckenmiller, Stanley, 181, 184
Duflo, Esther, 198
Dun and Bradstreet, 263
Dunbar, Willis F., 236

Easterbrook, Frank, 120
eBay, 154, 179, 182, 207
Ebbers, Bernie, 290, 292
Ebenstein, Lanny, 73
École Normale Supérieure, 67
Econometrica, 58
Economic Consequences of the Peace, The (Keynes), 40
"Economics after Neoliberalism" (Naidu, Rodrik, and Zucman), xi, xii
"Economics and Knowledge" (Hayek), 41
Economics Club of New York, 324
Economics for Inclusive Prosperity, xi
Economics of Welfare, The (Pigou), xi, 116–18, 124
Economist, The, 19, 106
Economy.com, 266, 312
Edgeworth, Francis Ysidro, 51, 193
Edinburgh University, 26
Edison, Thomas, 75
efficient market hypothesis, xvi, 86–91, 106, 167, 169, 184, 198, 204, 209; Lucas's adoption for entire economy of, 97, 101, 105; Mandelbrot's strictures on, 94, 96; speculative bubbles and discrediting of, 178, 181, 186
Eichengreen, Barry, 226, 332
Einstein, Albert, 65, 75, 119
Eisenhower, Dwight D., 137, 223
Eisner, Michael, 292
Elements of Pure Economics (Walras), 51
Elizabeth II, Queen of England, 299

Elliott Wave Theorist newsletter, 167
Ellison, Glenn, 178
Ellsberg, Daniel, 202
Emory University, 185
Engels, Friedrich, 57, 285
England: enclosure of common lands in, 149; street markets in, 25; *see also* United Kingdom
Enron, 200–201, 264, 290, 292
Environmental Protection Agency (EPA), 80, 121
Equifax, 312
equilibrium, theory of, *see* general equilibrium theory
Erasmus, Desiderius, 45
Erhard, Ludwig, 47
Euromoney, 295
European Central Bank, 20, 302
European Union, xv–xvi, 339, 350
"Existence of an Equilibrium for a Competitive Economy" (Arrow and Debreu), 67
externalities, 339; *see also* spillovers
Extraordinary Popular Delusions and the Madness of Crowds (Mackay), 36, 180
Exxon, 130
Exxon Mobil, 102, 272, 294

Facebook, viii, xv, xvi, 132
Failure of Capitalism, A (Posner), 337
Fama, Eugene, 86, 89–91, 101, 184–85, 356, 358
Fatal Conceit, The (Hayek), 47
Federal Bureau of Investigation (FBI), 17
Federal Deposit Insurance Corporation (FDIC), 163, 265, 329–30, 355, 374n
Federal Home Loan Mortgage Corporation (Freddie Mac), 11, 19, 212, 213, 242, 249, 253, 322–24, 331, 338, 339
Federal National Mortgage Association (Fannie Mae), 11, 212, 213, 242, 253, 322–24, 331, 338, 339, 341

Federal Reserve, 3, 6, 20, 22, 73, 103, 205, 226, 230–34, 244–45, 264, 322, 336, 344–45, 350; and Black Monday stockmarket crash, 105–106, 167, 227; COVID-19 pandemic response, xiii–xiv; derivatives markets and, 230–32, 283; Division of Monetary Affairs, 222; Friedman on role in Great Depression of, 76–78; funds rate cuts by, 221–23, 232–33, 240, 305; housing bubble and, 221, 238, 305–306; loans to banks from, 211, 302, 304–305, 313, 321; Lucas on, 100; Minsky on regulation of banks by, 216–17, 227, 268; Open Market Committee (FOMC), 221, 223, 333; regional banks of, 20, 223, 227, 233, 250, 254, 316, 318, 324, 331; and shadow banking system, 307; and subprime mortgages, 7, 11, 255–56, 265–66, 306; and Wall Street bailouts, xiii, 318–20, 324–41, 333, 341–42

Federal Reserve Act (1913), 319, 326

Federal Trade Commssion, 80

FICO scale, 244, 253, 254, 260

Fidelity Independent Adviser, 179

Fidelity Investments, 178; Magellan Fund, 179–80

Financial Accounting Standards Board, 308

Financial Analysts Journal, 89

Financial Markets, Money and the Real World (Davidson), 214–15

Financial Services Modernization Act (1999), 7, 229

Financial Services Regulatory Relief Act (2006), 284

Financial Shock (Zandi), 266

Financial Times, 6, 12, 280, 288, 296–97, 299

Finland, 321

First Franklin Loan Services, 257, 295

FirstPlus Financial Group, 252, 255

First Union Bank, 255

Fisher, Carl, 236

Fisher, Irving, 61, 77

Fisher, Richard, 233

Fitch Ratings, 262, 264, 297

Flaubert, Gustave, 335

Flood, Merrill, 142–43, 145

Foley, Duncan, 71

Fons, Jerome S., 263, 264

Food and Drug Administration (FDA), 80, 165

Fool's Gold (Tett), 280

Ford, Gerald, 6, 227

Ford, Henry, 75

Ford Motor Company, 126, 130, 139

Fortune 500 companies, 130

Fortune magazine, 248, 250, 295

Foster, Norman, 299

Foundations of Economic Analysis (Samuelson), 98

France, 4, 45, 157, 301

Frank, Barney, 325

Franklin, Benjamin, 235

Franklin National Bank, 216

Franklin Templeton Investments, 178

Freefall (Stiglitz), 352

Free to Choose (Friedman), 72, 80–81

free trade, ix, 31, 33–34, 37

French, Kenneth, 185

Friedman, Benjamin, 357, 359

Friedman, Milton, 7, 60, 72–84, 86, 88, 97, 107, 152, 206, 230–31, 349; antigovernment ideology of, 74–76, 80–81, 164, 165, 322; Coase and, 120; death of, 38, 72, 337; Hayek and, 46, 47; laissez-faire views of, 72, 76, 78, 174–75; Lucas and, 98, 100, 101, 103, 106; Nobel Prize of, 79; in Pinochet's Chile, 82–83, 129; Reagan and, 81–82; revisionist explanation of Great Depression by, 73, 76–78; Smith's influence on, 32–33, 38; utopian economics of, viii, 8, 346

Friedman, Rose, 32–33, 60, 73, 80, 81

Fuld, Richard S., Jr., 289, 290, 294, 295, 325, 337

"Full Employment in a Free Society" (Beveridge), 44

Galbraith, John Kenneth, 23, 40–41, 129, 134, 216

game theory, 10, 12, 65, 67, 71, 141–45, 152, 171, 246

Garn-St. Germain Depository Institutions Act (1982), 162

Garzarelli, Elaine, 167

Gates, Bill, 55, 131

GE Capital, 230, 330, 341

Geithner, Timothy, 318, 319, 324, 330–31, 333, 338, 342, 348, 350, 352

General Electric, 80, 121–22, 130, 179, 292

general equilibrium theory, 8, 50, 52, 63–65, 67–72, 78, 99, 101, 125, 152, 158

generalized autoregressive conditional heteroskedasticity (GARCH), 276

General Motors, 80, 130, 139, 283, 329

General Theory of Employment, Interest and Money, The (Keynes), xii, 14, 40, 98, 118–19, 169–70, 175, 176, 206, 207, 209, 298

GeoCities, 179

George Mason University, 198

Gerard, Harold, 189

Germany, 50, 285, 332, 358–59; Nazi, 45, 137

Glasgow University, 26, 192

Glass-Steagall Act (1933), 229, 342

Gleason, Jeffrey, 112

Global Crossing, 200

global warming, *see* climate change

Gödel, Kurt, 65

Goldman Sachs, 4, 102, 290, 315, 328, 330, 347, 350; and AIG bailout, 326; government safety net for, viii, 330, 333, 341; compensation of CEO of, 289, 343; credit default swaps of, 281; reduction in assets of, 311; subprime mortgage securities issued by, 260–62, 271; VAR models used by, 275

Goliath: The 100-Year War Between Monopoly Power and Democracy (Stoller), xvi–xvii

Google, viii, xv, xvi, 91, 132

Goolsbee, Austan, 254

Gorbachev, Mikhail, 43

Gore, Al, 112, 371*n*

Gorton, Gary, 308

Goskomsten, 43

Gosplan, 8

Government National Mortgage Association (Ginnie Mae), 212–13

Gramlich, Edward, 266, 340

Gramm-Leach-Bliley Act (1999), *see* Financial Services Modernization Act (1999)

Grateful Dead, 151

Great Crunch, 344, 346

Great Depression, 5, 40, 41, 62, 73, 107, 115, 206, 306, 334, 353, 358; Federal Reserve policies and, 76–78; financial statutes created during, 216, 229; laissez-faire and, 37, 76; unemployment during, 102, 103

"Greater Fool" theory of investing, 171

Great Moderation, 232

Greeks, ancient, 45

Greenberg, Alan "Ace," 314

Greenberg, Maurice "Hank," 292

Greenberger, Michael, 231

Greenspan, Alan, 8, 22–23, 25, 86, 122, 226–34, 265, 283, 306, 337, 342, 355, 357; bubbles and, 8–9, 11, 19, 227, 231–33, 240–41, 288, 336, 344; Congressional testimony of, 3–6, 240; deregulation advocated by, 4, 7, 20, 165, 229–30, 233; development of new financial products encouraged by, 13, 22, 226–27; funds rate set by, 222–23, 232; laissez-faire policy of,

37, 266; political career of, 227–28; as Rand's disciple, 5, 228–29, 234, 336; retirement of, 3, 234, 269, 283; Smith's influence on, 27, 36, 37, 228, 233, 286; on virtues of subprime mortgages, 254–55

Greenwald, Bruce, 163

gross domestic product (GDP), 99, 129, 222, 230, 313; of Chile under Pinochet, 83; decline in, 332, 333; health care spending as percentage of, 157; indebtedness relative to, 223, 225, 226; productivity and, 103; TARP as percentage of, 329; technical progress and, 135

Grossman, Sanford, 93–94

GSAMP TRUST 2006-NC2, 260, 261, 271

Gulf Oil, 130

Guttentag, Jack, 199

Haldane, Andrew, 317–18, 352–53

Hamilton, Alexander, 235

Hansen, Alvin, 45–46, 206

Harberger, Arnold, 83, 129

Hardin, Garrett, 148–49

harmony, illusion of, 8, 104, 256

Harrod, Roy, 174

Harvard University, 40, 44, 55, 91, 94, 100, 130, 155, 199, 182, 183, 202, 291, 322, 330; behavioral economics at, 198; Galbraith at, 41, 216; John F. Kennedy School of Government, 125; Joint Center for Housing Studies, 238, 249; Keynesians at, 83; Law School, 294, 340; Minsky at, 206; Pigou Club at, 115, 346; Summers at, 7, 23

Hasbro, 128

Has Globalization Gone Too Far? (Rodrik), xi

Hayek, Friedrich August von, 7, 38–49, 58, 74, 76, 84, 105, 117, 163, 190; death of, 38; "division of knowledge" conundrum of, 41, 54; Keynes criticized by, 39–40; laissez-faire views of, 39, 44–46, 58; Nobel Prize of, 38, 47; telecommunications metaphor of, 43, 86, 164, 303, 338

Hayek, Laurence, 47, 48

Hazlitt, Henry, 46

Hebrew University of Jerusalem, 194

hedge funds, 22, 180–83, 186, 208, 243, 297, 328, 341–43; Bear Stearns and, 297, 313; credit default swap losses of, 283; mortgage-backed securities purchased by, 253, 271, 281

Henry, Patrick, 235

"Herd Behavior and Investment" (Scharfstein and Stein), 177–78

Herring, Richard, 199

Hicks, John, 40, 175, 207

Himmelberg, Charles, 250

Hirshleifer, David, 190–91

Hispanics, 242

History Boys, The (Bennett), 335–36

History of Economic Analysis (Schumpeter), 51

Hitler, Adolf, 44, 45, 137, 222

Holland, 36

Home Depot, 25

Hong, Harrison, 178

Hoover, Herbert, 76

"Hope Now Alliance," 321

Hotelling, Harold, 62, 67

Household Finance Corporation, 252, 255, 297

House of Lords, 174

House of Representatives, U.S., 123, 284; Oversight and Government Reform Committee, 3

housing bubble, 19, 186, 225, 236–50, 267, 268, 270; collapse of, 305–306, 321; geographic spread of, 236; Greenspan's reluctance to acknowledge, 9, 19–20, 240; incentives and, 287; interest rates and, 221, 239–40; new types of

housing bubble (*cont.*)
  mortgages and, 243–47, 258–59;
  price increases leading to, 237–39,
  241; rational irrationality in, 11
Houthakker, Hendrik, 94
HSBC Bank, 18, 255, 297, 307
Hubbard, Glenn, 330
"Hubris Hypothesis of Corporate
  Takeovers, The" (Roll), 199
Hudson, Richard, 94–95
Hume, David, 45
Hurricane Katrina, 17, 18
Hutcheson, Francis, 26

IBM, 89, 92, 94, 130, 135, 262
Icahn, Carl, 130
imperfect competition, theory of, xii
Inconvenient Truth, An (documentary
  film), 112
India, 28, 29, 33, 169, 172–73
Indonesia, 13
Inefficient Markets (Shleifer), 183
inequality, ix, x, xvii, 28, 59, 64, 106
ING Direct, 315
Ingves, Stefan, 321
Inside B&C Lending, 253, 256
Inside Mortgage Finance, 260
Institute of Economic Affairs (IEA), 82
Institutional Investor, 89
Interior Department, U.S., 111
International Monetary Fund (IMF), 20,
  321, 332, 350, 357
Internet, 131, 132, 137, 204, 286; *see
  also* dot.com bubble
invisible hand, 26, 38, 64, 70, 87, 106,
  118, 125, 255, 286, 334, 337, 346
iPod, 29
Iraq War, 222, 232
Ireland, 4, 241, 332
Irrational Exuberance (Shiller), 19, 168
IS/LM model, 175, 207
Israel Defense Forces, 194
It's a Wonderful Life (film), 314

J.P. Morgan Bank, 6, 228, 229, 274, 276;
  279–81; Derivatives Department, 280;
  see also JPMorgan Chase
Jackson, Thomas Penfield, 131–32
Japan, 13, 29, 321, 330, 332; attack on
  Pearl Harbor by, 17, 18; deflation in,
  222; real estate and stock bubble in,
  186; stimulus packages in, 174
Jefferson, Thomas, 235
Jefferson Airplane, 151
Jegadeesh, Narasimhan, 185
Jensen, Michael, 291–93
Jevons, William Stanley, 50–52, 114
Jews, 73, 151; Nazi persecution of, 66
Johns Hopkins University, 82
Johnson, Lyndon, 125, 156, 336
Johnson and Johnson, 272
Jones, Paul Tudor, II, 180-81
Jorion, Philippe, 275, 278–79
Joseph, Keith, 7, 82, 285–86
Journal of Biological Psychiatry, The, 188
Journal of Business, The, 89
*Journal of Economic Behavior and
  Organization, The*, 198
Journal of Economic Perspectives, The,
  186, 190, 198
Journal of Finance, 90, 181
Journal of Law and Economics, 120
Journal of Political Economy, The, 153
JPMorgan Chase, 4, 265, 320, 342, 354;
  Advanta purchased by, 255; Bear
  Stearns acquired by, 316, 319, 337;
  government loans to, 330, 333;
  shadow banking system and, 307
Justice Department, U.S., Antitrust
  Division of, 129, 131, 132

Kahn, Alfred E., 286
Kahneman, Daniel, xii, 10, 193–98,
  201, 359
Kaldor, Nicholas, 40
Kaufman, Ted, 356
Kennedy, John F., 336

Keynes, John Maynard, viii, xii, 14, 98–99, 105, 168–76, 204, 335, 337, 360; "ambiguity aversion" identified by, 202; Beauty Contest theory of, 171–72, 177, 181, 182, 186; behavioral economics influenced by, 198; death of, 175; education of, 168–69; Greenspan's rejection of, 5; government intervention advocated by, 37; Hayek's critique of, 39–40; Minsky influenced by, 206, 207, 209; Pigou and, xi, 10, 115, 118–19; unpredictability acknowledged by, 276; utopian economics critiqued by, 172–73

Keynes, John Neville, 168

Keynes, Lydia, 40

Keynesianism, 45, 97, 100, 119, 323, 336, 349; "bastard," 175; blurring of distinction between monetarism and, 83, 85–86; Friedman's attack on, 73, 78, 82; government policies based on, 39; Minsky and, 205–207; New, 105, 106; post-, 207, 214; reality-based economics and, 176; recession models in, 103, 206, 173; neoclassical synthesis of, 152

Kindleberger, Charles P., 221

King, Mervyn, 355, 361

Knickerbocker Trust Company, 234

Kohlberg Kravis Roberts, 130

Kohn, Don, 22

Koopmans, Tjalling, 62, 66

Kozlowski, Dennis, 293

Krugman, Paul, 72

Krystofiak, Steven, 244–45

Kubik, Jeffrey D., 178

Kuwait, 313

Kyoto Protocol, 123

Labor Statistics, Bureau of, 155

Labour Party, British, 79

Laffer, Arthur, 7

Lagrange, Joseph-Louis, 58

Lahart, Justin, 205–206

Laibson, David, 198, 200, 203, 204

laissez-faire, 31, 41, 116, 308, 325; of Friedman, 72, 76, 78, 174–75; general equilibrium theory and, 50, 68; Greenspan and, 37, 266; of Hayek, 39, 44–46, 58; middle ground between collectivism and, 115, 136; of Mill, 33–34

Landlord's Game, The, 128

Lange, Oskar, 57–60, 61, 65, 206

Lausanne, University of, 51, 53

"Law and Economics" school, xii, xvi, 11

Lay, Kenneth, 290

Learned Hand, Billings, 129

Leeson, Nick, 230

Lehman Brothers, 294, 313, 319, 355; collapse of, ix, 3, 324–25, 328, 334, 337; compensation of CEO of, 289; subprime mortgage securities issued by, 253, 259–60, 262, 273

Lehn, Kenneth, 154

Lenin, Vladimir, 339

Leontief, Wassily, 206

Lerner, Abba, 57–59, 61, 63, 65

Levittown (New York), 18

Lewis, Kenneth, 289

Liberal Party, British, 44, 174

Liebniz, Gottfried, 75

Lincoln, Blanche, 356

Loan Performance, 243

Locke, John, 45, 46

Loewenstein, George, 198, 203

Lombard Street (Bagehot), 106

London interbank offered rate (LIBO), 311

London School of Economics (LSE), 39, 40, 44, 57, 58. 78, 82, 300, 345, 360

Long Beach Mortgage Company, 252, 253, 255, 257

Long-Term Capital Management (LCTM), 230, 277, 314

Lucas, Robert, 79, 97–107, 136, 176, 249, 345, 356, 371n

Lucent Technologies, 292
Luftwaffe, 137

Macaulay, Thomas Babington, 335
Mack, John J., 289, 304
Mackay, Charles, 36, 180
Macroeconomic Advisers, 302
macroeconomics, 19, 41, 76–77, 99,
    105–107, 152, 345
Macroeconomics (Miles and Scott), 136
Mad Money (television program), 304
Madoff, Bernie, 11
Magie, Lizzie, 128
Mail on Sunday, The, 29
Malkiel, Burton, 90–91, 96, 186
Mandelbrot, Benoit, 88, 94–96, 185, 276
Manhattan Project, 65
Mankiw, Greg, 115, 122–23, 346, 357
Mantel, Rolf, 70–71
Manual of Political Economy (Pareto), 53
"Market for Lemons, The" (Akerlof), 153
Market Signaling (Spence), 155
Markowitz, Harry, 91, 260
mark-to-market accounting, 308–309
Mark Twain Bank, 210
Marshall, Alfred, 36, 51, 115, 116, 152,
    169, 193
Martin, William McChesney, 344–45
Marx, Karl, xii, 57, 206, 285, 335, 336
Marxism, 39, 53, 57, 2
Massachusetts Institute of Technology
    (MIT), 20, 50, 83, 89, 125, 135, 151,
    152, 163, 177, 178, 183, 198, 221, 305
Masters, Blythe, 280
Mathematical Colloquium, 65
Mathematical Physics (Edgeworth), 193
Maximum Utility, Theorem of, 51
May, George S., 236
Mayer, Christopher, 250
Mayflower (ship), 235
McClure, Samuel, 203
McCormick, Cyrus, 75
McCulley, Paul, 206, 209

McCulloch, J. R., 34–35
McDonald's Corporation, 155
McGraw-Hill Companies, 263
Meade, James, 127
Meckling, William, 291
median household income, ix, 238–39,
    363n
Medicare, 156
Mellon Bank, 212
Mellon, Andrew, 349
Menger, Karl, 52, 65
Merrick, George, 236
Merrill Lynch, 139, 145, 294, 296, 304,
    311, 313; Bank of America purchase
    of, 324, 330; compensation of CEO
    of, 289; credit default swaps of, 281;
    First Franklin purchased by, 257, 295;
    risk-management system at, 269–70;
    shadow banking system and, 225–26;
    subprime mortgage securities issued
    by, 260, 262, 273–74
Merton, Robert, 230
MFS New Discovery Fund, 179
Michigan, University of, 57, 146, 194,
    266
microeconomics, 99, 152, 266
Microeconomics (Pindyck and
    Rubinfeld), 50
Microsoft Corporation, viii, 102,
    131–33, 179, 294
Miles, David, 136
Mill, John Stuart, xii, 33–36, 44, 46, 53,
    73, 116, 193
Millennium Bridge (London), 299–301,
    307, 309, 310
Milton, John, 45, 75
Minerals Management Service, U.S.,
    111
"Ministry of Production in the
    Collectivist State, The" (Barone), 57
Minnesota, University of, 74
Minsky, Hyman, viii, 205–12, 214–17,
    221, 225, 227, 234, 241, 243, 268,
    332, 340, 360

(Mis)Behavior of Markets, The
   (Mandelbrot and Hudson), 94–95
Mises, Ludwig von, 32, 39, 46
Missal, Michael J., 258
Mobil Oil, 130
Modigliani, Franco, 175
monetarism, 73, 78, 81, 83
Monetary History of the United States, A
   (Friedman and Schwartz), 76–77
Money Store, The, 255
Monnett, Charles, 112
Monopoly (game), 128
monopoly power, xii, xv–xvii, 10, 58, 75,
   102, 123, 126–32, 134, 136, 137,
   164
Montaigne, Michel de, 45
Monte Carlo simulation, 276
Monthly Review, The, 215
Mont Pelerin Society, 74
Moody's Investor Services, 262, 264,
   266, 271, 272, 301, 312
moral philosophy, 26, 192
Morgan, J. P., 128, 233
Morgan Stanley, viii, 4, 139, 145, 179,
   319, 328, 342, 343; Chinese equity
   in, 304, 354; compensation of CEO
   of, 289; Economics Department of,
   104; Federal Reserve and, 319, 345;
   reduction in assets of, 311; repayment
   of government loans by, 333;
   subprime mortgage securities issued
   by, 259–60, 273
Morgenstern, Oskar, 142, 194
Morris, Ian, 18
Mortgage Asset Research Institute,
   244
mortgage-backed securities (MBSs), 13,
   21
Mortgage Brokers Association for
   Responsible Lending, 244
Mozilo, Angelo, 246–47, 255
Munger, Charles, 282
Muolo, Paul, 252, 381*n*
Murphy, Kevin, 292

Muth, John, 100
Myrdal, Gunnar, 38

Nagel, Stefan, 180–82
Naidu, Suresh, xi, xii
NASDAQ, 18, 25, 181, 231–32
Nash, John, 67, 142, 145
National Academy of Sciences, 68
National Aeronautics and Space
   Administration (NASA), 137
National Association for Business
   Economics, 20, 104
National Association of Real Estate
   Boards, 74
National Bureau for Economic
   Research, 76
National Homeownership Strategy, 241
National Resources Committee, 73
National Socialism, *see* Nazis
Navy, U.S., Pacific Fleet, 17
Nazis, 44, 45, 66
Netherlands, 315
Netscape Communications, 132, 135,
   179
neuroeconomics, 202–203
New Century Financial Corporation,
   225, 245, 257, 258, 260, 266, 297
New Deal, 45, 73
New Industrial State, The (Galbraith), 129
New Republic, The, 45–46
New School, 71
Newsweek, 72
Newton, Huey P., 151
Newton, Isaac, 75, 119
New York Cotton Exchange, 94
New Yorker, The, 18, 104, 203
New York Mets baseball team, 196
New York State Common Retirement
   Fund, 180
New York Stock Exchange, 166, 297, 313
New York Times, The, 72, 74, 231, 254,
   263, 275, 296, 326, 333, 346; *Book
   Review*, 46

New York University (NYU), 70, 129, 189, 324; Stern School of Business, 343
New York Yankees baseball team, 196
Nightingale, Florence, 75
"NINJA" mortgage loans, 11
Nixon, Richard, 6, 79–80, 227, 336
Nobel Prize, 38, 47, 62, 79, 97, 102, 103, 120, 163, 198, 230, 261
noise traders, 182–84, 186
Nordhaus, William, 68, 114
Northern Rock, 303
Norway, 13, 321
Nothaft, Frank, 19, 249

Obama, Barack, xiii, 7, 123, 132, 157, 174, 254, 330, 333, 340, 342, 352, 353
Objectivist Newsletter, The, 228
Occupy Wall Street movement, xi
October Revolution, 57
oligopoly, 102, 126
"On an Economic Equation System and a Generalization of the Brouwer Fixed Point Theorem" (von Neuman), 66
O'Neal, Stan, 11, 274, 289, 295, 297, 304
On Liberty (Mill), 34
Only Yesterday (Allen), 236
"On the Economic Theory of Socialism" (Lange), 58
"On the Impossibility of Informationally Efficient Markets" (Grossman and Stiglitz), 94
Organisation for Economic Co-operation and Development, 334, 348
Organization of Petroleum Exporting Countries (OPEC), 49, 147
O'Rourke, Kevin, 226, 332
O'Toole, Bob, 167
Ove Arup, 299–301
Ownit Mortgage Solutions, 297
Oxford University, 26, 38, 114, 174, 300

Pacific Investment Management Company, 206
Padilla, Mathew, 252, 381n
Palin, Sarah, 348
paradox of thrift, 98, 173
Pareto, Vilfredo, 8, 53–58, 61, 63, 118
Pareto efficiency, 54–59, 63, 64, 67, 69, 101, 120, 134, 158, 163–64
Paris Agreement, xv
Parker Brothers, 128
Pasternak, Boris, 75
Paulson, Henry "Hank," 4, 307, 320, 321, 323–27, 330, 331, 333, 348
Pearl Harbor, Japanese attack on, 17, 18
Pender, Kathleen, 245
Penn Square Bank, 215
Pennsylvania, University of, Wharton School of Business, 93, 199, 250
Pentagon Papers, The, 202
Pericles, 45
Phelps, Edmund, 79
Philadelphia 76ers basketball team, 196
Philippines, 277
Phillips, A. W. ("Bill"), 78
Phillips Curve, 78–79
Pickens, T. Boone, 130
Pigou, Arthur C., xi, xiv, 10, 115–22, 124, 127, 164, 193, 360
Piketty, Thomas, x–xi
Pindyck, Robert S., 50
Pinochet, Augusto, 82–83, 129
Plato, 33, 192, 201
Plender, John, 288
Poland, 59, 80, 83
policy ineffectiveness proposition, 100
pollution tax, 354
polychlorinated biphenyls (PCBs), 121–22
Ponzi finance, 11, 209–12, 234, 245
Poor Law Amendment Act (1834), 33
Popov, Vladimir, 43
PortalPlayer, Inc., 29
Posner, Richard, 11, 120, 122, 337, 358
Poulakakos, Harry, 166
Poulakakos, Peter, 166

Poundstone, William, 145
Prechter, Robert, 167
predictability, illusion of, 13, 104, 275, 276
Prescott, Edward C., 103
President's Economic Policy Advisory Board, 81
Priceline, 171
Prices and Production (Hayek), 39, 40
Prince, Charles "Chuck," 11, 12, 289, 296–98, 304
Princeton University, 20, 65–67, 72, 90, 142, 143, 178, 180, 203, 254, 300; Institute for Advanced Study, 65
Principles of Economics (Marshall), 36
Principles of Political Economy (Mill), xii, 33, 35
prisoner's dilemma, 142–48, 206, 246, 296, 314
"Problem of Social Cost, The" (Coase), 119–20
productivity, 26, 28, 155, 227; agricultural, 149; growth of, random fluctuations in, 103–104; wages and, 59
protectionism, x
Proud Decades, The (Diggins), 38
Prudential Securities, 253

quantitative easing, 349
Quantum Fund, 180, 184
Quarterly Journal of Economics, The, 126, 153
Quesnay, François, 51

Rabin, Matt, 198
Radner, Roy, 70
Rajan, Raghuram G., 20–23, 291, 351
Ramsey, Frank, 64
Rand, Ayn, 5, 228–29, 234, 336
RAND Institute, 137, 142, 143, 145

Random Walk Down Wall Street, A (Malkiel), 90, 186
random walk theory, 88–91
Ranieri, Lewis, 253
rational expectations theory, 99–106, 126, 204
rational irrationality, 352, 360
RBS Greenwich Capital, 260
Reader's Digest, 46
Reagan, Ronald, 7, 21, 72, 81–82, 134, 162, 174, 228, 286, 336
reality-based economics, vii, viii, xi, xiii, xvi, xvii, 9–10, 124, 128, 138, 165, 176, 338, 339, 346, 359–60
RealtyTrac, 312
Reinhart, Vincent, 222
Renaissance Technologies, 315
"Report on Social Insurance and Allied Services" (Beveridge), 44
Republican Party, x, 24, 81, 122, 123, 137, 165, 227, 233, 323
Reserve Primary Fund, 327
residential mortgage-backed securities (RMBSs), 212, 214, 252, 257, 260, 261, 263, 264, 270–73, 281
Resolution Trust Corporation, 13, 162
Review of Economic Studies, The, 57, 66, 153
Revolution (Anderson), 81
Revolutionary era, 235
Ricardo, David, 33, 34
Rigas, John, 293
RiskMetrics, 275, 276, 278
Roach, Stephen S., 104, 345
Road to Serfdom, The (Hayek), 44–46, 74
Robbins, Lionel, 39, 40
Robinson, Joan, xii, 175
Rochester, University of, 197
Rockefeller, John D., 128
Rockefeller Foundation, 67
Rodrik, Dani, xi, xii
Roll, Richard, 198–99
Romans, ancient, 45, 85
Romer, Buddy, 135

Romer, Paul, 135–36
Ronald Reagan Presidential Library and Museum, 19
Roosevelt, Franklin Delano, 45, 73, 161, 163, 221
Roosevelt, Theodore, 128–29
Rosen, Harvey, 254
Roubini, Nouriel, 324
Royal Institute of British Architects, 299
Rubin, Robert, 20, 228, 231, 296
Rubinfeld, Daniel L., 50, 132–33
Rumsfeld, Donald, 227
Russia, 57, 83, 86, 255; communist, see Soviet Union
Rutgers University, 72

Saari, Donald G., 71
Sachs, Jeffrey, 83
Sack, Brian, 302
Samuelson, Paul, 357
St. Paul's Cathedral (London), 299
Salomon Brothers, 213, 253
Salomon Smith Barney, 178
Salzburg, University of, 47
Samsung Group, 29
Samuelson, Paul, 89, 98, 99, 106, 120, 152, 163, 175, 206, 216, 305
Sanders, Bernie, ix
San Francisco Chronicle, 243, 245
Sante Fe Railroad, 236
Sargent, Thomas, 100
Saunders, Anthony, 278
Savage, Jimmy, 88
Saving Capitalism from the Capitalists (Rajan and Zingales), 21
Savings & Loan (S&L) industry, collapse of, 13, 162
Scharfstein, David, 177–78, 182
Schlesinger, Karl, 65
Schlick, Moritz, 65
Schmalensee, Richard, xv
Scholes, Myron, 91, 93, 230

Schumpeter, Joseph, 44, 51, 209
Schwartz, Alan, 315
Schwartz, Anna J., 76–77
Schweitzer, Albert, 75
Science, 195, 203
Scott, Andrew, 136
Scott, Hal, 330
Scottish Enlightenment, 26, 27
Seale, Bobby, 151
Securities and Exchange Commission (SEC), 80, 90, 165, 266
Securities Industry and Financial Markets Association, 296–97
Seidman, L. William, 162–63, 228
Sen, Amartya, 55
Senate, U.S., 284; Banking Committee, 229, 231
Senior, Nassau, 33, 34
September 11, 2001, terrorist attacks (9/11), 17, 18, 197
shadow banking system, 214, 226, 272–73, 303, 307, 341
Shakespeare, William, 75
Shearson Lehman, 167
Sherman Antitrust Act (1890), xvi, 128, 132, 140
Shiller, Robert, 19, 168, 175, 237, 247–48
Shin, Hyun Song, 300–301, 307, 309–10
Shleifer, Andrei, 182–84
Shmelev, Nikolai, 43
Shultz, George, 122
Simons, Henry, 206
Sinai, Todd, 250
60 Minutes, 265
Skidelsky, Robert, 115
Smith, Adam, viii, xi, 8, 26–36, 72, 116, 136, 152, 196, 287, 346, 361; on banking, 163; death of, 33; divison of labor described by, 27–29; on duties of government, 31, 34–35, 75; Greenspan influenced by, 27, 36, 37,

228, 233, 286; Hayek and legacy of,
43–46; invisible hand metaphor of, 26,
38, 64, 337; moral philosophy of,
192–93; public goods addressed by,
30–31, 127
Smith, Debbie, 250
Smith, Vernon, 198
Smoot-Hawley Tariff Act (1930), 76
Socialism (Mises), 39
Socialist Party, 206
Social Security, 37, 45, 75
Société Générale, 326
Solomon, Amit, 178
Solow, Robert, 135, 152
Sonnenschein, Hugo, 70–71
Soros, George, 180, 184, 360
Soros Fund Mangement, 181
South Africa, 241
Southern California, University of, 292
Southern Pacific Railroad, 236
South Korea, 13, 29, 313, 337
South Sea bubble, 36, 180
Soviet Union, 8, 38, 43, 45, 57, 59, 80;
collapse of, 83; Ministry of Light
Industry, 43
Spain, 180, 241
Spamann, Holger, 294, 295
special-purpose vehicles (SPVs), 214,
272, 280
speculative bubbles, *see* bubbles
Spence, Michael, 155, 163
Sperry Lease Finance Corporation,
213
spillovers, xi, xiv, 10, 113–21, 123,
127–28, 164, 211, 283, 318, 339
Spitzer, Eliot, 296
Sputnik I, 38
Sraffa, Piero, 40
stability, illusion of, ix, 8, 104, 215, 226,
239, 304, 344
Stabilizing an Unstable Economy
(Minsky), 207, 217
Stack, Brian E., 179
Stalin, Joseph, 38, 44, 57

Standard & Poor's (S&P), 262–64, 271,
301; S&P 500, 87, 167, 179; S&P/
Case-Shiller Home Price Indices,
238, 247, 311, 333
Standard Oil Company, xvi, 128, 129
Stanford Magazine, 231
Stanford University, 62, 130, 135, 143,
159, 180, 197, 203, 232
Stansky, Robert, 179–80
State Department, U.S., 125
Statistical Research Group, 74
Stavins, Robert, xv
Stein, Jeremy, 177–78, 182
Stern, Nicholas, xiii–xiv, 112–13
Stern Report, 112–15
Stewart, Jimmy, 314
Stigler, George, 74, 98, 120, 129, 163
Stiglitz, Joseph, viii, 93–94, 104, 163–65,
352
Stoller, Matt, xvi–xvii
Strauss-Kahn, Dominique, 357
stress tests, 351
structured investment vehicles (SIVs),
214, 226, 272–73, 288, 303, 306, 341
Subprime Solution, The (Shiller), 247
Summers, Lawrence, 7, 23, 83–84, 228,
359
Superfund, 121
Swagel, Phillip, 322, 325
Swarthmore College, 187
Sweden, 13, 321, 330
Sweezy, Paul, 216, 332
Syracuse University, 178

Tableau Economique (Quesnay), 51
Tacitus, 45
Taft, William Howard, 129
Tahmassebian, Zareh, 248, 250
Taiwan, 29
Taleb, Nassim Nicholas, 278–79
Target, 25
Tate Modern, 299
Tax Reform Act (1986), 252

Taylor, John B., 233–34

Temporary Liquidity Guarantee Program, 330

Tennessee, University of, 214

Tett, Gillian, 280

Texaco, 130

Texas, University of, Austin, 185

Texas Instruments, 93

Texas Pacific Group, 130

Thailand, 13

Thain, John, 11, 313

Thaler, Richard, 197–98

Thatcher, Margaret, 7, 47, 82, 134, 285–86

TheGlobe.com, 171, 179

Theory of Games and Economic Behavior (von Neumann and Morgenstern), 142

Theory of Moral Sentiments, The (Smith), 192–93, 361

"Theory of Specualtion, The" (Bachelier), 88

Theory of Unemployment, The (Pigou), 118–19

3M Corporation, 224

thrift, paradox of, 98, 173

Thrift Supervision, Office of, 265

Thucydides, 45

Thünen, Johann Heinrich von, 50

Time Warner, 181

Titman, Sheridan, 185–86

Toshiba Corporation, 29

Toyota Motor Corporation, 126

trade, free, ix, 31, 33–34, 37

"Tragedy of the Commons" (Hardin), 148

Treasury bonds, 92, 213, 274, 277, 286, 290

Treasury Department, U.S., 4, 11, 74, 125, 265, 307, 322–26, 329, 330, 331, 351

Treatise on Money, A (Keynes), 40

Treatise on Probability, A (Keynes), 202, 206

Trichet, Jean-Claude, 20

Troubled Asset Relief Program (TARP), 329, 331, 333, 350

T. Rowe Price, 178

Trump, Donald, x, xii, xv, xvi

Tucker, Albert, 143–44

Tudor Fund, 181

Tufts University, 89

tulipmania, 36, 247

Turner, Adair, 360

Turning Point, The (Shmelev and Popov), 43

Tversky, Amos, xii, 10, 193–98, 360

Tyco Electronics Corporation, 293

UBS Financial Services, 269, 273, 279, 296, 304, 343, 354

United Kingdom, ix, 4, 27–29, 39, 45, 79, 115, 118, 303, 324, 336; Brexit referendum, xvi; Financial Services Authority, 317–18; Friedman in, 82; Hayek in, 39–41, 44–47; health care in, 157; India Office, 169, 172; Millennium Bridge project in, 299–301, 307, 309, 310; moral philosophy in, 192; nineteenth century, 33–36, 50–51; stimulus packages in, 174, 358; Treasury of, 37

United Nations, 197

"Use of Knowledge in Society, The" (Hayek), 42

U.S. Steel Corporation, xvi, 6, 128, 130, 228

utilitarian philosophy, 53

utopian economics, 8, 13, 14, 33, 117, 124, 335, 340, 346, 353; criticized by academic economics, x; COVID-19 pandemic policy response and, xiv, xvii; Greenspan and, 233, 241; influence of, xii; Keynes's attack on, 172; market failures and, viii, xii–xiii, xiv–xv, 318, 336, 338, 346; monopolistic companies and, xvi; reality-based economics versus, viii, 9,

24; triumph of, ix, 97–107; *see also* general equilibrium theory; invisible hand; rational expectations theory; *specific economists.*

Value at Risk (Jorion), 275
value-at-risk (VAR) models, 92, 274–79, 283, 334
Vanguard Group, 91
Vera, Chema, xvii
Versailles, Treaty of, 40
Victoria, Queen of England, 33
Vienna, University of, 39, 65
Vienna Circle, 65
Viniar, David, 275
Vinik, Jeffrey, 178–79
Volcker Rule, 354
Volcker, Paul, 103, 217, 336, 355
Voltaire, 102
von Neumann, John, 65–67, 142, 145, 171, 194

Wachovia Bank, 4, 255, 260, 265, 296, 330
Wald, Abraham, 65, 66
Wallace, Neil, 100
Wall Street Journal, The, 9, 184, 205, 320, 323
Wal-Mart, 25, 49, 181
Walras, Léon, viii, 8, 51–53, 57, 61, 64–67, 70, 114, 118, 346
Walters, Alan, 82
Warren, Elizabeth, 340
Washington, George, 235
Washington Mutual, 4, 246, 255, 257, 265
Washington University, 205; School of Business, 154

Waxman, Henry, 3–6
Wealth of Nations, The (Smith), 26, 35, 50, 192, 193
Weatherstone, Dennis, 275
Webvan, 181
Weill, Sanford "Sandy," 292, 296
Welch, Ivo, 190–91
Welch, Jack, 292
Wellesley College, 19, 247, 333
Wells Fargo Bank, 4, 214, 229, 265, 277, 330, 351, 354
White, William, 226
White House Council of Economic Advisers, 6, 20, 104, 115, 227–28, 254
Whither Socialism (Sitglitz), 164
Whitney, Eli, 75
Williams, John D., 143
William Volker Fund, 74
Wittgenstein, Ludwig, 39
Wood, Christopher, 18–19
Woodford, Michael, 105
Woolley, Paul, 360
World Bank, 28, 112
WorldCom, 200, 264, 290, 292, 293
World War I, 39
World War II, 17, 44, 59, 62, 66, 73–74, 221–22

Yale University, 19, 61, 62, 68, 70, 71, 77, 114, 168, 308; School of Management, 178

Zandi, Mark, 266, 312
Zeckhauser, Richard, 130
zero-sum games, 23, 142, 343
Zingales, Luigi, 330
Zucman, Gabriel, xi, xii